Tamed Agility

Matthias Book · Volker Gruhn
Rüdiger Striemer

Tamed Agility

Pragmatic Contracting and
Collaboration in
Agile Software Projects

 Springer

Matthias Book
Faculty of Industrial Engineering,
  Mechanical Engineering and Computer
  Science
University of Iceland
Reykjavík
Iceland

Volker Gruhn
paluno - The Ruhr Institute for Software
  Technology
Universität Duisburg-Essen
Essen
Germany

Rüdiger Striemer
adesso AG
Berlin
Germany

ISBN 978-3-319-82365-2   ISBN 978-3-319-41478-2   (eBook)
DOI 10.1007/978-3-319-41478-2

Printed on acid-free paper

This Springer imprint is published by Springer Nature
The registered company is Springer International Publishing AG Switzerland

Preface

Industrial software development is one of the major success stories of the twentieth century. Otherwise, software would not have been able to pervade other areas of life and business, established business models of entire industries would not have been swept away by digitalization, and the global success of Apple, Amazon, Google, Facebook, and eBay would not have been possible.

Software engineering, i.e., the design of larger and larger software systems based on engineering principles, enabled the development of software systems that seemed impossible just a couple of years ago. Therefore, any kind of fundamental denial of this success story is downright absurd (Osterweil et al. 2008). This fact cannot be changed, not even by numerous studies on the alleged state of the software industry, which were in some cases prepared under the flimsiest of conditions, as exposed, e.g., by Eveleens and Verhoef (2010), Glass (2006), or Jørgensen and Moløkken-Østfold (2006).

Yet, time and again, evidence is provided of projects that encounter difficulties—sometimes because the established software development practices have not been followed, sometimes because the individuals involved are too optimistic in their announcements and promises, and in some instances because the numerous individuals involved in a software development project do not have a uniform picture of the actual aim of the project.

It is astonishing that this happens relatively often and is not regarded as a rare exception. Obviously, problems can arise in other projects, not just in software development—airports are finished after serious delays or not at all, public construction projects become more expensive than planned, and trains cannot stop at all platforms. However, genuine project disasters, in the form of a multiplication of the project duration or cost, or in the form of canceled or rolled-back projects, seem to arise more frequently in software development than in other sectors.

Perhaps this is because the immaterial nature of software makes it more difficult to estimate the project state and makes the loss associated with a cancelled project less tangible. Perhaps it is also because software development projects (in which the relevant investment is "only" human resource cost) are often too ambitious and not overly concerned with lean solutions.

Perhaps it is also because the question on the nature of the software process can still not be answered definitively. Is it primarily a production process? Then, it can be structured from a Taylorist perspective, where detailed specifications are provided, such as in the car production process on an assembly line. Or is it a purely creative process, which is solely driven by the engineer's design talent? In this case, procedural specifications make little sense, in the same manner that the idea of a precise process to create a painting makes no sense. Software engineering seems to lie between these two poles. There are sections that must be clearly regulated and standardized, such as certain testing activities or configuration management. Others cannot be described using algorithms and cannot be supported by a heuristic process method, such as the approach to identify features to be developed at an early stage.

And then there is the phenomenon of uncertainty. Lehman (1989) provided a convincing argument that software projects are exposed to uncertainties; i.e., that during the course of development, situations could arise that were previously unforeseen (or at least uncertain to occur) and for which appropriate support was unknown. Lehman also noticed that, in most cases, these situations could not be identified in advance. Other authors also made this observation early on:

- "Uncertainty is inherent and inevitable in software development processes and products."—Ziv et al.'s uncertainty principle in software engineering (1996)
- "For a new software system, the requirements will not be completely known until after you have a working product."—Humphrey's requirements uncertainty principle (1995)
- It is impossible to fully specify or test an interactive system.—Wegner's lemma (1997)

In light of this finding, which is confirmed in practically every software project, terms such as "software factory" (Cusumano 1989) and titles of scientific articles such as "Software Processes are Software too" (Osterweil 1987) seem misleading or at least ambiguous. Software processes (at least for developing socio-technical systems) are insight-driven processes, they are comprised of more creative than algorithmic parts, and it is certainly the case that they are not precisely foreseeable (Gruhn and Urbainczyk 1998).

This in no way denies the existence of types of software that can be fully described. For example, embedded systems without human interfaces can be completely specified and created in line with the production paradigm.

However, this does not apply for socio-technical systems, for the simple reason that these kinds of systems do not end at the screen, but rather extend into the mind of the user. This does not just mean that software must be prepared for unforeseen user behavior. Rather, in socio-technical systems, the software is only a small part of a system comprised of human and mechanical participants that work together to perform complex processes. This interaction, into which software must seamlessly integrate, cannot be fully described and is also subject to constant change. In particular, when dealing with innovation, with the establishment of new business processes and services, and with the implementation of new automations, the design, implementation, and adaptation of software is a creative process, whose purpose requires continuous calibration. The development of these kinds of software solutions is not a production process, but rather a cognitive process, which is most likely to succeed when all stakeholders keep an eye on the common goal and pay attention to lean solutions.

Even if these solutions are of a technical nature, the goal they must support is anchored in the application domain and not in information technology (IT). Close communication between enterprise IT[1] and operating departments is unavoidable and essential for success in companies that develop software. However, it is often also characterized by different terminology and, especially, by different types of abstraction (and abstraction capacity).

However, the constant realignment of the project idea, the continuous consultation between enterprise IT and the application domain, and the rejection of the idea of a "software factory" (which suggests a completely predictable software production) also result in a few unpleasant conclusions. For example, the fact that the provision of a complete advance specification is not possible (and that the quest for this is doomed to failure), that there will be late requirements (which only arise during development or even after), that budget allocations and cost estimates are provisional, and that at the start of a project, it is impossible to know precisely what can be obtained and at what cost.

But is this really still necessary? Almost 50 years after the term "software engineering" was coined? After almost 50 years in which the "engineering" in "software engineering" defines a claim, namely the claim of reproducibility, reliability, and calculability? It appears to be so, as software development is still risky, projects still encounter difficulties and, when searching for the causes, the same reasons are constantly identified: a lack of understanding of the application domain, incorrect prioritization, and a lack of communication between the stakeholders (Curtis et al. 1988). Software processes are and will always be cognitive processes, but they must satisfy the expectations of production processes.

Structure and Audience of This Book

This is the challenge that this book deals with—the cognitive nature of software development, the necessity for a unified purpose, the concentration on lean software, the focus on added value, and the omission of the irrelevant. It describes specific instruments and methods enabling all stakeholders to develop a uniform understanding of the software to be created, to determine their genuinely essential requirements, and to deal with changes to this understanding and the requirements.

---

[1]By "enterprise IT," we refer to a company's enterprise IT department or to external contractors that perform this function.

The **Interaction Room** described in Part II brings all stakeholders together for this purpose—not to a table, but in a room where digitalization and mobilization strategies are jointly developed, where technology potentials are evaluated and where software projects are planned and managed. Why does this require a dedicated room? Because stakeholders can then communicate face to face rather than through e-mails. Because the room can be used to outline complex relationships in a comprehensible manner instead of having to laboriously write them up in great detail. Because there is only room for the most important issues. And because insights are not lost in short-term memory or huge documents, but concisely noted and constantly present. In short, because the Interaction Room makes projects visible and tangible.

The **adVANTAGE contract model** described in Part III ensures that the insight-driven and imprecise process of software development does not just function, but that it is allowed to flourish in a commercial environment, i.e., in a client and contractor relationship. In this model, changes to the project flow are not a reason for stress, but considered normal project events. The contract model ensures that stakeholders focus on generating maximum benefits, creating lean software, and distributing risk fairly despite (or with the aid of) all the changes.

How this can work during the day-to-day running of a project is shown in the **practical example** of the development of an inventory management system for a private health insurance company in Part IV. This is a complex system with, at first glance, an almost unmanageable number of business requirements, statutory conditions, stakeholders, and processes for general and special cases, embedded in the organically developed IT landscape of an insurance company from North Rhine-Westphalia. The example of the project kickoff and the first sprint shows how employees of the company and the IT contractor developed an overview of the project using the Interaction Room, how the design and development was managed, and how efforts were billed.

Ultimately, the success of every single software project, independently of the application domain and the technology used, depends on the **skills** of the stakeholders. Only if the stakeholders are prepared to talk to each other, interact with each other, respect different perceptions of value and effort drivers, reach compromises, pursue innovative solutions, and refrain from political maneuvers, can instruments such as the Interaction Room and adVANTAGE fully unfold their potential. Part V therefore finally describes the requirements profile that software engineers as well as domain experts must satisfy today.

Even though contracting and collaboration may be grounded in two different academic disciplines, they are inseparable in practice where all theory boils down to enabling people to work effectively with each other toward a successful product in a sustainable business relationship.

This book is therefore geared toward CIOs, project managers, and software engineers in industrial software development practice who want to learn how to deal effectively with the inevitable uncertainty of complex projects, who want to achieve higher levels of understanding and cooperation in their relationships with customers and suppliers, and who want to run their software projects at lower risk despite their inherent uncertainty.

Acknowledgments

The authors would like to thank Simon Grapenthin for sharing his extensive hands-on experience in facilitating Interaction Room workshops and training Interaction Room coaches in a wide range of business domains. We would also like to thank Sandra Delvos for countless hours of designing and revising the book's illustrations, and Alexander Lohberg and Anja Wintermeyer for their background research.

Reykjavík, Iceland   Matthias Book
Essen, Germany   Volker Gruhn
Berlin, Germany   Rüdiger Striemer

References

Curtis B, Krasner H, Iscoe N (1988) A field study of the software design process for large systems. Comm ACM 31(11):1268–1287. doi:10.1145/50087.50089

Cusumano MA (1989) The software factory: A historical interpretation. IEEE Software 6(2): 23–30. doi:10.1109/MS.1989.1430446

Eveleens JL, Verhoef C (2010) The rise and fall of the Chaos report figures. IEEE Software 27(1):30–36. doi:10.1109/MS.2009.154

Glass RL (2006) The Standish report: Does it really describe a software crisis? Comm ACM 49(8):15–16. doi:10.1145/1145287.1145301

Gruhn V, Urbainczyk J (1998) Software process modeling and enactment: An experience report related to problem tracking in an industrial project. In: Katayama T, Notkin D (eds) ICSE'98: Proc 20th Intl Conf Software Engineering, pp 13–21. doi:10.1109/ICSE.1998.671098

Humphrey WS (1995) A discipline for software engineering. Addison-Wesley, p 349

Jørgensen M, Moløkken-Østvold K (2006) How large are software cost overruns? A review of the 1994 Chaos report. Information and Software Technology 48(4):297–301. doi:10.1016/j.infsof.2005.07.002

Lehman MM (1989) Uncertainty in computer application and its control through the engineering of software. J Software Maintenance 1(1):3–27. doi:10.1002/smr.4360010103

Osterweil LJ (1987) Software processes are software too. In: Riddle WE (ed) ICSE'87: Proc 9th Intl Conf Software Engineering, pp 2–13

Osterweil LJ, Ghezzi C, Kramer J, Wolf AL (2008) Determining the impact of software engineering research on practice. IEEE Computer 41(3):39–49. doi:10.1109/MC.2008.85

Wegner P (1997) Why interaction is more powerful than algorithms. Comm ACM 40(5):80–91. doi:10.1145/253769.253801

Ziv H, Richardson DJ, Klösch R (1996) The uncertainty principle in software engineering. Technical Report UCI-TR-96-33, University of California, Irvine. http://www.ics.uci.edu/~ziv/papers/icse97.ps. Accessed 23 Feb 2016

Contents

Part I   Introduction

1   The Need for Tamed Agility 3
    1.1   A New School of IT 3
        1.1.1   Mobility..................................... 4
        1.1.2   Agility...................................... 5
        1.1.3   Elasticity 5
        1.1.4   Resulting Challenges.......................... 6
    1.2   Agile or Plan-Driven? 7
    1.3   A Pragmatic Middle Ground....................... 11
    1.4   Tamed Agility in Practice 13
    References.. 14

Part II   The Interaction Room

2   A Room for Ideas.................................... 17
    2.1   Key Interaction Room Principles..................... 18
    2.2   Involve Domain Experts 20
    2.3   Refine the Scope Continuously...................... 21
    2.4   Favor Relevance Over Completeness.................. 23
    2.5   Favor Clarity Over Syntactic and Semantic Precision......... 25
    2.6   Define Value and Effort Drivers 26
    2.7   Manage Late Requirements 27
    2.8   Manage Early Requirements........................ 29
    2.9   Reveal Uncertainties Early......................... 30
    2.10 Make Cost Changes Transparent..................... 32
    2.11 Analyze the Risk of Disasters....................... 33
    2.12 Build Trust Between Stakeholders.................... 34
    2.13 Visualize the Project's Progress 35
    References.. 36

3   Interaction Room Basics 39
    3.1   Method Overview................................ 40
    3.2   Canvases 41
    3.3   Annotations 43

	3.4	Variants...	48
	3.5	Stakeholders..	51
		3.5.1 Interaction Room Method Coach...............	52
		3.5.2 Interaction Room Domain Coach	53
		3.5.3 Process Owner	54
		3.5.4 Additional Roles............................	54
	3.6	Workshop Preparation	55
	3.7	Results and Follow-up Activities...........................	56
4	**Using an Interaction Room for Digitalization Strategy**		
	Development (IR:digital)................................		59
	4.1	Relevant Stakeholders	64
		4.1.1 Digital Business Expert	65
		4.1.2 Digital Technology Expert	67
		4.1.3 Interaction Engineer	68
	4.2	Partner Canvas...	69
		4.2.1 Methodology and Notation....................	69
		4.2.2 Annotations and Analysis.....................	72
	4.3	Physical Object Canvas	73
		4.3.1 Methodology and Notation....................	74
		4.3.2 Annotations and Analysis.....................	79
	4.4	Touchpoint Canvas	81
		4.4.1 Methodology and Notation....................	81
		4.4.2 Annotations and Analysis.....................	83
	4.5	Cross-Canvas Analyses	84
	4.6	Workshop Structure and Follow-up Activities..............	86
	References...		89
5	**Using an Interaction Room for Software Project Scoping**		
	(IR:scope)..		91
	5.1	Relevant Stakeholders	92
		5.1.1 Application Developer........................	92
		5.1.2 Operations Expert	92
		5.1.3 User	93
	5.2	Feature Canvas...	93
		5.2.1 Methodology and Notation....................	93
		5.2.2 Annotations and Analysis.....................	94
	5.3	Process Canvas...	95
		5.3.1 Methodology and Notation....................	96
		5.3.2 Annotations and Analysis.....................	99
	5.4	Object Canvas	103
		5.4.1 Methodology and Notation....................	103
		5.4.2 Annotations and Analysis.....................	106

	5.5	Integration Canvas	109
		5.5.1 Methodology and Notation	110
		5.5.2 Annotations and Analysis	112
	5.6	Cross-Canvas Analyses	114
	5.7	Workshop Structure and Follow-up Activities	116
	Reference		118

6   Using an Interaction Room for Mobile Application Development (IR:mobile) 119

	6.1	Relevant Stakeholders	120
		6.1.1 Mobility Expert	121
		6.1.2 Business Developer	121
	6.2	Persona Canvas	121
		6.2.1 Methodology and Visualization	122
		6.2.2 Annotations and Analysis	123
	6.3	Portfolio Canvas	124
		6.3.1 Methodology and Visualization	124
		6.3.2 Annotations and Analysis	125
	6.4	Touchpoint Canvas	127
		6.4.1 Methodology and Notation	127
		6.4.2 Annotations and Analysis	129
	6.5	Interaction Canvas	132
		6.5.1 Methodology and Notation	132
		6.5.2 Annotations and Analysis	135
	6.6	Cross-Canvas Analyses	137
	6.7	Workshop Structure and Follow-up Activities	138
	References		140

7   Using an Interaction Room for Technology Evaluation (IR:tech) 141

	7.1	Relevant Stakeholders	142
		7.1.1 Technology Expert	142
		7.1.2 Enterprise Architect	142
	7.2	Feature Canvas	142
	7.3	Process, Object, and Integration Canvases	145
	7.4	Cross-Canvas Analyses	145
	7.5	Workshop Structure and Follow-up Activities	146

8   Using an Interaction Room for Agile Project Monitoring (IR:agile) 149

	8.1	From Feature Canvas to Product Backlog	150
	8.2	Sprint Planning Workshops	151
	8.3	Requirements Exchange	152
	8.4	Risk Map	153

8.5   Progress Control   158
8.6   Cost Forward Progressing   159
References.   164

9   **Using Interaction Rooms Under Difficult Conditions**   165
9.1   Temporary Interaction Rooms.   165
9.2   Distributed Interaction Rooms.   167
9.3   Augmented Interaction Rooms   168
References.   169

10   **Summary**   171
Reference   174

Part III   The adVANTAGE Contract Model

11   **Framing Software Projects in Commercial Terms**   177
Reference   180

12   **Traditional Contract Models in an Agile World**   181
12.1   Fixed Price.   184
12.2   Time and Materials   187
12.3   Pay Per Use   188
12.4   Summary   191
References.   193

13   **Agile Contract Models**   195
13.1   Fixed Price per Iteration.   195
13.2   Fixed Price per (Whatever) Point   196
13.3   Money for Nothing, Change for Free.   197
13.4   Shared Pain/Shared Gain   198
13.5   Multi-stage Contract Models.   200
13.6   Summary   201
References.   202

14   **Key adVANTAGE Principles**   205
14.1   Commitment to Agility   206
14.2   Mutual Trust   207
14.3   Contractor's Willingness to Assume Risk.   209
14.4   Budget Security   210
14.5   Shared Pain   210
14.6   Efficiency Incentives   211
Reference   212

15   **adVANTAGE Procedures**   213
15.1   Initial Requirements Collection and Budget Estimate   213
15.2   Feature Prioritization and Sprint Definition.   215
15.3   Sprint Implementation and Controlling.   217

15.4 Sprint Inspection and Billing 221
    15.4.1 Full Completion of Sprint 221
    15.4.2 Partial Completion of Sprint 224
15.5 Planning the Next Sprint 224
15.6 Project Termination 226
15.7 Summary 227
Reference 228

16 adVANTAGE in Practice 229
16.1 Case Study: The BERGFÜRST Crowd Investing Platform 229
16.2 Fine-Tuning adVANTAGE Parameters 233
References 234

17 Summary 235

Part IV   A Sample Project

18 Case Study: The Cura Health Insurance Benefit System 241

19 Initial Project Scoping with the IR:scope 243
19.1 Project Vision 243
19.2 Identification of Stakeholders and Objectives 244
19.3 Feature Canvas 245
    19.3.1 Feature Identification and Canvas Population 245
    19.3.2 Annotation and Analysis 245
19.4 Process Canvas 248
    19.4.1 Identification and Prioritization of Business
            Processes 248
    19.4.2 Canvas Population 250
    19.4.3 Annotation and Analysis 252
19.5 Object Canvas 255
    19.5.1 Canvas Population 255
    19.5.2 Annotation and Analysis 255
19.6 Integration Canvas 258
    19.6.1 Canvas Population 258
    19.6.2 Annotation and Analysis 259
19.7 Cross-Canvas Annotation Analysis 260
19.8 Documentation and Follow-up Activities 261

20 Project Monitoring with the IR:agile 263
20.1 From Feature Canvas to Product Backlog 263
20.2 Risk Map 265
20.3 The First Sprint 267
    20.3.1 Planning the First Sprint 267
    20.3.2 Results of the First Sprint 267

20.4   Settlement Using adVANTAGE   269
20.5   Cost Forward Progressing   270
20.6   Using the Requirements Exchange   270

21   Lessons Learned   273

Part V   Conclusion

22   The Big Picture   281
     References   282

23   A New Skill Set   283
     23.1   General Software Technology and Methodology Skills   283
     23.2   New School of IT Skills: Mobility   284
     23.3   New School of IT Skills: Agility   287
     23.4   New School of IT Skills: Flexibility   288
     23.5   Business Development and Domain Knowledge   289
     23.6   Knowledge of Business Processes, Business Models,
            and Partnerships   290
     23.7   Insights and Experiences   291
     References   292

24   Outlook: Twelve Hypotheses   293

Appendix A: Interaction Room Workshop Agendas   295

Appendix B: Interaction Room Annotations   299

Appendix C: adVANTAGE Contract Template   313

Index   329

Part I
Introduction

The Need for Tamed Agility

1

Pragmatic, value-focused support for the design and implementation of complex IT projects appears more necessary than ever before, especially in times of ubiquitous digitalization, as "software is eating the world" (Andreessen 2011): In increasingly digital companies, the number of projects that is not heavily dependent on IT is constantly falling. The implementation of organization projects, projects for implementing regulatory requirements and merger and acquisition projects is also practically impossible without the involvement of IT—"every budget is becoming an IT budget" (Gartner 2012).

1.1 A New School of IT

IT has always involved automation, and IT has also always had a disruptive influence. Business models have always changed as a result of IT. Some disappeared, some only became possible in the first place. So is everything the same as it always was? Not entirely, because a number of factors are currently combining: The world is becoming more digital, data and applications are becoming mobile, and IT projects have to deliver quick results. Even during development, it must be possible to adapt their focus. Long project durations are undesirable, because the world has often changed so dramatically after a long project that it is difficult to know whether the originally promised benefits are actually generated. This leads to a change that is more radical than the slow progress of automation. Concepts that appeared promising yesterday are now a hindrance. It seems that enterprise IT has a new role and that it requires new or at least additional skills and capabilities.

Faced with technological disorder in the context of mobile technologies, broad digital transformation and elastic, cloud-based infrastructures, IT is no longer just a central means of production. Rather, enterprise IT is becoming an essential co-designer and co-creator of future solutions. In order to fulfill this role, it must

© Springer International Publishing Switzerland 2016
M. Book et al., *Tamed Agility*, DOI 10.1007/978-3-319-41478-2_1

assess the opportunities and risks of new technologies, talk to users and business departments, and know the challenges faced by the respective industry.

As a result, enterprise IT is changing from a pure service provider to an enabler and co-designer of business changes. Instead of just implementing an operating department's ideas, and instead of just providing defined services to an agreed quality, enterprise IT is taking on a consulting role. Based on its knowledge of technology costs and benefits, and of business challenges and opportunities, enterprise IT now works together with the operating departments to design solutions that can be implemented efficiently, that have innovation potentials, and that provide competitive advantages.

In other words: Enterprise IT is on the move. From the basement to the boardroom. It now has a say and takes responsibility. And it can only do this if it understands both technology and business.

Companies are currently facing huge strategic changes triggered by three key IT trends: mobility of clients and employees, agility in software development, and elasticity of IT infrastructure. These are the foundations that are increasingly defining the requirements of enterprise IT. And because an enterprise IT that satisfies these requirements has a different structure and different competencies than traditional enterprise IT, we call it the New School of IT. This is admittedly bold, but clearly states that the upcoming changes will go far beyond a normal level of change.

1.1.1 Mobility

Mobility is increasing across all industry sectors: Central business processes have mobile components, or at least components that can be mobilized. Clients and suppliers can be integrated using web-based applications or native apps and take over important parts of the business process. Mobile solutions need to be developed and delivered quickly. The aim is to rapidly launch new products or services on the market, often using a range of different sales channels.

Whether the mobility of data and applications demanded by users is always required, and whether it is socially and economically beneficial that the availability of humans is increasing, and that parts of the business process can be outsourced, is irrelevant for the question of whether enterprise IT must be able to develop and operate mobile applications. The trend toward mobility is a social trend, and the experiences gained in the private context are creating expectations in companies.

Consequently, enterprise IT must come to terms with the topic of mobility. This is exacerbated by the fact that mobility is often also an important driver for innovative applications, simply because the mobilization of data and applications can lead to structurally different applications and entirely new use cases, which makes the topic of mobility even more essential for enterprise IT. After all, the mastering of technologies that have the potential to trigger the next batch of changes in application landscapes cannot be outsourced and remains part of the enterprise IT's core business.

1.1.2 Agility

Innovative IT solutions can rarely be completely planned in advance and then "just" be implemented. Rather, they are based on the idea of permanent adaptation to new or clearer boundary conditions outlined by Ries (2011). And because the basic concepts of agile software development—fast and frequent delivery of software, concentration on source code as the central artifact of development, continuous communication with clients and users, and respect for application knowledge—benefit more than just mobile and other innovative applications, software is increasingly being developed with agile software process elements. Virtually, no software development of a relevant scale is either purely agile or entirely without agile elements (Boehm and Turner 2003). Common sense suggests that projects can vary significantly on the spectrum between strictly agile and strictly waterfall-oriented. Mary Poppendieck summarized this in her keynote speech at the 35th International Conference on Software Engineering (ICSE 2013) with the statement "agility without discipline cannot scale, and discipline without agility cannot compete."

Given that discipline can have different connotations, and given that a large number of people with a range of independent perceptions are involved in software projects of a relevant scale, certain standards are required to respond to different perceptions of the necessary discipline and restrict these perceptions to compatible ideas of discipline. A lack of compatible perceptions of discipline and their specific manifestation often results in misunderstandings. These can be countered by explicit rules and agreements, which then however represent the explicit discipline addressed by Poppendieck, i.e., an alternative to agile, personal discipline that is only based on a small number of principles. Overall, we are still faced with the problem that agile development approaches have to be supplemented by elements of requirements transparency in order to apply them to major projects in large organizations.

Probably the most popular approach to placing a square peg in a round hole and reconciling agility with the need for planning certainty is based on the Scaled Agile Framework (SAFe) approach introduced by Leffingwell (2011). However, significant doubts remain as to whether any of the original allure of agility remains in light of the extensive expansion, and also whether the implementation of SAFe in companies does not lead to completely erratic results, simply because SAFe is vague and non-specific.

1.1.3 Elasticity

Elasticity is the extension of agility from application development into application management, from the world of application software to the world of system software, infrastructure and hardware.

Infrastructures need to be elastic so that mobile applications, applications that are frequently extended with new functionality, and applications for end users can scale seamlessly—i.e., that they can deal with widely fluctuating (and also sharply increasing) user numbers without changing their behavior so drastically that the user is disturbed. Elasticity means that infrastructures can be scaled up as well as down.

Elastic infrastructures are also necessary to ensure that the benefits of agile software development do not dissipate: If agile development delivers new software every few weeks (or even days!), it must be released into productive use (or at least tested for its suitability to be released) just as often. If this does not happen and a new release is deployed only every few months, the development team's willingness to deliver features at short notice will run out quite fast. Continuous integration of software (Cusumano 1992) and the continuous release of new features—even in heterogeneous infrastructures (Humble and Farley 2010; Duvall et al. 2007)—are therefore required to ensure that agility will not remain restricted to the development side only.

There are many ways to ensure elasticity. Cloud solutions of many types and suppliers promise scalability. Security concerns about remotely hosted, externally managed data are numerous and often quite justified. Private clouds try to reconcile both—unlimited sovereignty over the data, and scalability as in a public cloud.

However, as is usual when trying to reconcile contrary positions, compromises cannot be avoided: A private cloud is not as scalable as a public cloud—but possibly sufficient for the application in question. And the complete sovereignty over all data comes at the price of a very high vertical IT integration—but maybe not all data's security is equally critical. The design of suitable private clouds (or comparable structures) therefore requires a sense of proportion, the critical consideration of killer arguments, the rational evaluation of risks and requirements and—in the solution domain—the automation of IT infrastructure provisioning mechanisms. Automation is particularly important here because it is the only way to avoid the susceptibility to errors and dependency on individual people that traditionally plagues provisioning processes.

1.1.4   Resulting Challenges

Mobility, agility, and elasticity influence each other; they entail, overlap, and reinforce each other: Mobile applications are subject to shorter release cycles and therefore require more agile process elements. Agile development depends on an elastic and easily provided infrastructure to ensure that the benefits of frequent releases reach users immediately. This interplay fundamentally changes the way IT works, and how it is understood.

However, this change is not just technical in nature. The New School of IT also means that the significance of IT in companies is changing. Seeing correlations, establishing new business models, reaching new target groups—the foundations for this are laid ever more often in IT departments. Enterprises are increasingly "digitizing" themselves, and in the process, enterprise IT increasingly emancipates itself from its role as the operating departments' assistant. Enterprise IT is driving the new developments instead of being driven by them.

The New School of IT also means that enterprise IT cannot focus exclusively on classical software systems anymore. Moore (2011) calls these systems the "systems of records." Systems of records are characterized by high transaction volume, clear persistence design, and a high degree of consistence. Besides these, we increasingly find "systems of engagement" that spill from the consumer world into the enterprise world. These are systems that consist more of mash-up architectures than traditional enterprise application landscapes, that are configured by users, that are easily adapted and frequently released, that focus on the user experience, and that are subject to a high degree of uncertainty regarding the next features that will be requested by users.

Development and operation of systems of engagement require other skills and approaches than systems of records. Therefore, start-ups follow other (more agile) software processes than large digital enterprises with stable business models. Things get difficult though when systems of records merge with systems of engagement, when flexibility and stability need to be reconciled, when stable, consistent, and scalable systems must be equipped with mobile interfaces. Neither an agile nor a classical development paradigm is quite suitable for this—rather, a mix is required: an enterprise IT from the New School of IT. This is an enterprise IT that has mastered both paces, that is founded on stable base processes, that can work with established technologies just as with new ones, and that can implement safe, robust operations processes just as well as short release cycles and continuous integration—and that has the expertise to decide which development paradigm is best suited to which problem.

The New School of IT requires companies to rethink not just their enterprise IT, but also their operating departments, business development, and management. The most extensive changes, as described in the previous chapter, are of a strategic nature. Dealing with them and taking advantage of the resulting opportunities is the top management's responsibility.

The New School of IT also exposes every IT project manager to uncomfortable challenges: How are IT projects affected when the operating department is not just sending down specifications from three levels up, but discussing with the engineers at eye level? What does it mean if system boundaries become blurred, if clients and suppliers become partners, if software development and business development go hand in hand? Where are these requirements reflected in the software development methodology?

1.2 Agile or Plan-Driven?

Traditional plan-driven approaches seem too rigid for these challenges. The attempt to provide excessively detailed, precise, and long-term preliminary planning seems less promising where the boundaries between strategy development and software development become blurred, where software development has to respond quickly to changing competitive situations and user expectations, where new technologies turn established service and operating models on their head. Rather, continuous alignment with user and management expectations, a lean product without super-fluous features, and the acceptance of continuous change is desired. This is typically the incentive to pursue an agile development approach.

Agile approaches describe a world in which higher priority is placed on pro-ducing working software than any other artifacts, in which communication between stakeholders is regarded as more important than the use of tools and modeling languages, in which the spoken word is assigned a higher value than written text, and in which an joint understanding of discipline and common sense ensure that all stakeholders cooperate effectively with each other (Beck et al. 2001). This departure from the illusion of strict planning certainty may appear threatening to number-driven managers (maybe also to seasoned IT managers), as it seems to involve an almost complete loss of control, perhaps even careless blind confidence in the team's overall ability to work things out. Is this desirable?

The agile literature promises huge increases in productivity, but only for those who unquestioningly subscribe to the agile "faith," it seems. Virtually no evidence-based studies are available. If an agile project works out, it is due to the agile method, but if it does not work out, it is due to insufficient faith, the narrow-mindedness of management, the rigidity of stakeholders, and other factors that cannot be measured (Meyer 2014). There is a lack of clear, scientifically founded studies on the usefulness of agile methods, especially studies that provide evidence of the wonderful descriptions of perceived increases in productivity such as the 90 % improvement touted by Schwaber and Sutherland (2012), to name just one example. By contrast, experience from major projects tends to show that while agile practices are useful, they also require a certain amount of planning certainty and functional restriction of the features to be developed (Ambler 2001; Cohn 2010).

Agile approaches do not guarantee success. The IT landscape in which the projects of the New School of IT operate is too complex. Excessive freedom is just as pointless for these kinds of projects as the attempt to define every detail in advance.

In particular, the rejection of advance detail planning, requirements elicitation and design work that is propagated by agile methods quickly reaches its limits in major projects in established IT landscapes: The integration requirements that are posed by a heterogeneous system landscape, and the attention to detail that is required for the correct implementation of established business processes, cannot be captured in a stream of high-level user stories. In particular, it is virtually impos-sible to arrive at correct solutions in an efficient manner, using only incremental cycles of client feedback. Rather, developers and domain experts require a joint overall understanding of the business processes and IT components in order to make appropriate architecture, design and technology decisions.

From a management perspective, agile practices, such as self-organizing teams and a lack of commitment to time and budget requirements, are problematic, especially in IT projects that are developed in a client–contractor relationship and not in-house: Employees in a start-up generally have sufficient intrinsic motivation to focus on a specific goal; and in internal projects, which are not overly critical to business, a detour here or there is forgivable (and may even promote innovation or at least instruction) as long as it does not exceed the budget framework. However, in complex projects, and especially in contractor relationships, a concrete idea of the target, direction, and expected effort of the project is essential in order to limit the economic risk for all stakeholders and ensure the smooth functioning of ongoing business operations.

A purely agile doctrine therefore does not quite seem to fit into the world of large companies: Giving up on detailed specifications altogether because it seems impossible to determine precisely which features can be delivered at which price is not acceptable for most clients. Careful advance consideration is always helpful, even if the results are known to be preliminary. The agile belief that talking is fundamentally better than writing may also be met with resistance in large companies, especially when dealing with complex software systems that are created by many stakeholders and supposed to be used for a long period of time. In such circumstances, the durability of the written word has its advantages. After all, despite a basic acceptance of the benefits of agile approaches, most clients still want to know roughly how expensive their software will be, which features can be delivered at what cost, and how long the development will take. As charming and unique as agile approaches may be in theory, in commercial practice they are quickly faced with reasonable expectations of planning certainty, coordination, and reliability.

Many of the aforementioned problems are due to an excessively dogmatic application of the agile principles, which does not take the reality of complex IT projects into account. However, this dogmatic approach can be relaxed without having to reject the key advantages of agility—responsiveness to changes and leanness of processes and products. Ultimately, in practice, strict adherence to the waterfall model is just as rare as the blind application of agile practices. Many approaches from the agile world can be logically applied in almost all projects, even in large and dispersed teams, and also in a manner that respects well-defined processes and synchronization points (Leffingwell 2011).

Upon closer inspection, many of the seemingly "radical" ideas in the agile literature are dampened by disclaimers not to overdo it, to communicate extensively and to apply common sense, but without specifying what a healthy balance of agility and planning might look like. There is certainly no panacea in this respect, as agile approaches differ depending on the project, stakeholders, and boundary conditions. Appealing for common sense is an obvious measure, but is unsatisfactory from a methodological perspective. It is certainly required, but is not an adequate condition for successful projects.

Boehm and Turner (2003) discuss dimensions of software development projects that may provide guidance for the decision of agile versus plan-driven methods for specific projects. These include purely local factors, such as project scale and criticality, as well as factors that relate to the corporate environment. Specifically:

- **Scale**: In agile projects, the focus is on the spoken word. Documents and models beyond the source code are regarded as deviations from the strict agile doctrine. But the spoken word has limited reach—only among small teams will the spoken word be sufficient to create joint understanding. Large projects with many stakeholders generally require written specifications in order to ensure that all stakeholders know what is required when. This is more plan-driven than agile. As a result, a general guideline is that small projects are more likely to consistently apply agile practices.
- **Criticality**: Does the system deal with money, human life, or even many human lives? If this is the case, a higher level of planning certainty, verification of software features, and proven comprehensive testing is advisable. Proponents of strict agility might argue that nothing can better lead to higher software quality than agile techniques. Let us assume that this is correct for a moment. Let us even assume that this applies not just to small, but also to large teams. Even then, the highest probability of correct software is not sufficient when dealing with safety-critical software. Sometimes, the correctness of the software has to be demonstrated. To do so, it must be specified. Yet, there is no place for this in pure agility doctrine. As a result, the following general guideline applies: The more critical a project, the more plan-driven elements and the more "big up-front" activities (Meyer 2014, Chap. 3) are required.
- **Dynamism**: The more dynamic the project context and the application environment of the software to be created, the greater the benefits provided by agile techniques. The strengths of agile techniques are particularly pronounced when a high level of dynamism is required. Dynamism may have completely different triggers: It may be caused exogenously, because a company's market, in which the software is to be used, is moving and it must be assumed that this movement will have an impact on the software (during its development or subsequent use). It may be organizational, because the company is currently being reorganized. Reasons for dynamism may also lie in the project, because certain requirements are fiercely contested, conflicts are foreseeable, or simply because an inadequate amount of domain knowledge exists. The latter form of dynamism does not necessarily have to affect the entire software equally. Perhaps some parts are well understood and easy to coordinate and others are not. As a result, a general guideline is that the more dynamic the context, the more a project tends toward agile techniques.
- **Personnel qualification**: While it would be desirable, not every team is fit for agile development. Agile development requires the involvement of clients, users, and the application domain. If the team does not have the relevant skills or know-how, the transfer of knowledge between users and developers generally has to be managed in a non-agile manner (i.e., via extensive specification documents), and often fails. A lack of domain knowledge by developers puts the project in jeopardy from the very beginning. If one still wants (or has) to take that risk, neither a purely agile or purely plan-driven approach is likely to work, and a situational mix of both approaches is required. The following general guideline applies: The greater the language difficulties between the development

team and users, the greater the dependence on an appropriate mix of agile and plan-driven instruments in order to compensate for this deficit.

- **Culture:** Companies with the same business purpose, same size, similar products, and the same market may differ culturally despite their commonalities. Cultural differences are often manifested in how errors and requirements for change are handled. On the one hand, some companies require the minutes of meetings to be signed by all stakeholders and, in some cases, the length of the change histories exceed the useful part of documents. On the other hand, some companies focus on recording just the key results. They accept the fact that some decisions cannot be transparent for all stakeholders, that back-and-forth discussion is required, and that decisions can simply be interpreted differently. Depending on an individual's perspective, these contradictions can either be referred to as "control-focused versus pragmatic" or as "careful versus casual." Both are just as partisan as the contradiction between "plan-driven versus agile." In fact, a company's culture often either propagates the use of agile techniques ("agility is genuinely necessary") or their limitation ("that level of agility is really not acceptable here"). A general guideline is that control-focused/careful company cultures generally tend toward plan-driven approaches and could benefit from agile injections, while the opposite is true for pragmatic/casual corporate cultures.

1.3 A Pragmatic Middle Ground

As we can see, the challenges of the New School of IT call for an approach that occupies a pragmatic middle ground between traditional and agile software development processes, i.e., an approach that does not attempt to guarantee planning certainty, trust, and value orientation based on comprehensive specifications, but that also does not expect these qualities to emerge automatically through the free interaction of forces.

Rather, large, digital companies require an approach of *tamed agility* in order to combine the necessary flexibility with essential rough planning (budget planning, portfolio planning, and IT controlling): Tamed agility is a middle ground for IT projects that can benefit from the flexibility of agile approaches, but must satisfy expectations with regard to business complexity, environment conditions, contractual requirements, etc., which make stricter preliminary planning essential.

Tamed agility combines techniques from agile approaches with planning and management methods. However, its primary aim is to ensure that all stakeholders develop a common understanding of what the essential requirements are at the start of a project, namely the requirements whose appropriate implementation determines the acceptance of the software (McMenamin and Palmer 1984). But how can these essential requirements be determined? How can they be separated from the many other, possibly also relevant, but non-essential requirements? And how can a vision of the future system be formed based on the knowledge of the essential requirements? This is impossible without abstraction, without temporary omission of irrelevant details, and a focus on the essentials—and it is especially impossible without a readiness for compromise and respect for application knowledge.

Before we look at how this can be achieved in software development, let us first take a step back and consider a situation that has nothing to do with software: Imagine a CEO who would like to understand what his new company building will look like and how it will function. He does not want to know exactly how the heating system will work, how thick the thermal insulation is, or how much air is exchanged by the ventilation system every hour. But he would like to know what the building looks like, where his office is, and what the view from his office is like. Probably, he is not aware of any of this and simply asks the project manager about the status of the building planning. She dutifully sends him 15 PDF files that provide information about everything: the view, the office layout, the building services, the access concept, and much more. The manager now realizes that he did not want this level of detail. After some back-and-forth discussion, it may turn out that a wood model stands in the project office and that the most important building plans have been attached to the office walls. Much better than 15 PDF files—not for every purpose, but certainly for the purpose of giving an idea and an anchoring point from which a range of further questions can be asked and answered.

This example shows that different communication situations require different models. A manager requires an overview model. This does not need to be formally precise, nor does it need to be overly detailed. Rather, it must support intuitive understanding. The authority processing the building application requires a model of the building to be constructed with precise dimensions and specifications. An approximate model is not sufficient in order to evaluate things like the maximum eaves height and compliance with clearance requirements. The building authority is less interested in other details though, such as the technical design of the installations, but those are relevant for the heating engineer. And even other models are obviously required for the interior design.

Software development requires models that are at least as diverse. This may be because the final artifact, the delivered software, is itself only a model of a section of the world. Models from which software is to be generated require a different level of detail and precision than models that only need to clarify the purpose, the core aim of the project, and the look and feel of the software to be created. Such models are especially required in the early phases of software construction. And this takes us back to the CEO who wants to understand his building: Just as 15 PDF files cannot help him, a manager who just wants to get an idea of a software project's core aim and state will not learn much from a 500-page specification.

As a result, we can conclude that vague, incomplete, perhaps even inconsistent models can be useful in the early phases of software development. In some cases, they may even be just the right communication tool. Completeness is not the aim in these early project phases. Instead, the aim is to find out what does and what does not belong into the software to be created. The boundary between the actual system and its context must be defined. And, in particular, the most important requirements must be identified, independently of their solutions. This is not just because these essential requirements must not be overlooked, but primarily because they clarify the key requirements for stakeholders with no knowledge of the application domain. Abstract models, which can be understood by all stakeholders, are particularly helpful for the initial requirements scoping of a software project.

Such an approach is most successful if the models are jointly prepared. If a model is *really* prepared *jointly* (rather than just one person preparing everything independently, and the others just approving the result), verbal communication and the joint struggle to find the best solution are unbeatable in terms of efficiency. Rough resource estimates are made based on the jointly prepared (and thus jointly understood) models (keeping in mind that this kind of estimate can only be rough and provisional).

Development then takes place using the necessary amount of agility, as late requirements are inevitable and priorities may change during development. Late requirements are exchanged for early requirements to ensure that the software being created does not become increasingly bloated. This not only means that new requirements are added, but that a continuous cleanup also takes place. Perhaps a bit less software may be enough after all, and the resource estimate is adjusted with every step toward a more solid structure and design of the software. In the design itself, the commercial risks are fairly distributed between the client and the contractor so that all sides are motivated to create the leanest possible software. This kind of tamed agility then no longer seems threatening, not even to the IT manager.

1.4   Tamed Agility in Practice

Tamed agility is not just a buzzword for another agile philosophy. It is manifested in specific instruments and procedures for the scoping, designing, development, and billing of complex agile projects, which are described in the following chapters:

The **Interaction Room** (Part II) helps teams obtain an overall picture of the business and technology, effort and risks, and the environment and dependencies without getting lost in extensive specification documents. The Interaction Room is not just a name, it is also a real, physical room. It is the central information and communication point in the project, where the focus is on the interaction between all stakeholders. Stakeholders outline models of the business processes to be supported and the data to be managed as well as the relevant application landscape on the walls of the Interaction Room. This occurs using free syntax, without specific notations, in a way all stakeholders understand. Particularly critical elements, i.e., special value, effort, or risk drivers, are highlighted with annotation symbols. These annotations allow the stakeholders to point out what is important to them and why. This occurs through personal interaction with one another, not through long-winded specifications or asynchronous communication. The live interaction results in a more direct development of a joint understanding of the scope of the project and the expected complexity of individual features, without the need for extensive documentation.

During the course of the project, the **adVANTAGE contract model** (Part III) then ensures that the agility that all stakeholders desire does not get trapped in rigid contracts, acceptance, and billing modalities, but that it is actually applied in practice as part of a fair cooperation between the contractor and the client. Sprints are planned in the Interaction Room, new and old requirements are weighed against each other, effort estimates are refined with a view toward the "big picture," and actual progress is compared to plans. The adVANTAGE model controls the sprint-based project billing and, in contrast to fixed-price or time and materials projects, ensures that the price risks are fairly distributed between the client and the contractor. All stakeholders are united in the goal of developing lean software, because additional effort is split between both sides.

References

Ambler SW (2001) Agile modeling and the Rational unified process (RUP). http://www. agilemodeling.com/essays/agileModelingRUP.htm. Accessed 23 Feb 2016

Andreessen M (2011) Why software is eating the world. Wall Street Journal, 20 Aug 2011. http:// www.wsj.com/articles/SB10001424053111903480904576512250915629460. Accessed 23 Feb 2016

Beck K et al (2001) Manifesto for agile software development. http://www.agilemanifesto.org. Accessed 23 Feb 2016

Boehm B, Turner R (2003) Balancing agility and discipline: A guide for the perplexed. Addison-Wesley

Cohn M (2010) Succeeding with agile. Addison-Wesley, pp 166-171

Cusumano MA (1992) Shifting economies: From craft production to flexible systems and software factories. Research Policy 21(5):453–480. doi:10.1016/0048-7333(92)90005-O

Duvall PM, Matyas S, Glover A (2007) Continuous integration: Improving software quality and reducing risk. Addison-Wesley

Gartner, Inc. (2012) Gartner says every budget is becoming an IT budget. http://www.gartner.com/ newsroom/id/2208015. Accessed 23 Feb 2016

Humble J, Farley D (2010) Continuous delivery: Reliable software releases through build, test, and deployment automation. Addison-Wesley

Leffingwell D (2011) Agile software requirements: Lean requirements practices for teams, programs, and the enterprise. Addison-Wesley

McMenamin SM, Palmer JF (1984) Essential systems analysis. Yourdon

Meyer B (2014) Agile! The good, the hype and the ugly. Springer

Moore G (2011) Systems of engagement and the future of enterprise IT: A sea change in enterprise IT. http://www.aiim.org/futurehistory. Accessed 23 Feb 2016

Ries E (2011) The lean startup: How today's entrepreneurs use continuous innovation to create radically successful businesses. Crown Business

Schwaber K, Sutherland J (2012) Software in 30 days: How agile managers beat the odds, delight their customers, and leave competitors in the dust. Wiley, p 6

Part II
The Interaction Room

A Room for Ideas

2

Obviously, software development is a form of modeling—after all, source code is ultimately just a model of a world view. Modeling requires abstraction, i.e., the omission of details. This omission does not just take place at a purely syntactic level. Much more important (and more difficult) is omission at the functional level, i.e., the decision on which section of reality the software should represent. The decision to omit certain functionality requires an understanding of the benefits that are expected from the software to be created. And it also requires a great deal of courage—because the nature of modeling and the uncertainty of software development mean that occasionally, the wrong things will be omitted. This courage is essential though, because including all conceivable ideas in the model to stay on the safe side (and implementing them in the product) leads to bloated software that is expensive to create and expensive to maintain.

Making reasonable decisions on a software's scope is only possible with domain knowledge. For example, let us assume that we have no idea of what the examination system at a university looks like. It seems extremely unlikely that we would be able to provide the correct responses to the question of what is required in an examination information system to be used by examination offices, lawyers, and university lecturers. In other words, a distinction between what is important and what is unimportant requires knowledge of the application domain.

This is where the Interaction Room comes into play. It brings all people responsible for developing the software product into the discussion. This most likely includes developers and future users as well as technology and business experts. They must develop a common idea of what the software to be developed must provide, what is essential and what is expendable, what is possible using the technology, and what should be left out. All this is necessary to ensure that the software is not just *correctly developed* (developers with a certain amount of experience can generally do this alone), but to ensure that the *correct software* is developed—software that provides the greatest possible benefits given the available resources. To evaluate this, developers must understand the objectives and priorities of future users. To achieve this, the Interaction Room (IR) does not follow the

© Springer International Publishing Switzerland 2016
M. Book et al., *Tamed Agility*, DOI 10.1007/978-3-319-41478-2_2

myths and rituals that are often seen in software engineering, especially those that
provide the illusion of completeness and consistency.

The Interaction Room is a physical room whose walls are covered with models
of business processes, business and physical objects, as well as user journeys and
system landscapes. It is a room in which communication is encouraged and facilitated, and whose finite walls make it clear that the focus must remain on what is
important. It is a room which makes it obvious that a business data model should
better contain 40 rather than 140 object types, and that 15 core business processes
can describe the purpose of the system more clearly than 50 special cases.

The work in the Interaction Room does not follow a completely closed
methodology (in the sense of a number of steps that lead from a problem to a
solution in a certain order). Rather, the following chapters describe a range of
method fragments that can be combined in different ways in different project
situations.[1]

An Interaction Room promotes moderated and targeted communication between
a project's stakeholders, focuses on what is important and ensures that required
features are evaluated and prioritized in light of the desired added value. The latter
occurs using annotations, which allow every stakeholder to express their ideas of
the key objectives and features of the desired solution. An Interaction Room supports the scoping of projects as well as the pursuit of project progress at a qualitative and quantitative level. It creates transparency and allows stakeholders to
jointly coordinate the direction of projects, respond to risks and changing expectations, and continuously work toward creating a lean software solution.

2.1   Key Interaction Room Principles

The Interaction Room ensures that the key principles of every project, namely
abstraction, value orientation, communication, and transparency, do not just remain
empty words, but instead become visible and tangible:

- The principle of **abstraction** demands a focus on the key relationships and
  genuinely essential decisions. The aim is to leave out details at certain levels of
  abstraction, while remaining aware that they will have to be filled in at a later
  date and that these details may subsequently play an extremely important role.
  Which details may be omitted, and where, is the subject of agreements,
  methodology, pragmatism, and common sense. In particular, models overloaded
  with details are more dangerous than incomplete models, especially in the early
  stages.
  In the Interaction Room, the abstraction requirement is manifested in the
  finiteness of the walls available for model sketches. It ensures that every

---

[1]However, for the sake of practicality, we will continue to refer to the sum of the individual
method fragments as the Interaction Room method.

stakeholder is aware that there is not enough space for every minor detail and that there is a need to focus on what is actually important.

- The principle of **value orientation** demands that the key criterion for the question of whether features are required, and the amount of effort to be spent on their implementation, is how important these features are for value creation within the business model to be supported by the software. Basically, this relates to nothing more than the decision on how the expensive activities of software development (such as specification, usability engineering, performance engineering, and security engineering) are focused on different software components. As a general rule, software is not used homogeneously (in the sense that all parts are used with the same intensity), it is not homogeneous with regard to risk (in the sense that all parts can cause the same losses), and it is also not homogeneous in any other quality. Given these inhomogeneities, it is important to keep software lean and focus efforts where they generate the most value.

  In the Interaction Room, value orientation is expressed by model annotations. They explicitly highlight particularly important features and their dimensions. A so-called requirements exchange (Sect. 8.3) also reinforces the awareness that all features have their price and that only the features that genuinely add value should be implemented.

- The principle of **communication** demands that all stakeholders are involved in defining the objective of a development project and in designing a software system. It is not necessary that every individual person has to be involved in every detail, but all groups should be represented in the relevant specifications and decisions. This involvement ensures that individuals consider the project to be "their" project, are committed to lean solutions, and participate actively.

  The Interaction Room acts as a central communication point and ensures that communication takes place face-to-face and at eye level, not just by exchanging e-mails and specifications. It is used to (re-)negotiate priorities, to assess the effects of late requirements, and to exchange early and late requirements. In short, it is used for everything that merits actual discussion, and everything that would remain a volatile unspoken perception rather than an explicit statement in written communication.

- The principle of **transparency** demands that preliminary or final specifications and decisions are made accessible to all relevant stakeholders (in the broadest possible sense). The same applies for risk considerations and qualitative and quantitative progress. Stakeholders only remain committed based on the principle of transparency. Only then can they understand and support decisions and interpret these appropriately during their detailed implementation.

  The Interaction Room displays the current state of the project at all times and represents the central orientation point and the basis for transparent structures and processes in the project.

These principles apply for all kinds of projects. However, software projects frequently have to deal with distinct challenges that prevent the consistent implementation of these principles. The following sections identify these challenges and describe the strategies and specific operationalizations that are employed in the Interaction Room in order to deal with them.

2.2   Involve Domain Experts

Curtis et al. (1988) documented that software development runs into difficulties (in the sense of project cancelations, significant delays, or budget overruns) more frequently the less knowledge the developers have in the application domain. In short, if you have no idea of what is going on, you should not be developing software. Although this realization was made more than 25 years ago and is just common sense, there is little reason to doubt that "adequate domain knowledge" is still not adequately considered as a factor for the success of software development.

The direct solution for the problem of inadequate domain competence seems clear: Only individuals who have understood the application domain, who have the same awareness of the problem, and who do not require an explanation of what is particularly important and difficult should be allowed to develop software. Access to genuine application domain experts should also be ensured at all times. This would be the perfect solution in an ideal world.

However, things are obviously much more difficult in real life: Perhaps a couple of experts who are fairly competent in the application domain are available. Perhaps it is even possible to temporarily involve an application domain expert with visionary foresight and an understanding of the issues. However, in most cases, a number of developers will not be entirely familiar with the application domain. And it is highly likely that the team's general, rough understanding of the problem will need to be supplemented with the details relevant to this particular project. In other words, it is almost always necessary to define business connections.

This knowledge transfer is not a one-way street though, where the business stakeholders hold all the solutions and the technical stakeholders just need to implement them. Rather, both the business and the technical side may have more or less feasible solution ideas that must be brought to a compatible level of abstraction. In the words of requirements engineering, this means that solution-independent requirements (i.e., based exclusively on the business application domain) and solution-based requirements (i.e., only able to be expressed based on a technical solution idea) have to be compared and aligned. Completely different stakeholder terminologies and backgrounds come together at these very early stages and require the involvement of all stakeholders in an insight-driven process.

The fundamental idea of the Interaction Room is that the application domain knowledge required for the project should be described in the simplest possible terms. Software engineering myths, such as completeness, consistency, and syntactic accuracy, must play a secondary role. The primary aim is to ensure that the problem being dealt with is clearly described, that the key relationships are noted, and that all stakeholders use the opportunity to indicate the aspects they perceive to be particularly important, difficult, or uncertain.

To make sure that every individual is actually involved, it is important that this communication takes place in an open environment and an atmosphere that is conducive to brainstorming, in which all stakeholders can talk to each other and express their ideas as they see fit, and where a hegemony of individual stakeholders is prevented. This allows individual and role-related priorities to be balanced and harmonized. All stakeholders, especially the business and expert representatives, must be placed in a position to express their ideas and objectives without barriers to entry. Being able to write and draw are the only requirements for participating in an Interaction Room. No modeling language needs to be learned, and no tools need to be used. The stakeholders create only box-and-line diagrams. This ensures the lowest possible barrier to entry, and thus prevents any one person from dominating the discussion due to their higher technical knowledge (in the form of language or tool skills).

> **Project challenge**: Thin spread of application domain knowledge.
> **Solution strategy**: Involve domain experts and enable them to discuss with technical experts.
> **Operationalization**: The IR method describes explicit expectations of the skills and attitudes of the stakeholders invited to the IR workshops (Sect. 3.5) and defines simple modeling languages that can be intuitively understood by all stakeholders (Sect. 3.1).

2.3 Refine the Scope Continuously

Systems of records must be integrated into the application landscapes of companies. Often, these integration tasks are particularly risky and difficult to assess. This is because the systems to be integrated are old, their interfaces are not well documented, and infrastructures that were not designed for this purpose need to fit together. However, integration engineering techniques (Gold-Bernstein and Ruh 2004) at least provide an overview of the integration tasks and allow the desired types of integration to be determined. This means that the boundaries of the system to be developed, its context, and the context boundaries can be defined and described, as shown in Fig. 2.1.

The *system context* is the part of the system environment that is relevant for defining and understanding the requirements of the relevant system. It provides useful features and systems to be integrated, which are available without having to

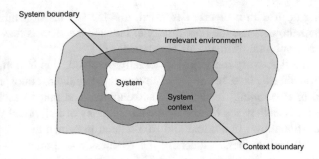

Fig. 2.1 System boundary, context, and external environment [adapted from Pohl and Rupp (2015)]

be created. The *system boundary* separates the planned system from its environment. It isolates the part of reality that can be shaped and changed as part of the development process from aspects in the environment that cannot be changed by the development process. A clear picture of the system boundary is only provided once the requirements are relatively stable. This may occasionally be the case after the initial scoping, but often takes until well into the implementation phase. This means that the boundary may also shift slightly in some instances: Parts of the system context may become part of the system because the feature originally assumed in the context is not available, or because the context cannot be adapted. Or, parts of the system are transferred to the system context because parts that were initially classified as "to be implemented" have been located in the context and do not have to be built from scratch. The *context boundary* ultimately separates the relevant part of a planned system environment from the irrelevant part, i.e., the part of the environment that has no influence on the planned system and its requirements.

But systems of records are only one side of the coin. The other side is the systems of engagement, whose features are generally not fixed at the start of a development project. Systems of this type tend to emerge rather than being strictly planned. It is virtually impossible to plan how these systems will be embedded into their environment. The integration requirements tend to grow in a similar manner to the functional requirements during the development process. A clear separation between the system to be developed, its context, and the external environment is not possible; the boundaries remain blurred.

This is not a bad thing, as long as all stakeholders are prepared to bear the resulting consequences. The consequences include the fact that the integration costs cannot be calculated in advance, and only coarsely even during development; that the system's architecture and its functional design are emergent, i.e., only arise during development; and that this means that some of the traditional planning and controlling instruments are ineffective.

Project challenge: Project boundaries remain fuzzy for a long time.
Solution strategy: Explicitly show and discuss what is part of the system and what is not.
Operationalization: The integration canvas (Sect. 5.5) provides an explicit view of the system under development and its interfaces with the environment.

2.4 Favor Relevance Over Completeness

In many projects, the key aspects are sprinkled over a 500-page document in which the 250 key business processes are noted, while the object model looks like a large wallpaper. These types of documents and artifacts are useful—for those who created them. It is likely that the author sorted, structured, and classified the information in the document meticulously. It is just a shame that virtually nobody is able to use these types of documents for their required purpose. How could they? Who is able to read 500-page documents and keep an eye on what is actually important? Yet, these kinds of documents are still reviewed and quality assured. The results generally get stuck at the syntactic level. Some areas have a large number of spelling mistakes, cross-references are missing in other areas, and there will certainly be something missing from the glossary. This kind of review does not provide any real benefits. How can it? First you need to know what really matters, what the essential requirements are. This "big picture," this abstract view, cannot be provided by a 500-page document.

Obviously, just outlining the "big picture" without providing any models and specifications with the relevant details can also not work. The devil is often in the details, and does it not seem reasonable to consider those features that appear difficult and tedious to implement in greater detail? For all the abstraction, is it not sensible to drill down into detail here and there? Sure, but where is the best place to start drilling? Is it where the ground is unknown and clarifications are expected from the drill down? Or is it not more tempting to drill where you will likely encounter what you expected?

Industrial project experience shows that detailed drill-downs often do not focus on the points that bear risks of disaster, but rather just those points where nothing unforeseen can occur anyway. This quickly leads to object models with a great level of detail in the representation of addresses and individuals, but not in areas relating to the retroactive cancelation of active contracts (or other difficult aspects). This may be due to the fact that humans prefer to focus on the known and because insight-driven processes require effort. Typical computer scientists (in the broadest sense) can model, so they model. However, they are not directly familiar with retroactive contract cancelations, but they are aware of the relationship between addresses, address supplements, and natural and legal persons (where they can even apply inheritance). Alas, drilling down at this point is comparatively useless. It provides no new insights and does not reveal any risks. Instead, it leads activity and attention away from the truly difficult parts.

But it gets worse. If the modeler has now exerted all their available modeling artistry in the address modeling, they generally want to present their model. A business representative is now confronted with compositions, aggregations, associations, and inheritances. After this, he has to present a typical customer support process. It seems only human that this, too, will now involve some exaggeration. Look at the position in which the business expert is placed. If the modeling of addresses is this complicated, then the business process should certainly not seem downright trivial? So the business expert shifts the focus from a typical process flow to the special case of a client who has already signed but wants to withdraw, wants to emigrate, but dies before crossing the border. The parity of useless complexity has been achieved; business and technology are both so complicated that they can never be understood by the other side. At this point, one refers to "analysis paralysis" (Langley 1995).

In the Interaction Room, there is no requirement to describe a system at such a level of completeness and detail. Stakeholders only need to specify the 15 key business processes (each with a maximum of 15 activities), the 40 key object types, and describe the 20 key systems to be integrated. Is this enough? Not only is this enough, it can already lead to all-day discussions even at this level of abstraction, while everything else just provides a distraction from what is important. Admittedly, it does not matter whether there are 15 business processes or 17, whether there are 40 object types or 45. But there are certainly not 150 business processes, no wallpaper-size diagrams and no 500-page documents. This focus on what is important works in the Interaction Room because models are sketched on whiteboards. The finite nature of whiteboards ensures that the principle of abstraction is embedded in the room.

Detailed considerations are naturally also permitted in the Interaction Room, but only where they promise knowledge acquisition and where they are clearly identified as drilling down beyond the big picture. Appropriate drilling points are identified after the abstract representation (first the abstract level, then the detail) based on the stakeholders' assessments of complexity and feasibility. Points are only considered as candidates for drilling down if they are assessed as complex, not completely understood and of uncertain feasibility by the majority of stakeholders.

Project challenge: Stakeholders get lost in discussions of details.
Solution strategy: Clearly highlight what is important and leave out what is trivial—favor relevance over completeness.
Operationalization: The finite nature of the Interaction Room's walls, and the limits on the number of artifacts suggested for each canvas,

enforces a focus on the most important points that can be modeled (Sect. 3.1). Model annotations highlight where drilling down into detail promises further insights (Sect. 3.3).

2.5 Favor Clarity Over Syntactic and Semantic Precision

Most software projects require the cooperation of business departments and enterprise IT. This sounds like communication difficulties might be involved: Different languages are spoken; common terms have different connotations; different perceptions exist in relation to the purpose and aim of abstraction and structuring. This problem is frequently aggravated by the fact that enterprise IT prescribes the tools to use for defining the common model. A business area representative then has to understand the difference between association, aggregation, and composition, even if all he wants to say is that a connection exists between the application and the contract.

Enterprise IT tends to move the modeling of application-related matters to familiar territory, generally without any malicious intent, which leaves the business departments in the dark. Nobody wants to learn the Unified Modeling Language (UML) or any other language. The business departments generally feel comfortable with box-and-line diagrams without specific syntax and semantics. This is naturally not a permanent solution—over time, models need to become more precise, especially at the difficult points, so they need to be assigned precise semantics. But not necessarily from the start, when the focus should primarily be on ensuring that no unnecessary communication barriers are established.

If the aim is to structure the communication process between enterprise IT and the business departments such that specialists can share their expertise in the simplest possible manner (so that every individual can express what they consider to be important), then entry barriers to describing business relationships must be kept as low as possible. Issues must be modeled so that application domain experts can participate without establishing unnecessary barriers. These kinds of unnecessary barriers particularly include instruments and modeling languages that distract from the content and focus on methodology and syntax.

Besides the barriers raised by modeling languages and instruments in communication between business areas and enterprise IT, it may also be the case that business stakeholders who feel forced to deal with this kind of information complexity, also feel that they must ensure that business relationships do not seem too trivial, and so attempt to overemphasize their complexity by detailing pathological marginal cases. This quickly leads to the escalation of complexity, which is diametrically opposed to the essential focus on basic relationships in the early phases.

The Interaction Room supports informal sketches and the use of basic cultural techniques—drawing, writing, annotating—that do not establish barriers in the early phases of alignment between business and IT experts.

> **Project challenge**: Correctness and consistency requirements of many modeling languages foster complexity and obscurity rather than clarity.
> **Solution strategy**: Focus on content rather than syntactic correctness and semantic precision of early models.
> **Operationalization**: The notation used on the Interaction Room canvases is deliberately limited to a minimum amount of syntax (Sect. 3.1).

2.6   Define Value and Effort Drivers

The first question that is almost always asked when developing software systems is: What is essential, which features are actually required, and which ones are indispensable? Indispensability in the sense of value orientation means that the features to be provided actually contribute to the company's value creation and that this value creation would be lower without the features (Wohlin and Aurum 2006). Only for very small and manageable systems can this question can be answered by a single individual. For larger systems, a single expert who can individually assess and decide what needs to be prioritized is generally not available. Rather, several experts need to be asked. This naturally leads to fuzzy criteria and discussions. Deciding whether an issue that is considered indispensable by one expert is actually indispensable, and deciding how the various indispensable features can be weighed against each other, requires considerable knowledge of the application domain.

And because the true value of software (anchored in the value created by the company using the software) is virtually impossible to measure, most attempts to measure the usefulness of software provide different results. Instead of measuring whether the developed software adds value and whether it is worth the effort to create the software, the productivity of the software development is assessed using measures that do not relate to the value added. The fact that counting code lines does not provide any information on the value of software is clear to anyone who knows the meaning of "copy and paste." The uselessness of function points (Behrens 1983) and weighted function points (McConnell 2006) is not immediately apparent, but becomes clear when you consider that the true benefit of software means achieving a business-related objective with as little effort as possible. The fact that the same objective can always also be reached with more user interaction and more database access is irrelevant. More complicated software does not necessarily provide greater benefits.

Unfortunately, traditional methods of measurement are only based on quantity. This sanctions precisely what is particularly important to us, rather than promoting it: Lean software that fulfills its purpose has the lowest possible function points and the least possible lines of code. However, the fulfillment of purpose in the sense of value orientation cannot be measured algorithmically. Fulfillment of purpose can only be assessed in light of the intended application. And this requires an understanding of what the user wants to achieve with the software. What is the added value? What is genuinely essential? Questions such as these have long been discussed [e.g., essential use cases (Constantine and Lockwood 1999) or value-based software engineering (Biffl et al. 2006)] without reaching any clear solutions.

The Interaction Room enables stakeholders to define different dimensions of "essential." Stakeholders from all areas indicate what they consider important and form a joint picture of the value drivers: What are the features based on which we are actually building the system? Who expects what from these features? What features does this kind of system need in order to run? Are these actually needed? This value calibration does not just occur once at the start of the project, but continuously. In doing so, the Interaction Room helps to ensure that the focus on values anchored in the application domain is omnipresent for stakeholders. The value of features also plays a key role during prioritization in the adVANTAGE contract model (Sect. 15.2).

> **Project challenge**: Losing track of the business value.
> **Solution strategy**: Define value and effort drivers and thus come to a joint understanding of what are the really important requirements of the project.
> **Operationalization**: In the Interaction Room, value, and effort drivers are highlighted by graphic annotations that are attached to model elements (Sect. 3.3).

2.7   Manage Late Requirements

A typical phenomenon is that of a late requirement: Regardless of the effort spent on the initial requirements analysis for information systems, it is virtually certain that additional requirements will arise during development; because information systems are sociotechnical systems, because user requirements change over time, or simply because new ideas are developed once the initial solution approaches are defined.

Changing requirements are a threat to projects [as described by Curtis et al. (1988)] but are unfortunately also inevitable. Changing requirements are risks inherent in software development—they cannot be prevented, they can only be managed.

Traditional responses to this dilemma all lead to what is commonly referred to as "change request theater", which still causes image problems for the software industry: Change request theater means that clients and developers split hairs over the question of what was and was not promised, what can and cannot lead to additional costs, and who is responsible for the additional costs.

This theater illustrates that striving for complete requirements for all stake-holders is futile. Should requirement documents be completely eliminated then, because it is clear that they quickly become outdated anyway? Or should we completely eschew the requirements analysis, because it is clear that it will not be complete and conclusive? If we leave responses tainted by agile myths to one side, the answer is clear: Requirements must at least be recorded when they relate to information systems that are to be used by a large number of people over a long period of time, or if the development process has to lead to a prescribed result. If both are not the case, then a requirement document may be dispensed with, if possible.

In the Interaction Room, late requirements are handled so that changes are initially dealt with at an abstract level. The model sketches describe the most important features of the software to be developed. Late requirements that are recorded at this level are very important as they affect the basic functionality. The effects of these kinds of changes must be discussed, both with regard to their business and technical impact as well as their effect on budgets, deadlines, and priorities. Other late requirements may arise, but are of a secondary nature. This does not mean that they cannot also have a significant effect in some cases, but they affect the structure and functionality of the system to be developed to a lesser extent.

An assessment of the impact helps evaluate the effort required for early and late requirements. The addition of late requirements is permitted, but must be balanced by the removal of early requirements to ensure that the project budget and schedule remain on course.

Project challenge: Illusion of requirements completeness.

Solution strategy: Evaluate late requirements based on their effort and include them only if they can be balanced by the removal of requirements that require a similar amount of effort.

Operationalization: In the Interaction Room, late requirements are managed by the requirements exchange (Sect. 8.3). The adVANTAGE contract model addresses the risks of late requirements through different risk distribution and budget security mechanisms (Sects. 14.3 and 14.4).

2.8 Manage Early Requirements

Everyone is aware that projects have to deal with *late* requirements. But (*too*) *early* requirements also exist. We understand early requirements as wishes that have only coincidentally reached the status of a valid requirement at the start of the project. Different types of coincidences are possible:

Perhaps a project has been delayed for an extended period of time. Now, none of the potential requirements requesters want to risk the possibility that their wishes remain unconsidered. In some cases, a requirements race arises based on the expectation that not everything will be implemented anyway. So every idea and wish, no matter how irrelevant, is thrown into the requirements pot. And if no one makes sure that ridiculous items are sorted out, this creates the beginnings of a monster project.

Things get particularly uncomfortable if individual requesters do not participate in the requirements race and restrict themselves to genuinely essential requirements. These requirements are then underrepresented in an incipient monster project and may be reduced even further if requirements are carelessly cut back. This means that not only have we created a monster project, but one with an incorrect focus— just because of the misguided conviction that every feature that reaches a requirement status is important.

But it may also be the case that someone has fueled the illusion that no late requirements will be accepted because a "final" requirements description is being prepared, so that the focus can then turn exclusively to software development. This is when the requirement race starts in earnest. Yet, the supposed complete requirements description is subsequently presented, adapted, improved, etc. In the meantime, the requesters, even those who did not want to be involved in the race, have the opportunity for detailed reflection on further wishes and potential software-bloating ideas.

This certainly does not lead to leaner software. Rather, the requirements pot is filled with all kinds of requirements that do not really belong there. As a result, the first essential step is to clean up and separate the important from the irrelevant. In doing so, one must not lose sight of the essential requirements (McMenamin and Palmer 1984). But even after cleaning up, the pot will still contain a number of requirements that do not need to be implemented at the end of the project. Because just as late requirements exist (those that are not considered necessary at the start of the project and which are identified as necessary during the project), so do early requirements (those that were considered necessary at the start of the project but which turn out to be unnecessary during the course of the project).

Typically, these kinds of early requirements are only removed as the delivery deadline approaches. Time is running out and someone finally asks: "Do we really still need to implement this?" However, by this point, a large number of (potentially unnecessary) requirements have already been implemented and the quantity of requirements that can still be eliminated is quite small.

To prevent this, the Interaction Room applies the rule that an early requirement to be eliminated must be identified for every late requirement that is added to the pot. Naturally, this type of requirements exchange does not solve every problem (e.g., that of an unequal requirements race remains), but it promotes a systematic approach to two problems:

- Every requester must consider how lean the software could be at an early stage. In the long term, this attitude means that the focus on complete, bloated software is redirected toward value-focused, leaner software.
- Insidious software bloating due to late requirements is countered by the continuous removal of early requirements.

Project challenge: Requirements are bloated from the start of the project.
Solution strategy: Continuously identify and eliminate premature requirements.
Operationalization: In the Interaction Room, the requirements exchange helps to weed out too-early requirements by encouraging to swap them against late requirements (Sect. 8.3). The adVANTAGE contract model targets the continuous adaptation of the project scope (Sect. 14.1).

2.9   Reveal Uncertainties Early

Even the most sophisticated software development plan prepared with the greatest care is generally not followed dogmatically. This is almost inevitable, as software development is an insight-driven process, which is confronted with significant inaccuracies, especially at the beginning. These inaccuracies affect the business requirement details, system and context boundaries (Sect. 2.3), and the skills of the stakeholders involved, their organizational corporate context, and their adherence to and faith in the method.

All these uncertainties are eliminated during the project; assumptions are gradually replaced by findings. During development, stakeholders learn what is actually required, what is particularly important to implement, and what can be left out. In this type of process, it is almost inevitable that new findings will lead to changes in the plan. Ultimately, the aim of the software development process is to eliminate inaccuracies and manage uncertainties.

The fact that uncertainty is unavoidable in every type of software project has been accepted for decades (Boehm 1981; Lehman 1989). However, two opposing philosophies have developed on how to correctly deal with this uncertainty:

Plan-driven approaches attempt to eliminate uncertainty at the start of the project by investing a huge amount of effort in precise requirements analyses and specification and design work. The idea that this detailed examination of the material leads to knowledge acquisition is undisputed. However, it remains questionable whether uncertainty can be eliminated to the extent suggested by the resulting mountain of paper; whether the effort to eliminate uncertainty has been applied efficiently (especially at the critical points); and which part of this effort becomes obsolete during the course of the project as the requirements change.

By contrast, agile approaches pursue the (almost fatalistic) approach that nothing can be done to counter uncertainty a priori and that issues are best eliminated gradually as they arise during the course of the project. Together with the principle of only developing precisely what you (or the client) have planned for the coming weeks and deliberately ignoring additional features, this is a perfectly consistent and efficient approach. However, it seems to be much better suited to startups, which develop their product fundamentals piece by piece on a clean slate, than for developing complex business components in a highly integrated system landscape.

In this case, tamed agility means choosing a middle path: Just as it is pointless to want to eliminate all uncertainty at the start of a project, it is also shortsighted to only eliminate uncertainty on an ad hoc basis, in areas where it seems urgent. Rather, the objective must be to establish an overview of where uncertainty exists at an early stage, in order to identify where risks are present and plan how these are to be dealt with: While a certain number of uncertainties can be eliminated by brief examination, others may require the involvement of experts or more comprehensive prototyping, while still others may have the potential to jeopardize the entire project. While this itself is naturally uncertain and remains in flux over the course of the project, it still helps to decide which uncertainties need to be eliminated at the start of the project, and which ones only have to be considered once they become urgent, in line with the agile model.

The prominent role of uncertainty means that one thing is certain: Uncertainty must be defined and managed. All stakeholders should be fundamentally prepared for the fact that uncertainty exists and that new areas of uncertainty can arise. A general rule for managing uncertainty is: Known uncertainties must be investigated (to turn uncertainty into certainty) and unknown uncertainties must be sought out (so that no late uncertainty surprises arise).

Project challenge: New insights overturn previous plans, jeopardizing the project's budget, schedule, or quality.

Solution strategy: Reveal uncertainties early so they can be eliminated and account for uncertainty in the contractual framing of the project.

Operationalization: In the Interaction Room, model elements can be marked with uncertainty annotations in order to express the need for clarification by stakeholders (Sect. 3.3). In the adVANTAGE contract model, uncertainties that manifest themselves in overspends or unfinished features are no reason for stress between the contract partners. Rather, they are an accepted project situation for which fair accounting modalities exist (Sect. 15.4).

2.10 Make Cost Changes Transparent

The genuinely unpleasant aspect of software development is that the final development expenses are not known at any time prior to the productive use of a full version of the software. Despite extensive attempts at making cost estimates more precise and reliable, despite increasing awareness of the difficulties and problems of cost estimation by COCOMO and successors (Boehm et al. 2000), despite numerous metrics [from McCabe (1976) to function points (Behrens 1983)] and despite fundamental appeals to quantify software development (Denne and Cleland-Huang 2003), the estimation of software development expenses remains one of the main sticking points in many projects. This is true even though genuinely risky activities, such as integrating the software into an application landscape or migrating legacy data, are often excluded in advance, and even though it is precisely these risky activities that have a significant impact on the overall efficiency of software development, introduction, and use.

The practice of industrial software development is still predominantly based on the principle of expert estimates. If these experts are adequately familiar with the technology and application domain, it is possible that they can provide the best estimate of all possible forecasts. However, during development, it often becomes clear that some things are more complicated than initially thought, while some may be simpler. Late requirements are added, and early requirements are removed. Expert estimates typically do not cover these unavoidable dynamics, as well as the experience gained during the project.

Still, consolidation makes sense: If we have an expert estimate at the feature level, and software development takes place iteratively based on a strictly interpreted Definition of Done, the unavoidable inadequacies of the initial expense estimate can be partially compensated by comparing the actual expense to the initial estimate and preparing appropriate projections. These numbers can then be made transparent to all stakeholders, and the knowledge gained can be applied to the expert estimate, so new forecasts will take into account previous forecast deviations.

> **Project challenge**: Stakeholders like to believe that project costs are fixed.
> **Solution strategy**: Make expected cost changes (and the reasons for them) transparent.
> **Operationalization**: The cost forward progressing technique constantly compares the current effort investment with the estimates and provides budget forecasts (Sect. 8.6). The adVANTAGE contract model controls the contractual handling of fluctuating costs by treating these kinds of fluctuations as the normal case, not as an exception (Sect. 14.1).

2.11 Analyze the Risk of Disasters

Some projects are somewhat more expensive than expected, while some are slightly less expensive. As long as these deviations remain within a certain corridor (such as ±10 % of the initial estimated value), they will raise eyebrows in management, but do not threaten the existence of the project. However, it is not the moderate deviations that pose a threat to software development projects, but the outliers: Projects that become twice as expensive, take twice as long as planned, or are canceled and rolled back. These kinds of situations involve significant loss potential; they tend to lead to legal disputes.

Such disasters are made possible by the Hiob principle: Almost everyone is aware that the success of the project is threatened, but no one is prepared to explicitly state this knowledge. Instead, progress and risk "traffic light symbols" are displayed in agreeable colors that can be easily communicated. Even if things look bleak, the project's executive-summary status indicator may be colored various shades of yellow, but will rarely look dark red. If at all, the difficulties are discussed at the coffee machine in a small intimate circle and without identifying any countermeasures.

This phenomenon can be overcome by requesting joint and mutually agreed project evaluations (which relate to both progress and feasibility as a whole): Who has identified risks and in which area, how are the features connected, what integration and data migration requirements exist for the software?

The Interaction Room deals with all these questions in such a way that consensus is promoted by synchronicity and that the actual problems are not ignored. An assessment is not provided by one individual and then commented on by another so that the first individual makes marginal changes. Otherwise, this always leads to the same result: Average risk and at worst a pale yellow traffic light symbol.

Rather, in the Interaction Room, a number of standard questions are jointly answered (by all stakeholders) to obtain everyone's assessment of possible risks. The risks are examined in various dimensions, and critical assessments are clarified.

This occurs at the start of the project and then at regular intervals. Explicit communication regarding the project status is made accessible to all stakeholders.

> **Project challenge**: Risks remain intransparent and catch the project by surprise.
>
> **Solution strategy**: Evaluate emergency indicators periodically and make all stakeholders aware of them.
>
> **Operationalization**: The Interaction Room provides the risk map (Sect. 8.4) as an instrument for continuous risk analysis.

2.12　Build Trust Between Stakeholders

Should software development be a matter of trust? Trust does not seem to be a component of traditional software process models; rather, software is created by the constant refinement of specifications, from the requirements document through to the specification and the code, where the documents to be produced by specific departments are defined as strictly as the individuals that require these documents.

The fact that these refinement steps are not mechanical processes, that they are creative and necessarily interdisciplinary activities to which application domain and technology experts can both contribute in equal measure, is often concealed. In process models such as the V model, the path from the idea to the working software seems more like a bureaucratic marathon. Whether a document is even sufficiently relevant and correct in order to use it as the basis for the next refinement step, whether a document's author and reader have understood its business and technical implications, is overlooked. Yet, in many cases, business departments and enterprise IT in major companies, clients, and developers in service contracts and even onshore and offshore parties in distributed development projects still operate as if specifications, including schedules, can simply be set in stone, and a perfectly functioning product can be expected by the deadline. (This naturally also displays a certain level of trust, though of a more naive nature than what one might wish for.)

The restrictions that developers occasionally feel put under by plan-driven software process models as a result of the specification requirements is countered by agile methods and their essentially complete elimination of specifications. They are replaced by close and intensive communication between all stakeholders, and especially, frequent feedback cycles with the client on requirements, prototypes, and releases. These feedback cycles focus on what is working and what the client likes, not what a document indicates. This practice works best in small, manageable, and especially tangible (interface-intensive) applications, whose progress can be clearly identified at the user interface. However, in large information systems, a great deal happens under the hood and is not directly accessible to the client, neither for review nor for precise description, whether written or verbal. No wonder that, in these circumstances, stakeholders from the operating area or management, who are not IT-savvy, lack confidence and trust that this kind of process can work, let alone that it can lead to predictable results.

> **Project challenge**: Stakeholders from business and technical departments can be adversaries.
> **Solution strategy**: Build trust between the stakeholders and encourage a feeling of joint ownership of the project.
> **Operationalization**: Cross-department communication is encouraged by joint project design and monitoring in all Interaction Room activities, which explicitly require stakeholders from a variety of backgrounds (Sect. 3.5). The adVANTAGE contract model allows clients and contractors to prioritize requirements during the course of the project transparently and reach mutually acceptable decisions (Sect. 15.2).

2.13 Visualize the Project's Progress

It is often difficult enough to specify the project objective and ensure that all stakeholders are committed to it. Constant monitoring then needs to ensure that this direction is maintained (or adapted by mutual consent) and that all stakeholders have the opportunity to follow the progress of the project. Without this kind of joint progress monitoring, the initially aligned expectations often begin to diverge. This occurs with absolutely no malicious intent by the stakeholders, simply because the developers have acquired knowledge that they do not share with the business stakeholders, or because the knowledge is imparted to business stakeholders and they become uncertain as to whether the initial project objective is still valid. If one or two misunderstandings and rumors are added to the mix, the initial harmonizing effect is quickly lost and the expectations of the stakeholders start to diverge. This is why central decisions must be coordinated and project progress (and regression) has to be made transparent.

The tracking of the project progress has two dimensions: Firstly, the purely expense-based, quantitative control of the project progress—primarily based on the agile adVANTAGE contract model (Chap. 15)—which predominantly provides information on the commercial side of the project. And, secondly, the content-related, qualitative side, which provides information on when specific features will become operational, which components are already complete and what the upcoming deliveries will look like (Sect. 8.5).

For business departments and future users, the qualitative dimension is often more important than the expense figures, budget overruns, and compliance. The business department's ability to assess the content-related progress is important for their expectations and confidence in the project. Without this confidence, the project mood can quickly change, quite apart from the fact that the development then quickly deviates from the expectations of the business departments. As a result, what has already been completed, how previously delivered software will be expanded in the future and how past, current, and future deliveries align with one another must be clarified and explained.

The project state is often particularly difficult to define at the start of the project because there is not much to see. Initial deliveries often consist of isolated dialogs and reports whose subsequent relevance is virtually impossible to assess. An Interaction Room supports the visualization of the project progress and the iden- tification of the results achieved in the context of the project by pasting achieved intermediate results (e.g., screenshots of implemented dialogs) directly onto the model sketches. This also allows individual dialogs to be assessed in their future context.

Project challenge: Stakeholders lack a clear picture of the project's state and progress.
Solution strategy: Visualize the project state continuously so all stake- holders are aware of its qualitative progress at all times.
Operationalization: Continuous progress control—in terms of feature completion, requirements management, and budget controlling—is sup- ported by the methods of the IR:agile (Chap. 8).

References

Behrens CA (1983) Measuring the productivity of computer systems development activities with function points. IEEE Transactions on Software Engineering 9(6):648–652. doi:10.1109/TSE. 1983.235429

Biffl S et al (2006) Value-based software engineering. Springer

Boehm B (1981) Software engineering economics. Prentice Hall, ch 21

Boehm B et al (2000) Software cost estimation with COCOMO II. Prentice Hall

Constantine LL, Lockwood LAD (1999) Software for use: A practical guide to the models and methods of usage-centered design. Addison-Wesley, ch 5

Curtis B, Krasner H, Iscoe N (1988) A field study of the software design process for large systems. Comm ACM 31(11):1268–1287. doi:10.1145/50087.50089

Denne M, Cleland-Huang J (2003) Software by numbers: Low-risk, high-return development. Prentice Hall

Gold-Bernstein B, Ruh W (2004) Enterprise integration: The essential guide to integration solutions. Addison-Wesley

Langley A (1995) Between 'paralysis by analysis' and 'extinction by instinct'. Sloan Management Review 36(3):63–76

Lehman MM (1989) Uncertainty in computer application and its control through the engineering of software. Journal of Software Maintenance 1(1):3–27. doi:10.1002/smr.4360010103

McCabe TJ (1976) A complexity measure. IEEE Transactions on Software Engineering 2(4):308–320

McConnell S (2006) Software estimation: Demystifying the black art. Microsoft Press, ch 18.2

McMenamin SM, Palmer JF (1984) Essential systems analysis. Yourdon

Pohl K, Rupp C (2015) Requirements engineering fundamentals: A study guide for the certified professional for requirements engineering exam – Foundation level – IREB compliant. Rocky Nook

Wohlin C, Aurum A (2006) Criteria for selecting software requirements to create product value: An industrial empirical study. In: Biffl S et al (eds) Value-based software engineering. Springer, pp 179–200

Interaction Room Basics

3

One of the main goals of an Interaction Room is to ensure that the abstract relationships within complex IT projects can be intuitively discussed and understood. This is achieved by roughly modeling a range of complementary perspectives of the project: Large model sketches on all the walls in the room display the focal points of communication in the Interaction Room. Business and technology experts jointly outline key application concepts, process flows, data structures, system landscapes, and user interfaces on large whiteboards, also referred to as canvases.

The different canvases in an Interaction Room help stakeholders discuss the structures, processes, and interfaces of an information system in the context of its application domain in an objective, yet pragmatic manner. The parallel consideration of the application domain and system from different perspectives helps stakeholders from all departments develop a common overall understanding of the system, identify dependencies, contradictions, and gaps, and establish mutual respect for requirements, complexity, and boundary conditions on both the business and technology sides.

This chapter covers three topics. Section 3.1 discusses the general methodological principles of the IR method, which deals with the idea of canvases (detailed in Sect. 3.2) and their pragmatic population. It outlines the relationship between the canvases and their use in different IR variants. Section 3.3 then presents the idea of annotations and their use in IR population, while Sect. 3.4 provides an overview of the IR variants. This is followed by a discussion of the stakeholder roles that are involved in all IR variants in Sect. 3.5. Finally, Sects. 3.6 and 3.7 discuss the preparation and follow-up activities of IR workshops.

© Springer International Publishing Switzerland 2016
M. Book et al., *Tamed Agility*, DOI 10.1007/978-3-319-41478-2_3

3.1   Method Overview

The population of an Interaction Room is not a closed method in the sense that a series of clearly outlined activities lead from a starting point to the target state. Rather, there are established method fragments, whose use has proven to be useful in certain starting situations. They represent the straight population path. Besides the straight path, exceptional situations during IR population, or even just specific boundary conditions in the individual project situation, may necessitate a different assembly of the project-specific approach from the individual method fragments. Good reasons for this type of modified composition should outweigh the consistent insistence on a defined method. However, the defined method should not just be scrapped without reason, as it is at least useful for condensing the know-how and experiences of numerous IR populations. A particularly liberal approach can be taken with the proposed order of method fragments, as long as no logical dependencies of the type "A must end before B, because B requires result A as an input" are affected. Relaxing the proposed order may often become necessary when stakeholders are stuck at a certain point, and a change of perspective (e.g., the partial population of a different canvas) is sufficient in order to resolve a sticking point and continue on with the original canvas.

In an ideal IR world, all models are created without any syntax specifications. This only works if all stakeholders have at least some experience in process and object modeling. This leads to the creation of more-or-less intuitive box-and-line diagrams without the need for discussion about their semantics. One reason for using a certain amount of notation specifications is that some stakeholders may have absolutely no modeling experience and may find it difficult if no specifications are provided. A second reason for the use of a minimum amount of notation specifications is that this prevents discussions on specific choices of modeling languages. These two important reasons clarify the need for a minimum amount of specifications on the use of symbols and their relationships on the different canvases.

This extremely pragmatic and imprecise modeling approach may be met with resistance by experienced modelers, who are often found among the technical stakeholders. In this case, it is important to remind all stakeholders that the canvases cannot represent a complete and correct specification, rather they can only promote an initial understanding of the subject matter. Notations should only be used to enable a simple introduction, and their use requires a similar degree of pragmatism. It is extremely likely that individual processes and structures will have to be completely specified in greater detail during the later design and development phases, which naturally place a greater value on the correctness of the syntax.

However, those kinds of specification are not developed in the Interaction Room and do not contribute to the team's overall understanding. Rather, they are used to communicate details for specific solutions between the dedicated experts.

One of the basic principles of the Interaction Room is the principle of abstraction, of a focus on the key issues instead of excessive detail. In the population of individual canvases, this principle is manifested in the form of volume rules (e.g., a maximum of 15 business process models in the process canvas with a maximum of 15 activities per business process model, and a maximum of 40 object types in the object canvas). These rules must not be interpreted too dogmatically. Ultimately, 17 business process models, each with 17 activities, are just as appropriate as 15 with 15 activities. However, it is important to ensure that the bending of the rules does not get out of hand. The sections on the individual canvases provide an overview of the specific limitations of scope.

When discussing the different canvases, stakeholders may occasionally address business or solution aspects that should be recorded, but which interrupt or distract the current discussion thread. In order to store this kind of information without diverting from the actual aim of the discussion, it can be noted on index cards and attached to a dedicated note area in the Interaction Room for subsequent consideration. It may be helpful to classify these statements, e.g., into outstanding issues, requests, detailed facts, depending on their type and number.

The IR coaches (Sects. 3.5.1 and 3.5.2) maintain the note area while populating the other canvases, which is always used if stakeholders provide information that needs to be recorded, but which would divert the current topic of discussion or which cannot be appropriately assigned to other canvases. This approach improves the cognitive freedom of stakeholders in their activities and allows them to hold open and free discussions, i.e., without having to worry that important (but currently excessively detailed or marginal) aspects (or those that are only relevant in special cases) are being disregarded. The note area also gives IR coaches the opportunity to ensure that discussions remain focused without appearing to use overly strict moderating measures and retain control over the flow of the workshop. Besides genuinely important statements, which may be addressed at a more appropriate point later in the workshop, and outstanding issues, which need to be clarified with other contact partners after the IR workshop, the Interaction Room also allows detailed knowledge that is not specifically relevant to the workshop to be recorded without the discussion necessarily having to return to the issue at a later date. This also allows the IR coaches to diplomatically eliminate the disruptive potential of irrelevant statements without frustrating stakeholders if necessary.

3.2   Canvases

Common to all IR variants is that facts are noted in an abstract and concise form. This occurs on different canvases depending on the IR variant. These canvases are briefly introduced in this section, while details on the canvases are then discussed when they are first used in the IR variants. Figure 3.1 provides an overview of the relationship between the canvases used. It shows that the different canvases are linked to each other and that individual canvases are used for different IR variants.

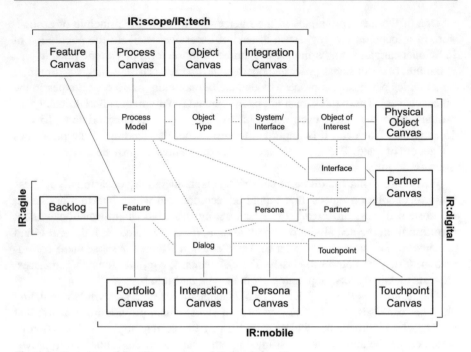

Fig. 3.1 Overview of the IR canvases and their relationships

- **Partner canvas**: The partner canvas is used to identify the partners connected with the company to be digitalized and describes their interfaces with the company (Sect. 4.2).
- **Physical object canvas**: The physical object canvas is used to identify objects that provide the conditions or other events on the duration, directly in the business process of the company to be digitalized, or which are to be controlled by these business processes (Sect. 4.3).
- **Touchpoint canvas**: A touchpoint canvas describes the order in which a partner of the company to be digitalized uses specific channels to contact the company (Sects. 4.4 and 6.4).
- **Feature canvas**: The feature canvas describes the features and properties of a software system. This may be an existing software system or one that is yet to be developed (Sect. 5.2).
- **Process canvas**: The process canvas provides an outline of the key business processes. The focus is on the central processes, while an abstract view is generally taken of exceptions and special cases (Sect. 5.3).
- **Object canvas**: The object canvas identifies the most important types of objects to be managed and defines correlations (Sect. 5.4).
- **Integration canvas**: The integration canvas identifies the software systems to be integrated with the software system being built. It specifies the key features of the interfaces to these systems (Sect. 5.5).

- **Persona canvas:** Personas are descriptions of individually assumed users. They are specifically described in great detail in order to convey a tangible image of the assumed users (Sect. 6.2).
- **Portfolio canvas**: In the portfolio canvas, new services and offers to be developed are embedded in the context of the existing company portfolio and then reviewed to confirm whether this provides a coherent overall picture (Sect. 6.3).
- **Interaction canvas**: The interaction canvas describes the interactions that take place between the mobile software and the user (Sect. 6.5).

3.3 Annotations

Once the project material has become tangible by populating the canvases, the next step is to identify aspects that make the software development complex, time consuming, and uncertain or that have another critical impact. Annotations are attached to the model elements on the individual canvases, which clarify what the stakeholders deem important and difficult in various dimensions. This assessment is easily missed in business process and software system models that are not qualified in greater detail. It is often not immediately clear which aspects are particularly relevant or critical for the success of the project and whether these are

- activities and functions that are particularly important for the value added by the company or the software system to be developed,
- business or implementation aspects that are considered particularly complex or not yet adequately understood, or
- business or technical boundary conditions that need to be taken into account during implementation.

Annotations are a tool that can be used to reveal all the aspects that remain invisible in traditional process and system models. The placement of annotations on the canvases in the Interaction Room ensures that stakeholders are aware that the annotated challenges must be dealt with and helps to define the identified values, efforts, and risks at specific points in processes and systems. This helps to ensure that they are not lost during the project. The background information recorded for each annotation (Appendix B) also provides valuable notes on the type of annotated challenge, which is helpful for problem-solving as well as for prioritizing and effort estimates. It is therefore advisable to use annotations on all canvases and consider them as part of the big picture, rather than just in isolation, in order to obtain an impression of the effort and complexity of the entire project and ensure that no aspects and relationships critical to the success of the project are overlooked.

A key aim of the population of an Interaction Room is to raise awareness of the individual impressions of added value, complexity, risk, and uncertainty at an early stage in the project, to clearly display these in models and discuss them in the team. This allows stakeholders to gain a better understanding of the project challenges and establishes the foundation for more reliable effort estimates and prioritization.

Explicit visualization of a project's value and effort drivers is achieved by using annotations on the IR canvases with a range of symbols that act as "warning signs" for aspects that need to be clarified or considered during the project. All annotations are available to stakeholders in a physical form, as magnetic symbols, pasted symbols, stamp symbols that can be easily placed on all relevant canvas elements.

Every annotation expresses a certain type of challenge, a quality feature, such as safety requirements, a design feature, such as an external interface, as well as "gut feelings," such as a particular complexity or uncertainty.

Annotations give an impression of the significance, efforts, risks, and uncertainties inherent in the individual elements of the application domain and the desired technical solution. These assessments are particularly valuable as they remain hidden in traditional software and process models, firstly because they do not provide an opportunity to express this information, and secondly, because the demand for completeness and correctness in formal modeling languages forces the modeler to specify facts in greater detail than is actually possible at such an early stage. Traditional modeling may lead to the active masking of complexity and uncertainty that can lead to unforeseen additional effort at a later stage in the project.

The annotation technique in the Interaction Room ensures that all stakeholders explicitly discuss value, effort, and risk drivers at an early stage. It also visibly anchors the insights generated by this discussion in the Interaction Room's overview diagrams, which can be understood by all stakeholders. An annotated, informal object canvas provides a much better picture of the project complexity than a complete UML diagram without annotations, even for individuals who are not familiar with the project material.

Information on what the annotation specifically relates to, its specific requirement, and the benefits of implementation, or the damage that may be caused if it is not considered, are recorded in the workshop. These assessments may be used to derive initial starting points for prioritization, more detailed business/technical research, and the necessary specification refinements on certain points as part of the follow-up activities to an IR workshop.

The question of "how" the implementation is to take place is deliberately excluded when specifying the annotation (e.g., "How should the annotation be considered as part of an implementation?"), as this would preempt a discussion in the solution domain. It is too early to tackle this question in an IR workshop. A solution discussion on every annotation would also quickly exceed the workshop timeframe. The Interaction Room exclusively aims to create an awareness of the points at which detailed solutions are required for non-obvious requirements.

Canvas annotations can be analyzed at an early stage. This generally leads to suspicions and the discovery of implausibilities, rather than strict errors. The discussion of these matters often uncovers differing perceptions among stakeholders, which can then also be promptly eliminated.

We distinguish between three key classes of annotations:

- **Value drivers** define aspects whose implementation is expected to influence the system's desired business value or user value, e.g., the potential for increases in productivity, but also the risk of reputation damage. They express the value delivered by certain system or process parts, whether these are values relevant to the software provider, such as reputation or financial gain, or performance or excitement factors perceived by the user. These value contributions are typically not distributed equally across the system—rather, some components make key contributions, which justify the development of the entire system in the first place, while other components only perform a secondary or supporting function. The business value and user value annotations can be used to highlight the key value-added contributions from a provider or user perspective.

- **Effort drivers** define boundary conditions or requirements to be reflected in the implementation of the system to be developed. These are often quality features, such as special time or security requirements, but they can also be functional requirements, such as the decision to perform a certain task automatically or manually. Annotations for effort drivers give stakeholders the opportunity to express aspects that are not as tangible as specific features, but whose implementation may be just as time consuming and whose consequences may be just as far-reaching for design and architecture decisions. They counteract the lure of the seeming precision of formal modeling languages. These kinds of languages encourage stakeholders to primarily focus on describing tangible aspects of the system: What must the system do? What data does it need to process? How should it work? There is a danger that stakeholders will fall into the trap of an "anything goes" mentality. Everything is relatively easy to define and plan on paper, so the high-level design quickly becomes a request program. The efforts, risks, and uncertainties that lurk in the implementation are quickly consigned to the background. This ends in a model that looks solid and seemingly only has to be programmed, but which shows no sign of its inherent complexity and contradictions as well as incomplete features. For example, a component for processing contractual modifications is quickly specified in a traditional manner and seems relatively harmless in process and structural diagrams. However, the information that these kinds of modifications occur more frequently at certain reference dates and subsequently multiply the normal system load, that failures due to system overload cannot be tolerated for reasons of reputation, and that modifications have to take place within a legally defined timeframe means that the component is considered in an entirely different light. It requires significantly higher efforts than assumed at first glance and has a much more demanding architecture, as it may require load distribution mechanisms. It is virtually impossible to represent these aspects in traditional system models. However, annotations allow stakeholders to highlight these aspects precisely where they occur, in the process and object models on the Interaction Room canvases.

- **Uncertainty** is a special type of annotation that is used at the end of a canvas annotation in order to allow every stakeholder to define aspects that have not yet been adequately understood. It ensures that stakeholders can also express impressions that are normally not even considered in software specifications. Namely, that certain aspects are not yet understood, that they require research, or that expertise is lacking in the team. In short, that the painstakingly prepared specification contains gaps or that it may even be incorrect. Challenging stakeholders to disclose this assessment is one of the keys to risk management in the Interaction Room.

Canvases are typically annotated once the canvases have reached an initial, stable modeling state. One canvas is annotated at any a time. This may take place in a single or multiple annotation rounds. In each annotation round, stakeholders have ten minutes to distribute a specific set of annotations (e.g., in the form of adhesive or magnetic symbols) to the canvas based on their personal assessment. Generally, no more than five symbols should be used during an annotation round, as the meaning of the symbols may be confused otherwise. If more than five annotations are available to annotate a canvas, separate annotation rounds with a maximum of five symbols each are recommended. The IR coaches determine the symbols to be affixed to the canvases in each annotation round.

This annotation process is performed independently, without comment and completely unmoderated. Stakeholders affix annotation symbols to model elements that they deem particularly important, time consuming, or critical. Every stakeholder may paste any number of annotations to the annotated canvas, even if the annotated elements already have similar or different annotations from other stakeholders.

However, the IR method coach must note that the annotations should not be used to define general implementation difficulties or overarching boundary conditions, but just employed to highlight specific problem areas. For example, it is not sensible to assign security annotations to every step in a process, as these are generally overarching requirements, whose ubiquitous labeling with annotations does not lead to additional insight, but just to additional modeling and interpretation overheads. Highlighting individual elements that involve special or additional challenges with annotations provides a much greater benefit.

While annotation symbols already provide a rough indication of the type of challenges at the points marked in the process or system, additional information that reflects the precise characteristics of the annotation in the specific context is required for a solid assessment.

In order to learn more about these characteristics, the IR method coach looks through all the annotation symbols following the unmoderated annotation round and asks who affixed the annotation to the relevant element and why. The author of the relevant annotation briefly explains their rationale for the label, and the other stakeholders are given a brief opportunity to express objections. If the stakeholder who placed the annotation wishes it to remain in place, it is attached to the canvas and numbered. The specific characteristic that the stakeholder wanted to note (e.g., particular access peaks at particular times, indicated by a high-use annotation) is also noted in the workshop report under this serial number. Appendix B provides an overview of all the annotations together with typical detailed questions that should be answered in the report. If there is a need for further discussion about an annotation, it is also assigned an uncertainty symbol and discussed at a later date outside the workshop. If no stakeholder wishes to explain an annotation (because they have changed their mind in the meantime), or discussions lead to the conclusion that the noted aspect is irrelevant, the annotation is removed from the canvas. This annotation technique can be repeated across multiple annotation rounds that focus on different annotations.

However, the last annotation round is always exclusively reserved for the uncertainty annotation. This annotation should not be considered in the previous rounds, as stakeholders may not be prepared to openly communicate uncertainty about a system or business aspect with which they feel they should be familiar. However, in the last annotation round for every canvas, the IR method coach states that every stakeholder must attach at least one uncertainty annotation to the canvas. This "mandatory annotation" prevents the effect of stigmatizing those who admit uncertainty and also ensures that all stakeholders take the time to reflect on whether all outstanding issues have been addressed.

Practical experience shows that uncertainty annotations are frequently also affixed to elements that have not previously been the subject of controversial discussion, or to which different annotations were affixed, but for which all stakeholders agree that there is a need for clarification and specification. As a result, the uncertainty annotation can also be used to identify a potential "elephant in the room," i.e., a problem that no one previously wanted to address.

As is the case in the other annotation rounds, the IR method coach once again goes through all the uncertainty annotations in succession and asks each stakeholder to describe the perceived uncertainty. If it turns out that stakeholders in the team clearly have the knowledge to resolve this uncertainty, the uncertainty is removed, as this is not a problem for the entire team, but only a local lack of understanding. The team reaches a decision on the removal or retention of the annotation (it is definitely retained if doubt remains). If no stakeholder in the team can resolve the uncertainty, it is noted in the report, just like the other annotations, ideally mentioning a responsible individual who will introduce the necessary steps to eliminate the uncertainty (e.g., clarification of strategic issues with management, consultation with external business, or technology experts for specific problems).

3.4   Variants

In the preceding sections, we presented the basic principles of the IR method, which we derived from the traditional challenges faced by software projects. We distinguished between the initial specification of the objective of a development project and monitoring the progress of a project using an Interaction Room (scoping versus monitoring). The use of the individual IR elements in different project situations has resulted in the formation of five independent IR variants, which combine the IR instruments in different ways:

- The **Interaction Room for Digitalization Strategy Development (IR:digital)** is the starting point for identifying innovative projects and their scoping in the context of a broadly understood digitalization. The interaction of experts in the actual business domain with experts for various digitalization technologies is crucial in this variant. This is true because many of these technologies have not been tried and tested over a number of years so there is no uniform concept of what it can achieve. However, they often have the potential to fundamentally change existing business models or even enable new services. And this can only be defined with mutual cooperation, by preparing scenarios and ultimately assessing the business case. In the IR:digital, it is particularly important that the feasibility and enforceability of the business model (if it is modified by the digitalization) are systematically reviewed. Often, there are fantastic ideas for digital services that no one wants to pay for or which require an extremely large marketing budget. These kinds of solutions, which need to be eliminated, are identified in the IR:digital just like the more viable ones. The IR:digital is the starting point for the scoping of innovations and can be seen as a preliminary stage for more specific considerations in other IR variants.
- The **Interaction Room for Mobile Application Development (IR:mobile)** is based on the organization's known business processes and focuses on the question of the points at which these business processes and their supporting applications and data can be usefully mobilized. This covers technical issues (what effort is required to mobilize certain data and applications?), dedicated mobilization risks (security, redundancy, and consistency of data), and primarily also questions of feasibility (who can and should use a mobile application, and does a willingness or interest even exist in view of the context in which it will be used?). The IR:mobile requires the involvement of mobilization experts, especially those that have an idea of what can be expected of mobile users, what they enjoy, and what they are used to from other mobile applications. The IR:mobile gives direction to what can sometimes be vague attempts to mobilize data and applications with different interpretations so that the stakeholders can pursue a common goal. The IR:mobile can lead directly to an IR:scope in that the identified mobilization potential results in specific process changes and software designs. All instruments that are used in the IR:agile for project monitoring can then also be used for mobile software development.

- The **Interaction Room for Technology Evaluation (IR:tech)** evaluates current technologies, predominantly in the context of elastic infrastructures, for their application potential to provide better technological support for existing business processes and models. The IR:tech addresses the perceived innovation density in the technical space and reflects on the fact that users and business departments are increasingly thinking and reasoning in technological dimensions. Examples of technologies in this context (or even just technological buzzwords) are big data, NoSQL, and continuous integration and delivery. These kinds of buzzwords thrown around by the popular press and tech small talk quickly create the feeling that "we need to have a look at this." The IR:tech aims to support precisely this discussion, evaluate technologies based on their potential, and potentially outline application scenarios (only if a general value proposition appears plausible in the specific company context). In contrast to the other IR variants, IR:tech contains a component that is clearly aligned to an understanding of technology. It also contains the method-based element of "taking a broader view," which means that application scenarios in other sectors are systematically considered for the respective technology. If a specific potential benefit of a technology is identified in the IR:tech, the technical and business modifications that the introduction of the technology would involve can be detailed in a subsequent IR:scope.
- The **Interaction Room for Software Project Scoping (IR:scope)** starts with a project idea and helps the stakeholders involved focus on a common goal (scoping). The project aim (the software to be developed) typically displays characteristics which suggest the application of elements of agile software development. For example, it is clear that the requirements are incomplete and that they will continue to develop during the course of the project, that human interfaces are involved (in the form of dialogs, reports), so that late requirements are unavoidable, and that the priorities have to constantly be adjusted to the level of knowledge. In this kind of situation, the aim is to combine the diversity of ideas and perceptions, reconcile the objectives, and ensure that the stakeholders are committed to a joint idea of the software to be developed. This kind of consensus can then be used as the starting point for the actual project, which is ideally monitored in the IR:agile.
- The **Interaction Room for Agile Project Monitoring (IR:agile)** supports the consistent monitoring of relevant phenomena for the entire duration of the project. The IR:agile typically follows on from the IR:scope. The IR:agile focuses on the dynamism of requirements, indicators of project disasters (and their development over time), the planning and controlling of iterations, and transparent cost monitoring and control. The dynamics of the number of requirements must be monitored by the requirements exchange (Sect. 8.3) and the adVANTAGE contract model (Sect. 15.2) for the entire duration of the project, but often only becomes prominent and visible toward the end of the project. Cost control is a different matter. Its application particularly leads to interesting options for action in the initial implementation activities, while the

cost control and projection options are generally less influential toward the end
of the project, but even more important as money starts to get tight at the end.

In summary, the IR:digital fulfills a particularly business-based role, as it is used
to identify digitalization potentials within or adjacent to the current business model.
These kinds of potentials often lead to the development of more mobile solutions
(which can be supported by the IR:mobile) or the desire to use specific new
technologies (which can be evaluated in the IR:tech). If the application of the IR:
digital does not point to mobile solutions or the use of new technologies, it is likely
that the reference points identified in the IR:digital point to the application of the
IR:scope. Figure 3.2 displays this relationship as a diagram. It displays the project
phases in which the different IR variants are applied. The IR:digital is used to
identify digitalization opportunities in the broadest possible sense, while the
specific configuration then provides the focal point for a digital strategy. The IR:
digital is frequently the starting point that leads to the specification of roughly
outlined ideas for software systems to be developed, mobile software systems, or
the use of elastic infrastructures. The duration of the preparation, implementation
and follow-up for an IR:digital workshop typically extends over a longer period of
time than in other IR variants.

The IR:digital is not required if the project goal is more narrowly defined from
the beginning. In this case, the IR:mobile (if an idea for mobilizing parts of a
business process exists) or the IR:tech (to investigate the opportunities for using
elasticity technology) can be used as the starting point. These two are also optional,
as the IR:scope is the ideal starting point (if an idea for a software system to be
implemented in known technology already exists) for a software development
project that does not involve any special mobile or technological challenges. What
is common to all four variants is that the starting situation is characterized by vague
perceptions by all the stakeholders involved and that the harmonization of these
perceptions can be an important step along the path in implementation projects.

Project scoping in the IR:scope can be followed by tamed agile development
with appropriate monitoring of the development in the IR:agile. This may take place
at different times in the project. The IR:agile monitoring is scaled down if stakeholders have the impression that the requirements are stabilizing and that costs and
risks are under control. However, a "small" IR:scope workshop may need to be held
at the start of every sprint in order to define the tasks to be completed in the sprint.
In general, it is sensible to continue monitoring for the duration and simply adjust
the frequency and intensity of the monitoring to the maturity of the project situation.

Fig. 3.2 Sequence of IR variants along the life of the project

Although the IR variants build on each other and can naturally be linked in the above manner, IRs can also be employed independently. The initial population of every Interaction Room leads to results that do not necessarily have to be used as part of software development projects, but which provide independent benefits in different applications.

3.5 Stakeholders

The Interaction Room method is predominantly focused on providing an area for moderated and focused discussion between the various stakeholders in order to reach and document joint decisions. This requires the right cooperation by the right people when populating an Interaction Room. "Right" has different dimensions in this respect: The stakeholders must have the necessary competence. Business experts must be familiar with their business, technical experts must be familiar with the technologies to be applied or assessed, and developers must know the processes and tools required for development. It is also important that stakeholders have the necessary decision-making power. Generally speaking, they should have the authority to reach decisions on issues that require a decision to be made. Limits to this authority naturally exist, especially in large organizations with hierarchical structures, where follow-up discussions are required and decisions have to remain provisional. But this must not become the norm as it otherwise reduces IR population to a more-or-less non-committal collection of incomplete decisions. Ultimately, stakeholders must have the business expertise and the decision-making power and must also be prepared to make decisions. Procrastinating and avoiding commitments may be useful and prevent errors in some cases, but it must not be allowed to get out of hand in the IR. It is just as important to ensure that stakeholders can represent and debate their business position, but are prepared to consider the perspectives of other departments and take new paths. It is clear that the selection of stakeholders for an IR population is an extremely important step.

The population of an Interaction Room is moderated and methodologically managed in order to ensure that the right stakeholders can cooperate effectively, that they adhere to suitable abstraction levels, and do not get caught up in detail. The tasks of stakeholder selection, moderation, and methodological management are performed by two IR coaches. The IR method coach is responsible for the methodology, while the IR domain coach has broad knowledge of the sector in which the IR population will take place. The positions of the coaches should be assigned externally where possible. External means that they are external to the context of the project. If the company has a certified IR method coach, the role can be assigned to this individual, as long as he or she is not a stakeholder in the project context. In principle, the role of the IR domain coach can also be assigned to a company employee, but only if all stakeholders agree that the candidate has broad knowledge of the sector and that their view is not clouded by company politics.

All IR variants affect a company's business processes, regardless of whether digital improvement opportunities are sought (IR:digital), whether mobilization potentials are to be identified (IR:mobile), whether software development is planned (IR:scope) or managed (IR:agile), or whether new technologies are to be evaluated (IR:tech). Knowledge of the current and targeted business processes is essential in every single case and is the responsibility of the process owner.

The roles of the IR coaches and the process owner are described in the following sections, which also provide an overview of the roles that arise in the IR variants.

3.5.1   Interaction Room Method Coach

Although the activities in the Interaction Room are not based on a closed method that defines precisely when and with whom an activity should take place, an IR does require method knowledge, especially for the initial population. This method knowledge is required to ensure an efficient population and allows a certified IR method coach to coordinate the diversity of stakeholders, reconcile various interests, and reach decisions. The IR method coach obtains the required practical experience through a certification process. His or her tasks include the following:

- Ensuring that all stakeholders in the population of the Interaction Room are given adequate opportunity to express their perceptions and objectives, and that all are involved in creating the canvases. Of particular importance is ensuring and maintaining an open and fair discussion atmosphere, reining in dominant stakeholders and encouraging reticent individuals.
- Enforcing the following communication rules:

  - One item of communication at a time, even if a large number of individuals are involved, and even if a large number of outstanding issues need to be clarified. The discussion must allow all stakeholders to participate at all times.
  - Secondary issues are recorded, but do not dominate the discussion: The varying stakeholder backgrounds mean that many topics will be assigned different levels of importance. However, not all issues are equally important for a balanced IR population. The IR method coach ensures that the topics discussed target the workshop's objective.
  - No final assessments; every opinion is valid: In particular, annotations should help to identify the essential requirements. The items that are deemed essential depend on which features stakeholders consider important and why this is the case. In order to find out, it is important that all opinions are aired. This can only be ensured if all opinions are accepted as valid points for discussion. In particular, the discussion of an individual opinion makes sense if it appears far-fetched by the majority of stakeholders.

- Separating the important from the irrelevant in order to ensure that the canvases provide orientation and to prevent details from being overvalued. The method coach generally requires the support and assessment of the IR domain coach in this respect. The method coach must support a focus on the key elements when preparing every canvas and constantly push against the demand for completeness.
- Ensuring the correct application of the IR method fragments to make sure that the methodological requirements are not ignored. The open approach to the IR method allows individual method fragments to be brought forward or skipped, depending on the individual situation; however, limited scope exists within the method fragments. For example, if a business process model is annotated, this takes place in line with the annotation rules. The flexibility of the method means that it is not always easy to strictly enforce the core principles of the method. This is the task of the method coach.
- Managing the available time to ensure that the overall objective set for the IR workshop is achieved. For example, this may mean that discussions are terminated in order to make sure that all canvases are created. Wherever a time issue is identified, the IR method coach is responsible for reconciling competing objectives and working toward consensual prioritization.

3.5.2   Interaction Room Domain Coach

Whenever a company requires matters to be documented, criteria to be identified, and assessments to be performed, there is the risk that historic frictions and rigidities may arise, that the importance of details may be overstated, and that sight of the big picture is lost. At the time that this risk materializes, it is often difficult to return to a higher level of abstraction and assign details according to their relevance.

The IR domain coach ensures that the IR population does not get lost in company-specific details, which appear important in the company context, but which are ultimately much less relevant than assumed by the stakeholders. The domain coach questions disputed business details by integrating them into the big picture. This task can only be performed successfully if the other business representatives recognize the business expertise of the domain coach and approve of the big picture that this individual puts forward. Consequently, the domain coach must have profound business knowledge of the sector and be in a position to convert the jargon used by the individual company to general terminology, as well as have rough knowledge of the current sector trends. Their task is to work together with the IR method coach to push toward compliance with an appropriate level of abstraction and review the validity of business arguments. In particular, patterns of reasoning along the line of "it has always been like this here, we don't need to bother trying that here, the board wouldn't approve" require a response by the IR domain coach and a look into the underlying business substance.

3.5.3   Process Owner

The role of process owner is often varied, given that IR populations frequently relate to more than a single-core business process. Process owners have the power to interpret the current processes and are aware of their structure and their associated problems. However, a process owner must not only be able to describe the ideal process form, rather (and much more importantly) they must be familiar with the process from beginning to end, how it is implemented in the company, without having to rely on process documentation or hearsay. Yet, the process owner must still be able to describe the process with a sufficient level of abstraction. The process owner is supported by genuine users when dealing with sensitive process details (e.g., in the IR:mobile). Up-to-date, practical knowledge is required in all situations and must be distinguished from vague, unconfirmed preconceptions.

3.5.4   Additional Roles

Table 3.1 lists the various roles that are required in the different IR variants. A fundamental distinction is made between external and internal appointment. In principle, externally assigned roles can be assigned internally, if project externality and independent expertise are ensured. Internal appointments cannot be replaced, as these roles involve the introduction of specific knowledge of company details. The roles that arise in all IR variants have already been discussed above, while the roles that are not used in all IR variants are described in the variants in which they first arise.

Table 3.1 Stakeholder roles in the Interaction Room variants

Role	External	IR:digital	IR:scope	IR:mobile	IR:tech	IR:agile
IR method coach	X	X	X	X	X	X
IR domain coach	X	X	X	X	X	X
Process owner		X	X	X	X	X
Business developer		X		X	X	
Application developer			X	X	X	X
Operations expert			X	X	X	X
Digital business expert	X	X				
Digital technology expert	X	X				
Interaction engineer	X	X		X		
User			X			X
Mobility expert	X			X		
Enterprise architect						X
Technology expert					X	

3.6   Workshop Preparation

There are several IR variants as well as a certain range of requirements for the involved stakeholders. However, a number of commonalities also exist in the preparation of IR populations. This includes the fact that the underlying project goals need to be outlined in advance in order to ensure targeted and productive discussion in the Interaction Room.

A simple method for providing an abstract description of the project goal is the "press release" format. This text, with a maximum length of one page, is not intended to be made public, but formulated so that it could be understood by any interested layman. The text provides information on why the client wants to develop the respective software. It focuses on the goals, can certainly be on the bold side, and conveys the overarching goal. It also clarifies whether the project goal is to develop something new, replace a legacy system, migrate a system, undertake business or technical analysis, or engage in strategy development. Despite this seeming lack of precision, the "press release" has a unifying effect, as it can be repeatedly consulted during the IR population and the project in order to check whether the project is still on track to achieve the goal and to ensure that all stakeholders are committed to the goal.

The IR coaches should first discuss the following points with the project owners in order to ensure that they can appropriately classify the context in which an IR population takes place:

- What problems do company projects typically face (e.g., requirements management, stakeholder communication, degree of integration, user acceptance)?
- Which aspects are expected to be particularly critical in the planned project?
- What are the essential insights that the IR population needs to address (e.g., target definition, requirements analysis, user analysis, process analysis, architectural design, prioritization, effort assessment)?
- Do complex dependencies have to be resolved when integrating old and new components?
- Do innovative solutions need to be developed for new services? Or is an initial analysis required in order to identify the optimization potential of existing processes?
- Which departments and stakeholders are likely to be the drivers, which are likely to be the laggards, and which will be the enablers of changes?

The responses to these questions give a picture of the expectations and challenges that will be encountered in the project, and represent a logical basis for the IR population. IR coaches classify the perceptions, fears, and areas of focus of the individual stakeholders, while the behavior of the individual stakeholders can be sorted in a general context.

These insights can be used to adapt the canvases and the effort required for population, annotation, and the discussion of the model elements, to the specific starting situation. The fragments of the IR method can be combined to form an Interaction Room workshop that is precisely tailored to the "pain points" of the project under consideration.

In some cases, the responses to the above reflective questions also help to select the most suitable IR variant. The IR:digital provides the ideal starting point where the initial focus is on developing the digital business model (Chap. 4). If a specific mobile app is to be developed, the IR:mobile is better suited to the mobile-specific analysis and design activities (Chap. 6). And the IR:tech is the tool of choice if the aim is to investigate the potential of new technologies, such as big data, for existing systems (Chap. 7).

Another important measure to prepare the Interaction Room is stakeholder selection. While the roles to be filled are generally predetermined (Sect. 3.5.4), the individuals that fill the roles have to be identified and instructed in the IR population.

3.7   Results and Follow-up Activities

The models created in the Interaction Room are generally documented so they can also be converted to a specific syntax if desired. This allows the level of detail of the documentation to be adapted so that certain canvases are documented in more or less detail. All models are generally documented, and annotations are recorded together with the justifications defined when discussing the annotation. Documentation ensures that results achieved and decisions reached in the Interaction Room are permanently available. It also ensures that these results are available in any subsequent software development or decision-making processes. For example, the results of an IR:digital population are often used in strategic decisions or portfolio processes, while the results of an IR:scope are frequently used in traditional specification processes. Even the natural continued use as part of an IR:agile may require the interim retention of the IR:scope results, simply because there may be gaps between the IR:scope and IR:agile. The documentation of IR results aims to ensure that they can be integrated into all kinds of subsequent processes.

Figure 3.3 shows the relationships between the various IR canvases and artifacts. The feature canvas on the left side is used to create a product backlog. Annotations from the feature canvas and annotations from the process canvas are included in the

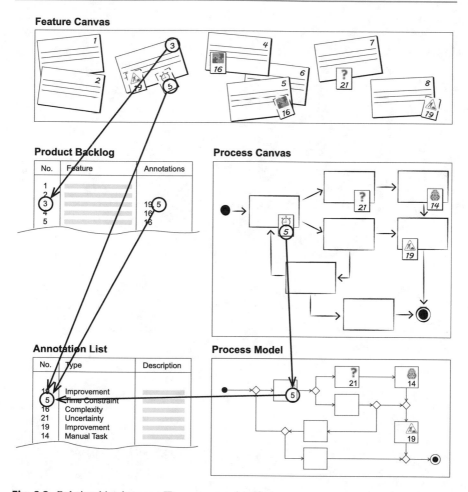

Fig. 3.3 Relationships between IR canvases and artifacts

annotation documentation. Process models are digitized as part of the documentation. The documentation format is flexible and can be adapted to the specific requirements of the process model subsequently used for development.

Using an Interaction Room for Digitalization Strategy Development (IR:digital)

4

Digitalization is a multifaceted term. Digitalization includes "normal" automation, which is the long-standing objective of IT. But digitalization also drives the mobilization of data and applications, because once data is available in digital form, there is a desire to access this data from anywhere—and people who have become accustomed to ubiquitous access to data will continue to push for more digitalization. Digitalization thus drives mobilization and vice versa. Digitalization also includes the direct integration of physical objects with business processes that are based on information from the real world. Westerman et al. (2014) distinguish two dimensions that have a significant impact on the efforts of companies in the area of digital transformation:

- **Digital capability** refers to the systematic investigation of the potential for digitalization, which ultimately clearly indicates where and how to invest in digital transformation. This naturally requires knowledge about products, marketing channels, and essential customer requirements, as well as available implementation technology, to prevent media disruptions, automate interfaces, and integrate objects from the real world directly into the business processes.
- **Leadership capability** refers to the acceptance of the emerging nature of new solutions, and the idea that all stakeholders are aware that the transformation of a business model with a focus on digitalization is even less plan-driven than other IT projects. Scope must be provided for experiments, without losing focus on digitalization. This focus must be directed from a central position, and it must be constantly supported and continuously clarified.

For enterprise IT, this requires new methods to determine and assess digitalization potentials, and it must be able to convey ideas of the specific concept of digitalization and its importance for individual user groups. It must find flexible paths for developing emerging systems and managing the associated development and business processes. It also has to be familiar with traditional digitalization technologies and architectures.

© Springer International Publishing Switzerland 2016
M. Book et al., *Tamed Agility*, DOI 10.1007/978-3-319-41478-2_4

The Interaction Room for Digitalization Strategy Development (IR:digital) supports the identification of digitalization potentials. It plays a particularly important role for companies that may already be digital, or which are on the path toward becoming digital companies.

By digital companies, we mean companies whose core business processes across almost all activities are primarily dependent on correctly functioning IT and whose products are exclusively digital.

Based on this definition, insurance companies, banks, and telecommunication companies are all digital companies. They have no, or virtually no, physical dependencies, and the products are almost exclusively digital (if you abstract from marginal issues, such as printed policies, account statements, and invoices). By contrast, logistics companies are not purely digital companies, because the transportation of goods primarily depends on the physical nature of the goods. The automotive industry is also not digital, because even though the production process depends significantly on IT, the final product is still mostly dependent on assembling physical components. It is impossible to manufacture a car without any sheet of metal, even if you have the most cutting-edge IT.

IT and digitalization are naturally also playing an increasingly important role in non-digital sectors. However, these are still primarily bound to the laws of physics and physical objects. Interestingly, these residual physics (or the residual relevance of physical objects) are a driver of digitalization beyond "normal" automation and mobilization, as it is precisely these objects that are becoming increasingly connected and integrated into purely digital communication structures. We refer to the resulting systems as cyber-physical systems.

- **Automation** refers to the fact that mechanisms and activities that previously required the intervention and cooperation of humans will be able to do without this cooperation in the future, because decisions, data transmissions, and inspections will be replaced by algorithms. In order to be able to pursue automation, both the inputs (for the purpose of algorithmic processing) and the outputs of automatic activities must be digitally represented. In other words, the fundamental purpose of IT, namely automation, necessarily promotes digitalization.
- **Mobilization** means that business process activities can be performed at different locations which are not yet known at the start of the process. This also means that the information and documents required for the business activities need to be made provided at arbitrary locations. Since those locations are not known in advance, the provision of data must occur spontaneously. Making information available anywhere is only possible in digital form, however. In other words: Mobilization promotes digitalization. But the question of what is driving the trend toward mobilization remains. This appears to be due to a technology-induced change (at some point, telecommunication became available in the necessary quality, quantity, and at an acceptable cost) that occurred in society and which is also attractive for parts of the population who are not IT-savvy, thanks to attractive, easy-to-use terminal devices. Digitalization

potentials as a result of mobilization are considered in greater detail in the
IR:mobile (Chap. 6).

- **Cyber-physicalization** means that objects from the real world are able to
communicate digitally. Machines and devices can provide continuous information on their status, status changes, capacity reserves, and maintenance
requirements, or communicate in another manner, using telecommunication that
is essentially available worldwide. They may communicate with each other, or
with a control system. This is also made possible by Internet-based communication. The distinctive feature is that information modeling is no longer
required: Instead of storing the status of physical objects in information systems
(which requires the models of the objects in the information system to be
updated and kept consistent with the real world using business processes,
exception handling procedures, and human interaction), a request can always be
sent to physical objects in cyber-physical systems if current information is
required. Figure 4.1 illustrates this paradigm shift.

This obviously only works in a few situations. The use of modeling is the safer
option if statements have to be made about the entirety of all objects and if these
statements have to be 100 % correct. But communication with physical objects

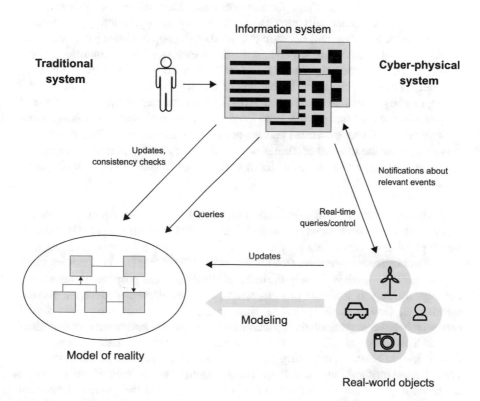

Fig. 4.1 Paradigm shift from traditional to cyber-physical systems

is a realistic option if a response from 95 % of the objects is considered sufficient when a request is sent to a large number of objects, and a certain amount of
imprecision is acceptable.

Ideas from the world of cyber-physical systems have shaped the term "Industry
4.0" (Schwab 2016), whose protagonists talk of the fourth industrial revolution
(after steam engines, electricity, and IT). The digital availability of information
opens up the potential for innovative features and services via a range of items
(not just industrial machines, but also alarm systems, domestic technology,
copiers, and, of course, the refrigerator) on a smaller scale, not just on an
industrial level. The fact that this data has to satisfy different consistency
requirements, that it may have different origins, that it may exhibit different
levels of reliability, and that its evaluation places great demands on business
relevance, statistical knowledge, and plausibility checks, makes its digitalization
particularly challenging. But one thing is clear: It is certainly a huge driver of
digitalization.

A variation of cyber-physical systems, with significant additional potential, is
the idea that physical objects do not just have to be physical items, but can also
be people. People count their steps, record their whereabouts, and report their
medical and vital data. Health insurers offer special rates for people who are
keen to exercise and report their movements. Data protection, privacy, and
ethical arguments naturally play an important role when developing these kinds
of services. But they will not stop the trend. Ask people whether they consider
privacy to be important, super-important, or extremely super-important. Most
will respond "extremely super-important." Then ask whether they might consider accepting a couple of limitations of privacy (in return for a discount, the
opportunity to win an iPad, a few miles in the customer loyalty program), and
you will soon see that privacy is no longer as super-important. Wearables, social
networks, and user-generated content are driving digitalization. The question is
not whether the Internet of Things will be joined by an Internet of Humans, but
rather the rules according to which it will operate (Schmidt 2015; Davies et al.
2015).

A variant of the cyber-physicalization digitalization driver exists in increasingly
digital corporate worlds in which automation and mobilization are prevalent and in
which physical objects do not play a major role (for example, in banks and lotteries,
as well as insurance companies to a limited extent). This involves the concentration
of information, which is already digitally available, for the purpose of supporting
decision making in business processes, and for the purpose of deriving recommendations. One example is banks, which can be regarded as completely digital
and which have a particularly concentrated amount of information about their
clients. This information is reflected in the account statement. It allows a range of
conclusions to be drawn regarding the client's behavior and financial position. With
very little algorithmic effort, a bank could identify that a bank client spends a
relatively high portion of their free budget on traveling, that their financial freedom
is increasing, and that a rail card may be worthwhile (admittedly with a certain

amount of uncertainty due to cash payments). Most banks currently do not do this for reasons of trust, the assessment of the importance of privacy, and for reasons of data protection. However, the data protection argument could be eliminated by obtaining client consent. As always, the next level of digitalization can take place in companies that are already digital by condensing digital information, which leads to new services.

Different business sectors differ in their attitude toward digitalization drivers due to the differing levels of automation of the business processes. The attitude toward mobilization also varies from sector to sector. The differences in digitalization affinity are also due to the different levels of importance of physical objects. In the manufacturing industry, it is obvious that business processes control physical objects. In service companies, physical objects must first be identified by searching for the objects to which the services relate. Because some service companies are entirely disconnected from the real-world objects at a certain level of abstraction, they use condensed objects (e.g., banks) or purely artificial objects (e.g., lotteries and discount systems); that is, their business purpose is purely virtual. There is no upper limit to this hierarchy—while banks are detached as a whole, investment banks are even more abstract than retail banks. The world of companies detached from objects is not flat, but has an inherently hierarchic structure.

The distinction based on the degree of abstraction of digitalization is particularly important because the vulnerability of the business model also increases with the degree of digitalization. A completely digital company depends on good products, appropriate marketing channels, and functioning IT. These factors are generally easier to replicate (and improve!) than the non-digital portion. For example, it is easier for a new market participant to establish an insurance company than an automotive company. However, a range of factors protect digital companies from these kinds of threats. These include the brand and the associated trust, widely distributed, physical touchpoints with the client (points of sale, ATMs, local agents), and the behavioral pattern of clients, which are slow to change.

The left side of Fig. 4.2 shows the traditional model: Information about physical objects is stored in an information system. This information system is used to execute business processes and reach decisions. A considerable amount of effort is spent on ensuring that the physical object models in the information system are kept up-to-date. Structural changes to physical objects are difficult to replicate in the information system, since they require model modifications.

Moreover, consistency conditions, which apply to almost all physical objects, are introduced in modeling. Dealing with exceptions related to temporary or one-time infringements of consistency conditions, make both the persistence and the algorithms in information systems complicated. A significant part of the effort to create, maintain, and operate information systems is spent on dealing with these kinds of exceptions. Often, it turns out over time that some of the original consistency conditions, which were originally deemed significant, are gradually lost, or even worse, bent out of shape. The incremental bending of data to satisfy consistency checks is generally the easiest way to ensure the impossibility of maintaining

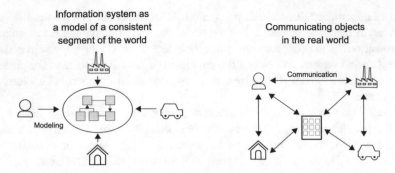

Fig. 4.2 Modeling real-world objects in an information system

the model, which leads to the problem of effort explosion much more quickly than necessary and desired.

The right side of Fig. 4.2 displays the alternative model. Instead of using a central model, the relevant real-world objects (which may also be interrelated) used by the company are identified. They may also be proactively reported as a result of particular status changes. However, no attempt is made to keep all information about all objects that may be required at some point consistent at all times. This eliminates the need for a coherent, closed model of the world and makes it clear that no perfect concept of consistency can be forced upon the real world. Physical objects are more diverse and colorful than their modeled replicas. This also has an impact on the algorithms. Instead of a strict concept of consistency of the data, a certain amount of robustness and fault tolerance is required in the algorithms. This is generally easier to control than creating closed world assumptions by communication standards and protocols.

4.1 Relevant Stakeholders

Besides the essential IR coaches with their method and domain expertise, and the process owners who are responsible for the business processes to analyze for digitalization, the IR:digital also requires the assignment of the roles of digital business expert, digital technology expert, and interaction engineer. The digital business expert identifies the prospects for digitalization and its change potential for complete business models across the different sectors. The digital technology expert is familiar with the technologies used as part of digitalization projects, both those that are more focused on the mobilization of data and applications and those that lean more toward cyber-physical systems. The interaction engineer considers the scenarios put up for discussion by the digital business expert and digital technology expert from a strict user perspective. The three roles specific to the IR:digital are discussed in the following sections.

4.1.1   Digital Business Expert

Different industries introduce completely different digitalization solutions, which all face individual digitalization challenges and questions:

- General insurance companies identify people as medically insured objects and collect data. But how can this data be secured against unauthorized access and against manipulation?
- Neobanks analyze the budget positions of their clients and suggest changes. But to what extent does the client consider this to be supportive, and when does it become invasive? Is the client prepared to pay for this kind of service? How is the independence of recommendations ensured?
- Carmakers collect data on the usage and driving behavior of their cars and also try to sell insurance. But do clients want a manufacturer as an insurer? Can rates and products be calculated by carmakers? Furthermore, insurance companies are also interested in pay-as-you-drive concepts and are removing the principle of solidarity by pricing risks individually. Does this mean the fundamental principle of an entire industry is up for discussion? And, if yes, how do markets typically reshape themselves?
- Amazon, Google, eBay, and Apple are collecting so much data about the actual behavior of people that the meaning of traditional market research is changing.
- Music publishers still exist, but they generally no longer earn money by selling music, but rather from concerts and memorabilia. Are these cash flows enough for them to allow the sale of music to be transferred to iTunes and others? Or is music no longer purchased individually, but rather provided as a service via Spotify?
- Who do clients in general accept to receive recurring bills from? Their bank, their telecommunication provider, or their energy supplier?
- Newspaper publishers are establishing portals, often with a regional focus. Clients are not used to paying for this content, but enjoy using it. The circulation of regional print media is falling across the board. Is the provision of content via paper still appropriate? Would a publisher sell more paper-based newspapers if it offered mobile and digital content?
- Didn't Neckermann produce the most fantastic mail-order catalogs right up the end? During the initial e-business/e-commerce hype, wasn't it obvious that emotional goods, such as shoes and cars, would not be able to be sold over the Internet?
- Germany's national soccer league is still playing soccer. But the question of who can afford Ronaldo either depends on the wallets of oligarchs and sheiks, or on the question of which club can market and bill for licensing rights in Asia. In other words, it also depends on appropriate digital monetarization.

Digital business experts are familiar with the types of questions mentioned above. They know the answers that are currently favored in sectors and companies.

They know the answers that were favored in the past and have investigated whether the responses have changed over time. In short: They are aware of the opportunities and risks of digitalization (with respect to automation, mobilization, and cyber-physicalization) in existing business models and can transfer challenges and solutions from other industries to the situation in question.

The digital business expert primarily operates by asking the right questions. These questions relate to the following topics:

- **Business model**: Are digitalization trends threatening the current business model? Can new sources of income be developed based on new services or products?
- **Competition**: What digitalization initiatives have been implemented in the industry? How are market leaders responding? What innovations have been introduced by niche providers in the industry? Are there any new market participants from outside the industry?
- **Brand**: How can the brand and image be transferred to new offers? (This represents a great advantage over new market participants!) How can the current client base be approached with new, additional services and products?
- **Legacy issues**: How can historic obligations be eliminated in view of new potentials? (This is often required in order to establish simple digital solutions. If this simplification is not successful, there is a risk that new market participants will gain an advantage.) How can the sinecures of current client advisors and sales channels be dealt with? How can the cannibalization between new and old channels be avoided?
- **Acceptance**: Is the client prepared to accept a new digital approach and/or new products and services? Do emotional or organizational hurdles exist? What are the perceived data protection problems, and do plausible solutions with simple explanations exist?
- **Monetarization**: Who is prepared to pay for what? Are these cash flows sufficient to cover the design and operating effort? What associated income models are conceivable? Are premium services and products available? The monetarization discussion is delicate, as this is precisely where a number of business models and services fail. A critical review must confirm whether the benefit perceived by end customers (often measured as convenience, which is difficult to assess) is large enough to induce them to pay. In all Internet-based businesses, the payment hurdle is initially higher than justified by the actual price. Clients hesitate to establish cash flow relationships with new suppliers due to trust and uncertainty. But even if the decision is made that the payment hurdle can be overcome, the question of whether an adequate number of clients can be reached remains. This often requires an enormous marketing and advertising budget, or a brand that is already strong. In short: The monetarization of end customer businesses is difficult, especially because large Internet players can set up a range of services. If a service is easy to replicate, its monetarization is decidedly questionable. But, even if the business model does not target the end customer,

an eye must be kept on the distribution of the revenue between the partners, the prices for the different types of clients, the commissions for sales partners, and the design and operating costs. New products and services naturally change during their development. Ries (2011) describes this phenomenon as one that is virtually inherent in IT-based innovations. Consequently, the issue of monetarization has to be answered time and again and cannot be decided conclusively at the beginning of the digital transformation. And, unfortunately, there is always a chance that the response may be negative.

- **Introduction**: How can new digital models be introduced to the market? How can they be tested? Who is able to establish and evaluate appropriate A/B tests? What expectations exist with regard to the development of earnings and the customer base? Is the organization resilient enough to adapt to changes in income and business models?
- **Monitoring**: How can the successes/failures of new digital solutions be measured? What are the variables and how can the associated values be automatically determined? Who are these values reported to, and how?

4.1.2 Digital Technology Expert

The digital technology expert is aware of the potentials, levels of maturity, and the key application scenarios of current digitalization technologies. This includes trends and technologies in the context of mobile applications, in the interaction design and in the elasticity context in the broadest possible sense. No classifications currently exist in the context of elasticity, matching operating models, and persistence options in the technology world. Digital technology experts obviously have to be familiar with cloud-like structures and operating models (regardless of whether this relates to private or public clouds). They must also be familiar with non-relational storage concepts and be able to classify these concepts, and they must be able to assess the application opportunities of technologies from the sphere of "big data" (Hashem et al. 2015). The digital technology expert assesses the technical feasibility of the resulting ideas. His or her tasks include the following:

- The digital technology expert checks whether automation technologies, mobilization of data and applications, and cyber-physicalization, i.e., the integration of physical objects into the business processes, can help improve these business processes. The digital technology expert's focus is on the applied technologies. For the aspect of cyber-physicalization in particular, he or she considers all real-world objects that are present in a company's information system, and reviews their integration and management potential.
- The digital technology expert looks at the interactions identified by the interaction engineer and checks which of these interactions can and should receive mobile support. This involves the following questions:

- Is the provision of data and applications possible from a security perspective? What is the public perception of the sector-specific security position?
  Do regulatory provisions or sector-specific regulations have to be taken into
  account? What potential losses and probabilities of occurrence are connected
  with corruption, unauthorized access to the data, and loss of data?
- In what context do these interactions occur? In this case, "context" combines
  all the associated exogenous factors, which can have a significant influence
  on the correct structure of an interaction.
- Will mobile data only be read, or also recorded/manipulated? Do precautions
  need to be taken in case telecommunications are unavailable? What types of
  inconsistencies and which inconsistency periods may arise, and which can be
  tolerated? Are competing manipulations of the data possible from an organizational perspective, and can they be eliminated?

4.1.3   Interaction Engineer

The interaction engineer is required because many of the solutions identified in the
IR:digital are new and potentially involve new interaction possibilities. This
includes gestures, voice commands, and inputs via innovative devices (wrist-
watches, glasses, etc.). The new interaction possibilities need to be coordinated to
ensure that all devices have similar modes of operation. They also need to be
coordinated with traditional interaction possibilities based on the WIMP
(Windows-Icons-Menus-Pointers) paradigm to ensure that the user experiences a
consistent as well as uniform interaction concept. Multimodal interactions are often
employed in new digitalization solutions, which are based on the opportunities
offered by cyber-physical or mobile solutions (e.g., simultaneous voice and touch
operation). The intuitiveness of these kinds of interactions must be critically
reviewed.

The interaction engineer also focuses on business processes, which often represent the overarching context of individual interactions, without being a priority
for in-house or external users. If these interactions do not have a uniform structure,
the user interface will be confusing. In all these situations, the digital solution must
be observed from the perspective of the potential users, their cognitive load must be
taken into account, and media or interaction disruptions must be critically examined. If this task is left to the technology experts, there is a risk that the focus will
drift away from the user and turn to the testing of gadgets. On the other hand, if this
task is left to application domain experts, the focus can quickly turn to business
relationships. The interaction engineer's role ensures that the focus remains on the
user.

4.2   Partner Canvas

The IR:digital uses three canvases:

- The **partner canvas** is used to identify the key partners and their interfaces to the company.
- The **physical object canvas** (Sect. 4.3) is used in order to identify the specific physical objects and their integration into internal business processes.
- The **touchpoint canvases** (Sect. 4.4) are used in order to identify the sequence and channels the respective partner uses to contact the company.

The partner canvas provides information on the types of partners, clients, or users (hereinafter referred to as partners) with whom information or physical objects are exchanged. Partners typically include clients, suppliers, and business partners. Up to ten of the most important partners are identified when creating the partner canvas, which contains all the business processes (without detailing them) that occur within the company. The external interfaces for these business processes are then identified. This reveals the data and products that are supplied externally, as well as the data and products that are purchased externally, and specifies the communication partners.

4.2.1   Methodology and Notation

Partner interfaces are classified into input and output interfaces. On the partner canvas, all interfaces are noted on an ellipse that represents the organization's boundary. The interfaces between the organization and the outside world are added to this ellipse as circles. They are linked to the business process activities that the interfaces supply, or from which they obtain information. Internal parts of the business process are not displayed. All partners who have access to the interfaces and who contribute to the interfaces are noted outside the ellipse. Figure 4.3 shows an example of a partner canvas.

To populate the partner canvas, the organization's core business processes are considered one by one, and the interfaces involved are recorded in order to identify all the relevant interfaces. The interfaces are then investigated in order to determine whether physical objects are affected by an interface. In Fig. 4.3, for example, the interface between broker and rates on the left boundary can be described as follows:

Rates are provided to brokers in the BiPRO XY4001 format. This occurs monthly and is generated proactively by the insurance company. The exchange of rate information is documented and archived.

This description indicates the object being exchanged, the exchange format, how often the exchange takes place, and the additional regulations that apply. This specific example may be a reason for automation, however, no physical object, whose integration in the business processes may be worthwhile, can be identified.

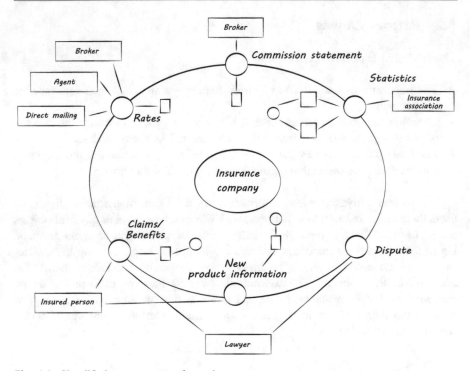

Fig. 4.3 Simplified partner canvas for an insurance company

For another example, an interface similar to the following example may arise in the manufacturing industry:

Machines are delivered to clients, including the operating instructions, a description of the technical features, and a maintenance agreement. Everything is provided by the company and made available online. Access to the information is not recorded.

This description once again indicates the typical information on how an interface is handled. It also confirms that a machine is delivered. This is certainly a physical object. The use of life cycle information about this object within the internal business processes requires further investigation.

Every partner touchpoint with the company is recorded based on the following categories, in order to ensure the systematic collection of interfaces:

- **Partner**: Which partners are involved?

    - Example: An insurance company that wants to identify its digitalization potentials identifies the roles of all the individuals that it contacts. This may include policyholders, sales representatives, brokers, and lawyers.

- **Interfaces**: Which partners use which interfaces?

  – Example: Brokers and interested parties access the product information.

- **Business process**: Which business processes is the partner involved in? How are the interfaces accessed and supplied?

  – Example: A broker interacts with the insurance company in various business processes, such as in the consulting/pricing, contract conclusion, commission settlement, and claims settlement processes.

- **Frequency**: How often does this type of interaction occur?

  – Example: The broker has a monthly interface for commission settlement and is more frequently involved in contract conclusions than claims settlement. Contracts are either concluded in the broker's office or (more often) at the policyholder's location.

- **Terminals/Media**: What types of terminals are involved in the interaction, and what types of input/output media are important?

  – Example: In some cases, the consulting/pricing and contract conclusion processes may be mobile processes and are executed using tablets. Otherwise, laptops and desktop PCs are used.

- **Skills**: Can it be assumed that the interacting individuals are only occasionally involved in the process (and therefore require a great deal of support and training), or do they quickly become experts and expect maximum efficiency?

  – Example: A broker quickly reaches the status of an expert in the consulting/pricing and contract conclusion processes (due to the process frequency). The same is true for the provision settlement process (due to the special interest). However, more assistance must be provided in claims processes.

- **Communication properties**: What types and formats of objects and documents are exchanged, and in which direction? Does this take place in analog or digital format? How often is an interface used, and what service levels and response times have to be ensured? Do security requirements exist? Does the exchange have to be documented?
  A company's partners identified this way are then naturally classified into partner groups. For example, an insurance company has insured individuals, sales representatives, and brokers, which are identified in the interface descriptions. This represents an initial differentiation of a company's outside world, without having to specify personas, as is the case in design thinking

(Brown 2009) or in the IR:mobile. Yet, the additional division of partner groups may be prudent in certain situations. Perhaps large and small brokers exist, which should be kept separate for the purposes of the partner canvas. However, in contrast to personas, the subdivision continues to provide homogeneous groups of partners. Any further breakdown does not occur in the IR:digital, as no specific services are established for specific target groups. This kind of detailing takes place in the IR:mobile (Chap. 7).

4.2.2   Annotations and Analysis

The annotations in Table 4.1, which relate to interface/partner pairs, are used to annotate the partner canvas.

In the analysis of the partner canvas, the following points should be examined:

- Have all relevant interfaces to every partner been recorded, or do gaps exist? This may particularly occur along the chain of defined interfaces. If a partner receives information via an interface, this poses the question of what the partner

Table 4.1 Annotations for interface/partner pairs on the partner canvas

Symbol	Name	Interpretation
	High use	Information may be exchanged across the individual interfaces at different frequencies. The more often an interface is used, the greater the focus on the interface. The high use annotation indicates that an interface is frequently used, or at least that a large number of objects occasionally use this interface to communicate.
	Accuracy	Some, generally commercial and contractually based relationships require the exchange of absolutely precise information. The consistency of information exchanged over these kinds of interfaces is extremely important, as inconsistencies lead to misunderstandings and can lead to economic losses. Other interfaces focus on providing information on issues and events without the need for a correct description. The accuracy annotation indicates which interfaces need to satisfy high accuracy requirements.
	Reliability	The interfaces/partner pair has to satisfy certain service levels. This may relate to the speed of communication via the interface or even the importance of ensuring that information exchanged using this interface is not lost. The reliability annotation provides information on these and associated relationships. The type of reliability is then covered in the detailed discussion of the annotations.
	Security	Security has many aspects. The type of security requirement must therefore be identified when addressing security concerns. The security annotation at a partner/interface pair can be used to indicate that the individual stakeholder considers a certain interface to be critical to security. The discussion of the annotation then identifies the nature of the individual security concern. This may relate to data integrity requirements, protection against unauthorized access, or the integrity of content.

then does with the information and whether a response is provided. If a response is provided, this response has to return to the company via another interface.

- If the number of interfaces with a partner leads to a diverse range of annotations, this situation must be explicitly discussed with the partner to make sure that they are aware of this variation. It may be perfectly fine and proper for one interface to be extremely critical to security, while another is not. A plausibility check should take place in the case of large annotation ranges in order to correct any annotation gaps/errors.
- If a model element has been assigned at least three of the four attributes used, a detailed review is required to check whether any feasible technical solutions exist to guarantee the necessary qualities.
- If intensive back-and-forth interfaces exist with a partner (i.e., an interface to supply goods to a partner, another for receipts, and yet another for additional deliveries), a plausibility check must confirm whether the splitting of the overarching business process is desirable and unavoidable.

4.3 Physical Object Canvas

Many digitalization opportunities arise due to the fact that information about physical objects no longer has to be transmitted in models (typically information systems). Instead, real, physical objects can be requested directly, or data can reveal their status. In this section, we use the term "object of interest" (OoI) in order to clarify the digitalization driver for the integration of physical objects into business processes. An object of interest refers to an object whose direct integration into a company's business processes has the potential to significantly simplify these business processes. In the vast majority of cases, an OoI is a physical object, but it may also be an individual, who is prepared to provide information on status, location, and context. In rare cases, an OoI may also be a purely virtual object that effectively acts as a proxy for a physical object. It is distinguished by the fact that it delivers status data (either continuously or on request) for evaluation at a different point, and its ability to receive control data.

OoIs are identified and described using the physical object canvas. It identifies up to ten of the most important OoIs, whose direct integration into the business processes can lead to significant simplifications or new business models, as well as consider their life cycle and identify events that could lead to data deliveries. To identify the ten key OoIs, it may be necessary to define additional candidates and then gradually reduce the larger quantity down to the most important candidates.

An OoI may also be a human, for the continuous delivery of data, or on request. Equipped with wearables, watches, or other mobile devices, human actors deliver data that generally only has to be evaluated, not stored, in order to respond to certain situations or introduce other measures.

4.3.1   Methodology and Notation

The IR:digital is not focused on detailing how business processes change due to the direct integration of OoIs. Rather, it is more important to determine the extent of the impact of OoIs on the process landscape and identify business processes that may benefit from OoIs (potentially also from different types of OoIs). As a result, these dependencies are primarily accessed via the OoIs and not via the business processes.

OoIs are initially determined based on the partner canvas. This involves the consideration of all interfaces between the company and the outside world identified in the partner canvas. The first category of objects includes those that are explicitly produced and delivered, and those that are explicitly supplied to the company externally. This type of physical object tends to play an important role for producing companies.

However, OoIs that are indirectly dependent on the services provided by a company can also be identified, especially if the service (such as home insurance, or the provision of a printing service) relates to a relevant physical object (such as to a residential building or a printer). In this case, we use the term "service-based OoI."

In some purely digital companies, OoIs cannot be identified by interface analysis or by service-based considerations (as is the case for banks and lottery companies, for example). These kinds of companies are completely disconnected from real-world objects, and their operations are based exclusively on virtual objects. In this case, reference is made to the objects that condense the physical objects or processes. A bank does not have any physical objects, and a bank's services are also only based on virtual constructs. But the central "account" object does exist. And this object condenses information on a perspective of the real "human" object (the perspective that is defined in cash flows). Changes to this condensed object can be identified as status changes, which may result in the introduction of certain measures, just like status changes in physical OoIs. These are referred to as virtual, condensed OoIs.

Interface analysis and the systematic observation of these interfaces for physical OoIs, service-based OoIs, and condensed OoIs enable a basic number of OoIs to be identified, even if they do not directly relate to standard types of interfaces.

OoIs that are directly related to physical objects are generally easy to identify because they are either delivered by suppliers or to clients. They occur as a standard type at a specific interface. This includes OoIs that have a direct impact on the company as products (cars, refrigerators, and machines).

Service-based OoIs can be identified by observing the objects purchased for service products: What is the object to which business interruption insurance relates? This will generally be a piece of equipment, in which case the insured object is a physical OoI. Cars are OoIs, i.e., physical objects, to which the service "third-party vehicle insurance" provided by an insurance company relates. The service "maintenance of the heating system" relates to a heating system, while the service "managed printer" relates to printers.

This collection of OoIs along the external interfaces allows the vast majority of OoIs to be identified. Certain additional OoI candidates may be concealed within the internal business processes. This may include machines and plants in a producing company. While they generally have to be delivered at some point, these kinds of deliveries may not be included in the partner canvas because machine deliveries are rare. They can be identified by searching for physical objects under internal administration. This will generally only lead to the identification of a small number of new OoIs, but this addition makes sense in order to complete the set objects identified via the tour of the interfaces. The additional use of the object canvas is recommended (Sect. 5.4) if this addition leads to the impression that a large number of relevant OoIs have been detected internally. A review of the objects in the object canvas for their OoI potential also leads to the systematic identification of internal digitalization potentials.

Two additional objects are automatically included in the number of objects of interest to be investigated:

- The "client" object, as relevant events may occur during the client's life cycle that connect him or her with the company's products and services. These may also be identified by considering the products (and should be identified at the company interfaces and so already be included in the number of OoIs to be investigated). However, this minor methodological redundancy is accepted in order to prevent gaps at central points.
- Therefore, the second default OoI is the "product" object. With service- and product-oriented companies, this OoI is highly likely to appear in the interfaces in any case. But with companies whose objects are entirely disconnected from the real world, it can easily happen that the actual product does not appear in the examination of the interface; therefore, its examination is explicitly requested.

For companies disconnected from real objects, it often happens that the total number of objects to be examined is actually limited to the two default objects "product" and "client."

A sufficiently complete number of OoIs should exist after this step. Each OoI is examined to determine whether it could generate data about its state during its life cycle that could be relevant, legally usable, and profitable for the company's business processes. Key indications are supplied by the following life cycle questions:

- What location changes is the object subject to during its life cycle?
- What state changes does the object experience during its life cycle?
- What context information for the object exists at runtime? Can this be collected digitally?
- What important events occur during the life cycle of the object?
- What happens at the end of the object's life cycle, and what causes it to be dissolved?

- What other objects does the OoI being examined come into contact with, and does this result in direct communication situations?

All situations in which people are the objects of interest are subject to especially close examination, based on the privacy questions that follow.

- What data is automatically collected about the behavior of people (movement behavior, navigation behavior, usage behavior in regard to devices)? Such data may already be in concentrated form. One example is the "account" object in the context of a bank. Such an object can be viewed as the concentration of account holder behavior.
- For what purpose is this data used? Is the type of use transparent for the person whose data is used, and does the person agree?
- What benefits for the data owner can be generated with this data? Are there services, discounts, or status changes that are offered to the data owner? To what extent do these services or discounts make the client relationship stronger?
- How can abuse be prevented? What risks are associated with prohibited access to the data (image impairment, financial damage, loss of confidence)?
- Is it possible to comply with all requirements and directives for handling personal data?
- Does the (partial) anonymization of personal data ensure adequate data privacy on the one hand, and does it still permit meaningful use on the other hand? What type of anonymization can be carried out automatically?

After these two sets of questions are examined, OoIs with a high OoI potential and without excessive privacy concerns are left. These are examined to determine whether the OoIs are technically capable of providing information about their state in the broadest sense, and how expensive their configuration could become. How this information could be used in the current business processes is examined. Whether new business processes become possible based on this information and whether this data could be exploited in other ways, possibly also externally, is examined as well. Here a review is required—typically by the digital technology expert—to determine how to deal with the fact that not all objects of interest may be accessible at all times, how the volume of information supplied by multiple OoIs can be statistically summarized, what telecommunication means are required, what telecommunication costs may be incurred, and what security issues need to be taken into account.

After all determining factors are examined, a number of OoIs remain that can be considered for integration into the business processes. Which business processes may be affected is examined for each of these OoIs. This is done by free association based on the question: How can current information about the state of an object (for example, a machine, usage behavior of a person, navigation behavior of a person, location behavior of a person, wind power station, car, solar cell, alarm system, or salesperson consulting behavior) be supplied to the company's business processes at any time?

We will discuss some examples of OoIs and their potential in the following:

- A person—considered here as an OoI for a health insurer—undergoes a medical examination with the use of medical devices. The devices used in the process are able to supply diagnostic and administrative information directly for diagnostics and cost settlement, with no media breaks. This means a magnetic resonance tomography (MRT) device can report directly to the health insurer, indicating what body region of which patient was examined with an MRT and for how long.
- An MRT—considered here as an OoI for a manufacturer of medical devices—transmits its operating times to the manufacturer for the purpose of monitoring maintenance intervals and scheduling service personnel in a timely manner.
- An MRT—considered here as an OoI in the sense of hospital equipment—automatically transmits the result data to the responsible medical specialist with reference to the patient who was examined.
- A building air dryer—considered here as an object supplied by a facility management company—transmits its location to the company every 30 min so it always knows what unit is located where. If the device is in motion (its location is currently changing), a message is sent to the recipient when the device is being moved. The message includes the location, time, and distance to the destination, so the recipient does not have to reserve half days for receiving the device. The device is also subject to relevant state changes (for example, the condensate reservoir is almost full). This state change is sent to the current operator as a reminder to empty the reservoir.
- A forklift—considered here as an object supplied by a forklift manufacturer—supplies information about its use (driving characteristics and lifting performance) to the manufacturer, enabling the development of new services such as "lifting as a service" and preventive maintenance. Individual pricing for these services is possible depending on the respective user behavior.
- A dog—considered here as an OoI of a dog food manufacturer (identified by examining the life cycle of the OoI "dog food")—supplies vital signs. These are offered to the dog owner in concentrated form. The dog owner can control the whereabouts and exercise profile of his dog.
- Construction machines—considered as OoIs in the sense of operating equipment of a construction company—report their location when they are moved. If this happens within a certain window, for example at night, an alarm is triggered.
- A car—considered as an OoI supplied by an automobile manufacturer—reports details regarding signs of wear to the authorized dealer. This enables the dealer to offer tailor-made maintenance services. Sales is informed when signs of wear exceed a certain frequency. After a certain service life, the life cycle is assumed to end soon and sales efforts are intensified.
- A car—considered as an OoI supplied by an automobile manufacturer—reports the intensity of use for certain features (such as park heating, steering wheel heating, and driving mode selection). If it turns out that they are frequently

ordered by the basic population of clients but rarely used, then this information is not relevant for the individual "car" object but may be relevant for advertising, marketing, pricing, and even usability engineering.

- A machine—considered as an OoI supplied by a machine manufacturer—supplies information about the ambient temperature, relative humidity, and other context parameters. Based on this information and the information about maintenance intervals, the manufacturer can make applicable improvements to its products.
- A machine—considered as an OoI of an operator—reports available production capacities to a platform used to assign orders and participates in order auctions.
- A photovoltaic system—considered as an OoI operated by an energy company—supplies information about its state in order to optimize maintenance intervals and verify the plausibility of supply remuneration settlements.
- A person—considered as an OoI of an insurer—reports his vital data to the health insurer. Depending on the state of health, immediate therapeutic measures or also just statistics can be derived.
- The central "account" object is an OoI in a bank. While an account is not a real object, it has the greatest proximity to the "client" object out of all objects managed by the bank. The "account" object in a way reflects a dimension of the actual OoI "client", being the dimension of the client's behavior that results in transactions.

After the population of the physical object canvas, OoIs have to be identified for which the relevant events, the data to be supplied and the affected business processes are specified. One also has to note whether the OoIs proactively report individual events to supply data or whether they have to be queried (reactive from the OoI perspective). Figure 4.4 shows a corresponding list for the OoI "machine" of a machine manufacturer.

In addition to the effect on existing business processes, one also needs to examine what additional business processes that did not even exist without the new, broad data base now become possible. Processes in product engineering based on usage behavior or client complaints are an example. Sometimes new products or services are also conceivable based on the newly developed data sources. For example, it is typically possible to not only sell a machine but to offer service models focusing on the performance of the machine. This, however, is only possible—and in particular, can only be priced in a meaningful way—if information is available stating which machines are used how and in what situations. This can vary significantly depending on the context and client. Furthermore, the only way to easily determine this is with machines that send regular reports about how they are used. Therefore, such business models only become possible in the first place when detailed information about OoIs is collected. Other business models can consist of selling data that is collected, or making it available for statistical purposes. Special attention should be paid to data privacy and proprietary rights with all these supplementary business models.

OoI Machine	
Event:	Installation
Data:	Place, Time, ID, Worker
Delivery:	proactive
Affected business processes:	Equipment management, Marketing
Event:	Malfunction
Data:	Place, Time, Type of malfunction
Delivery:	proactive
Affected business processes:	Equipment management, Product management, Maintenance
Event:	Repair
Data:	Time, Type of repair, Cost, Technician
Delivery:	proactive
Affected business processes:	Maintenance, Relaunch management
Event:	Test
Data:	Test identification
Delivery:	reactive
Affected business processes:	Maintenance, Relaunch management

Fig. 4.4 Example of an object of interest described on a physical objects canvas

4.3.2 Annotations and Analysis

The annotation of OoIs on the physical object canvas is performed with the help of the annotations in Table 4.2.

In the overall view, the following competing annotations are considered suspect—OoIs annotated this way should be examined in view of these conflicts:

- **High use and time constraint**: The high-use annotation means that many of the OoIs can occur at the same time. The time constraint annotation means that the information supplied by the OoIs requires further processing within a defined time. Together these factors impose a scalability requirement on the central infrastructure. One needs to examine whether this can be achieved with reasonable means.
- **Reliability and flexibility**: The reliability annotation means that the OoIs are outside the full control of the central system and that the assumed probability of failure for the OoIs could be a problem for the functionality of the overall system. The flexibility annotation means that the formats of the data to be supplied are expected to change. Both together can mean that data deliveries—especially after format changes—could be prone to error. In such situations, each change should be covered by a suitable test strategy as a minimum.

Table 4.2 Annotations for objects of interest on the physical object canvas

Symbol	Name	Interpretation
	Business value	The value creation potential of the OoI is considered to be particularly high—whether through the creation of new products or services, by optimizing existing processes, or through derived business models such as the resale of collected data.
	User value	The resulting solution would serve the requirements of clients or partners particularly well, so that interacting with the OoI would become especially attractive or practical for them.
	High use	The annotated OoI may (at least at certain times) appear in especially high numbers, or the information supplied by this object may cause a high data volume and/or a high delivery frequency. An example could be wind turbines in a region which all suddenly report that they are now shutting down due to adverse weather conditions.
	Time constraint	Data supplied by the annotated object requires further processing in fixed, defined, and usually also short time periods. One example is a car that sends an emergency call triggered by the sensor of the activated air bag. This information has to be processed quickly and asynchronous wait time must be avoided.
	Reliability	OoIs are decentralized elements of an overall system. They have different origins and play roles of different importance in the overall system. Whether the assumed probability of failure for the individual occurrences of the OoI is considered problematic for the overall system is specified for each OoI. Mobile traffic light systems that respond to events and report when the signals change are an example. If complete monitoring is considered important, and it is assumed that too many errors will occur during data transmission, this can be emphasized by this annotation.
	Accuracy	The data to be supplied by the OoI, which tends to contain errors due to its diverse origins, needs to be adjusted to meet the correctness requirements of the internal business processes prior to further processing. An example may be vitals data of persons covered by health insurance that needs to be reviewed in regard to relevance for discounted premiums: Such data comes from many different persons and is generated and transmitted by numerous different devices and apps. One can expect many different versions and deviations from defined formats here. A need for adjustments prior to further processing has to be taken into account.
	Flexibility	The corresponding objects are intended to supply defined data according to their life cycle analysis, but the content, format, and frequency of data deliveries can be expected to change sometimes based on technology, regulatory, or data privacy changes.
	Complexity	Integrating the OoI would lead to especially complex solutions. This may be due to the fact that data is difficult to capture at the OoI, the data structure makes evaluation difficult or integrating the OoI in a digital system poses special design challenges for other reasons.

- **High use and accuracy**: A scalable data volume that requires adjustments prior to processing can indicate a potential performance problem. Therefore, the calculation complexity of the adjustment should be examined.

4.4 Touchpoint Canvas

The purpose of the touchpoint canvas is to analyze, for a maximum of five partners, what probable contact sequences exist, which events trigger the contacts, and on what channels or in what contexts they occur. This means the interfaces from the partner canvas are arranged in typical perception sequences in reference to a specific partner.

There is a separate touchpoint canvas for each of the most important partners up to a total of five. Every touchpoint canvas lists up to ten so-called touchpoint events. A touchpoint event is an event that triggers a contact. Each touchpoint canvas differentiates five to ten access channels or contexts in which contacts can occur. The information shown here is also referred to as a customer safari or customer journey map by other approaches [which are in turn loosely derived from service blueprints (Shostack 1984)] that focus on the client as well.

4.4.1 Methodology and Notation

The objective of the touchpoint canvas is to determine potential interaction breaks from the perspective of the most important partners, up to a maximum of five, and to determine whether the individual service for and touchpoints with each partner form a coherent and plausible picture. Requiring the partner to select different access channels depending on the touchpoint is to be avoided. The interaction with the company should appear consistent to the partner. Special attention is paid to those touchpoints where there is a risk that the interaction may be terminated because the partner is irritated, unable or unwilling to overcome a usability hurdle. These touchpoints are called trust points.

For the five most important partners (one of these is always the partner "client"), the touchpoint events that cause the partner to come into contact with the company in question are placed on a timeline (the horizontal axis of the canvas). Here, the term timeline is not to be interpreted in terms of a strict linearization of the contacts. It can branch and also bend back, for example, when an exception occurs at a touchpoint requiring the return to a previous touchpoint. However, documenting a complete sequence of contacts that reflect the handling of all exceptions is not the goal, as it would mask the regular flow too much.

A notation is made for each touchpoint event, documenting through what channel and in what context the contact can be supported. Here it is possible that more than one channel can be considered for a touchpoint event. If this is the case, choosing the channel is up to the partner as a rule. At least the assigned interfaces from the partner canvas have to show up for each partner. Channels and contexts can be noted along the vertical axis using so-called touchpoint lanes. While access channels in particular are noted in the lanes within the scope of the IR:digital, context information primarily appears as lanes when the touchpoint canvas is used in the IR:mobile (Sect. 6.4). We typically differentiate the following touchpoint lanes:

- **Real objects**: This lane is chosen when OoIs are exchanged.
- **Paper**: This lane is chosen when paper is exchanged.
- **Electronic messages**: This lane is chosen when electronic messages are exchanged.
- **Web**: This lane is chosen when a partner obtains information on the organization's Web site. It is possible to differentiate between mobile and stationary Web access (especially in the context of the IR:mobile).
- **Social media**: This lane is chosen when information is obtained or exchanged using social media.

The number of touchpoint lanes can be expanded. An insurance company may, e.g., add the lane "client service center" for clients, while a bank may add the lane "ATM."

The touchpoints are entered in the coordinate system as simple circles. They show which channels support the touchpoint events. Placing a touchpoint event on the canvas indicates a contact that takes place in the context named by the lane or using the named access channel (which usually designates a certain media class such as Web and mobile). Trust points, i.e., touchpoints with a risk of terminating the interaction, are marked by double circles.

By default, one of the five partners to be examined is the partner "client." For this partner, the life cycle of the OoI "client" examined in the physical object canvas corresponds to the label of the horizontal axis on the partner touchpoint canvas for the partner "client."

Figure 4.5 shows an example of the touchpoint canvas. Interfaces from the partner canvas are sorted according to two dimensions. Two of the touchpoints are identified as trust points.

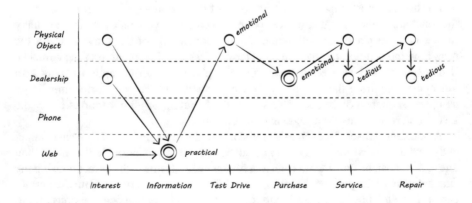

Fig. 4.5 Example of touchpoint canvas for a client buying a car

4.4.2 Annotations and Analysis

Instead of assigning value and effort annotations, each recorded touchpoint is evaluated from the partner perspective on an emotion scale encompassing the attributes "tedious," "necessary," "practical," "desirable," and "emotional":

- **Tedious**: The partner perceives touchpoints as tedious that require interaction where this is not necessary from the partner's perspective. Touchpoints that are considered necessary can still easily be perceived as tedious if they are poorly implemented though. This means it takes longer to use them than it should from the partner's perspective, they are not perceived as robust or reliable, or they cause uncertainty for the partner ("Did it work correctly?"). When all employees have to respond to the registration for a company event (and not just the expected ten percent not attending), that is tedious, because it is perceived as not necessary. A conference system where the reviewer remains uncertain whether his opinion was recorded, until he receives an e-mail a few minutes later, is tedious, because it is poorly implemented.
- **Necessary**: Some touchpoints are necessary and accepted as such. When the client wants to buy something in an online shop, he has to identify himself and enter a delivery address. A good implementation ensures that the client is willing to accept this "bureaucratic" step.
- **Practical**: Necessary touchpoints are perceived as practical, especially at the start of their implementation, if they make other activities obsolete. Paying a parking fine for an American rental car can be quite difficult, because the foreign renter usually does not have a check he can just put in the mail. On the other hand, if there is a QR-code-based mobile app for paying parking tickets by credit card, the convenience of this application may even overshadow the unpleasant occasion.
- **Desirable**: Some touchpoints do not even exist yet with full functionality, but are desired by the partner. This results in a genuine touchpoint expansion request. For example, a client may have the idea that informing his bank once of a change of address should automatically inform all companies with direct debit authorization of the changed address. The touchpoint "client informs bank of address change" exists in such a situation. However, the expanded functionality is not available yet. This makes "desirable" a difficult classification because it mixes the evaluation of existing with the desire for future functionality. It is, however, especially useful as well, since it provides a direct indication of potential for improvement.
- **Emotional**: The partner is emotionally involved in some touchpoints. This can have various reasons, whether one is calling a complaint hotline, picking up a new car from the manufacturer, checking into a hotel after a long journey, or rebooking a flight because of a missed connection. Ideally, such touchpoints need to be especially robust with a friendly user interface.

Figure 4.5 shows the partner touchpoint canvas of an automobile manufacturer's client. It begins with interest in the product, which can manifest itself through numerous channels, and continues with a test drive, which includes a real object (the car in the test drive). The purchase takes place on site. The "service" touchpoint can occur through four lanes: On the one hand, the service appointment is made by telephone or Web, on the other hand, the actual service is performed at the dealership and involves a real object (the car). "Repair" is also listed as a touchpoint. The attributes listed on the emotional scale exhibit a significant spread. At least the purchase is perceived as pleasant and emotional for most buyers, and emotional involvement of the client can be expected on occasion for the repair as well. Even this simple annotation shows that, from the perspective of the automobile manufacturer, the goal is to follow the initial positive touchpoints with other positive ones in order to maintain client loyalty beyond the life cycle of a car. The classification of the "information" touchpoint as a trust point is interesting: If the client fails to obtain enticing information about products and their configuration, or is unable to determine prices quickly enough, there is a risk the customer may lose the desire to buy so the budding business relationship fails to be consummated.

The analysis of touchpoint canvases usually does not result in any identification of problems. Instead, their examination provides indications of suspicious facts that require closer analysis. Typical suspicious facts are as follows:

- A lot of back and forth between the touchpoint lanes, which can disrupt the uniform impression or indicate media, breaks in the execution of actions.
- Numerous selection options at individual touchpoint events (vertical lines that intersect several lanes), since this can confront the partner with the cognitive burden of selecting the right channel or recalling which one was chosen last.
- Many interfaces classified as "desirable," since this indicates functional gaps.
- Many Web-based interfaces classified as "emotional" since there is a risk of the company being blamed for access problems caused by a lack of telecommunications coverage. In particular when the client is emotionally involved, this can lead to annoyance which is virtually impossible to rectify.
- Any interface classified as "tedious." If the partner perceives an interface as tedious, it should either be eliminated or automated, or its necessity should be made clear.
- Any tedious trust point since terminating the interaction is an immediate threat here.

4.5 Cross-Canvas Analyses

During population of the IR, the analysis of the individual canvases used in the IR: digital has usually led to suspicions and self-evident improvements. Preparing and improving the models is followed by a second analysis step, in which an analysis across the various canvases is performed. We differentiate between completeness analysis, annotation analysis, and the verification of plausibility.

The **completeness analysis** examines whether the model elements determined in a canvas are picked up in other canvases. This does not have to be done for all model elements, only for the essential ones. There may be good reasons if certain model elements are not examined further even though they appear relevant from the perspective of an individual canvas. The completeness analysis merely intends to verify that there are good reasons for perceived gaps. Some examples for suspicion of incompleteness are as follows:

- Do important partners (with many and intensively used interfaces) appear in the partner canvas, but their life cycle is not described in a touchpoint canvas? Typically, the most important partners should appear as anchor points of touchpoint canvases.
- Do objects occur in numerous or at least intensively used interfaces without being shown on the physical object canvas? If this is the case, supplementing the physical object canvas should typically be considered.
- If there are OoIs with many relevant events, do these events also appear in touchpoint canvases? If this is not the case, it indicates that the examined touchpoint canvases are not sufficiently focused on the OoIs' potential. In this case, it can be useful to consider in what touchpoint canvas scopes the OoIs would appear, and to describe these (even if we are probably not going to implement them anytime soon).

The **annotation analysis** examines whether the interplay of annotations used in partner, physical object, and partner touchpoint canvases indicates suspicious facts and inconsistencies. The following constellations could indicate the need for clarification:

- Combinations of annotations on interfaces and annotations on OoIs are almost always suspect if they are not well coordinated:

  - An interface that supposedly has to withstand a high load, and an OoI exchanged over the interface that does not generate a high load do not fit together. The actual load and performance requirements should be examined.
  - A security–critical interface used to exchange an OoI for which high flexibility is assumed also appears awkward, since the security mechanisms potentially have to be adapted for every change of the OoI. In this case, it usually makes sense to describe the security requirements in detail.
  - An interface to be used for handling a high load, and an OoI to be exchanged over this interface where strict time restrictions have to be met does not fit together at first glance. The load scenarios should typically be examined more closely.
  - An interface for which high reliability is demanded and an OoI that is marked as critical regarding the probability of failure (using the reliability annotation) may not fit together from the perspective of overall system reliability.

- If an OoI is annotated with a high business value, and the events named for the OoI do not appear in at least one partner touchpoint canvas, one should question how the assumed business value will be realized.
- Events from the life cycle of OoIs with attractiveness annotations can appear in partner touchpoint canvases. If the corresponding touchpoints there are annotated as "tedious," this begs the question for whom it is attractive to use the OoI? Such annotation combinations often conceal situations that are not equally attractive for all stakeholders. Often, attractiveness for the organization in fact contradicts attractiveness for the user. This can be the case, e.g., when data capture is externalized. While this can mean savings for the company, it may be tedious for the user. Measures are typically required to establish a balance of attractiveness between the stakeholders.

In the **verification of plausibility**, several questions are asked where the answers can provide indications of additional improvement potential:

- Is it possible that the information collected through the interfaces is easy to digitize, while the internal business processes themselves are not the object of automation?
- Should activities be automated, but not all their inputs/outputs be digitized?
- Do the annotations on the OoIs match the business process activities requesting them? (This can only be examined if corresponding details were captured in addition on the process canvas).

These analyses and the verification of plausibility can uncover gaps, contradictions, and possible inconsistencies. They cannot be eliminated through algorithms as a rule. The main goal of the overall analysis is to point out improvement potential early on.

4.6   Workshop Structure and Follow-up Activities

The presentation of the canvases in the IR:digital in the preceding sections was accompanied by notes on how to populate them individually. The interplay involved in populating the canvases of the IR:digital has not been discussed yet. This is not merely a question of the sequence, but especially a question of interrelationships since it is helpful to collect and record knowledge directly on another canvases as it comes to light while populating a canvas. This interrelationship and integration is among the benefits of synchronous modeling in the Interaction Room. In order to achieve it, a workshop in the IR:digital should follow the method described below. A suitable agenda for the population of the IR:digital over the course of two days is found in Sect. A.1.

- Classification of the company being examined to make it clear how the OoIs can be identified on the physical object canvas.

  - Result: type of company in terms of digitalization

- Creation of the partner canvas with collection of all OoIs that appear while describing the interface.

  - Result: partner canvas, initial entries on the physical object canvas

- Annotation of the partner canvas in one annotation cycle and analysis

  - Result: annotated partner canvas and indications of suspicion

- Determination of the five most important partners on the partner canvas. A touchpoint canvas is later created for at least these five partners. The touchpoint canvas for the partner "client" is always among these.
- Consideration of available technologies to obtain an overview of what is technically feasible. Such a consideration is necessary because the possibilities of many digitalization technologies (especially those related to the trends of mobilization, cyber-physicalization, and the evaluation of summarized life cycle objects) often cannot be assessed by the stakeholders in an IR:digital workshop, so that an excursion into the solution domain can help to inspire ideas about digitalization potential in the application domain.
- Creation of the physical object canvas through a systematic consideration of all interfaces, taking into account the OoI "product" and the OoI "client."

  - Result: initial physical object canvas

- If applicable, determination of additional OoIs through consideration of all elements on the object canvas, and their abstraction. This means that when few OoIs can be identified through the partner canvas and it is suspected that additional OoIs are concealed in the information systems, an object canvas (Sect. 5.4) is created and a search for OoIs is performed there.

  - Result: physical object canvas

- Annotation of the physical object canvas, and analysis of annotations

  - Result: annotated physical object canvas and indications of suspicion

- Reduction of the physical object canvas to the ten most important OoIs.
- Examination of the OoI life cycles and determination of the information that can be supplied, as well as its use in the partner canvas (data from which OoIs are supplied to which business processes; where can OoIs be controlled?).

- Result: detailed description of the OoIs that were identified in the physical object canvas

- Creation of touchpoint canvas

  - Population of touchpoint canvas for the partner "client"
  - Annotation and analysis of the touchpoint canvas for the partner "client"
  - Result: annotated client canvases and indications of suspicion

- Creation of touchpoint canvas, at most for the four most important partners from the partner canvas

  - Annotation and analysis of each touchpoint canvas
  - Result: annotated touchpoint canvas and indications of suspicion

- Higher-level analysis of the canvases that were created

  - Completeness analysis
  - Annotation analysis
  - Verification of plausibility
  - Result: indications of suspicion resulting from overall IR:digital population

- Deriving the digitalization focal points from the touchpoint canvases and their analysis, establishing key activities and priorities for the subsequent approach, ranking the OoIs, interface characteristics, implementation objectives

  - Result: ranking of digitalization approaches

- Formulating "press release"-style summaries for the top five implementation suggestions.

  - Result: brief descriptions of project ideas

At the end of IR:digital population, prioritized and evaluated proposals for key activities and/or projects have been defined in the context of digitalization. These fall into the category of mobile-driven, technology-driven, or classic development projects. In the first two cases, more detailed specification using the IR:mobile or IR:tech is meaningful if there is a defined risk structure and the analysis results in heterogeneous stakeholder objectives. In case of a classic development project, it makes sense to set limits with the help of the IR:scope, thereby establishing the requirements for development support using the IR:agile.

Other ways to proceed are also conceivable: Obviously, it is possible to develop a project outline identified in the IR:digital further using other methods than an IR. The documentation resulting from an IR population can serve as valuable input for virtually any requirements, design, or architecture work. Subsequent process steps should only be aware that the results of the IR:digital are abstract, may still include inconsistencies, and that further refinement will be required further down the road.

References

Brown T (2009) Change by design: How design thinking transforms organizations and inspires innovation. HarperBusiness

Davies N et al (2015) Security and Privacy Implications of Pervasive Memory Augmentation. IEEE Pervasive Computing 14(1):44–53. doi:10.1109/MPRV.2015.13

Hashem IAT et al (2015) The rise of "big data" on cloud computing: Review and open research issues. Information Systems 47:98–115. doi:10.1016/j.is.2014.07.006

Ries E (2011) The lean startup: How today's entrepreneurs use continuous innovation to create radically successful businesses. Crown Business

Schmidt A (2015) Societal discussion required? Ubicomp products beyond Weiser's vision. IEEE Pervasive Computing 14(1):8–10. doi:10.1109/MPRV.2015.15

Schwab K (2016) The fourth industrial revolution. World Economic Forum

Shostack GL (1984) Designing services that deliver. Harvard Business Review 62(1):133–139

Westerman G, Bonnet D, McAfee A (2014) Leading digital: Turning technology into business transformation. Harvard Business Review Press

Using an Interaction Room for Software Project Scoping (IR:scope)

5

While agile process models encourage frequent communication with stakeholders, they are relatively silent on how to ensure that this communication will lead to valuable, actionable insights. The Interaction Room for Software Project Scoping (IR:scope) fills this methodical gap in agile process models: It provides a communication forum for all stakeholders in the project, enables the business and technical substance to be made visible and comprehensible, documents ideas and risks, and offers methodology guidelines to focus communication on the project aspects that are actually critical. All of this is accomplished in a deliberately pragmatic framework that does not add methodical ballast but integrates naturally with the agile approach.

As described in Sect. 2.1, one of the main objectives of an Interaction Room is to make the complexities of large IT projects intuitively comprehensible. This is accomplished by sketching out models of various, complementary perspectives of the project: Large model sketches on all walls of the room are at the center of all communication in the Interaction Room. Business and technology experts jointly map the key system and user interfaces, process sequences, and data structures on large whiteboards.

The various canvases of an Interaction Room help stakeholders deal with the structures, processes, and interfaces of an information system in the context of its business domain in a guided but pragmatic way. Parallel views of the business domain and technical systems help stakeholders from different backgrounds to develop a joint understanding of the system. Dependencies, contradictions, and uncertainties can be identified, and mutual respect is established for requirements, context, and complexity, both on the business and on the technology side.

Once the project material has been made comprehensible this way, the next step is to identify aspects that make system development complex, costly or uncertain. Annotations are added to the sketches for this purpose and analyzed to derive recommendations for detailed requirements analysis and risk management.

© Springer International Publishing Switzerland 2016
M. Book et al., *Tamed Agility*, DOI 10.1007/978-3-319-41478-2_5

The IR:scope supports the development of a joint understanding of the initial business and technical situation as well as the value-driven documentation of requirements and their critical discussion. To achieve this, representatives of all project stakeholders (Sect. 3.5) join in the Interaction Room in a series of workshops.

5.1   Relevant Stakeholders

In addition to the IR coaches and the process owner as representatives of the business side (Sects. 3.5.1–3.5.3), the technical stakeholders who will build and operate the system—application developers and operations experts—also have to be taken on board in the IR:scope. The business side includes user representatives as well. Their roles are described in the following sections.

5.1.1   Application Developer

The application developer is one of the key representatives of the technical stakeholders on the team and ensures that questions regarding the software process and implementation technology can be answered competently. To fill this role, it is not that important whether this stakeholder is an actual software developer on the project team, or an outside expert who has in-depth knowledge of software engineering in general and the company architecture in particular. It is crucial, however, that the application developer is able to classify apparently infeasible ideas as such in a timely manner. He consistently monitors the feasibility of planned software solutions, in terms of whether they can be created and integrated. Together with the operations expert, he is responsible for making sure that the imagination of process owners, business developers, and technology experts does not run wild.

5.1.2   Operations Expert

Like the application developer, the role of the operations expert is a restraining one. He is responsible for evaluating whether proposed software solutions can be put into productive operation in a timely manner. The operations expert keeps an eye on costs even more than the application developer. For example, he points out early on if certain service levels for certain platforms/base systems can become expensive, if they deviate from the organization's IT strategy specifications or entail other risks. Depending on the organization, the application developer and operations expert may be the same person.

5.1.3 User

In addition to the process owners for the affected business processes, the IR:scope should also include users of the software being created who are familiar with the business processes in day-to-day practice. They know to what extent the defined processes deviate from the practiced ones, what exceptions often occur in practice, and which steps require particular effort. Furthermore, they are able to provide feedback as to how well the planned solutions address concrete application problems, conform to the reality of their work, and so on.

5.2 Feature Canvas

Documenting the requirements for the software being created is the first step in the population of an IR:scope. This is done on the feature canvas, a wall used to collect and prioritize the requirements to be implemented in the project.

The stakeholders typically collect several dozen requirements to be implemented in the project from their perspective. No more than half a dozen core aspects are then selected from this collection for a detailed discussion in the IR:scope, as described in the following sections.

5.2.1 Methodology and Notation

In order to establish a consensus between the workshop participants about the scope of the software to be developed in the project, the requirements of all stakeholders are collected on the feature canvas. The IR coaches invite the stakeholders to note their requirements for the project and the problem areas they perceive in the project on index cards and to pin them to the canvas.

The phrasing of these requirements does not need to be as complete and precise as user stories (not to mention the documentation of requirements in classic requirements engineering). This is because concrete implementation tasks are not yet being derived at this stage. The goal is merely to develop an overview of the general requirements that need to be implemented in the project. Noting keywords and phrases describing certain business processes or application functions that need to be supported or considered by the planned system is sufficient.

In pinning the cards to the feature canvas, the stakeholders are asked to consolidate their contributions as pragmatically as possible by removing cards with duplicate information and grouping cards related to aspects of the same business processes. The IR coaches can support this process by identifying conceivable clusters of requirements and/or core processes in cooperation with the stakeholders responsible for the project while preparing for the workshop and placing appropriate cluster headlines on the feature canvas at the outset.

Once all stakeholders have contributed their cards in such an unstructured brainstorming session, the requirements are discussed by the stakeholders to make sure everyone interprets them in the same way. Next, the requirements are prioritized according to where the stakeholders see the most urgent need for clarification and refinement. The annotations presented in the following section assist with this process.

5.2.2   Annotations and Analysis

The stakeholders first add the annotations in Table 5.1 to all cards on the canvas (not only their own) which they consider especially worthy of discussion.

The annotations pinned to the canvases are subsequently discussed and stated more precisely by the stakeholders—for example, the user value can be classified according to Kano (1984) depending on user expectations:

- **Must-be qualities** are fundamentally expected by the user. While their presence is not perceived positively, the user would be disappointed if they were lacking.
- **One-dimensional qualities** are utilized by the user to differentiate between offers. The quality of their implementation can have both a positive and a negative impact on user satisfaction.

Table 5.1 Annotations for requirements on the feature canvas

Symbol	Name	Interpretation
	Business value	The requirement is very valuable from a business perspective. For example, the requirement may make a special contribution to productivity, the external image, sales figures, or similar. A cross-selling function, for instance, can be of special business value for an online shop ("other clients also bought…").
	User value	The requirement has a high value from the user perspective—for example because it expresses a fundamental expectation and covers a key requirement of the user (making it a reason to use the software being created), or because it makes a special contribution to the satisfaction of users with the software. For example, the requirement to enter and view product reviews can be a key driver of user value for an online shop.
	Complexity	Implementing the requirement poses special business or technical challenges. This may mean that the business domain is subject to complicated process or structural specifications, that the integration of technical components is complicated, or that developing algorithms is especially difficult. One example in an online shop may be the requirement to display the most helpful product reviews for the user first.
	Uncertainty	There is uncertainty regarding the background or embodiment of central business or technical aspects of the requirement. This uncertainty may be related to specific points, such as clarifying whether an online shop will accept only debit or also credit cards. It may also be of an overall nature, for example stating that the legal regulations for returning goods in international trade are still unclear and their impact on the software being developed has to be determined.

- **Attractive qualities** are not expected by the user—while their lack is not viewed negatively, the user is impressed if they are present.

These annotations help better identify value, cost, and risk drivers: Business and user value are clearly value drivers, while the complexity and uncertainty annotations at least indicate a higher cost, but usually also a higher risk.

The annotations are especially useful for prioritizing the requirements for discussion in the IR:scope:

- Cards with one or more value driver annotations should be given a higher priority because they describe features that are the reason for developing the software in the first place, or the reason why users choose this software at all. Understanding them is essential for project success.
- Cards that are not only marked as value drivers but also marked as cost and risk drivers (e.g., in the combination of user value and complexity) are especially critical: Here the expected use of the feature is endangered by the risk that the complexity of the business material could lead to unsatisfactory or incorrect solutions. This makes it all the more important to understand the material, state the requirement precisely if applicable, and test the solution thoroughly following its development.
- However, the combination of complexity and uncertainty annotations also indicates that a requirement should be discussed in greater detail in the Interaction Room since these points pose a special risk for the success of the project. Not only is the implementation expected to be difficult, but some of its details are not known yet.

That being said, the priority of the requirements is not determined merely by the number and type of annotations. It is determined by the stakeholders using a prioritization method such as card sorting. Here the stakeholders gradually arrange the requirement cards in order of priority by taking turns inserting a card into the sequence or changing the position of a card in the row. This gradual addition and repositioning of one card at a time per stakeholder continues until none of the stakeholders see any further need to change a card position, which means a consensus regarding the prioritization has been found.

The features assigned the highest priority in this manner are then examined in more detail in the IR:scope from the perspectives of the other canvases, as described in the sections that follow.

5.3   Process Canvas

The process canvas is dedicated to visualizing the business processes that are relevant for the software system under development. Domain experts sketch out the processes that the system supposed to support, automate, or participate in.

A process canvas is not intended to precisely and fully specify every business process. What is important is to reach a consensus among the participating business experts with regard to how a process is typically handled in practice (or how it should be handled), what data is produced, and which interfaces exist to participating system components, roles, and subsequent processes. To keep the presentation concise, and to prevent the discussion from being sidetracked by non-constructive details, the scope of the process canvas should not exceed a maximum of 15 processes with up to 15 steps each.

Frequently, this step (which initially is not even about a technical implementation and/or support of the processes) bears considerable potential for discussion. For example, officially specified processes may deviate from those actually followed in the company, or processes may have never been formally documented, but just established or evolved over time. Establishing a consensus regarding these process sequences is the first step toward understanding the requirements for IT, evaluating the design or strategy decisions and choosing technical solution options. The process canvas supports this as described in the following sections.

5.3.1 Methodology and Notation

Stakeholders with very different experiences in process modeling come together in an Interaction Room. These stakeholders typically include both technology experts, for whom abstract models are an everyday form of communication, and domain experts, who are able to deal with complex case situations but have no experience with documenting them in abstract diagrams. In order to equally involve both sides in the population of the process canvas and utilize all of their knowledge, the method's participation threshold was kept purposely low.

The IR method coach merely explains the purpose of the process canvas at the outset and then selects the processes to be sketched together with the stakeholders, based on the requirements previously prioritized on the feature canvas (Sect. 5.2).

The processes are then sketched jointly by the stakeholders. Ideally, the stakeholders work together on the whiteboard to get the discussion going. However, it may be useful if the IR domain coach takes care of modeling based on the stakeholders' input until the stakeholders overcome their apprehension of shared modeling and gain experience with the desired level of abstraction.

No specific notation such as UML or BPMN is prescribed to sketch the processes. Whatever notation is intuitively understood by all stakeholders or agreed on ad hoc is permitted. In practice, this usually leads to the use of a greatly simplified version of UML activity diagrams that express the essential concepts of process sequences (Fig. 5.1):

- Individual process steps (activities) are shown by rectangles.
- The sequence of activities (control flow) is indicated by arrows.
- Execution alternatives (branches) are indicated by labeling the arrows with conditions.

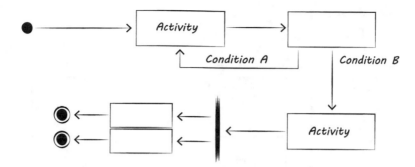

Fig. 5.1 Notation for process canvases

For the clearer presentation of more complex processes, the IR method coach can also introduce the following symbols as needed:

- A bar perpendicular to the control flow direction indicates the beginning or end of a parallel process.
- A black disk marks the beginning of the process.
- A circled black disk marks the end of the process.

To keep the modeling flow as intuitive as possible, and avoid disrupting it with syntax specifications or diagram refactoring, strict compliance with UML requirements (such as branching only on diamond symbols, bringing all branches back together with equivalent symbols) is omitted since the process semantics usually become clear from the context anyway.

Figure 5.2 shows an example of a simple process canvas, which was developed by a mixed team of business and technology experts without the explicit introduction of a notation in order to develop a joint understanding of a process for regular rate reviews by a health insurer.

Here the process was outlined at a high level, showing the steps required for rate restructuring including possible alternatives without specifying the exact implementation of the individual steps in detail. Even though it will be necessary to refine the details in the course of the subsequent implementation (e.g., to specify how the restructuring criteria will be reviewed in concrete terms), the existing presentation is sufficient as orientation for business and IT experts in discussing the fundamental requirements for the individual steps.

The IR coaches moderate modeling in multiple ways: They ensure that an abstraction level is maintained that is suitable for comprehension by all stakeholders—the presentation must not become so trivial that the characteristic structures, points of contact, and uncertainties are concealed, but neither should the sketches be so detailed that specialized knowledge is required to understand them. In choosing the right abstraction level for any IR canvas, it must always be avoided that the stakeholders "cannot see the forest for the trees."

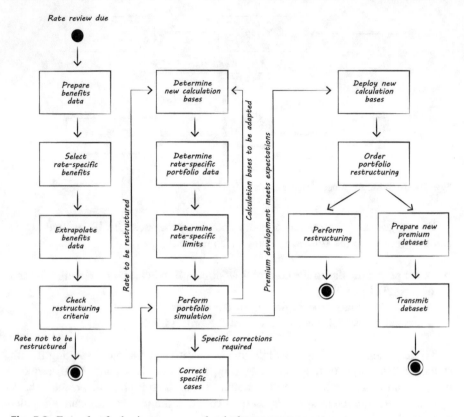

Fig. 5.2 Example of a business process sketched on a process canvas

In order to achieve this, the coaches not only make sure that the process steps are described with a meaningful granularity (in particular, the stakeholders should not succumb to the temptation of modeling every interaction step with the information system as an individual process step). The IR domain coach in particular also curbs discussions that lose themselves in technical details or specialized business cases and ensures that the process canvases primarily reflect the standard case for handling a process. Handling exceptions and other special situations are not necessarily required for the desired fundamental understanding of a process and are often actually counterproductive in obtaining that understanding. They should therefore only be modeled if they occur frequently and if they are expected to have a significant influence on subsequent design decisions. That being said, it is often more helpful to merely point out the underlying "disruption factors" with an annotation (Sect. 3.3), so the problem can be explored later.

However, the IR coaches should definitely follow up if they perceive points in the course of modeling where the stakeholders fail to communicate clearly— whether these are uncertainties about process details, contradictions/gaps in process conditions, misunderstandings or diverging model interpretations, or process segments nobody "dares" to model. These communication weaknesses often result in comprehension gaps which can lead to problems in the subsequent course of the project. Here the IR coaches have to put their finger on the problem early on and encourage the stakeholders to close the identified gap by either correcting or expanding the model outline, or adding a suitable annotation to indicate the need for further discussion.

Furthermore, the IR method coach in particular is responsible for involving all stakeholders equally in the discussion—which not only means encouraging quieter stakeholders to participate in the discussion in order to benefit from their knowledge, but especially also restraining overly dominant stakeholders to prevent them from controlling the formation of independent opinions.

Finally, the IR method coach is also responsible for maintaining an overview of the relationships between the process canvas and the other canvases and for monitoring the consistency of the contents. In keeping with the pragmatic modeling approach, the consistency requirement is not to be understood dogmatically: Not every structural detail affected by a process also has to appear on an object or integration canvas. However, the obviously important elements should be found in both views in order to emphasize which system components are integrated into what process and which data structures are handled by the processes.

This different standard is also reflected by the scope of the process diagrams produced in the Interaction Room, which is limited by the space available on the whiteboards on the one hand and the cognitive capacity of the stakeholders on the other hand: A process canvas typically will not contain more than 15 processes with up to 15 steps. More complex canvases cannot really be developed in the course of an individual IR population workshop. If the business domain is more complex, it should be developed in a series of workshops that each focus on specific sections of the process landscape.

5.3.2 Annotations and Analysis

The process canvas describes the essential sequences in the business processes being examined but (just like classic modeling languages) does not provide clues on how to evaluate the individual process steps: Which steps are especially complex? Which ones are especially time critical? Which ones are subject to special constraints? Which steps are not understood yet?

Business experts who deal with these processes on a daily basis have unconsciously internalized all of this additional information, while it is entirely unknown to the technical stakeholders, who also have no way to simply derive it from any formal models. At the same time, the business experts do not recognize where technical pitfalls may be in the implementation of the processes, while those are often obvious to technical stakeholders at a glance.

In order to make this qualitative business and technical knowledge explicit to the whole team, the IR:scope provides all stakeholders the opportunity to add annotations to the elements of the process canvas, in order to highlight particular value and effort drivers. Table 5.2 shows the spectrum of annotations for process steps on the process canvas.

Only five to seven annotations out of this palette should be provided to the stakeholders at a time, in order to avoid overwhelming them with a choice of too many annotations. For the first annotation round, recommended annotations include business value, user value, policy constraint, complexity, and one or two other effort-driven annotations matching the type of business (e.g., the high use and time constraint annotations, or the security and flexibility annotations). If the IR domain coach has the impression that other aspects are relevant for the processes being annotated, additional annotation rounds with up to five other annotations each can follow. However, the uncertainty annotation is only assigned in a final, dedicated annotation round as described in Sect. 3.3.

Following the annotation of the process canvas, the stakeholders explain and discuss the annotations they have assigned to the process steps. Detailed knowledge about constraints, value, and effort drivers that would normally remain concealed in the minds of individual stakeholders is thereby explicitly stated and recorded. The form in Fig. B.4 can be used to record the precise localization, characteristics, and motivation for each annotation.

The analysis of the individual annotations and combinations of annotations spanning several process steps provides valuable insights for prioritizing and esti- mating the effort required for the process steps' IT support:

- **Isolated business value or user value annotations** on process steps not car- rying any effort annotations show that a process step is central for the provider or user of the system, but does not appear to be associated with complicated implementation requirements. Therefore, it can be considered a "quick win" that can be realized without major difficulty.
- **Isolated effort annotations** obviously constitute warnings of particularly high conceptual or implementation requirements. The effort needed to implement them should be especially carefully considered when no value annotation associates particular priority with the process step.
- **Combinations of various annotations** should be viewed critically, since they can increase risk as well as effort. The combination of value and effort anno- tations, e.g., is always considered particularly risky, since an especially valuable part of the process is subject to particularly high complexity. When a process step is marked with both the automation and business value annotations, it can be assumed that the desired automation will not only required above-average effort to realize, but that it also needs to be of especially high quality in order to actually produce the business value expected from the process step. Failing to obtain the required quality bears the risk that the desired business value (and therefore one of the key objectives for building the application in the first place) will not be achieved. This constitutes a risk which needs to be explicitly monitored in the course of project risk management.

Table 5.2 Annotations for process sequences on process canvases

Symbol	Name	Interpretation
◈	Business value	The process step generates or supports particular value for the company. Or the process step is one of the reasons why the process as a whole is being executed in the first place. The risk assessment in the course of an insurance company's quotation process is an example of such a step.
👥	User value	The process step is of particular value for the person executing it. This value can be aligned with the values and objectives of the company (e.g., an immediate confirmation of coverage in response to an insurance application saves both the insured and the insurer time-consuming inquiries and discussions), but the value may also be contrary to the company's business objectives (e.g., a potential client wants the validity period for an offer to be as long as possible, while a company wants it to be as short as possible).
⎍	High use	The process step is performed particularly often and therefore demands an above-average amount of resources (such as personnel, materials, or IT). High use may constitute continuously high demand or intermittent peaks in demand. This may include plannable events such as handling the holiday business in the retail sector or the cutoff date for renewing motor vehicle insurance at the end of November, or unplannable events such as lottery jackpots or natural phenomena.
⏱	Time constraint	The process step has to meet specific time constraints such as fixed processing times or deadlines. Even though information systems are seldom subject to real-time requirements, it is common for certain process sequences to be subject to deadlines, compliance with which should be enforced or at least supported by the software. Examples are cancelation and payment deadlines in electronic commerce.
🔒	Security	The process step has to meet special security requirements, such as restrictions on participants who are authorized to carry out the step, the sensitivity of the data being processed, or the personal assignment and non-repudiation of the action that is carried out. In the maintenance of patient files for example, a requirement may be that only certain roles are permitted to view these files and that any changes can be traced to their author.
🔗	Reliability	The process step has to be carried out with especially high reliability, which means errors are not permitted in its execution, and the possibility to execute it has to be guaranteed at all times. This can mean, for example, that the principle of dual control is applied to ensure a step is carried out correctly, or that substitution rules are in place in case the participant who is primarily responsible for the step is absent.
🪨	Flexibility	It is foreseeable that the process step will not always be executed exactly as specified, but that it will have to adapt to new conditions in the future and/or will be adjusted by the performer depending on the situation. This may, for example, be the case in health care, where treatment or rehabilitation processes cannot be firmly defined but depend on individual diagnoses, or in other business domains where, e.g., legal changes, the introduction of new products, or the discontinuation of old payment methods can be foreseen.

(continued)

Table 5.2 (continued)

Symbol	Name	Interpretation
	Mobility	The process step is to be executed on mobile devices. This annotation is helpful when the mobilization of a process is planned in the Interaction Room. It allows the stakeholders to identify early on which elements are to be provided on mobile devices and what continues to be available through classic channels. For a public transport company for example, this could apply to process steps such as purchasing and validating passenger tickets.
	Automation	The process step is to be automated. In digitalization projects in particular, this annotation can be used to indicate which process steps currently taking place off-line will be supported by IT in the future. This may, for example, include simple processes such as address changes, but also more complex functions such as automatic confirmation of coverage in an insurance company.
	Manual task	The process step can and will not be automated. Even in the course of ongoing digitalization, there will be process steps that require human expertise, for example to make decisions based on numerous criteria and to handle exceptions. Examples of such processes include underwriting complex risks in reinsurance and making decisions about therapy measures in rehabilitation.
	Policy constraint	The process step is subject to certain legal or organizational constraints that have to be taken into account in the redesign or technical implementation. A variety of such policy constraints is possible, such as consumer protection rules for investment transactions prescribed by the Markets in Financial Instruments Directive (MiFID) and international directives for handling goodwill cases.
	Complexity	Executing the process step is more complex than it may appear at first glance. Experts have to be involved in order to carry it out (or technically support it). The complexity of the process step will usually manifest itself in business aspects (such as calculating duties for international trade).
	Need for improvement	The process step is to be redesigned in order to optimize it or adapt it to new requirements. Many motivations are possible for this change. The improvement may be the core of the planned project because it is necessary to enable other conversions, or it may be an opportunity when a process is being modernized anyway.
	External resource	The process step is carried out by a participant outside the own organization. For example, e-commerce providers may use third-party providers to obtain information about client creditworthiness. The annotation indicates risks arising from depending on third-party providers, such as occasional non-availability or changing contract models.
	Uncertainty	There is uncertainty regarding central aspects of executing or supporting the process step. This may include rather precise questions for which answers still need to be obtained (e.g., up to what delivery weight an online shop wants to offer free shipping of orders), or broader issues that remain unresolved (such as how certain youth protection directives will be implemented in shipping). The difference between the complexity and uncertainty annotations is that a complex problem has already been largely understood and identified as elaborate, but in contrast to uncertainty, no essential questions remain unanswered.

- Process steps that not only have a value and/or effort annotation but also an **uncertainty annotation** are considered especially critical. In this case, the value and/or effort symbolized by the annotation is combined with the risk that the process step and/or requirement for it has not been adequately understood by the team yet. This can lead to delays in realization or even incorrect implementation if the uncertainty is not adequately resolved.

Besides examining the process steps individually, it is just as important to examine several semantically related and interdependent steps. An potentially critical combination such as an external resource that delivers an essential business value not only exists in this perspective when the corresponding annotations are attached to the same element, but also, for example, when a value creation activity in a process canvas follows an activity carried out by an external participant. If the external resource is not available, this affects downstream activities. In case of activities identified as adding especially high value, this can lead to undesirable function or quality impairments. One should therefore always examine whether upstream activities introduce specific challenges that are no longer taken into account downstream. For example, a policy constraint highlighted by an annotation in one process step may impose specific data privacy requirements—in this case, stakeholders should make sure that downstream steps are marked with corresponding security annotations, to make sure the privacy requirements will be considered there.

5.4 Object Canvas

While the process canvas presents the dynamic process sequences of the application domain, the focus of the object canvas is on the business data and artifacts that are handled by these processes. Rather than presenting a complete and precise object model, the object canvas shall provide a high-level overview that enables all stakeholders to understand the involved data structures as intuitively as possible. With a scope of no more than 40 object types, the object canvas does not need to reach the level of detail of a traditional class diagram, but just provide an overview of the information landscape for the application domain. A pragmatic methodology and notation similar to the process canvas are used to establish this overview.

5.4.1 Methodology and Notation

Various strategies for pragmatically outlining the object canvas are possible depending on the application domain and project focus:

If the domain and project are primarily defined by *data structures* (e.g., when the processes largely consist of reading and writing data), it is recommended to begin population of the IR:scope with an object canvas. In an initial brainstorming session, a handful of data objects that are considered especially central for the project is collected from the stakeholders. Using these as a starting point, the stakeholders then identify additional, related objects until they have the impression that a sufficiently complete picture of the project-relevant data structures has been drawn.

If, however, the domain and project are more strongly defined by the *actions* of various participants, i.e., by business processes, then modeling should begin with the process canvas as described in Sect. 5.3. All objects affected by the process steps are noted on the object canvas—initially only as a loose, disconnected collection. After the process canvas is complete, the stakeholders begin to structure the terms on the object canvas by including relationships, adding more objects, and removing irrelevant and/or redundant terms.

A formal notation such as UML class diagrams is deliberately eschewed for the sketching of the object canvas, to keep the learning curve as flat as possible and allow stakeholders who are not familiar with formal modeling languages to participate without fear of syntax requirements. Instead, stakeholders are encouraged to use the minimal notation shown in Fig. 5.3 with the following elements:

- Rectangles represent object types that are relevant in the application domain.
- Lines represent non-directional relationships between the data.

These very generic semantics were chosen to avoid assumptions about the type of data described in the sketches. The data symbolized by a rectangle may be a class in the sense of object-oriented analysis, but also an attribute of such a class (it is premature to decide at this point which data will ultimately be implemented as a class and which as an attribute). The rectangle may also represent a document that contains unstructured information, or an abstract concept with no direct equivalent in the implemented information system.

The representation of the relationships between data as plain lines is just as generic. Arrowheads are purposely omitted from the basic notation since their semantics in data structures are not as clear as in process sequences: An arrow between two model elements could be interpreted as "is part of" or "contains," alternatively as "generated by," "influenced by," or "depends on," or have other contradictory meanings. The undirected line merely expresses an intuitively identified relationship which needs to be stated in concrete terms in more detailed models to be created later in the project. However, it does not suggest a specific meaning (which would vary between the various objects anyway).

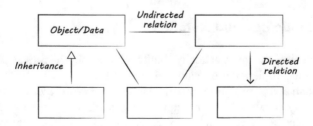

Fig. 5.3 Notation for object canvases

If necessary, object canvases can, however, be refined with additional notation elements, in order to clarify relationships in especially complex data structures:

- Directed relationships can be represented by lines with open arrowheads. In this case, the semantics of the relationship should be noted on the arrow in verb form (e.g., "includes").
- Inheritance relationships can be represented by lines with closed arrowheads, with the arrow pointing to the superclass, similar to UML.

Inheritance relationships and multiplicities should be used sparingly and only where necessary to clarify relationships between certain data structures. An object canvas can and should not be refined into a detailed class diagram in an IR:scope.

Even in the expanded notation, the specification of aggregation and composition relationships is discouraged since the syntax and semantics of the UML notation for these concepts can be easily misunderstood by stakeholders with no modeling experience. Where necessary, aggregation or composition relationships can be shown by correspondingly labeled directional links or appropriate multiplicities.

Figure 5.4 shows an example of a simple object canvas that was developed by a mixed team of business and technology experts in order to establish a common understanding of the concepts and elements of a portfolio management system for a health insurance company.

This canvas gives an overview of the most important concepts needed to describe insurance rates, but without specifying a concrete implementation (e.g., in the form of an object-oriented or relational structure). While information such as "price level" and "tax deductibility" will probably be modeled as simple attributes of a "rate" object, the "insurance terms" and "service description" are likely unstructured text documents that cannot be captured in object structures. However, all that matters in this presentation is to show the domain-specific data and relationships that need to be represented in the software under development.

The IR coaches have two tasks while outlining such an object canvas: Firstly, they have to ensure that all stakeholders have the same understanding of the terms used on the object canvas. Stakeholders from different domains frequently have slightly different interpretations of a certain term without being aware that other interpretations may exist. If this becomes apparent in the course of the discussion, the IR domain coach is responsible for establishing a common definition with the stakeholders.

Secondly and especially for areas of the application domain that are already well understood (and where everyone can join the discussion), it is typically very tempting to record too many trivial details on the canvas. In contrast, the sketches for aspects that are less well understood are often quite superficial. This poses the risk of misunderstandings down the road: When the model is examined later, it is no longer clear whether the areas that appear deceptively manageable actually have such a simple structure, or whether the creators of the model lacked knowledge of their actual complexity. Areas of the model that appear very dense at first glance can also suggest a level of complexity that does not exist upon closer examination. It is the responsibility of the IR coaches to keep an eye on such imbalances and

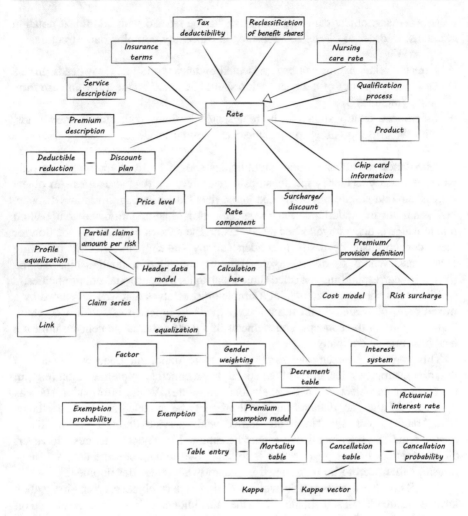

Fig. 5.4 Example of a simple object canvas

focus the discussion on aspects that are especially complex or not sufficiently understood yet.

5.4.2　Annotations and Analysis

Supposedly simple object models often conceal a considerable amount of domain knowledge, constraints, uncertainty, and stakeholders' gut feelings that cannot be explicitly expressed in formal modeling languages such as the UML. However, this informal additional information is at least as important for the correct implementation of the data structures as the details specified in an object model. In order to express such valuable background knowledge explicitly, the stakeholders can add the annotations shown in Table 5.3 to the object canvas.

The annotation of the object canvas typically begins with the business value, user value, policy constraint, and complexity annotations along with one or two other effort annotations related to the application domain (such as the accuracy, security, flexibility, and external resource annotations). Additional annotations can be assigned to the model in subsequent rounds as needed.

Following the annotation of the object canvas, the IR domain coach asks the stakeholders to explain and discuss the annotations they assigned to the model elements. The detailed comments made in this process are recorded, so they are available later in the project. The analysis of the individual annotations and their combinations on various data structures also provide insights for prioritizing and estimating the implementation effort. In addition to the obvious effort implied by annotations such as accuracy, security, and flexibility, not only combinations of value and effort drivers but also combinations of certain effort drivers have to be considered as especially effort- or risk-intensive:

- While the combination of the flexibility and manual task annotations, for example, appears unproblematic (and in fact, each of these annotations may suggest adding the other), the combination of the flexibility and automation annotations is particularly critical: While data is to be captured and/or processed automatically on the one hand, structural changes to this data are already foreseeable. This is expected to require additional effort either to design sufficiently flexible data structures in advance or to adapt them again later—with the added risk of incompatibilities or errors creeping in during flexible design or subsequent alterations.
- Conflicts between annotations can also be considered warning signals: A data structure marked with the invariability or deprecation annotations as well as a value or effort annotation such as flexibility, mobility, or business value is expected to realize a (new?) functional requirement or business value on the one hand, but is apparently classified as a legacy component on the other hand, for which no further development seems reasonable. This requires either the realization of elaborate adaptation or replacement mechanisms for the affected data structures, or a reassessment of the strategic value of the legacy system.
- Beyond the combinations and collisions of individual annotations, examining the canvas as a whole can also be revealing: Larger areas without annotations are suspect—rather than assuming that everything is clear to all stakeholders in this area, it often appears more likely that none of the stakeholders thought hard about such areas and identified challenges that may still be concealed there. This sometimes becomes clear in the course of an uncertainty annotation round, when question marks are suddenly placed in model regions that were previously lacking annotations.
- The informative value of annotations assigned too ubiquitously also has to be considered critically: At the start of an annotation round, the IR method coach points out that a correctness requirement naturally applies to all data, but that the

Table 5.3 Annotations for data structures on the object canvas

Symbol	Name	Interpretation
	Business value	The data is of particular value for the provider of the software system. This can apply, e.g., to client user profiles in an online shop.
	User value	The data is of particular value for users of the software system. Customer ratings in an online shop are an example of this.
	Accuracy	The data is subject to particularly high requirements with regard to timeliness, precision, or consistency. Typical examples include the timeliness of prices for securities, the precision of sensor data, or the consistency of cached data.
	Security	The data is particularly sensitive and therefore needs to be protected against unauthorized access or loss. Protection can take a variety of forms such as encrypted transmission, creating backups, or electronic signatures.
	Flexibility	The data is subject to foreseeable structural changes, for example due to technical or legal evolution. Such flexibility is especially important for companies offering purely digital products: Insurance companies, for example, have to maintain numerous contract variants for several product generations in parallel. The situation is similar, e.g., for mobile telecommunication service providers, although they can handle the conversion of legacy contracts to current contracts more pragmatically.
	Mobility	The data is to be obtained or made available on mobile devices. This annotation is especially relevant when the data volume for the mobile devices is high or subject to demanding timeliness requirements, or when transmitting data captured on mobile devices to a central back-end is critical.
	Automation	Data capture or processing is to be automated. This annotation is especially relevant for digitalization projects when legacy data is to be made accessible for digital processing.
	Manual task	The data is available in a format that is not suitable for automatic processing. Examples include text documents or other unstructured data sources where preparation for automated processing is not possible due to their semantic complexity or not desirable since the process in question will continue to be handled manually.
	Policy constraint	Obtaining, processing, or storing the data is subject to particular business or technical basic conditions. Examples include retention periods and requirements for the type of data that needs to be captured for executing a process (e.g., bookkeeping and accounting regulations).
	Complexity	The structure or processing of the data is more complex than it would appear at first glance. This annotation is helpful when stakeholders are tempted to model complex data structures in detail in the Interaction Room instead of limiting themselves to the big picture. The annotation can indicate which of the model elements that all appear simple at first glance harbor especially high complexity.

(continued)

Table 5.3 (continued)

Symbol	Name	Interpretation
STOP	Invariability	The data structure can/must not be changed (e.g., because it comes from an unchangeable legacy system). Especially in migration or adaptation projects where "greenfield" software development is not possible because of constraints established by an existing software landscape, it is important to maintain an overview of where there is design freedom and where existing structures have to be respected.
	Deprecation	The data will not be available anymore in the future (e.g., because the data source will cease to exist). This annotation is used mainly in migration and adaptation projects to indicate which data structures have to be replaced by new structures in the future and what data will no longer be available to the new system.
	Need for improvement	The data requires structural or qualitative revision (e.g., to enable new types of analyses). Altering existing data structures is a drastic change that can be highlighted early on with this annotation. Among other things, it requires careful deliberation about the migration of data in old structures and the adaptation of all components working with this data.
	External resource	The data comes from an external source. This means it is necessary to take into account that this source (e.g., an external currency converter) may not always be available, or that the influence on its quality and business model may be limited.
	Uncertainty	There is uncertainty about central aspects of the data structure or content. This uncertainty may be of a specific nature (e.g., regarding value ranges or validation rules for certain data types), but it can also affect larger parts of the design, for instance when it remains unclear in a logistics system what data is needed to describe international freight traffic.

accuracy annotation should only be applied to structures requiring unusually high attention. Yet some stakeholders tend to be generous when assigning annotations. If annotations are assigned to more than a third of the model elements, the IR coaches should question which elements are actually special value or effort drivers that demand above-average attention.

5.5 Integration Canvas

The integration canvas shows the system under development in the context of its neighboring systems. This clarifies communication with and dependency on other components of the system landscape. Typically, the canvas has a star-shaped structure with the software system under development in the middle, connected to the related systems by arrows. Like the other canvases, the integration canvas has to remain manageable rather than getting out of hand and becoming a complete infrastructure model. Therefore, it presents the software being developed in the context of at most 20 important related systems.

5.5.1   Methodology and Notation

While the stakeholders sketch the process and object canvases, the integration canvas is typically filled in parallel: External components or organizations that play a role in process steps are arranged on the integration canvas around the software being developed. Data that is produced or consumed in process steps and exchanged with external participants is recorded on the object canvas in the form of data objects and as arrows systems on the integration canvas.

The notation of the integration canvas is limited to a minimum syntax as shown in Fig. 5.5:

- Rectangles represent components of the system landscape or other components that the system under development (shown in the center) needs to communicate with.
- Arrows represent the direction of data flows between the components. The transmitted data entities are noted as arrow labels.

Even though the appearance of the integration canvas is largely defined by the data flow arrows, it differs from classic data flow diagrams in several ways.

For one thing, the purpose of this canvas is merely to show what data is exchanged with which components, but not to model all data flows in the system landscape. For this reason, data flows between the related systems are omitted, putting the focus on data exchanged with the software system under development.

Whether the communicating components are internal or external to the organization, and whether they are technical, institutional, or human communication partners, is also not differentiated. The aim of the integration canvas is just to create awareness of the relationships, so the stakeholders can form an overall understanding of the dependencies and responsibilities between the components.

The types of data that can be exchanged with these communication partners are correspondingly broad: The arrow labels can describe structured or unstructured data of any kind. However, stakeholders should ensure that any data noted here is reflected on the object canvas as well, to arrive at a comprehensive picture of the system's data structures.

Fig. 5.5 Notation for integration canvases

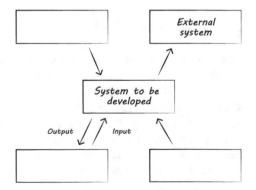

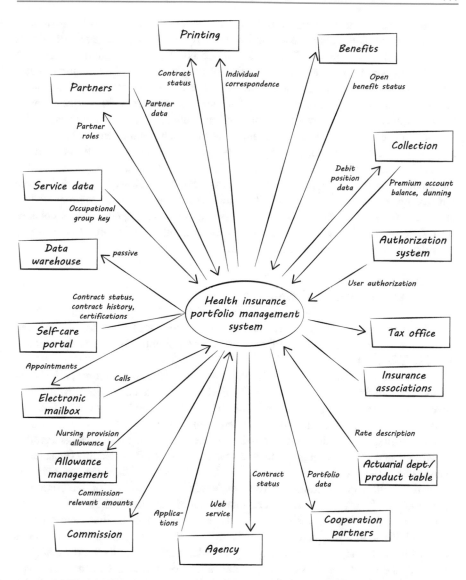

Fig. 5.6 Example of an integration canvas

In the spirit of pragmatic modeling, the data flow arrows in the integration canvas do not depict the exact communication protocol but limit themselves to the main direction of the data delivery (if the component in the project focus, for example, requests creditworthiness data from an external rating agency, only the incoming arrow with the label "credit report" is drawn, but no outgoing "credit report request" arrow).

Figure 5.6 shows an example of a simple integration canvas for a health insurer's portfolio management system which was created by business and technology experts in the course of an IR:scope population.

The related systems shown here are both components internal to the insurance company (such as the commission and benefits systems) and external participants and services such as the tax office and insurance associations. Communication with the related systems is therefore quite varied. It may consist of the structured, automated exchange of data (access to rate descriptions in the product table for instance) or the manual transfer of unstructured data (such as reports to insurance associations). At the abstraction level of the interaction canvas, the only relevant aspect for the stakeholders is what data is exchanged with which components. The concrete exchange formats and protocols are precisely specified in the system design later on.

Parallel modeling of the process, object, and integration canvases ensures that the business world to be supported by information technology is examined from three complementary perspectives: What processes occur, what data is processed by them, and with what external components is this data exchanged? The IR coaches are tasked with maintaining an overview of the content in these three canvases and pointing out gaps or contradictions that arise.

5.5.2 Annotations and Analysis

Stakeholders can mark especially critical aspects that will need to be observed during the integration of the various system components, using the annotations listed in Table 5.4.

The integration canvas is initially annotated with the annotations policy constraint, complexity, external resource, invariability, and need for improvement. If necessary, the IR domain coach can let the stakeholders add further annotations for other challenges in the course of subsequent annotation rounds.

The ensuing explanation and discussion of the annotations provides background knowledge and reveals requirements and constraints that often remain concealed in classic presentations of a system landscape. Using the integration canvas, they can be made explicit in the minds of the stakeholders responsible for integration or operation. Analyzing the individual annotations and their combinations on various components also provides insights about the effort and risks of integrating them.

In addition to the effort and risks already represented by the individual annotations (such as the risk that an external resource provider may change its interface at short notice, or the effort required to react to the failure of a critical external resource), combinations of different annotations in turn indicate especially great effort:

- A combination of the high use and external resource annotations implies an especially high risk: Not only is the developed system subject to a high load—this load is in fact transferred to an external component over which the operation has no control. If the external resource fails, a high number of users are affected with potentially serious consequences.

Table 5.4 Annotations for components on the integration canvas

Symbol	Name	Interpretation
	High use	The component or interface is continuously or occasionally subject to heavy loads. This is typically the case when a process step involving an external contractor or participant is executed particularly often, for example when reports are exchanged regularly between social insurance organizations.
	Security	The component or interface has to meet special requirements to protect its functionality or data against attacks or loss. Depending on the conceivable dangers or attacks, it may, for example, be necessary to encrypt communication to protect against unauthorized access, or to design the external components redundantly.
	Reliability	The component is subject to especially high availability requirements. Depending on the concrete requirements of the software being developed, this may mean that the duration and frequency of failures are not permitted to exceed a certain threshold, or that the component must be designed with redundancy to switch to a backup component in case of failure. This may result in additional requirements to ensure data consistency between the redundant components.
	Mobility	The component needs to be available on mobile devices. This annotation is useful to represent the distribution of the system components across mobile devices and the back-end using the integration canvas. Components with a mobile availability requirement typically result in higher development and testing effort to ensure compatibility with various mobile platforms.
	Policy constraint	The component or interface is subject to special business or technical constraints. These could, e.g., include legal restrictions on the location where cloud applications are hosted.
	Complexity	Handling the component or interface is more complex than it appears at first glance. The annotation indicates that integrating the component requires special effort—for example because data formats have to be converted, or because the exchange format or communication protocol being used is particularly complex.
	Invariability	The component or interface can/must not be changed (for example because it is a legacy system). This restriction is often found in enterprise IT landscapes that developed organically. Their legacy systems are to remain unchanged since adaptation and quality assurance would demand excessive effort (provided that the required expertise still exists within the company).
	Deprecation	The component will no longer be available in the future. In migration and adaptation projects in particular, this annotation can be assigned to components that are to be replaced in the course of the project or will be eliminated in the future.
	Need for improvement	Certain aspects of the component or interface have to be adapted or optimized. This need for improvement can consist of work required to make the main project objective possible, or optimizations that can be realized in the course of conversion work which is planned anyway.

(continued)

Table 5.4 (continued)

Symbol	Name	Interpretation
◐	External resource	The component is an external resource, so there is limited influence on its availability and quality. At what point a component is considered external depends on the possibilities for influence within the scope of the planned project: Even components that are managed within the company but not part of the planned project may need to be designated as external. In other situations, it may be sufficient to only designate components as external if they are actually operated by independent organizations. The annotation is recommended in both cases if a loss of control and reliability risks are expressed due to the externality of the component.
?	Uncertainty	There is uncertainty about central aspects of the component or interface, for example regarding concrete details of the communication protocol or more general questions regarding the ways and means to integrate an external service.

- Combinations of the mobility and complexity annotations appear critical as well: If the mobile connection of a certain component as such represents a major technical and process challenge, the mobilization of a component already identified as complex appears especially critical. Taking a closer look at the challenges associated with this mobilization project in an IR:mobile could be worthwhile.

5.6 Cross-Canvas Analyses

The annotations provide initial indications of where difficulties might lurk in the course of the project, where additional expertise needs to be developed, and what areas leave little room for compromise.

In addition to examining individual canvases, an overall view of all canvases in the Interaction Room is worthwhile as well. The annotation patterns described in the preceding sections can be applied here again. Semantically related or interdependent model elements with colliding or mutually reinforcing annotations may not just be found on the same canvas, but also on different canvases: For example, if a process step is annotated with high business value on a process canvas while the system responsible for data provision to that step is marked for deprecation on the integration canvas, alternative solution for obtaining the required data in the future must be discussed.

In addition to such annotation combinations and collisions distributed over more than one canvas, the individual canvases should also be examined for possible challenges that are not taken into account in the corresponding place on another canvas—for example, if a certain data structure is marked as security-critical on the object canvas even though no corresponding annotations appear on the process canvas, and no need for corresponding security precautions in the respective components is indicated on the integration canvas.

The following combinations of concrete annotations send strong signals for looming future problems, some of which may manifest themselves in the course of the system's development, while others may only become apparent when the system is put into operation. While these annotations could easily be identified as critical combinations when applied to the same model element, their combination is often not apparent when examining an overall canvas or relationships between several canvases. Therefore, an overarching review of all canvases should explicitly consider the following combinations of annotations:

- **Security and flexibility**: Recurring difficulties or at least additional effort can be expected in the system's life cycle in order to adapt the security precautions to changeable processes, architectures, technologies, and so on. Strategies should be developed to isolate the security infrastructures from the changeable elements of the system as far as possible.
- **Security and external resource**: All stakeholders need to be aware that typi-cally, security can only be guaranteed within the boundaries of their own component, but is expected by the user of the system as a whole. Measures need to be developed to minimize the loss of control at the system boundary as far as possible.
- **Deprecation and business/user value**: The stakeholders need to ensure that the identified value can be provided even after the component is replaced. There is, however, a risk that the annotated value aspects may be restricted at least temporarily.
- **External resource and business/user value**: The stakeholders need to be aware that the value emphasized by the annotation is provided by a component on which the organization has limited influence. There is a risk that the corresponding function may later be provided in a manner that no longer meets the requirements for creating value. The stakeholders therefore need to consider whether the corresponding function could also be provided by components operated internally with greater control.
- **Complexity and business/user value**: The emphasized value is to be provided by a component that is more difficult to implement than the average component. This leads to a higher risk, and sufficient resources should be provided to mitigate the risk.
- **Flexibility and business/user value**: The emphasized value is to be created by a component for which the requirements and realization are expected to be subject to significant change. This bears the risk that the value cannot be provided with adequate quality anymore after future changes.

Finally, the combination of uncertainty annotations with other annotations is considered especially risky: In this case, a value, effort, or risk driver is already known, but an uncertainty associated with this challenge (or another challenge that could affect the realization of the element) may lead to unforeseen problems or additional effort.

Some annotations are in direct opposition to each other—if they are combined, the constellation should be critically reviewed, potential misunderstandings should be clarified, and an alternative representation should be sought:

- **Invariability, deprecation, and need for improvement**: Each of these annotations excludes the other two, since simultaneously retaining, changing, and replacing a system is not reasonable.
- **Invariability and flexibility**: The challenges emphasized by these two annotations are incompatible, indicating either a misunderstanding between the stakeholders or the need to reclassify the affected business aspect or technical component.

Such inconsistencies, especially when examining several canvases in combination, are quite common due to the pragmatic modeling processes of the IR:scope. The IR coaches should not attempt to interrupt the cognitive flow with constant consistency requests during the modeling and annotation rounds, but strive to resolve them during the subsequent discussion of annotations. It can also be helpful to transfer the annotations from one canvas to the linked elements of another canvas in especially critical areas during a more intensive subsequent analysis of the overall picture.

5.7   Workshop Structure and Follow-up Activities

The process of populating an IR:scope with models and annotations is relatively flexible and not subject to a large number of rules. In general, the initial definition of project objectives culminates in the writing of a fictitious "press release" that can be used by the IR domain coach to refocus the stakeholders whenever the discussion tends to get sidetracked. Then, the requirements are collected and prioritized in more detail on the feature canvas.

What happens next depends on the project and the orientation of the participating stakeholders: The process, object, and integration canvases have to be filled in order to develop the business domain and IT landscape in which the project will take place. However, the sequence in which this happens is not fixed but depends on which canvas promises the most intuitive path to understanding the domain.

For many information systems, the simplest approach is to access the domain by outlining the business processes on the process canvas, while the object and integration canvases are filled loosely "on the side" whenever insights about data and system structures are gained in the course of process modeling. If the system being developed is more back-end-centric, less user-oriented, or even involves system or data migration, it may be more helpful to approach the requirements through the objects that will be managed by the system. In this case, the stakeholders need to ask, while modeling the object canvas, which related systems supply this data (to be sketched on the integration canvas) and which processes deliver and handle the data (to be sketched on the process canvas). This approach can be easier for the stakeholders, especially when the business experts tend to grasp their domain by examining concrete cases, forms, and documents rather than by reasoning about generic business processes. Using the integration canvas as the primary canvas is less common, but indicated, for example, when the project focus is on replacing a legacy component with a new solution.

While the primary canvas is outlined cohesively as the stakeholders, for example, move through a process step by step, the content of the other canvases populated on the side initially remains fragmentary. The other canvases are completed when work on the primary canvas is finished, and missing data structures and relationships are added.

Selecting a "leading" canvas for the stakeholders to focus their modeling efforts on while populating the other two canvases in parallel and subsequently completing them has proven itself as an efficient way to obtain a sufficiently complete and consistent description of the domain—without asking the stakeholders (who are usually less skilled in modeling) to complete three separate modeling cycles.

Stakeholders with classic modeling experience may object that continuously keeping all three views (processes, objects, and integration) consistent with each other and discussing them in the overall view is complex and hardly realistic. This objection is certainly justified when working with detailed, formal models (e.g., in the UML). However, giving up the completeness and precision requirements in the Interaction Room and radically simplifying the notation syntax and modeling depth makes a parallel examination possible. Especially in the early project phase, this high-level view delivers more valuable insights than attempting to model all aspects in detail.

The annotations assigned by the stakeholders after the process, object, and integration models are sketched also make an essential contribution to these insights. In several annotation rounds, annotations are first added to the primary canvas and then to the other canvases, as described in Sect. 3.3.

The parallel examination of processes, data, and system components, as well as the annotation of important value and effort drivers, leads to the development of a high-level overall understanding of the system relationships by all stakeholders. Misunderstandings about structures and processes are avoided, while inconsistencies, gaps, and redundancies become apparent early on. This overall understanding is not just essential for deriving reliable recommendations for the subsequent project phases, but also helps to highlight unanswered questions, existing risks, and important basis conditions more completely and concretely.

Completing the IR:scope population marks the transition from project scoping to project implementation. At the end of such a workshop, a high-level list of requirements and a high-level system model have been developed. While these are not yet complete, they are supported by all stakeholders, and all of the stakeholders should have the impression that at least the most critical points have been resolved, the most essential questions have been answered, and the major uncertainties have been identified.

In other words, a more detailed specification of some aspects is likely still required, and more questions are sure to arise during the conceptual design and development process, but there should be no more big surprises or major conflicts. Above all, the value, effort, and uncertainty annotations identify what aspects subsequent refinement steps should focus on, so that precise modeling results in genuine insights rather than merely constituting a diligent but routine piece of work. Assigning, explaining, discussing, and recording the annotations can therefore be viewed as the most important step for gaining insights in the IR:scope. No other modeling technique can achieve insights so early and document them as precisely.

Depending on the project's complexity and constraints, detailing the model sketches developed in the IR:scope can take place in the course of a classic requirements engineering and specification process. The advantage is that the effort can now be invested precisely on the aspects previously annotated as critical, instead of being poured indiscriminately into the creation of a system specification of full breadth and depth. Agile project management with the help of the IR:agile can follow directly as well. Here the refinement of the requirements and specifications is realized from sprint to sprint (Sect. 8.2).

Reference

Kano N et al (1984) Attractive quality and must-be quality. J Japanese Society for Quality Control 14(2):39–48, ISSN 0386-8230 (in Japanese)

Using an Interaction Room for Mobile Application Development (IR:mobile)

Expectations for mobile applications have changed significantly in the last few years. The simple urge to "have an app too" has grown into the strategic question of how mobile applications can contribute to the success of a company.

This strategic question is based on the realization that the information and communication patterns of employees and customers have changed over the years: Accessing information and completing transactions anytime and anywhere has become an everyday reality. Like our keys and wallet, the smart phone is always with us, and always online. Access speeds and costs, device performance and usability no longer constitute obstacles—neither for demanding tasks nor for recreation. People organize a significant part of their economic and social communication using mobile devices today.

Private experiences with mobile applications establish expectations among customers and employees that are transferred to the business domain: The possibility of mobile support results in an expectation of mobile support, even if there is no intrinsically mobile aspect in the business. How these expectations can be met economically—and especially how entirely new business models can be developed through the innovative use of the mobile channel—is the great, disruptive challenge that digital companies face today.

Leveraging the potential of mobile applications for the success of a company requires

- Consistently focusing on the users' needs, expectations, and altered behaviors;
- Effectively putting the new technical capabilities of mobile devices to use;
- Taking the company's existing structures and processes into account, and thinking through the required adaptations.

This means that the challenges of mobile application development cannot be boiled down to technical questions such as "Web-based or native app?" or choosing the "right" mobile operating system. They mainly lie in the critical examination of

© Springer International Publishing Switzerland 2016
M. Book et al., *Tamed Agility*, DOI 10.1007/978-3-319-41478-2_6

suitable product variations, entirely new forms of addressing and supporting customers, and changes to the company's business processes and business models.

New information and communication patterns enabled by mobility are, however,
still clashing with proven patterns of product and service offerings, established
marketing approaches and business processes, both in the business departments and
enterprise IT. Established patterns have made the company successful in the past
and are therefore deeply anchored in the minds of decision makers and company
structures.

Even the relatively young companies of the Internet economy occasionally have
a difficult time responding to the expectations and demands of users in the mobile
world. This is illustrated by Facebook's long search for monetization options for its
mobile application (Carmody 2012). Large companies from traditional industries
such as banking, insurance, media, and health care exhibit even greater inertia.

Initiating the changes required for the mobilization of processes and business
models in established companies requires equal amounts of business expertise,
conceptual skills, creativity and technical know-how. Experience has shown that
the various stakeholders in a company can only contribute their respective expertise
to the development of a mobile strategy or concrete applications in a joint, highly
interactive process without working against or past each other. The Interaction
Room for Mobile Application Development (IR:mobile) offers the corresponding
methodical framework.

The objective of an IR:mobile is to develop the vision of a mobile application
that is tailored to the needs and requirements of the targeted user groups. Due to the
special opportunities and challenges associated with mobile devices, but especially
because of the wide variety of contexts in which a mobile app can be used, its
development requires much more intensive preparation and awareness of the users
and fields of application than what is required for the development of classic
information systems. The conceptual design of a mobile application can therefore
usually not be realized in an IR:scope (Chap. 5), but requires the methods of the
IR:mobile.

6.1 Relevant Stakeholders

An IR:mobile mainly requires the roles that are also used in the IR:scope: The IR
method coach (Sect. 3.5.1) is skilled in applying the IR:mobile methodology and
leads the discussion while the IR domain coach (Sect. 3.5.2) is familiar with the
business domain and ensures that the IR elements are used as effectively as possible
to answer the most difficult questions of the domain. In addition to these external
experts, several internal experts are essential: The process owner (Sect. 3.5.3) is
responsible for the business processes targeted by the mobile solution. Application
developers (Sect. 5.1.1) and operations experts (Sect. 5.1.2) are in charge of
developing and maintaining the solution. Among these, the representatives of the
developer side in particular should already have mobile implementation know-how.

The same applies to the interaction engineer (Sect. 4.1.3) who, in addition to general usability expertise, mainly has to be familiar with the interaction possibilities and limitations of mobile devices.

In addition, however, discussion in the IR:mobile also requires special mobility and business development know-how. This is why the roles of mobility expert and business developer described in the following sections are added.

6.1.1   Mobility Expert

The mobility expert is one of the team's innovation drivers. He or she is familiar with the technical possibilities of mobile devices, knows what functions are available on which devices, and how mature and useful they are in practice. The mobility expert is far from being a hardware nerd or platform evangelist: It is much more important for this role to have an intuitive feel for the new possibilities offered to the user by the technology, to know what makes mobile users tick, how they act and entertain themselves, and what they expect. The mobility expert works closely with the business developer and usability expert—with the former to discover and develop new economic potential of mobility for the company and with the latter to not only make the mobile solution user friendly, but to make even demanding mobile users enthusiastic about it.

6.1.2   Business Developer

The business developer has to be familiar with the company's business strategy. He or she has to know the composition of the clientele and the strategic requirements for the further development of products and services. The business developer has to be familiar with the market in order to assess the planned further developments of competitors' business models. Based on this knowledge and expertise, the business developer participates in the IR:mobile in order to identify digitalization potential and mobilization solutions. The role's tasks also include comparing ideas for new products, services and customer groups directly to the company's strategic direction and helping to prioritize them.

6.2   Persona Canvas

Work in the IR:mobile focuses mainly on the strategic and conceptual preparation for the development of a mobile application, rather than on examining concrete processes, data structures, and technologies. In order to understand the initial situation, the users, and their needs, and to derive an interaction concept from this, the stakeholders in the IR:mobile work on four canvases:

- The **persona canvas** examines the various user groups who will work with the mobile application and elaborates their individual needs.
- The **portfolio canvas** (Sect. 6.3) examines the market environment of the company's own and competitors' services against which the new mobile application will have to assert itself.
- The **touchpoint canvas** (Sect. 6.4) shows how users will work with the mobile application in various day-to-day business situations.
- The **interaction canvas** (Sect. 6.5) serves to visualize the first drafts of dialogs that shall implement the planned functionality.

Like any Interaction Room, work in the IR:mobile begins with the definition of the project objective in order to focus the subsequent discussions. The stakeholders prepare a statement for this purpose at the abstraction level of a fictitious "press release" (Sect. 3.6), outlining the initial situation and requirements for the mobile application being developed.

To align the business and user value of the planned mobile app closely with the needs of the target group(s), the future users are the first focal point of the IR:mobile: What are their preferences, what annoys them, what are their wishes and needs?

6.2.1   Methodology and Visualization

In contrast to the development of classic business information systems, whose target groups (employees and/or business partners of the company) are comparatively homogeneous and well known, and whose representatives can be invited directly into the team (Sect. 5.1.3), the target groups for mobile applications are often more fragmented, and not all of them can be represented on the team.

In order to make the users present and alive in the design process anyway, the workshop participants develop personas (Cooper 2004). These are detailed profiles of fictitious users representing the typical user groups. A persona is more than an anonymous participant in a sample scenario. It includes a back story that allows the stakeholders to put themselves in the person's position and phrase requirements from that person's perspective. The detailed back story is intended to help a stakeholder go beyond just nominally putting himself in the place of "the user" while subconsciously projecting the stakeholder's own opinions onto the user. Instead, the stakeholders shall be made aware of how the users are different from them, and what differing requirements the users could therefore have.

The stakeholders explore the personas through a number of guiding questions: What is relevant for the assumed users? How are they connected? How do they communicate privately, how in business? What are the different users' life situations like? What are their general and relevant needs?

While everyone usually participates in a joint discussion in the IR:mobile, it can be helpful to let the stakeholders work in small groups to develop the personas.

Experience has shown that this leads to a more diverse spectrum of different personas than a discussion in a large group, whose creativity is quickly channeled into common patterns. To focus the work on the most important target groups, no more than five personas should be developed in the IR:mobile.

The characteristics of each persona are recorded in a "portrait" summarizing the persona's personality and expectations:

- **Basics**: Name, age, marital status, and occupation.
- **Profile**: Demographic information, personality, specific technical knowledge, and special skills.
- **Activities**: Responsibilities and typical activities at work, private activities (volunteering, recreation); interaction partners and interaction channels at work and in private life; and ways to procure information, use of media, and expectations for (technical) products.
- **Needs**: Need for information, security, and recognition.
- **Values**: Ideals, demands on self and others, and positive and negative factors influencing decisions.
- **Personal goals**: Intrinsic motivation, role models, and aims in life.

After the personas are developed in small groups, they should be presented to all stakeholders and discussed as a team so all stakeholders can familiarize themselves with all personas. In order to do so, the portraits are posted on the persona canvas in poster form. Feedback from the discussion is then integrated into the persona descriptions.

6.2.2 Annotations and Analysis

Usually, not all types of users will use the planned mobile application to the same extent. Depending on the application domain, the primary target group will tend to consist of new or experienced users, technology or business-minded users, and occasional or power users. Therefore, the relevance of the individual personas should be weighted, indicating how critical the requirements and expectations of each group are expected to be for the overall design of the mobile application.

In order to accomplish this, the relevance of the personas is evaluated with business value annotations by the stakeholders in the course of the discussion, as described in Table 6.1.

The number of annotations assigned to each persona provides a first impression of the stakeholders' assessment of that group's relevance. The final weighting of the personas is performed based on this background in the course of a brief team discussion.

During the later annotation of the other canvases, care should be taken to assign user-related annotations such as user value mainly from the perspective of those personas that received the highest weighting in this step.

Table 6.1 Prioritizing personas with value annotations

Symbol	Name	Interpretation
◆◆◆	Business value	The persona is one of the primary target groups for the mobile application. In a marketplace application, for example, registered buyers and sellers of goods can constitute two different primary target groups while unregistered (anonymous) users and administrators are secondary target groups.

6.3   Portfolio Canvas

The stakeholders in the IR:mobile next explore the desired scope of the mobile application's functionality by analyzing the current service and product landscape of their own company and the industry.

Agreement should also be reached regarding the fundamental ambitions for the mobile solution: What are the activities of competitors in this field? What level of innovation is desired? Does the company want to establish novel, mobile-specific service offerings, or even business models, or is a mobile presence and keeping up with the offers of competitors the primary objective? Both can constitute successful strategies, but the desired result has to be clear. Otherwise, there is a risk of prioritizing resources incorrectly, or of various stakeholder groups' differing ambitions leading to conflicts and frustration.

6.3.1   Methodology and Visualization

Initially, the stakeholders obtain an overview of the competition—not in the form of abstract market figures, but by exploration and visualization of various service offerings. They take a critical, distanced look at the services currently offered by their own company. In large companies in particular, employees may be more familiar with their own intranet than with the breadth and depth of the information and services provided to customers.

Printed screenshots of apps and Web sites, printouts of service offerings, printed forms, and brochures—everything that is suitable for making the current landscape of the company's own and competing services tangible is used to visualize the various offerings. The illustrative material is posted on the portfolio canvas, clustered by topics and providers as shown in Fig. 6.1. Up to six clusters (for the own company and up to five competitors) with a maximum of six artifacts each should be formed in order to maintain an overview and focus on the most important players in the market.

The participants then discuss which existing and new services will be offered additionally or exclusively through mobile applications. Even at this stage, different stakeholders with varying levels of business expertise and technology affinity will have different expectations that need to be weighed.

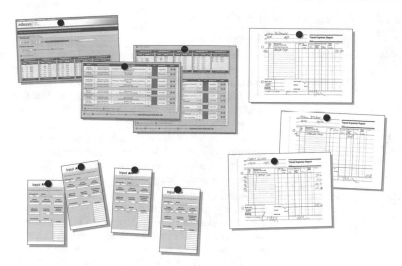

Fig. 6.1 Example of a simple portfolio canvas

6.3.2 Annotations and Analysis

To facilitate these deliberations, the stakeholders add annotations to the artifacts on the portfolio canvas, highlighting what appears valuable to them and where they see innovation potential, a need for changes or gaps. The annotations in Table 6.2 are used for this purpose.

These annotations can be added to visualizations of both the company's own and third-party offerings on the portfolio canvas, in order to not only highlight aspects of the own offering that can be improved, but also draw inspiration from competing offerings.

Analyzing the annotations assigned to the portfolio canvas provides a first impression of the scope and benefits of the identified mobilization opportunities:

- The **business value** and **user value** annotations identify specific value drivers that can arise from mobilization in the company's own service portfolio or that may already have been realized in competing offerings. Effort annotations are deliberately not yet assigned to them at this point, so as to initially focus the discussion on expectations rather than concrete solutions.
- The **innovation** annotation sends a mixed signal: On the one hand, offering an innovative feature that was previously unavailable in the market but provides a special added value for users is a powerful value driver. But on the other hand, innovations are typically associated with a higher implementation and acceptance risk.
- The **need for improvement** annotation also serves as an indicator of additional effort. It identifies business or technical aspects that have to be adapted in order to support mobilization. This annotation, however, is initially not to be understood as a restrictive counterpart to the value annotations, but merely as an

Table 6.2 Annotations for artifacts on the portfolio canvas

Symbol	Name	Interpretation
	Business value	The mobilization of the annotated element makes an important contribution to the company's business objectives. Field service technicians of an energy supplier, for example, can record descriptions and location data of power line and transformer faults more precisely and efficiently using a mobile application than on paper.
	User value	The mobilization of the annotated element creates a special benefit for the users. A public transport company, for example, can enhance client convenience by selling electronic tickets using a mobile application.
	Innovation	The mobilization of the annotated element promises or realizes a particular innovation potential. This means the annotation identifies the "highlights" of the mobilization project. These are often entirely new services that only become possible through mobile access or the technical capabilities of the mobile device. An example is the ability to show additional information related to a camera image taken with the mobile device, making orientation easier for tourists in a foreign city.
	Mobility	The annotated element (such as a service, information, process etc.) shall be mobilized. This annotation identifies artifacts on the portfolio canvas that illustrate processes or data which are currently not available for mobile use but where mobilization is desired.
	Need for improvement	The annotated element has to be changed in order to support mobilization desired here or at another point. Mobilizing processes is not always possible directly. It may require adaptations in the process being examined, as well as in related processes. For example, mobilizing the ticket booking process of a public transport company also requires mobilization of the ticket validation process.

indication of which other process elements must not be disregarded during the later development of a concrete solution (and only then will it possible to estimate the corresponding effort).

Identifying the mobilization needs and opportunities is, however, just one function of the portfolio canvas. Identifying and discussing possible innovations and process adjustments also tests the willingness of the company to engage in the changes that mobilization brings with it. Both supportive and restrictive conditions in the company are discussed.

In the flow of brainstorming, the discussion can easily drift too far from possible changes in the current portfolio to the solution domain. New processes for new features are quickly suggested off the cuff, while other ideas are nipped in the bud with the killer argument of established policy constraints. It is therefore the responsibility of the IR coaches to initially keep the discussion on the level of building awareness of the opportunities, obstacles, and objectives of mobilization in light of the current service portfolio. A more detailed examination of users and usage contexts on the persona and touchpoint canvases is required before diving into the solution domain.

6.4 Touchpoint Canvas

With the insights from the portfolio and persona canvases, the picture of the initial situation and target groups for the planned mobile app is complete. The next step is to understand how the system can support users in various activity phases. On the touchpoint canvas, the stakeholders mentally follow the personas step by step in the course of so-called user journeys and analyze their needs at each step: When does the user interact with the company's services? What are the conditions at these points like? What motivates the user to access the mobile application? What options does the mobile app offer to the user? Which factors determine whether a user will "stay with us" or is lost?

6.4.1 Methodology and Notation

These user journeys are drawn up for one to five of the most important personas, and outlined on touchpoint canvas: The stakeholders describe in which situations (touchpoints) the user comes into contact with the business domain and/or the company, and how a mobile application can support the user at these points. The stakeholders look for answers to a number of questions at each touchpoint:

- When/how often is the touchpoint visited (timing, trigger)?
- What does the touchpoint look like, what are the conditions there (location)?
- What communication options exist at the touchpoint?
- What are the user's questions and needs?
- Is this a trust point, meaning that this is where the user decides whether or not to continue using the service?

In particular, when the touchpoint is a trust point, i.e., a point where the user could terminate the interaction with the application, additional questions have to be answered:

- What aspects make the touchpoint a trust point?
- What needs of the user require special attention here?
- Are these needs due to the mobile interaction, or of a more fundamental nature?

Identifying the various stations along the user journey not only requires an examination of how the currently offered services are utilized by the user. The stakeholders should also identify new contact situations where the user gains the opportunity to access the service through the particular features of the mobile channel. These can include contacts initiated by the user out of personal interest, and contacts that are initiated by the company through the mobile application in new usage contexts. The mobile app should therefore not be viewed as a complementary communication channel that exists in parallel to the existing contact options, but as an expansion of these. The stakeholders are therefore asked to develop ideas for concrete mobile services that provide the best possible support for users: At what points of the user journey is it possible to better respond to user needs, where can added value be created for them, where can new services be offered to them, and where may it be possible for them to have new positive experiences?

The sequence of user interactions is recorded on the touchpoint canvas of the Interaction Room as described in (Sect. 4.4). As in the IR:digital, up to ten touchpoints per user journey are arranged in a coordinate system of touchpoint events and touchpoint lanes that describe the interaction triggers and interaction channels. The situation is briefly described for each touchpoint: Where is the user located? What is the user doing? What are the ambient conditions?

Figure 6.2 shows an example of a simple touchpoint canvas with user journeys for a passenger and train conductor.

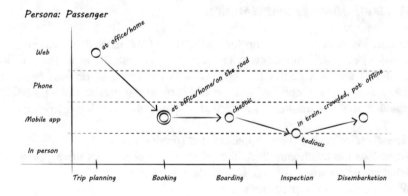

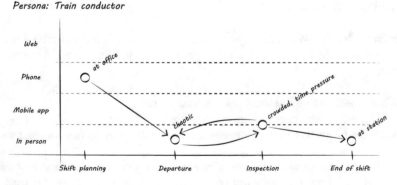

Fig. 6.2 Example of a simple touchpoint canvas

Both use different channels to prepare for the train trip through different activities—on the passenger's side, from trip planning to booking a ticket, from boarding at the correct platform to ticket inspection and ultimate disembarkation, and on the conductor's side, from shift planning to multiple departures and ticket inspections to the end of the shift. The touchpoints are described with the ambient conditions. At the time of ticket inspection, for example, conditions on the train are often crowded, a network may not be available, and the inspection is bothersome for the travelers since it interrupts other activities.

The booking step also constitutes a trust point for the traveler. Another means of transport could be chosen for the trip at this point (e.g., because taking the train appears more expensive but no faster than traveling by car, or because there are no more attractive connections to the desired destination). Both personas are involved in the touchpoint event "validation," which means this is a personal interaction but with the use of mobile devices (insofar as mobile booking was used).

The IR coaches should ensure that the detail level of touchpoints does not get out of hand, resulting in the precise modeling of a business process: On the touchpoint canvas, the focus is not on modeling a concrete process sequence (which will be examined in a later step) but on how a certain persona experiences a specific activity (such as a train ride), and in what situations the persona comes into contact with the planned mobile application.

6.4.2 Annotations and Analysis

After outlining the user journeys, the annotations in Table 6.3 are assigned to the touchpoints in order to highlight critical aspects that need to be observed at these points of contact.

The annotations are debated in a discussion moderated by the IR domain coach, and their precise characteristics and backgrounds are documented according to the schema in Appendix B. They constitute an important starting point for the initial estimation of effort and prioritization of features in later stages of software development.

Even at this stage, examining the overall picture of the annotated user journeys for the various personas reveals points that deserve special attention in the detailed conceptual design phase:

- The user journeys of different personas will typically converge in some touchpoints but diverge in others. For touchpoints included in the user journeys of more than one persona, the degree to which the annotations match should be examined:

  - When different personas visit the same touchpoint for the same reason, they usually perform the **same activity** there (e.g., a regular and occasional traveler purchasing tickets). The corresponding touchpoints should have the

Table 6.3 Annotations for touchpoints on the touchpoint canvas

Symbol	Name	Interpretation
	Business value	Particular value is created from a business perspective at the touchpoint. Such a value driver will often be the motivation to consider the development of a mobile application at all. For a media company, it may for example be worthwhile to develop an app that informs users live about events in the course of football games. Even if this function has no immediate monetary benefit, it can ensure that the user does turn to other media providers to satisfy his mobile information needs but remains loyal to the brand which he is already familiar with on classic channels.
	User value	Particular value is created from the user's perspective at the touchpoint. Such added value for the user can take many forms, ranging from a uniquely mobile feature (such as a navigation aid in an unfamiliar city) to a function that conveniently covers a user's spontaneous need for information or service (such as booking a cinema ticket).
	Innovation	A novel form of interaction or business transaction is realized at the touchpoint. This innovation can be based on the technical possibilities of the mobile device (e.g., augmenting a live camera image by displaying additional information), or it can consist of a novel business channel (such as identifying a rented car by a printed barcode and transmitting the access code by text messaging).
	Reliability	The reliability of interaction at the touchpoint is of particular importance. This is especially crucial at trust points (touchpoints where the user may terminate use of the mobile service or turn to a competing service), since disruptions can have a massive impact on the entire user journey. If, e.g., the mobile purchase or validation of a train ticket does not work reliably, the entire user journey for the use of public transportation is at risk or associated with high frustration potential.
	Attractiveness	A special usage incentive should be offered at the touchpoint. Measures to increase attractiveness are especially interesting for touchpoints that users tend to resist visiting—either because the interaction step is unavoidable (such as paying for a pay-and-display ticket) or because it is voluntary but bothersome (such as participating in a survey). If high business value depends on the touchpoint (e.g., collecting insights about user preferences), incentive measures should be considered. These can make the touchpoint more attractive or valuable for the user—for example, by making the interaction playful, awarding loyalty points, or through other mechanisms.
	Need for improvement	The interaction at an existing touchpoint should be improved. This annotation can be used in particular when the existing mobile support of touchpoints shall be enhanced in a project (e.g., replacing static public transport schedule information with an application that takes the current position of buses and trains into account), or when the business processes underlying the touchpoint have to be adapted in order to their mobilization.
	Uncertainty	Some aspects of the touchpoint are not yet adequately understood. Examples include local ambient conditions, or the concrete information needs of the user in the respective situation.

same annotations in this situation. If this is not the case, possible reasons for the deviations should be examined (e.g., the business value of the touchpoint may be much higher for the frequent traveler and therefore annotated only in his user journey).

– When different personas visit the same touchpoint for related reasons, they often perform **complimentary activities** there, which means they interact with each other (e.g., validation of a passenger's ticket by the conductor). In this case, it is not unusual for the touchpoint annotations in the user journeys to be different. However, one should review whether the complimentary aspects of the interaction are meaningful in relation to each other.

– When different personas visit the same touchpoint for different reasons and carry out **different activities** there, one should examine whether this is actually the same touchpoint or whether different touchpoints for the respective activities should be defined in the individual user journeys.

- The combination of the value annotations **business value** and **user value** indicates a touchpoint of especially high priority:

  – When the business value and user value annotations are combined on touchpoints in the same user journey, the interests of the provider and user converge. This is an especially strong argument in favor of mobilizing the corresponding aspects (e.g., the ability to book tickets online means greater convenience for travelers and lower costs for the public transport operator).

  – When the same touchpoints with value annotations are found in the user journeys of different personas, this also implies a special priority because more than one target group can be satisfied by implementing the corresponding feature.

- **Innovations** are usually only worthwhile if they offer a concrete benefit, because they are inherently risky:

  – Innovation annotations should ideally occur in combination with **business** or **user value** annotations, or at least contribute to the **attractiveness** of the system.

  – Innovation annotations that stand on their own need to be critically examined to determine whether the assumed effort to implement the innovation is justified.

  – Innovation at touchpoints that require especially high **reliability** are also worthy of examination, since ensuring reliability alone often requires significant effort already. This is likely to be increased to an extent which cannot be estimated reliably when implementing a risky innovation.

The user journeys outlined on the touchpoint canvas lead to a number of requirements for the mobile application being developed. Instead of noting these directly on the feature canvas of an IR:scope, thereby launching the detailed planning stage of software development, it is worthwhile to first utilize the more in-depth understanding of the user perspective obtained by the IR:mobile stakeholders to sketch initial outlines of the user's interaction with the mobile application, as described in the following section.

6.5   Interaction Canvas

The interaction canvas offers stakeholders the opportunity to roughly outline the user experience (UX) that the planned mobile application will offer, based on the ideas they developed during the population of the touchpoint canvas. Like all canvases of an Interaction Room, the interaction canvas does not claim to produce a complete interaction concept and sophisticated screen design. This is and remains the responsibility of specialized UX designers. Based on the preceding detailed consideration of personas and user journeys, the IR:mobile stakeholders do, however, have a comprehensive picture of the usage contexts in which the application will be typically accessed. This puts them in an ideal position to outline possible solutions for the user interaction, which can later be refined by UX experts.

6.5.1   Methodology and Notation

The stakeholders outline their vision of the dialogs that the user shall interact with by drawing "storyboards" on the interaction canvas. Depending on the technology of the mobile app, a dialog may refer to a Web page (in Web apps) or a screen (in native apps).

Each dialog is visualized as a rectangle, representing a section of the screen or the entire length of a Web page. Within the dialogs, the desired content and/or input elements (text, input fields, buttons, and illustrations) are sketched simply and without a formal notation. The layout of the elements in a dialog plays may serve as an initial suggestion for future screen layouts. Rather than defining exactly what the dialog will look like and where which elements will be placed, the goal is to develop a feeling for how many user interface elements can reasonably fit on the screen.

This approach of sketching user interface mockups or storyboards is not new. However, the dialogs of modern applications are rarely static—some dialog elements may change depending on user interactions, without switching to a whole new dialog (e.g., by loading a new Web page). Simple notes and symbols such as arrows can be added to the sketch to indicate such localized changes. Since dynamic user interfaces come in infinitely diverse forms, and a precise specification of the interface is not our goal at this point, the IR:mobile deliberately does not define a set of methods or symbols for this step. Instead, any symbols understood in the same way by all stakeholders can be used to show how a dialog should change.

If the changes within a dialog are so extensive that presenting them in the same sketch would become too confusing, several versions of the dialog can also be

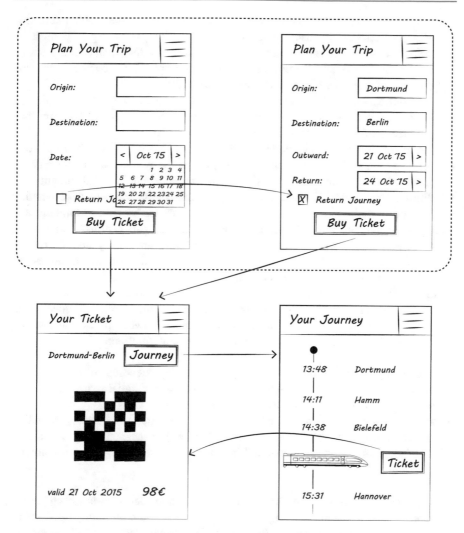

Fig. 6.3 Interaction canvas with the storyboard view of a changeable dialog

outlined and linked by arrows. A dotted line is drawn around the various sketches of the same screen to emphasize these are different views of the same dialog, rather than independent dialogs.

Figure 6.3 shows an example of a dialog for planning and booking a train journey. As indicated by the arrows, the dialog "plan your trip" changes when users check the "return journey" box, adding a selection box for the return journey date. The dialogs "your ticket" and "your journey" are independent dialogs though (i.e., separate Web pages, if this was implemented as a Web-based mobile app).

For clarity, the modelers have refrained from explicitly showing further navigation and interaction options here, such as opening a menu by tapping the top right corner, or backtracking along the dialog. The rationale is that such interaction options are more easily made understood by describing that, e.g., "it must be possible to return to the home screen from any dialog," rather than spelling out all the necessary arrows and thereby obfuscating the application-specific interaction options that may not be obvious to every stakeholder.

To ensure that the stakeholders focus on the essentials in the course of modeling, the interaction canvas should not contain more than ten dialogs and no more than three versions of changeable dialogs should be outlined.

The interaction canvas can under some circumstances serve as an alternative to the process canvas. It may especially be helpful as the primary driver for gaining insights into the application domain when the stakeholders (all pragmatism notwithstanding) have a difficult time with the comparatively abstract presentation of the process canvas. This may be because they are accustomed to thinking and acting in concrete business transactions based on existing paper forms. In particular, for the development of new mobile applications that are highly defined by the design of their user interface, initiating modeling through the interaction canvas can be easier than through the process canvas.

In the initial modeling of interaction and process canvases, and in deriving one of these canvases from the other, an important task of the IR method coach is to make the stakeholders aware of the subtle differences between process and dialog sequences, which are important for finding an efficient solution:

- **Business processes** typically encompass sequences extending over hours, days, or weeks, with several participants working together. Parallel sequences are not uncommon and may be affected by external influences.
- **Interaction processes** on the other hand only encompass sequences extending over minutes or at most hours, with only one participant interacting with a user interface. Parallel actions or external interventions in the dialog sequence are not common.

Even though these differences seem apparent at first glance, it has been shown that consistently maintaining the right abstraction level while outlining processes of either kind is not easy in practice (especially for stakeholders with little modeling experience). In modeling business processes, the level of detail quickly moves to individual dialog steps, especially when the stakeholders are feeling their way through the new development of a process step by step, guided by their personal vision of the planned IT system.

When the IR method coach recognizes that the granularity of a process canvas is moving to the dialog flow level, he can either attempt to guide modeling back to the process level (if he has the impression that the dialog details are not contributing any new insights), or suggest actually modeling the dialog flow first instead of the process (if he has the impression that the stakeholders find it easier to approach the domain this way).

The reverse case (choosing too high of an abstraction level for modeling an interaction canvas) tends to occur rarely. At most it can indicate that the stakeholders consider the details of the interaction steps insignificant and want to mentally explore the overall process in particular. If the IR method coach has the impression that the desire to suppress interface details stems from wanting to avoid an uncomfortable examination of domain details that are not understood yet, he should attempt to motivate the stakeholders to explore precisely those details. If on the other hand the IR method coach has the impression that the interface details are viewed merely as a time-consuming manifestation of process details which are already known, he should suggest moving directly to process modeling in order to focus on the big picture.

A more common problem in the modeling of interaction canvases is that the stakeholders lose themselves in irrelevant details, for example, when discussions erupt about the placement of individual dialog elements on the storyboards. Similar to object canvases, there is a risk with interaction canvases that trivialities are extensively illustrated since their modeling is seductively simple and seemingly productive. Meanwhile though, the actually challenging elements (such as the visualization of complex information relationships or the realization of intuitive gesture control) are not examined in sufficient depth. Here, the IR method coach is responsible for noting early on when the discussion strays into irrelevant details, and for guiding it back to the exploration of interaction aspects that are not yet sufficiently understood.

6.5.2   Annotations and Analysis

The annotations in Table 6.4 can be used by the stakeholders to highlight especially critical aspects on the interaction canvas.

In the first annotation round, the IR coaches offer the stakeholders only the business value, user value, and comprehensibility annotations plus one or two additional annotations that appear to be especially relevant for the application domain. The focus can be expanded to include additional annotations in subsequent annotation rounds as needed.

Unlike the annotations on the remaining IR:mobile canvases, the annotations on the interaction canvas are not intended primarily to support strategic decisions about the direction of the mobile application. Instead, they identify concrete value and effort drivers that will have to be considered in the course of implementation. The detailed discussion and documentation of the characteristics and background of these annotations should therefore follow the schema in Appendix B.

The annotations on the interaction canvas also illustrate the points that require special attention during the later refinement of the dialog outlines:

- Clearly the dialog elements annotated with the **correctness**, **comprehensibility**, **attractiveness,** and/or **flexibility** effort drivers require an especially detailed UX design, since challenges that go beyond fundamental usability requirements have been identified here.

Table 6.4 Annotations for elements on the interaction canvas

Symbol	Name	Interpretation
	Business value	The dialog, feature, or dialog element makes an essential contribution to the value of the mobile application for the operator. This annotation is used to identify model elements for which the mobile application is being realized in the first place, differentiating them from purely supportive features.
	User value	The dialog, feature, or dialog element is especially desirable for users and/or has the potential to invoke great enthusiasm among users. This annotation can be used to identify model elements that are expected to cause users to work with the mobile application. The high-quality implementation of such elements is especially critical at trust points to avoid losing users.
	Innovation	The dialog, feature or dialog element constitutes a special business or technical innovation. In addition to business innovations such as providing a novel, location-based service, this annotation can also identify technical innovations such as the use of gesture control in the mobile application. It therefore symbolizes both above-average enthusiasm potential and possible higher risks related to implementing the function.
	Accuracy	Ensuring correct input in the dialog (element) is of special importance. While robustness to prevent incorrect input is a fundamental requirement and therefore normally not annotated, this annotation can be used, e.g., to identify input that needs to be verified with special care, or particularly complex input validations. The annotation can also point out that, when sensor data is used, e.g., GPS-based location data may be unavailable or of limited accuracy.
	Usability	The comprehensible presentation of and/or the intuitive interaction with the dialog (element) is of special importance. This annotation should be used to highlight special usability challenges that go beyond the common, basic requirements for the user friendliness of interactive systems. Examples are the input or visualization of especially complex data.
	Attractiveness	The form of presentation or interaction with the dialog (element) is intended to create a special incentive to use the feature. This annotation picks up the attractiveness annotation on the touchpoint canvas to identify points where a special incentive to execute certain process steps should be created, for example, through the use of gamification techniques (Deterding et al. 2011).
	Flexibility	The presentation and/or function of the dialog (element) must be adaptable to various usage contexts. These may consist of different target groups with varying requirements or abilities (e.g., different fields of responsibility, languages or skills), but also different usage situations (e.g., at work, during leisure time). Suitable adaptation of the presentation or functionality is required for these cases.
	Uncertainty	The design of this feature is associated with especially high uncertainty. On the interaction canvas, this typically consists of more comprehensive questions regarding the exact business requirements for the dialog (e.g., what data exactly needs to be requested). Design uncertainty of the kind "in what corner should this button be" is deliberately ignored on the interaction canvas, since visual design is only defined in concrete terms later on by a UX designer.

- Special care is particularly required for dialog elements that were not only annotated with effort drivers, but also with the value drivers **business value** and/or **user value**.
- The **innovation** annotation combined with the effort drivers mentioned above indicates especially high risk. Innovation annotations that stand on their own should be examined similarly to the examination of touchpoints. The innovation annotation should always appear together with another annotation as a rule, which justifies the implementation of an innovative technology and the associated additional effort.

6.6   Cross-Canvas Analyses

In addition to the insights gained from the population of the individual canvases (as described in the preceding sections), a number of insights can also be derived from the cross-canvas examination of the sketches and annotations in the IR:mobile:

- During population of the canvases, the extent to which the previously defined characteristics of the **personas** are reflected in the user journeys and dialog sketches should be repeatedly reviewed. It is all too easy for stakeholders to argue primarily from their own perspective in the course of the discussion, rather than putting themselves in the position of the personas. In particular, for the annotation with value drivers, care should be taken to relate the stated user and/or business values to concrete personas.
- Regular reviews should also be performed to determine how the mobile application that emerges during the population of the touchpoint canvas and interaction canvas integrates into the market landscape described on the portfolio canvas: Does it depict features that were identified as particularly important and value-adding? Does it contain features that were perceived as "challenging" in practical tests, and should therefore be realized in a different, better way? Does it encompass features that differentiate the own offering from that of competitors?
- Following the annotation of the **user journeys**, briefly assessing the benefits is worthwhile: How difficult does it seem to implement the user journeys of the various personas?

  - User journeys that contain virtually no value drivers and are possibly even assigned to personas of low relevance may be sources of premature requirements. Their implementation would be associated with great effort but fail to make a major value contribution for most users. It should be examined whether they can be put on hold.
  - User journeys that suggest a high effort (e.g., because of the need for various changes or innovations on their touchpoints) are most likely justified when they are assigned to personas of high relevance. Persona relevance is therefore an essential criterion for prioritizing touchpoints that otherwise have comparable value and effort ratings.

- A similar benefit assessment is also recommended for the **interaction canvas**: Dialogs that are elaborate to realize should only have a high priority if they implement touchpoints of personas with a high relevance. Otherwise, putting them on hold is recommended.
- The consistency of annotations between the interaction canvas and touchpoint canvas also has to be examined:

  - Since the dialogs sketched on the interaction canvas outline the concrete characteristics of the interaction on the touchpoints, the value and effort annotations on the touchpoint canvas should be found on the interaction canvas. This consistency does not have to be exact, complete, and precise, since not all requirements for a touchpoint can be broken down to specific dialog elements. But if the requirements for the dialog and touchpoint deviate from each other significantly, the plausibility of the annotations should be reviewed.
  - While the user journeys are persona-specific, the dialogs of a mobile application often will not be separated strictly by personas but combine the requirements of all personas. After outlining the dialogs, one should therefore ensure that the requirements of all personas (according to their weights) are meaningfully combined on the interaction canvas. Since an interaction canvas only illustrates sections of the mobile application's interface as a rule, special attention should be paid to inconsistencies in the implementation of requirements.

- The annotations on the interaction canvas are assessments assigned at the most detailed level of the IR:mobile, which means they are on an abstraction level comparable to the annotations used in the IR:scope. When an IR:mobile is followed by an IR:scope, the annotations on the interaction canvas should therefore be included in the cross-canvas annotation analysis of the IR:scope as well. This means one should examine whether value and effort annotations on the interaction canvas are consistent with the process and object canvases of the IR:scope.

6.7 Workshop Structure and Follow-up Activities

Clarifying the project vision, the outset and the orientation points of each Interaction Room discussion is of special importance in the IR:mobile. The mere impulse that "we also need an app" is too vague, while focusing on the mobilization of specific processes right away (without more detailed considerations regarding value contributions and user groups) is too hasty. In contrast to classic software solutions that cover numerous requirements, a mobile application focuses on covering a handful of closely described requirements as effectively as possible. The legwork has to be completed with corresponding diligence to avoid investing a lot of effort into an application that fails to meet the needs of the market.

Using the previously described canvases, the vision of the mobile application is defined in concrete terms step by step during the discussion of user types, the service portfolio, usage contexts, and interaction techniques. The corresponding methodology can be summarized as follows:

- Mapping and weighting personas to represent the intended target groups for the mobile application,

  - Result: Insights about the characteristics and needs of the most important user groups;

- Exploration of the current service landscape, using the organization's own service portfolio and the services of the leading competitors as examples,

  - Result: Visual overview of the interfaces (paper forms or software dialogs) for the service offerings of the most important market participants on the portfolio canvas;

- Annotation of the portfolio canvas with value and effort drivers in the various interface implementations,

  - Result: Suggestions for worthwhile strategic directions of the organization's own mobile application;

- Outlining the user journeys of the most important personas on the touchpoint canvas and identification of the personas' touchpoints with the service portfolio,

  - Result: Understanding of the user activity sequence and ambient situation at the touchpoints; ideas for required features of the mobile application that cover the users' needs at the touchpoints;

- Annotation of the touchpoint canvas with value and effort drivers on the various touchpoints,

  - Result: Initial insights regarding recommended priorities and expected development challenges;

- Outlining dialogs for the most important touchpoints on the interaction canvas,

  - Result: Initial solution ideas for the interaction requirements of the users under the ambient conditions identified on the touchpoints;

- Annotation of the interaction canvas with value and effort drivers on the various dialogs,

  - Result: Initial insights about setting priorities and expected development challenges for the UX of the mobile application.

The actual implementation of the application conceived in this manner then is a software project—the IR:mobile therefore transitions into an IR:scope, with the focus shifting from the definition of requirements to the concrete effects on processes, data structures, and system components, as well as the value and effort drivers that have to be known for project planning and risk management.

For the transition between the IR:mobile and IR:scope, the requirements that can be derived from the touchpoint canvas and interaction canvas therefore serve as the starting point for the population of the feature canvas. The annotations on the touchpoints and dialogs can already be used for an initial prioritization and to estimate the effort required for the features.

Processes, data, and backend interfaces of the mobile application are then planned in more detail using the tools of the IR:scope. To what extent existing business processes have to be redesigned or expanded and how to handle data required and generated by the mobile application are examples of questions that arise in this process.

The user journeys and dialog outlines previously created in the IR:mobile should be carried over into the IR:scope. They make the application vision tangible for the stakeholders on the one hand and, on the other hand, ensure that the processes and data are based on the intended usability of the mobile application, rather than constraining the user experience by the underlying process and data structures.

References

Carmody T (2012) Facebook: The last great company of the desktop age, playing catch-up in a mobile world. Wired, 2 Jul 2012. http://www.wired.com/2012/02/facebook-mobile/. Accessed 23 Feb 2016

Cooper A (2004) The inmates are running the asylum: Why high tech products drive us crazy and how to restore the sanity. Pearson Education, Chap. 9

Deterding S, Dixon D, Khaled R, Nacke L (2011) From game design elements to gamefulness: Defining "gamification". In: Lugmayr et al (eds) MindTrek'11: Proc 15th Intl Academic MindTrek Conf: Envisioning Future Media Environments, pp 9–15. doi:10.1145/2181037.2181040

Using an Interaction Room for Technology Evaluation (IR:tech)

7

In order to succeed in the long term, a company must not just continuously adapt to business challenges and opportunities, but also keep on top of relevant technical innovations. It can afford neither to be left behind by technical progress, nor to blindly follow every trend. The continuous evaluation of new technologies therefore is a significant strategic task: The company has to analyze the business value that would be added by adopting a new technology, but also needs to consider what investments are required to implement it, and whether this effort would be justified by the expected benefits.

What makes this analysis problematic is that it cannot be performed by any department in the company on its own. While the enterprise IT has the necessary know-how to identify promising technologies and estimate their integration effort from a technical perspective, it lacks the domain expertise to assess the business value of the technology, let alone to identify potential business innovation it enables. Conversely, the business department (even if it has already heard of buzzwords such as cloud computing or big data) lacks the expertise to assess how such technologies could realistically alter its business, or what technical basic conditions and restrictions would have to be observed during their introduction.

The consequence is that promising topics are either not pursued further because neither side recognizes the full potential, or that an attempt is made to implement an ad hoc solution that realizes the potential poorly and leads to unnecessary effort, frustration, and possibly even abandonment of a technology initiative that would actually have been beneficial.

In fact, the adequate evaluation of technologies requires cooperation between operating departments and enterprise IT, enabling both sides to obtain an overview of the possibilities, requirements, and basic conditions of the other side. This makes it possible reach a substantiated decision on whether and how the new technology should be implemented. The Interaction Room for Technology Evaluation (IR:tech) provides a suitable infrastructure and methodology tool to answer these questions purposefully and with minimal effort.

© Springer International Publishing Switzerland 2016
M. Book et al., *Tamed Agility*, DOI 10.1007/978-3-319-41478-2_7

7.1   Relevant Stakeholders

In addition to the IR coaches, business and technology representatives work together in an IR:tech. These obviously include the application developers and operations officers on the IT side, in addition to the previously described roles of the business developer and process owner for the processes expected to be affected on the business side. In the IR:tech, these are complemented by the role of the technology expert who can provide an objective picture of the possibilities and limits of the new technology, and the enterprise architect who maintains an overview of the company's entire system landscape. The latter roles are described in more detail in the following sections.

7.1.1   Technology Expert

The technology expert has a broad overview of the state of the art and current trends in enterprise IT. In particular, he has experience with the practical use of the new technology being analyzed and is able to provide the other stakeholders with an assessment of the implementation scenarios it is suited for and the prerequisites that have to be met. Filling the technology expert role externally is recommended so that he can make suggestions on the use of technology unimpeded by company politics or organizational blindness, even when they collide with established processes and ways of thinking.

7.1.2   Enterprise Architect

The enterprise architect is responsible for analyzing and optimizing the company's architecture, i.e., the processes actually used in the company and the IT systems that support them. His goal is to make the business processes as efficient and flexible as possible with the help of IT support. Together with the business developer and process owners of the specific processes that are targeted, the enterprise architect in the IR:tech helps evaluate new technologies and assess their benefits.

7.2   Feature Canvas

Analyzing the application potential of new technologies as well as adaptations required to adopt them in business processes requires an examination of process, data, and integration structures. The canvases of the IR:scope are therefore also used in the IR:tech, albeit in a slightly different way.

Similar to the IR:scope, the feature canvas in the IR:tech serves to clarify the project contents and define expectations for the new technology. The methodology used for collecting, clustering, and prioritizing the requirements is the same as in the IR:scope. However, the feature canvas of an IR:tech with a maximum of 30 requirements is typically less comprehensive than one in an IR:scope, since the fields of application for the new technology are usually more narrowly defined.

The only difference is the number of annotations available to highlight the requirements: While only the business and user value as well as the complexity and uncertainty of the planned features are annotated in an IR:scope, a larger selection of annotations is available in the IR:tech. This makes it possible to highlight aspects directly that are to be supported or considered by the new technology. The available annotations are shown in Table 7.1.

Table 7.1 Annotations for requirements on the feature canvas of the IR:tech

Symbol	Name	Interpretation
	Business value	The feature is of high value from the company's perspective. In the IR:tech, this annotation is mainly used to highlight functions that are optimized or made possible in the first place by the technology being evaluated. For a transport company for example, this could be the ability to schedule vehicles on secondary lines more economically by recording and evaluating passenger streams more precisely using big data technologies.
	User value	The feature is of high value from a user perspective. In the IR:tech, this annotation also applies primarily to delight and performance requirements that become possible based on the technology being evaluated. For a vehicle owner for example, this can be a system that derives the load on vehicle components from a variety of sensor data and then recommends individually tailored maintenance intervals.
	Innovation	Using the new technology in this feature facilitates a special functional or business innovation. This annotation identifies features that could not be realized without the technology being evaluated, but that are also associated with special effort and risks because they are so new. A decision for or against the new technology can often be based on a cost/benefit assessment of these features.
	High use	The high load to which this feature is exposed continuously or temporarily (e.g., due to a high frequency of use), or that would be caused in downstream systems by using the technology (e.g., due to recording and processing a large number of events or a high volume of sensor data), has to be taken into account.
	Time constraint	Time restrictions have to be considered when applying the technology under evaluation. These could be business requirements (such as response times), or they could be inherent in the new technology (e.g., the validity period of predictions derived from sensor data).

(continued)

Table 7.1 (continued)

Symbol	Name	Interpretation
	Security	Special security requirements have to be considered when using the technology under evaluation. These requirements may have to be satisfied independently of the new technology (such as data privacy requirements), or they may be added or intensified by the technology (e.g., privacy requirements for insights derived from aggregated user data).
	Reliability	Special reliability requirements have to be considered when using the technology under evaluation. These requirements may have to be satisfied by the feature independently of the new technology (such as availability, which may be delegated to third parties using a cloud solution), or may be introduced by the technology (such as the informativeness of prediction data that downstream systems rely on).
	Flexibility	Special functional or structural flexibility must be provided by the technology under evaluation. In a big data solution for example, this could be a requirement to interface with numerous different sensors or data sources whose quantity and availability fluctuates at runtime.
	Policy constraint	Special legal or organizational conditions have to be met by the technology under evaluation. For example, the evaluation of a cloud solution may be subject to restrictions regarding the countries in which data centers may be located, and which organizations and authorities have access to the data.
	Complexity	Realizing the feature poses special business or technical challenges. Typically, this annotation in the IR:tech points out complexity that results from using the new technology in a certain feature in the first place. It can also used to emphasize one of the above annotations, or to point out a different challenge which is not covered by these annotations.
	Uncertainty	There is uncertainty regarding the implementation of business or technical aspects of using the technology for this feature. Examples include specific open questions (such as the sizing of a cloud solution) or more fundamental issues (such whether sufficient data can be captured by a big data solution to derive informative insights).

In an initial annotation round, the stakeholders should focus on adding the business value, user value, innovation, basic condition, and complexity annotations to the canvas. Additional annotation symbols can be offered by the IR coaches for marking the canvas in subsequent rounds, based on likely technology or domain challenges.

In the context of the IR:tech, the innovation annotation which identifies an especially innovative system aspect is of special importance. It combines the semantics of several annotations: On the one hand, it promises a high business value (e.g., regarding company image and/or productivity) and also a high user value (in the form of one of the software solution's performance characteristics).

But it also implies a significant risk, since by definition, there is no practical experience with using the new technology for the planned purpose yet, so that effort and benefit estimates will be very inaccurate. Finally, innovations are always associated with a high degree of uncertainty as well, which is also implied by this annotation.

7.3   Process, Object, and Integration Canvases

The central elements of the IR:tech are the process, object, and integration canvases for modeling the processes, data structures, and related systems affected by the introduction of the new technology. The modeling methodology and notation of these canvases correspond to the IR:scope, but the modeling focus—other than in the IR:scope—is not on the overall process and system landscape, but on the specific structures that can benefit from using the new technology. The sketches on these canvases are correspondingly compact.

Which of the canvases is the "leading" canvas and focal point of modeling, and which canvases are populated on the side, mainly depends on which perspective is influenced most by the technology being evaluated. When it comes to recording and evaluating big data in the company, the object canvas appears to be a suitable starting point. If greater flexibility is to be established on the basis of cloud computing, the integration canvas can help identify candidates. And when the outsourcing of complex functionality using a software-as-a-service model is under debate, the process canvas is the best place to start.

The modeling, annotation, and interpretation of the canvases are largely the same as in the IR:scope. But assigning and analyzing the annotations in the IR:tech mainly focus on value and effort drivers that are conditional on the new technology, or are intensified in its context. In the analysis of big data technologies, for example, these could be annotations on the aspects of capacity utilization, correctness, flexibility, and external interfaces.

7.4   Cross-Canvas Analyses

The main aspect to observe in the cross-canvas analysis is where challenges or potential marked on one canvas affect other canvases, and what effects they have there.

If the IR:tech is, e.g., used to evaluate a company's possible fields of application for big data technologies, then the corresponding data structures will likely be modeled and annotated mainly on the object canvas. Here it is important to remember that this innovation does not only take place on the data level, but also requires non-trivial functionality for recording and evaluating the data at the process level. Data is recorded in certain process steps (which requires a corresponding set of software components for data recording, aggregation, and storage). The data is evaluated and used for decision making in other process steps (which requires corresponding evaluation and decision-making algorithms).

Ultimately, analyzing the canvases from an overall perspective has to answer the question of whether introducing the new technology actually promises a monetizable business model, rather than merely leading to a technically interesting "gimmick" that creates little added value. The value and effort annotations distributed across the canvases can serve as valuable indicators for this.

7.5   Workshop Structure and Follow-up Activities

At first glance, the work in the IR:tech appears identical to that of the IR:scope—the stakeholders use the feature canvas to communicate about the project requirements and then outline the most important business and system structures on the process, object, and integration canvases. But there are two essential methodical differences compared to the IR:scope:

- For one thing, the IR:tech does not focus on presenting the overall system, but only those aspects that are most affected by the new technology. Following the definition of the project objectives on the feature canvas, the stakeholders therefore mainly examine those processes and data structures on the other canvases in which the objectives can be implemented with the new technology.
- For another, the IR:tech explicitly differentiates between modeling the target and current states: After the population of the feature canvas, the current state of the relevant process, data, and system structures is initially outlined on the process, object, and integration canvases. Annotations are then added to these models in order to highlight the opportunities and challenges of the new technology.

Based on these insights, the stakeholders now discuss approaches for the new technology. If, for example, the application potential for big data is to be evaluated, the stakeholders first identify the data required to achieve the desired objectives. This data is then localized on the object canvas—either it is already recorded there (in this case, the team needs to investigate whether the current data source is adequate or if measures to make it more precise are required), or it is not being recorded yet (in this case, the team needs to establish how this data can be captured and related to already established data structures). If the data does not originate from business processes, software systems, or other digital sources, but manifests itself in physical objects, it can be helpful to first outline a physical object canvas like the one used in the IR:digital to correctly localize the data sources (Sect. 4.3). The stakeholders then discuss the process steps in which the data is produced, recorded, and processed.

The insights from this evaluation process are outlined on the current state canvases, transforming them into representations of the target state: On the process, object, and integration canvases, the stakeholders outline how data structures, processes, and component links have to change in order to implement the solutions that were just developed for the objectives formulated initially. Annotations are then again assigned to the resulting target representations, but now with a focus on the feasibility of implementing the proposed solutions.

This leads to the result of the IR:tech—the business and IT stakeholders develop a joint understanding of how a new technology can meet the expectations established for it, what changes this would require in the process and system landscape, and whether the expected benefit would justify the implementation effort.

These insights can lead to a better-substantiated technology recommendation for management. The annotated canvases clearly illustrate what the solution would look like, what the associated opportunities and challenges are, what effort can be expected, and what the starting points for introducing the technology are. If a decision to implement the new technology is made on this basis, the canvases created in the IR:tech can serve directly as the starting point for a more in-depth examination of the business and technical implementation in the IR:scope (Chap. 5).

Using an Interaction Room for Agile Project Monitoring (IR:agile)

8

An Interaction Room is often used in the earliest project phases in order to understand the problem domain, prioritize problem aspects, conceive solution strategies, and prioritize their implementation steps. As shown in the preceding chapters, an IR:scope or IR:mobile can initially assist with project scoping, which means helping to establish a joint understanding of the project domain and a shared vision of the solution among all stakeholders: What business processes are we talking about? How do they have to be adapted? Into what system landscape does the solution have to be integrated? What compromises does this require? What usage contexts have to be considered? How can business and user expectations be combined most profitably for both sides? The Interaction Room then helps state a concrete vision for the solution, develop target processes and structures for it, and identify and resolve dependencies and conflicts between components, but also between business and technology aspects.

Such an initial Interaction Room population results in a requirements document and an initial system specification. While these documents are not yet complete, they are supported by all stakeholders, all of which have the impression that at least the most critical points of conflict have been resolved, the most essential questions have been answered, and the major uncertainties have been identified. In other words, the specification definitely has to become more detailed, and questions are sure to arise in the conceptual design and development process, but there should not be any major surprises and conflicts.

In the subsequent course of the project, the Interaction Room is now transformed from a scoping into a monitoring tool: It helps to focus the work of the team, maintain risk and requirement management, keep an eye on the budget and assess the progress. This is accomplished in the IR:agile, as described in the following sections.

Modeling work on the canvases is not as prominent in the IR:agile. While the models remain present in the room along with their annotations (as results of the IR: scope), they mostly serve as a visible orientation in the overall project and a constant reminder of value and effort drivers. But aside from refining points in the

© Springer International Publishing Switzerland 2016
M. Book et al., *Tamed Agility*, DOI 10.1007/978-3-319-41478-2_8

course of sprint planning meetings (Sect. 8.2), the canvases stabilize—while design work continues at a fine-grained level, this is done using classic modeling tools. The Interaction Room meanwhile represents the big picture.

In the transition from the IR:scope to the IR:agile, elements for monitoring and controlling the project become more prominent instead—these instruments include the requirements exchange (Sect. 8.3), risk map (Sect. 8.4), cost forward progressing (Sect. 8.6), and adVANTAGE (Chap. 15). The extent to which these instruments are used depends on the scope and maturity of the project—as soon as the stakeholders have the impression that the requirements are largely stable, the risk monitoring instruments of the IR:agile are often scaled down. The requirements exchange and adVANTAGE, meanwhile, are both fundamentally relevant during the entire course of the project, but usually gain most prominence and visibility as the end of the project approaches. Conversely, cost forward progressing yields most interesting insights during the initial implementation activities in particular, but becomes less influential toward the end of the project. In keeping with ongoing reprioritization, IR:scope activities may occasionally be inserted into an IR:agile to better understand the details of individual sprints, e.g., when the next agile iteration (sprint) is prepared. The insights obtained in these IR:scope segments are then adapted to inform the risk and cost monitoring tools of the IR:agile.

8.1   From Feature Canvas to Product Backlog

In preparation for agile project management methods such as Scrum, the feature canvas created in a preceding IR:scope or IR:mobile is transformed into a product backlog. This requires an elaboration and completion of the listed features, as well as an estimation of efforts per feature. In both of these steps, stakeholders need to be aware that the number of features and the effort estimates are still likely to change.

- **Elaboration and completion of features**: Before agile development with the help of the IR:agile can begin, the features collected on the feature canvas have to be reviewed for completeness. Of course, this does not mean entertaining the illusion that the feature list can be finalized, but only that all features which are known and have already been discussed up to this point are actually documented, which may not have been done diligently as part of the IR:scope or IR:mobile since the focus was merely on collecting the most important features. It is also possible that the population of the other canvases helped identify new features without consistently recording them on the feature canvas. But before agile development begins, it is time to clean up and compile everything that is already known. Therefore, the feature canvas is updated according to the current state of knowledge, in order to establish a starting point for development.
- **Effort classifications**: The effort per feature is estimated in person-days as precisely as possible at this point. Estimates can be omitted in certain cases (e.g., when they depend on a technology choice that is yet to be made). In such cases,

justification is required for the entire unestimated feature, stating why an estimate was not possible. If this exception is made for several features, the team should, however, consider whether the transition to development was perhaps premature, and if the uncertainties should be resolved first.

The transition from the feature canvas to the backlog does not mean that the features have to be elaborated to the point of writing user stories. This step is deliberately omitted to avoid that format specifications prevent anyone from defining desired features. Rather, the possibly reduced precision of features (compared to user stories) is accepted in order to keep the barrier for defining features as low as possible.

A set of features that either have estimates or reasons why they could not be estimated then forms the backlog, which is used as an important starting point for further work in the IR:agile.

8.2   Sprint Planning Workshops

The overall processes and system structures outlined in the initial scoping phase is now refined in each sprint to facilitate the upcoming implementation. Still, developing complete, precise class, and process models is not the goal of the Interaction Room. Instead, the IR:agile ensures that the stakeholders maintain an integrated view of the business and technology, structure and dynamics, integration and interaction aspects as they explore the implementation of specific features in more detail.

In the course of sprint planning, the IR:agile mainly helps with the task breakdown, i.e., the segmentation of the initially recorded, higher-level features or user stories into fine-grained, concrete development tasks. If this step would completed by the IT stakeholders alone, the developers could easily be tempted to focus on detailed technical solutions, without being aware of business questions that may also require clarification. The IR:agile therefore ensures awareness of the tasks on both sides: On the canvases transferred from the IR:scope, the stakeholders define their understanding of the features coming up in the next sprint in concrete terms by refining the model sketches. The separate examination of processes, data, and interfaces along with the annotation of value and effort drivers (in the same manner as in the IR:scope) helps to plan necessary work on all these levels as explicit tasks and to estimate the related effort in more detail.

As demonstrated in practice, ongoing work in the Interaction Room leads to continuous focus on the value to be created by the software, based on the target vision for the project, a more informed task breakdown, and therefore to more realistic estimates of work effort (Grapenthin et al. 2014). This reduces unplanned effort and unexpected conflicts, thereby lowering the project risk.

8.3   Requirements Exchange

The idea of the requirements exchange is that late requirements are only added when early requirements can be omitted. Even though late requirements are unavoidable, the requirements exchange counteracts "fattening" of the software being developed by encouraging the elimination of features. Late requirements are approved more readily the more solidly they are "financed": When a late requirement with an estimated scope of n person-days appears, it is accepted without objection if a requirement with a scope of n person-days which has not been realized yet is considered eligible for omission. Such an elimination decision must of course be supported by the stakeholders who previously introduced the requirement which shall now be omitted. The process becomes really simple when the stakeholder for the late requirement is also the stakeholder for the requirement swapped out in return—then the stakeholder can almost decide the exchange alone (the product manager who is ultimately responsible for creating a coherent piece of software, all exchanges notwithstanding, still has to agree).

The simplicity and charm of the requirements exchange and the underlying assumption that early and late requirements can be kept in balance is obviously a simplification. A number of problems can occur:

- Early requirements may already have been implemented and—even if they are identified as eligible for omission—cannot be used to "finance" late requirements anymore. This can in fact happen easily if early, superfluous requirements are not identified until late in the process. It is especially vexing since effort was not only expended for the realization of requirements that could be omitted, but because they have already been implemented in the software and therefore also need to be tested and then tested again in subsequent releases. The idea of the requirements exchange is to continuously search for what can be eliminated by having individual late requirements trigger this search. This ensures that the search for early requirements will not be postponed until the remaining project time clearly becomes too short. The requirements exchange instrument therefore means the search is conducted as early as possible. The only better way would be if requirements that can be omitted would not be assigned the requirement status in the first place.

- Some stakeholders want late requirements and propose other stakeholders' earlier requirements as financing. Permitting this can easily lead to fights among the team members. Financing requires a consensus, and sometimes the IR coaches together with the product manager have to help find this consensus. In general, nothing is omitted without the approval of the relevant stakeholders.

- Late requirements are financed by omissible early requirements, but the product manager views the omission as putting the software at risk. This is difficult for the product manager. If the stakeholders agree to the exchange (whether one stakeholder is exchanging within his set of requirements or several stakeholders are willing to exchange among each other), but the product manager does not agree because he believes the requirement that is up for omission to be essential, then the exchange is not permissible. How to deal with the late requirement remains open. Looking for other financing is the first step. If this is unsuccessful, the product manager can easily be obligated to examine a requirement that is not financed and to provide additional financing if necessary.

- There is no more financing potential because there are simply more late requirements than early requirements which are eligible for omission. This can happen since there is, after all, no natural balance between early and late requirements. It is important for the originator of the late requirement to actively look for financing. The standard mechanisms for handling late requirements apply after that. Effects on the budget and schedule are made transparent, and sponsors are sought for the necessary additional budget.

These problems show that there cannot be an algorithmic solution that consistently ensures that late and early requirements balance out in the sense of an invisible hand of the market. Yet the requirements exchange makes a significant contribution to preventing software fattening, simply because the originator of a late requirement is prompted to think about what can be omitted. Since omitting requirements is offset at the effort level, requirement proposers will even start to think about how their late requirement can be designed so their implementation requires only little effort, which makes financing easier. For solution-specific requirements in particular, which is what we are increasingly dealing with in the course of development, striving for requirements that are easy to implement can be an important tool for creating lean software.

The requirements exchange is integrated into the IR:agile through the dynamics of the backlog. Based on the estimated person-days, a late requirement can only be exchanged for one or more requirements being omitted if the estimate for the late requirement is less than or equal to the sum of estimates for the requirements being omitted. This instrument is an important element of the adVANTAGE contract model (Sect. 15.5).

8.4   Risk Map

Software projects that get somewhat more expensive than planned are annoying but usually not the end of the world. Things get difficult when a project becomes disastrous, that is to say it takes twice as long, costs twice as much or reaches a point where planning reliability becomes nonexistent. Fortunately, projects do not reach such a state all of a sudden. Numerous indicators can warn of an impending disaster before it occurs.

The risk map of the IR:agile illustrates the risk of a project disaster. Initially, it comprises the following dimensions, which are evaluated based on the insights and experiences from the population of the IR:scope:

- **Accessibility of (internal) client** (internal coordination, sponsorship, decisiveness, and decision-making ability): If the client (whether an actual external or an internal client) has complicated decision-making processes that are not comprehensible from the outside, sponsorship for the project is not pronounced, and the client generally has difficulty making reliable decisions promptly, this is considered a disaster indicator. Whether this is the case can often be deduced from impressions gathered over the course of the IR:scope population. Major discussions about minor details, tedious decision-making processes and extensive involvement of stakeholders from across the organizational chart are suspicious characteristics.
- **Focus on most important business processes**: If agreeing on the 15 most important business processes (one of the early steps in the population of the process canvas) has been difficult because the stakeholders had highly diverging views all along, this is considered a disaster driver. If the diverging ideas only existed at the beginning of the IR:scope population, but could then be resolved in the course of the IR population, the disaster risk has been mitigated by the IR: scope. Ultimately, it is up to the IR coaches to assess whether a sufficient understanding has been reached, or whether ideas continue to diverge under the surface, so an increased risk of disaster remains.
- **Consensus about system boundaries**: A review of the integration canvas sketched in the IR:scope can help to evaluate whether the system boundaries have been clearly established. If this is the case, the required effort can be estimated much more reliably than if the system boundaries are vague. If stakeholders' opinions on which features belong in the software diverge and cannot be fully aligned in the Interaction Room, there is an elevated risk of disaster.
- **Coverage of essential features**: The collection of features on the feature canvas is usually limited by the time spent on this step in the IR:scope workshop—the more time is given to stakeholders, the more features they will come up with. Even if the list of features is still incomplete, the stakeholders should, however, have the feeling that the essence of the system is covered. As long as this is not the case, the collection of features should continue. Otherwise, the incompleteness of the list of essential features must be considered a disaster driver.
- **Consensus about feature benefits**: If the user value and business value annotations on the feature canvas indicate highly divergent stakeholder opinions on which features provide which benefits, the stakeholders are obviously not in agreement about the objective that shall be achieved by the project. This is a major disaster driver.
- **Consensus about feature effort**: The effort required to implement the listed features should be estimated in person-days before transitioning from the IR: scope to the IR:agile. If this turns out to be very difficult, or if it takes a long time to reach a consensus, this may indicate that the stakeholders' understanding of the features is not uniform. This is a disaster driver.
- **Consistency of annotations**: As described in Sect. 5.6, the annotations of all canvases populated in the IR:scope should be analyzed on an

element-by-element, canvas-by-canvas, and cross-canvas level. If an exceptionally high number of potential improvements, ambiguities, and suspicious constellations are found in this analysis, this is a disaster indicator insofar as such issues indicate unconsolidated stakeholder perceptions regarding the system tasks and benefits.

While the above indicators can be assessed right at the beginning of an IR:agile, based on the experiences from the IR:scope, the following additional indicators are initially set to neutral values, and evaluated only later in the course of continuous project monitoring with the IR:agile:

- **Use of requirements exchange**: As described above, the inclusion or rejection of requirements that are introduced after the project's initial stages is facilitated by the IR:agile's requirements exchange. While the requirements exchange helps to prevent a runaway project scope, its constant use until late into the project can also indicate a risk factor—namely that the client is lacking a reliable vision of which features exactly the project resources should be invested in. This risk dimension is especially critical when new requirements of significant scope are added but "financing" (in terms of early requirements to be swapped out) cannot be found. On the other hand, an entirely static set of requirements (i.e., no use of the requirements exchange at all) can also indicate a communication problem: Possibly there is nobody on the client side who is really caring about the software being developed, and there are no late requirements due to a sheer lack of interest.
- **Structural changes to the canvas contents**: The IR:scope is all about outlining the big picture of the system being developed. Upon the transition to the IR:agile, this picture is expected to have reached a certain degree of stability. But if the canvas contents continue to change significantly even in the IR:agile, then it appears that a consensus has not yet been reached regarding the system fundamentals. This criterion continues to gain importance as the project progresses.
- **Difficulties with sprint planning**: The planning of each sprint or iteration in the IR:agile is based on the product backlog and the canvases sketched in the IR:scope. To derive reliable technical implementation tasks from these, the stakeholders need to have the same perception of risks, value drivers, and benefits of the software being created. Difficult and protracted sprint planning is a disaster indicator.
- **Divergence in cost forward progressing**: Cost forward progressing (Sect. 8.6) provides continuous forecasts and extrapolations of effort estimates to the team, based on their previous performance. If the two series of forecasts produced by cost forward progressing do not converge toward one value, there is a risk of disaster.

Other dimensions that can indicate a project disaster are not IR-specific and have little to do with the chosen development approach. They include the experience and knowledge of the project team (especially the project manager) in the application domain and chosen technology, and the question of how well the team's level of agility matches the level of agility that would be appropriate for the project. Both too much and too little agility can put a project at significant risk. In the first case, stakeholders may push for final decisions that nobody wants to make. In the second case, excessive insistence on consistent documents can cause stakeholders launch battles about documents and lose sight of timely software development.

Figure 8.1 shows the general outline of the risk map, including the above-mentioned criteria. On each of the eleven axes, the disaster points can be allocated in the respective dimension on a scale of 0–10. The overall map area indicates how high the risk of disaster is considered to be. There are no algorithmic rules for assigning or evaluating disaster points though—rather, they serve as an informal indicator to raise awareness and track the development of risk factors as the project progresses.

Figure 8.2 shows the risk map for a project after the initial IR:scope population. In addition to this initial assessment, the criteria have to be reviewed periodically as the project progresses. As an example, Fig. 8.3 shows the risk map of the same project at a later time. At this time, values have also been assigned to the dimensions which were neutral in Fig. 8.2.

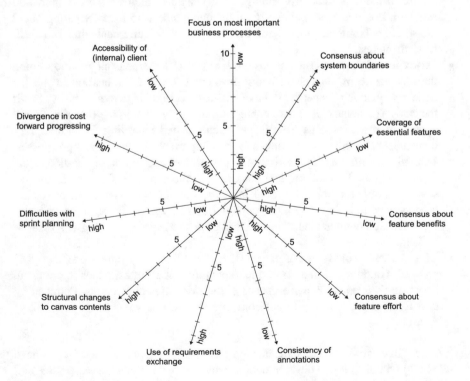

Fig. 8.1 General outline of a risk map

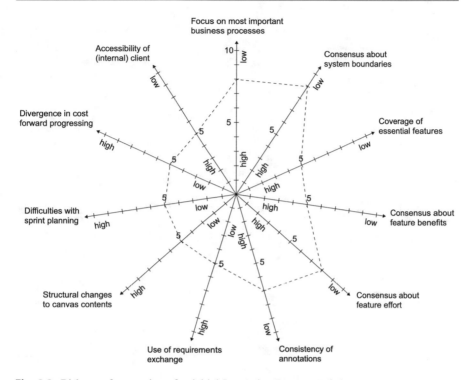

Fig. 8.2 Risk map for a project after initial Interaction Room population

The sum of disaster points can be calculated for Figs. 8.2 and 8.3. Even though there are some changes regarding specific risks, the total remains at 67 points. Project managers should take care not to assign too much formal value to this number, however: Since the assignment of disaster values is purely qualitative, the absolute number of disaster points is quite meaningless. But if it is high from the outset, if the assessments for specific disaster dimensions change drastically, or if gradual but sustained trends are observed, then examining the contributing risk factors in more detail is definitely recommended.

Obviously, continuous maintenance of a risk map should not be the only risk management technique employed in a project—Moran (2014), e.g., suggests a broad spectrum of additional techniques for risk identification and management. The risk map, meanwhile, is a simple tool that helps stakeholders to stay aware of issues that could otherwise remain ignored for too long while the team just "muddles through." Striving to bring the sum of the disaster points down sprint after sprint provides a motivation to deal with structural issues that require long-term commitment to remedy.

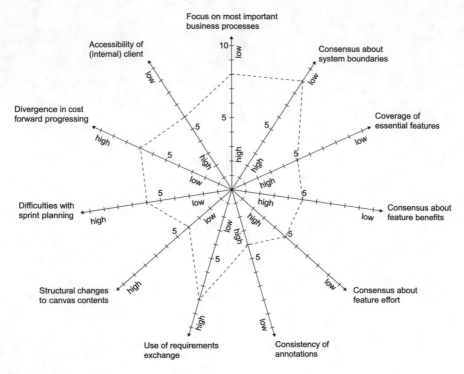

Fig. 8.3 Risk map for a project at a later stage

8.5   Progress Control

In the course of the IR:scope, the Interaction Room is initially populated with high-level sketches of the process, object, and integration canvases that make up the project framework. Parts of this big picture subsequently take concrete form during the sprint planning meetings in the IR:agile: Processes and data structures are refined, requirements become user stories, and user stories become tasks. The canvases in the Interaction Room reflect this development:

- While the initial sketches were still defined by a high degree of uncertainty, the architecture decisions become more concrete over time. The more parts of the system are cast in code, the more stable the design becomes. This is made clear on the canvases by attaching finished artifacts (such as screenshots of implemented dialogs, or detailed diagrams of modeled processes and data structures) to the sketches on the canvases. These attached artifacts show at a glance which parts of the system have already been built and which ones are still in the planning stage.

- Design and realization changes can also be represented this way: When a new version of an artifact is released (such as a revised dialog), its printout can be attached to the canvas on top of the previous version. This not only makes it possible to trace the version history of key artifacts by leafing through the printouts—the thickness of the stacks of printouts also indicates parts of the system that are subject to ongoing changes (a potential trouble spot for the stability and quality of adjacent components), and which parts of the design are already solid.

Obviously, the printouts attached to the canvases cannot replace a version control system for the detailed management of all project artifacts. They merely serve as rough points of orientation for the implementation progress and change history, and therefore form a tangible index of the most important project artifacts—a tool that visualizes the project progress intuitively, beyond the abstract burndown charts.

8.6 Cost Forward Progressing

The cost of software projects is characterized by certain dynamics. Estimates change, expended efforts turn out differently than estimated, and late requirements are added so that a higher overall budget is needed. The total costs of a project are only known exactly at the end—and even then it can be hard to define when exactly a project has actually ended.

Experience has shown that every assessment of project costs is an inaccurate snapshot, as it merely represents the current state of the situation. In contrast, a series of estimates over time is usually more reliable than any individual estimate, since a series makes it easier to see whether the estimates converge, or whether the probability of meeting a forecast is even sufficiently high. The Interaction Room helps to improve the quality of estimates by eliciting risk and complexity drivers about the features to be implemented (in the form of annotations). In addition, the adVANTAGE contract model encourages consistent tracking of effort estimates and actual expenditures (Sect. 15.3). The IR:agile combines these inputs in the cost forward progressing method to derive extrapolations and a series of qualitative, comparable estimates.

The calculations of cost forward progressing work with three types of parameters of differing credibility:

- $IE(f_i)$ is the **initial estimate** of the effort for a feature f_i (where i is the identifying number of the feature), which has only been sketched roughly in the IR: scope. This estimate is made during the transition from the IR:scope to the IR: agile when the product backlog is derived from the feature canvas and the initial estimates are added. It is informed by the "big picture" and annotations on the canvases.

- $DE(f_i)$ is the **detailed estimate** of the effort for a feature f_i before it is implemented. This estimate is made in the course of a sprint planning meeting in the IR:agile, when the sprint backlog is compiled for the next sprint. It is informed by the considerations that go into the task breakdown for each feature, as well as experiences from any previous sprints.
- $AE(f_i)$ is the **actual effort** that was invested into implementing a feature f_i. This value is recorded after the end of a sprint, when the feature has been completed and accepted by the client.

Of these parameter types, only the initial estimates $IE(f_i)$ for all features are defined at the start of a project, while the detailed estimates $DE(f_i)$ and actual efforts $AE(f_i)$ remain undefined initially. Formally speaking, if we assume that F represents the set of all features in the project and the dom operator yields a mapping's domain, the following applies initially:

$$\text{dom } IE = F; \quad \text{dom } DE = \emptyset; \quad \text{dom } AE = \emptyset$$

Now let us assume that 100 features were identified in an IR:agile—i.e., $F = \{f_1, \ldots, f_{100}\}$—for which initial estimates were made as shown in Table 8.1. Let us assume that the sum of all these initial effort estimates in the example is

$$\sum_{f_i \in \text{dom } IE} IE(f_i) = 2000 \text{ person-days (PD)}.$$

If a detailed estimate is now made for five features at the start of a sprint, the corresponding $DE(f_i)$ are assigned concrete values, as shown in Table 8.2.

The estimate of the total effort can therefore be rendered more precisely by adding up the most current defined values for all features. Since

$$\text{dom } IE = \{f_1, \ldots, f_{100}\}; \quad \text{dom } DE = \{f_1, f_2, f_3, f_4, f_5\}; \quad \text{dom } AE = \emptyset$$

now applies for the domains of our estimates, we can define the overall estimate OE as the sum of the most current known values, i.e., as

Table 8.1 Initial estimates for a sample project

i	$IE(f_i)$	$DE(f_i)$	$AE(f_i)$
1	10		
2	20		
3	10		
4	20		
5	10		
6	25		
7	30		
...			

Table 8.2 Detailed
estimates added in the course
of sprint planning

i	$IE(f_i)$	$DE(f_i)$	$AE(f_i)$
1	10	20	
2	15	25	
3	5	15	
4	10	25	
5	10	15	
6	25		
7	30		
...	...		

- the sum of the initial estimates *IE* known from the outset, insofar as they have not been superseded by detailed estimates, plus
- the sum of the detailed estimates *DE* that are already known, insofar as they have not been superseded by actual efforts, plus
- the sum of actual efforts *AE* that have already been expended.

In the example, the updated overall estimate is therefore

$$OE = \sum_{f_i \in \mathrm{dom}\ IE \backslash \mathrm{dom}\ DE} IE(f_i) + \sum_{f_i \in \mathrm{dom}\ DE \backslash \mathrm{dom}\ AE} DE(f_i) + \sum_{f_i \in \mathrm{dom}\ AE} AE(f_i).$$

The calculation above can be viewed as a "computer scientist's forecast": It is based on the assumption that any deviation is a local phenomenon, which does not imply conclusions regarding the estimates for the other features.

However, the detailed estimate for a sprint not only provides more precise information of the effort expected in the current sprint. It also shows how far off the initial estimate was. Accordingly, it seems plausible to correct the initial estimates of *all* features according to the deviation between the initial and the recent detailed estimate.

In the example, the initial estimate for the first five features was 50 person-days. This was rendered more precisely as 100 person-days in the detailed estimate (presumably based on a more in-depth examination of the requirements and challenges as part of the task breakdown). While the straightforward addition in the "computer scientist's forecast" leads to a revised total effort of 2050 person-days, one would have to assume a total effort of 4000 instead of 2000 person-days based on the revision of the initial estimates, since a sprint appears to take twice as long as initially estimated.

In general, this "statistician's extrapolation" can be calculated as follows: For all features for which we have detailed estimates, we first calculate the average deviation ΔIE between the detailed and initial estimate:

$$\Delta IE = \frac{\sum_{f_i \in \mathrm{dom}\ DE} DE(f_i)/IE(f_i)}{|\mathrm{dom}\ DE|}$$

The initial estimates of all features that do not have detailed estimates yet are multiplied by this factor. This results in the revised initial estimates

$$\forall f_i \in \text{dom } IE \backslash \text{dom } DE : IE'(f_i) = IE(f_i) \times \Delta IE.$$

As the project progresses, the actual effort expended in a sprint can be used to revise the detailed estimates of features that have not been implemented yet in the same manner:

$$\forall f_i \in \text{dom } DE \backslash \text{dom } AE : DE'(f_i) = DE(f_i) \times \Delta DE$$

$$\text{where} \quad \Delta DE = \frac{\sum_{f_i \in \text{def } AE} AE(f_i)/DE(f_i)}{|\text{def } AE|}$$

The "statistician's extrapolation," i.e., the overall effort forecast corrected for estimation errors, is therefore calculated as

- the sum of the revised initial estimates IE', insofar as they have not been superseded by detailed estimates, plus
- the sum of the revised, known detailed estimates DE', insofar as they have not been superseded by actual efforts, plus
- the sum of the efforts already expended AE

or in brief:

$$OE' = \sum_{f_i \in \text{dom } IE \backslash \text{dom } DE} IE'(f_i) + \sum_{f_i \in \text{dom } DE \backslash \text{dom } AE} DE'(f_i) + \sum_{f_i \in \text{dom } AE} AE(f_i).$$

Tables 8.3 and 8.4 show an example of four features initially estimated at 20, 25, 15, and 10 person-days. In Table 8.3, we see how these values develop with progressing detailed estimates and implementation. The respective most current values (bold) are added up to calculate the "computer scientist's forecast."

In Table 8.3, we see the calculation of the IE and DE deviations. Their application in Table 8.4 leads to corrected estimates $IE'(f_i)$ and $DE'(f_i)$. Adding up the

Table 8.3 Cost forward progressing with "computer scientist's forecast"

i	$IE(f_i)$	$DE(f_i)$	$AE(f_i)$	i	$IE(f_i)$	$DE(f_i)$	$AE(f_i)$	i	$IE(f_i)$	$DE(f_i)$	$AE(f_i)$
1	**20**			1	**20**			1	20	**30**	
2	**25**			2	25	**50**		2	25	50	**60**
3	**15**			3	**15**			3	**15**		
4	**10**			4	**10**			4	**10**		
OE = 20 + 25 + 15 + 10 = 70 PD				OE = 20 + 50 + 15 + 10 = 95 PD				OE = 30 + 60 + 15 + 10 = 115 PD			
				$\Delta IE = \frac{50}{25} = 2$				$\Delta IE = \left(\frac{30}{20} + \frac{50}{25}\right)/2 = 1.75$			
								$\Delta DE = \frac{60}{50} = 1.2$			

Table 8.4 Cost forward progressing with "statistician's extrapolation"

i	$IE(f_i)$	i	$IE(f_i)$	$IE'(f_i)$	$DE(f_i)$	i	$IE(f_i)$	$IE'(f_i)$	$DE(f_i)$	$DE'(f_i)$	$AE(f_i)$
1	**20**	1	20	**40**		1	20	35	30	**36**	
2	**25**	2	25	50	**50**	2	25	43.75	50	60	**60**
3	**15**	3	15	**30**		3	15	**26.25**			
4	**10**	4	10	**20**		4	10	**17.5**			
OE = 70 PD		OE' = 40 + 50 + 30 + 20 = 140 PD				OE' = 36 + 60 + 26.25 + 17.5 = 139.75 PD					

respective most current values (bold) in Table 8.4 results in the "statistician's extrapolation," i.e., the revised overall estimate.

By applying both the "computer scientist's forecast" and the "statistician's extrapolation" to the total feature set, the effects of changes to the feature set caused by late requirements can also be represented: As long as proper "financing" is maintained using the methods of the requirements exchange, the total effort does not change due to changes to the feature set. Forecast changes result only if precise "financing" of late requirements by swapping out early requirements cannot be achieved.

Figure 8.4 shows the development of the two predictions obtained through cost forward progressing for a project in progress. We see the initial estimate at the transition from the IR:scope to the IR:agile as the anchor point, as well as eight additional measuring points. At two of these measuring points, we have expansions in the form of late requirements that could not be financed by swapping out early requirements (once with an initial estimate, once with a detailed estimate).

Overall, we see that the "computer scientist's forecast" increases moderately at first (while the "statistician's extrapolation" increases dramatically). A stable level appears to have been reached starting at the fifth measuring point. At the final measuring point, we see the effect of a detailed estimate turning out to be significantly below the initial estimate. This effect has a mild impact on the forecast and a pronounced impact on the extrapolation. In the subsequent course of the project,

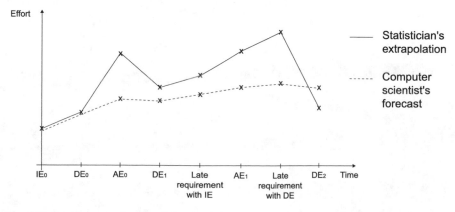

Fig. 8.4 Development of extrapolations and forecasts over time

when the overall uncertainty decreases, the "computer scientist's forecast" therefore may be the more plausible prediction since it does not have as great an impact on the overall estimate. Overall, the actual effort likely lies in a corridor between the two predictions. However, does not seem likely that the actual efforts will drop back to the initially estimated level.

References

Grapenthin S, Poggel S, Book M, Gruhn V (2014) Facilitating task breakdown in sprint planning meeting 2 with an Interaction Room: An experience report. In: Rabiser R, Torkar R (eds) SEAA'14: Proc 40th Euromicro Conf on Software Engineering and Advanced Applications, pp 1–8. doi:10.1109/SEAA.2014.71

Moran A (2014) Agile Risk Management. Springer

Using Interaction Rooms Under Difficult Conditions

9

The preceding chapters have shown that an Interaction Room in its different variations is a valuable tool for the orientation and alignment of interests of all stakeholders, from the earliest preliminary stages of a project to its conclusion. Setting up a separate Interaction Room for each project will, however, not be possible in many companies for practical reasons—perhaps there are insufficient meeting rooms available exclusively, or the team members work in geographically separate locations, or a complete Interaction Room does not appear necessary to solve the problem in question.

However, the individual elements of an Interaction Room are modular and lightweight enough to be customized to various project and room situations. The following sections provide suggestions for dealing with typical situations where setting up a complete Interaction Room seems infeasible.

9.1 Temporary Interaction Rooms

The most common objection to using an Interaction Room is that the organization cannot spare a dedicated room for the entire project term. This objection may be justified depending on the project scope and complexity. However, complex projects with strategic objectives, major integration challenges, and numerous stakeholders are usually exposed to such high cost and quality risks that reserving a room for the project is a worthwhile investment.

At least the initial workshops which only take a few days—usually an IR:digital for strategy development and an IR:mobile or IR:scope for project scoping, for example—should definitely be held in dedicated room. Ideally, this is a conference room equipped as an Interaction Room. This means it has large whiteboards on all walls and annotations as magnetic or self-adhesive symbols. It should be located on as neutral ground as possible—i.e., not in the heart of the IT or operating department, so the workshop does not turn into a "home game" for either side. Both sides

© Springer International Publishing Switzerland 2016
M. Book et al., *Tamed Agility*, DOI 10.1007/978-3-319-41478-2_9

should engage with each other. Equipping some conference rooms as Interaction Rooms is worthwhile for all companies that frequently deal with complex IT projects.

If a conference room equipped as an Interaction Room is not available, a room can also be temporarily "upgraded" to an IR with mobile whiteboards or self-adhesive whiteboard film. However, this solution typically does not provide as much freedom for sketching as a dedicated Interaction Room, which may subconsciously dampen the creativity of the stakeholders.

If the Interaction Room is only available for the scoping phase but not for the entire course of the project in the form of the IR:agile, the most important question is how to preserve and further develop the insights from an IR:digital, IR:mobile, IR:tech, or IR:scope. These insights are twofold in nature: For one, the analysis of the model sketches and annotations following an IR population typically results in a document with recommended actions. It identifies the major value, effort, and risk drivers as well as uncertainties and makes recommendations on how to take them into account in the subsequent course of the project (Sect. 3.7). This document should be made available to all stakeholders. Project management has to ensure that the points listed there are actually implemented or resolved.

In addition, taking high-resolution photographs of all canvases after each day of an IR workshop is recommended. These serve as the starting point for the concrete modeling of especially critical system elements and process steps. Often it is helpful to neatly reproduce the handwritten canvases including the annotations in a modeling tool, to make them easier to read (but without any interpretation or further development!). To avoid losing the overall impression of these annotated model sketches in the course of the project, printing out the photographs or reproduced canvases in poster size, and posting them in a room where they are present for as many stakeholders as possible is recommended (if mobile whiteboards or whiteboard film were used, the originals can be used directly). This may be the developer team room, or even a kitchenette or corridor, making it possible to spontaneously gather in front of the canvases in order to discuss current issues with the overall project context as a backdrop. However, transferring the canvases to another whiteboard in the team room is also conceivable, where they can be developed further in the course of the project.

The result is a visual excerpt of an Interaction Room in the team room. While this may only offer a perspective on a part of the project (when there is not enough space to transfer all the canvases), and editing is perhaps not as convenient (if only printed posters are available instead of whiteboards), it does at least serve as a central communication platform for the project stakeholders. Orientation in the project, the identification of design decisions and their effects, and perhaps most importantly, retaining the knowledge of all annotated value, effort, and risk drivers are facilitated this way.

The team can also decide to hold the regular sprint planning meetings as small IR:scope workshops in order to better understand the business and technical aspects of the features that will be tackled next. Instead of holding the sprint planning meeting with the limited resources of the IR excerpts in the team room, using a fully equipped Interaction Room with its generous space for half a day is recommended. The posters in the team room should be updated at this time as well, so the new sprint starts with a fresh overview of the entire project and the focal points of the current sprint. The team room posters collected from one iteration to the next in this manner, together with the burndown charts of the sprints, constitute a readily accessible summary of the work performed by the team. This also makes them suitable as a starting point for sprint and project retrospectives.

9.2   Distributed Interaction Rooms

As described in the previous section, an Interaction Room should ideally be available to the entire team for the duration of the project term. This makes the project with its objectives, context, challenges, and current status tangible to all stakeholders at all times and facilitates discussions.

But often, this ideal situation cannot be realized when various team members work in different places. Even in the simple case described above, when a project does not have a dedicated Interaction Room but posters of the canvases are put up in a team room after the workshops, the question arises which perspectives belong in which team room. Do the process canvases go to the business experts and the integration canvases to the developers? Do only the developers get all of the canvases, since they ultimately have to build the system? Or do both sides get a copy of all canvases? How are they posted at the different locations, and how are all canvases subsequently kept consistent?

These problems worsen when the project stakeholders are not just located in different departments within the same building, but are distributed across various sites, making it impossible to just drop in on your colleagues to discuss a problem in front of the canvases.

Concrete strategies for transferring the Interaction Room methodology to distributed teams are highly dependent on the team composition at the various sites, and on the required closeness of cooperation. Some guidelines can, however, help to support communication as effectively as possible, even under these difficult conditions:

Communication between the stakeholders is most important at the outset of any project. In the early phases, when the project objective and substance are being defined, the stakeholders who will have to work together for the project are usually just getting to know each other better. Developing a collaborative general atmosphere is essential in this phase, so that company departments do not isolate themselves from each other and formulate adversarial expectations, but instead jointly define a product and project while becoming familiar with and respecting the challenges faced by each other, so that possible solutions are developed in cooperation. However, such a basic attitude of joint project ownership and a creative atmosphere that promotes innovative solutions cannot develop over a distance but only through personal communication. This means there is no way around a personal, joint workshop for the initial Interaction Rooms—an IR:digital, IR:mobile, IR:tech, or IR:scope. Even when this means some stakeholders have to travel, the resulting team spirit and common understanding of problems and solutions is definitely worth the investment, especially in complex projects.

Following these workshops, the question arises how the insights that were jointly developed in the Interaction Room can be utilized and further developed most effectively at the various sites. Reproducing the visualizations from the joint Interaction Room at the various sites forms the foundation—ideally again in dedicated Interaction Rooms equipped with whiteboards, if necessary only by putting up posters in distributed team rooms (Sect. 9.1). To provide a complete picture of the project at each location, all canvases should, however, be reproduced at all sites. Even if the team at a certain site is only responsible for a certain area (an operating department for example will likely have little to do with integration questions), a complete overview helps to maintain awareness of the dependencies between one's own area and those of the other teams. Everyone also sees the complete picture during teleconferences this way.

The model sketches on the canvases of the local Interaction Rooms are going to develop separately according to the main activities of the various teams. This is intentional and natural on the one hand—each team can use its Interaction Room to better visualize the parts of the project it is responsible for. However, it is essential to ensure that the planning and development remain compatible with each other. Mutual visits between the teams are therefore recommended at regular intervals, in order to coordinate the state of work and subsequent planning and to align the sketches in the Interaction Rooms with each other at the key structural joints.

It is apparent that such a distributed approach does not lend itself to the same close cooperation and direct communication about effort, dependencies, and potential solutions that is possible in a common Interaction Room. However, at least the function of an orientation framework for the entire project and a visualization instrument for local design planning and the local project progress are supported more effectively even by distributed Interaction Rooms than if the teams only use classic means of communication such as a central issue tracking software.

9.3   Augmented Interaction Rooms

As described above, the effectiveness of working in distributed Interaction Rooms is primarily restricted by separating the modeling work of the teams at the various sites. While occasional reconciliation meetings can keep the rough overall framework consistent, this is tedious and error-prone. Hidden dependencies are often missed, especially in major projects.

Digitizing the Interaction Rooms is a convenient way to enable a more straightforward exchange and reconciliation of models between the various sites. So-called Augmented Interaction Rooms (AugIRs) use large-scale interactive displays instead of whiteboards (Kleffmann et al. 2014a). These can be marked with electronic pens like a whiteboard, making them as intuitive to use as classic whiteboards. In fact, the displays surpass classic whiteboards when it comes to drawing convenience, since they support the straightforward, gesture-controlled movement of drawing elements or the entire drawing area, making the restructuring of sketches and the flexible use of space much simpler compared to classic whiteboards.

When Augmented Interaction Rooms are available to the teams at the various sites, digitally prepared sketches can be easily exchanged between different locations. Conference calls are also supported, allowing distributed teams to work on the same canvases simultaneously. Asynchronous work is simplified as well (with corresponding AugIR software): While the teams work with "their" canvases locally, they can be notified automatically of collisions or the violation of dependencies with the canvases of remote teams.

Setting up an Augmented Interaction Room is worthwhile even when all of a company's teams work at the same site, since this solves the problem of individual teams requiring the exclusive use of rooms. Since the sketches and annotations are no longer prepared physically but digitally, the current state of a whole Interaction Room can be saved and later restored at the push of a button (Kleffmann et al. 2014b). This allows several teams to use an AugIR in parallel (in different time slots), instead of having to make do with photographic records and printed posters.

Clearly, the infrastructure required for a digital Interaction Room with several interactive displays in whiteboard size is no small investment. It does, however, offer the greatest number of project teams the opportunity to benefit from the Interaction Room methodology. The more constructive, risk-aware, and value-oriented project work enabled by this should lead to improved product quality, which soon offsets the infrastructure investment.

References

Kleffmann M, Book M, Gruhn V (2014a) Supporting collaboration of heterogeneous teams in an augmented team room. In: Lanubile F, Ali R (eds) SSE'14: Proc 6th Intl Workshop on Social Software Engineering, pp 9–16. doi:10.1145/2661685.2661688

Kleffmann M, Book M, Hebisch E, Gruhn V (2014b) Automated versioning and temporal navigation for model sketches on large interactive displays. In: Kim S, Hung CC, Hong J (eds) SAC'14: Proc 29th Annual ACM Symp on Applied Computing, pp 161–168. doi:10.1145/2554850.2563668

Summary

10

The Interaction Room serves as a platform for communication between all project stakeholders. While this is of central importance in agile process models, it is usually hardly organized and usually focuses entirely on technical details. In the Interaction Room on the other hand, the perspectives of all stakeholders—domain experts, developers, operations experts, managers, and users—are expressed, recorded, and jointly discussed. Shared modeling and annotation provokes and channels exactly the discussion that is required by all agile methods as a central element, but hardly promoted by their methodology.

Different Interaction Room variants lend themselves to different project situations. Figure 10.1 illustrates the characteristics of software development projects that suggest high usefulness of an IR:scope or IR:agile. The top half of the figure shows the criteria for a project's affinity for scoping in an IR:scope, while the bottom half shows the criteria that determine a project's affinity for monitoring with the help of an IR:agile. The less dominant a project is in a certain dimension, the less need there is for using an Interaction Room. None of these criteria result in the strict inapplicability of the Interaction Room, nor in a strict necessity of its use. These are merely rough guidelines that may need to be overridden by specific characteristics of individual projects.

The following criteria are used in Fig. 10.1 to ascertain a project's Interaction Room affinity:

- **Centrality**: A software development project can be carried out with various degrees of centrality. Here the question is how the persons involved in development are distributed across sites. Having all persons at one location is a fully central model, enabling communication between the stakeholders at any time without expending travel time and incurring costs. The Interaction Room as a means of personal communication benefits from such a central organization. In more decentralized organizations, the application experts may be in a different location than the developers, or the developers at a different location than the specifiers and architects. Using the Interaction Room is nevertheless possible in

© Springer International Publishing Switzerland 2016
M. Book et al., *Tamed Agility*, DOI 10.1007/978-3-319-41478-2_10

Fig. 10.1 Suitability of a
project for the IR:scope or
IR:agile

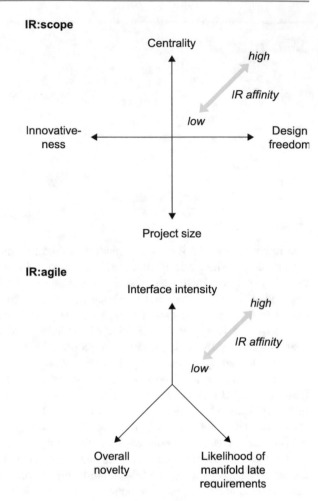

such situations, but usually demands greater logistics, organizational and other
efforts, as discussed in Sect. 9.2.

- **Innovativeness**: Software can support novel business processes or administer
  new products and clients. It can also enable fundamentally new business
  models. The software being developed is associated with business innovations
  in all of these situations. Corresponding software development is defined by the
  fact that innovations on the business side go hand in hand with previously
  unknown software structures. On the other side are software development
  projects that supplement existing software systems while retaining their structure. Innovation plays a minor role here; what needs to happen is usually readily
  conceivable. In between there is a large variety of projects with specific innovation focal points, those intended to adapt off-the-shelf software to company
  specifics and those that "only" support a release change from one software

version to the next. Generally, the more innovative the business domain, the more important it is to coordinate the features and structure of the new software with all stakeholders—and the more useful it is to support precisely this coordination with an IR.

- **Design freedom**: Closely related but nevertheless distinguishable from innovativeness is the freedom to design the software being developed. Even software that is not innovative from a business perspective can offer significant design freedom in its details, which requires coordination. This may relate to the structure of the business processes that have to be supported, the organization model and also the interfaces. When deciding whether an Interaction Room will be useful for the project, it is therefore also important to consider whether such the design freedom requires coordination between various participating groups and persons. If this is the case, then the Interaction Room is a suitable instrument.

- **Project size**: The size of the software being developed influences the communication intensity of the software process. "The larger the software, the greater the number of stakeholders" may not be accurate in special cases, but works as a general guideline. An Interaction Room may constitute excessive overhead for the development of a software that can be built by a few developers within a few weeks. Meaningful scoping of software that is developed by dozens of developers over the course of a year or more, on the other hand, may not be possible with just one Interaction Room, but require the IR instruments to be applied to hierarchically structured subprojects.

- **Interface intensity**: Whenever software has numerous interfaces to users, the coordination of these interfaces is crucial for acceptance. In other words, realizing a printer driver usually requires less back and forth than realizing an interface to a human user. Interfaces to humans not only include dialogs, but also reports and documents of many kinds. When software is defined by many such interfaces, a variety of late and competing requirements is likely. These interfaces as a set also require the establishment of an interaction paradigm. Should user guidance be optimized, should users even have the opportunity to record inconsistent data? Should they be supported to achieve maximum efficiency, or is a pleasant user experience most important? In short, the more interface-intensive the application, the more does its design depend on having the stakeholders agree on an interaction paradigm. The Interaction Room can contribute to this (e.g., with the interaction canvas). To state the argument from the opposite perspective: when we are talking about a purely technical software with no user interaction, there is hardly a starting point for the IR instruments.

- **Likelihood of manifold late requirements**: Late requirements are virtually unavoidable in any project. Nevertheless, the question of how undefined and potentially change-intensive the initial requirements are is relevant for establishing the appropriate agility level. In largely clear situations, it makes sense to put more effort into the initial requirements documentation than in cases where a variety of requirements that cannot be foreseen precisely is expected.

- **Overall novelty**: Software that is functionally and structurally novel is virtually impossible to specify in advance. Here Ries' (2011) paradigm applies—the purpose of the software only becomes clear during development, so that a meandering development process must be permitted in order to obtain the maximum possible benefit. Clinging to the initially planned purpose of the software is often harmful in such innovative situations, since it impedes moving toward something even more useful. When software is not only innovative in specific details, but even in its core goals, this has a significant influence on the dynamics and volatility of even fundamental requirements.

In addition to these dimensions that make using the Interaction Room more or less attractive, there are some strict exclusion criteria. These include the unavailability of domain experts, a strictly plan-driven conceptual world (even though this should no longer exist today), and clients who simply do not want to be bothered during the development process. This is because gaining new insights through interdisciplinary communication, or permitting the vagueness and flexibility that make the Interaction Room such an effective communication catalyst, are not possible under those circumstances.

Reference

Ries E (2011) The lean startup: How today's entrepreneurs use continuous innovation to create radically successful businesses. Crown Business

Part III
The adVANTAGE Contract Model

Framing Software Projects in Commercial Terms

11

As described in the preceding chapters, the Interaction Room offers a number of practical instruments for stakeholders in software projects. At their core, they all revolve around the challenge of dealing with uncertainty in various phases of software development. While uncertainty is unavoidable, it can be effectively addressed in teams through communication. In Chap. 2.1, we discussed why communication is almost certainly *the* central task in software projects: because people have different levels of understanding of a domain, because they usually lack a clear vision at the outset, because they easily get lost in details and do not have a clear idea of the drivers that determine the value and cost of the software being developed, and because requirements are never permanently stable (if they appear to be precisely known at all).

The Interaction Room is an expression of the conviction that facing these conditions is preferable to pretending that we can adequately specify software in one go (especially for socio-technical systems). As a framework for systematic but not formal communication in agile software projects, the Interaction Room has proven itself in numerous project situations. It serves as the central, physical forum and methodic guideline of the agile project village—in the form of the IR:digital, IR:mobile, or IR:tech in the early strategy development phases, in the form of the IR:scope for concrete project scoping and in the form of the IR:agile during project implementation.

While the Interaction Room addresses the key *constructive* aspects of a software project, we have however not yet addressed the general *commercial* conditions under which agile software projects take place. In this chapter, we will examine these conditions in more detail and show how they can be addressed to deal with the unavoidable uncertainty in software projects.

First off, we need to be aware that there are not only differences between how plan-driven or agile methods affect the economic aspects of a software project, but also in how company boundaries (i.e., boundaries between legally independent economic units) influence project activities.

© Springer International Publishing Switzerland 2016
M. Book et al., *Tamed Agility*, DOI 10.1007/978-3-319-41478-2_11

			Project character	
			Plan-driven approach	Agile approach
Mode of cooperation		External service provider		
		Mixed teams		
		In-house development		

Fig. 11.1 Possible commercial settings of software projects

Figure 11.1 illustrates various commercial situations, depending on the character and cooperation model of the software project. Let us examine the project character first; in other words, let us look at both ends of the spectrum between a plan-driven and an agile approach from a business perspective:

- In **a plan-driven approach**, we assume that some documents (product briefs, specifications, or similar artifacts) exist in the early phases of the software project, providing a reasonably reliable, stable basis for calculating the realization effort. These types of projects cannot be disregarded, even in a book on the topic of tamed agility, since they do of course still exist quite commonly. Consider purely technical systems, especially for critical applications: Surely, it would be preferable to clearly specify the software for pacemakers and driverless cars before the programmers and then the testers get to work on them. Late, surprising requirements should not occur at all or at least very rarely in such systems, or at least be so non-critical that they can be postponed to future releases. But examples for reasonable plan-driven development can be found in socio-technical systems as well: Many software products are developed this way (with long-term advance product management, where the product characteristics for numerous different future use cases are clearly specified). Commercial aspects play an important but not all too complicated role in all these cases. As long as a basis for estimating the required realization effort exists, we are dealing with "normal" estimation uncertainty that depends on numerous factors (Jørgensen and Moløkken-Østvold 2004)—the quality and detail level of the underlying documents (product brief, specification), the experience of the estimator, and so on. The risk associated with this estimation uncertainty lies with the developing company, according to the cooperation model (see below).
- **Agile methods** take into account the fact that software development is a process of gaining insights. Here, it is an accepted basic assumption that software cannot be specified conclusively or that this specification would have to be so elaborate that the software might as well be realized in the same timeframe. In fact, it is the essential characteristic of agile methods that usable systems are developed

quickly in short cycles, which can then be provided to the clients for feedback that forms the basis for development of the next iteration. Skipping the preparation of comprehensive documents does however also lead to the difficulty that an informative advance estimate cannot be prepared. This is not a problem as such, since a calculation basis in the form of a product brief full of holes would be highly unsound anyway, leading to nothing but unreliable estimates of effort that are more like guesswork. Either way, we are dealing with risk which is often significant.

The mode of dealing with the cost risks that arise from the "normal" estimate uncertainty in the plan-driven process, or associated with the inherent unpredictability of future developments in agile process models, depends to a large extent on the type of cooperation model between software users and software developers.

- The simplest case is that of **in-house development**. Users and developers work for the same company in this scenario. The company's internal application development is commissioned by one or more operating departments. Regardless of the chosen method, risks arising from the project are borne entirely by the company realizing the project. Management will be interested in an assessment of the risks, but the investment decision is not going to depend on how these risks are virtually distributed between the departments.
- This book mainly examines the case of an **external service provider**, which means an external company is commissioned to build the software. Choosing the method (plan-driven vs. agile) is of crucial importance in this case. If a plan-driven process is chosen and a somewhat reliable calculation basis exists, the risks are clearly distributed: The client bears the risk of late or changing requirements, and the contractor bears the general software development risk. This includes, for example, insufficiently qualified staff deployed in the project, resulting poor quality of results and high cost of rework, liability risk in case of gross negligence, and so on. In contracts for these types of projects, everything is ultimately decided by the quality of the product brief. It is consulted and interpreted in case of disputes, for example, to determine whether features that were not implemented are described there or not. The legal consequences are clearly defined depending on the evaluation of the content. That is also why suppliers are able to offer building software at fixed prices in such scenarios. They believe they can estimate their general software development risk. All that remains is the question of whether the product brief is considered detailed enough to use it as a calculation base. Agile situations are much more difficult to assess in this regard, since detailed product briefs do not exist here by definition, so a calculation base is lacking. We will examine various contract types based on this background in the next chapter.
- The **cooperative performance structure** is an even more complex case, for example, when developers of a supplier work in mixed teams with developers of the client. Surely, the simplest way to deal with this situation would be for the client to bear all risks, merely purchasing resources from the contractor in the

form of "body leasing." The billing model for this is very straightforward and has been used thousands of times. But there are also cases where the client would prefer somewhat more responsibility and readiness to assume risk on the part of the contractor. We will see later that this is a special case of the external service provider model with a few special rules.

Reference

Jørgensen M, Moløkken-Østvold K (2004) Reasons for software effort estimation error: Impact of respondent role, information collection approach, and data analysis method. IEEE TSE 30 (12):993–1007. doi:10.1109/TSE.2004.103

Traditional Contract Models in an Agile World

12

First, we want to examine typical contract models that are familiar from plan-driven software projects. We initially assume a classic external service provider model, which means a project structure with a client who is both user and creator of the requirements and a contractor who is the developer and supplier. The client and contractor are separated by a company boundary. This is important in the examination of various contract models, since such a company boundary separates

- two different legal entities: We are examining various contract models here. Contracts are not only intended to describe the rules of working together, but also to define the consequences that result if at least one of the contractual partners does not abide by the agreed rules. A legal dispute is the result when this occurs. Initially, it can be negotiated between the persons in charge at the two companies, possibly with the involvement of legal advisors. When this fails, the entire organization structure of the relevant legal system is available to help the adversaries assert their rights and to balance their interests. In contrast to in-house development, the client and contractor do not depend on resolution between the conflicting parties. If the matter is not resolved, the parties can petition the courts and ask an independent judge to render a binding decision.
- two different economic units: While there is one management structure in case of in-house development, combining both sets of interests (the user and requirements author, and the developer) and being able to prioritize and therefore resolve conflicts in case of disputes, this is not the case with the external service provider model. Here the client and contractor each have their own company management, with their own respective objectives focusing on their own company. Rather than focusing on the overall best solution in case of a conflict, the focus will be on satisfying the respective local interests.

However, let us first examine the positive case of proper and successful completion of the contractually agreed software project. Here the contract serves to define the relationship between the contractual partners, their respective obligations

© Springer International Publishing Switzerland 2016
M. Book et al., *Tamed Agility*, DOI 10.1007/978-3-319-41478-2_12

and the objectives of working together. Contracts for custom software development therefore typically cover at least the following:

- **Project objective**: What is the intended result of implementing the project? What type of software is supposed to be developed and by when? Where (in what referenced document) is the desired project result described?
- **Roles of the contractual partners**: What are the respective responsibilities of the client and contractor? How are these responsibilities defined positively (by naming work tasks) or negatively (by excluding tasks)?
- **Obligations of the contractual partners**: What delivery obligations arise from the roles mentioned above? Obligations are by no means limited to the contractor side (creating and delivering the product, i.e., the software), they also exist on the side of the client (duty to cooperate in the project and pay the project price, see the various compensation models below). The duties of the client to cooperate are frequently discussed in particular, even in projects that go well. A "receiving" rather than "providing" mentality often develops on the client side. This is psychologically comprehensible since the client is the customer or buyer of the delivery object. However, this delivery object has to be created in the course of custom software projects, a process which requires the client's involvement. Regulating this in detail and as conclusively as possible in the contract is therefore not just a legal requirement, it also promotes an understanding of the project character from the outset.
- **Compensation model**: Usually included under the client's obligations, the compensation model can at times be defined in a separate section of a contract for software projects—all the more because simple compensation models are often unsuitable for agile projects, as we will see below. The more agile the project and the less the project results are defined in advance, the more complex the models for compensating the work of the contractor usually become.
- **Legal consequences in case of actions that violate the contract**: Software project contracts are normally within the context of the general legal framework for contracts of work and labor in the respective jurisdiction. This means that many fundamental rules for dealing with actions that violate the contract as well as liability issues are already established in detail. Naturally, the contracting parties can agree on other provisions that define concrete requirements or deviate from discretionary aspects of contract law. In agile software projects, for which the delivery object is naturally defined poorly or not at all, the question of defective delivery is of major importance. Cases in which the client can refuse acceptance of the delivery object have to be defined. This is associated with legal consequences such as supplementary performance, replacement, abatement, the payment of damages, and so on. If describing the delivery object with sufficient clarity is not possible (the normal case in agile projects), taking this into account correspondingly in the contract is all the more important. A classic contract of work and labor is often out of the question here. Instead, the project has the nature of providing a service, which does not have to mean however that the contractor assumes no risk whatsoever in regard to project success.

We have to differentiate between service contracts and contracts for work and labor. Fixed price contracts are often equated to contracts for work and labor, and the other way around. But a contract for work and labor does not have to call for a fixed price compensation model. Neither are service contracts always settled on a time and materials basis (although this is common and popular). In fact, the relation between the compensation model and contractual framework is orthogonal, as shown in Fig. 12.1.

According to the freedom of contract principle, the client and contractor can agree on virtually any provisions within this coordinate system. The commercial dimension leaves even more design freedom than the legal one, where the laws of most countries at least specify the general outlines for the design of contracts.

As long as the planned project implementation process is not disrupted and the services are provided by the contractor according to the contract, meaning the project proceeds positively, the choice of the contract type is economically neutral and therefore largely insignificant. However, the two contract types—contract for work and labor versus service contract—distribute risk entirely differently between the client and contractor. In practice, this is mainly revealed by errors in the calculation and by defective performance.

In case of a contract for work and labor, the contractor owes the delivery of a certain result in the form of creating a work with specific, contractually established characteristics. We are talking about (IT) projects in which certain requirements have to be fully implemented at a fixed (or maximum) price and by a fixed date (and the legal consequences under a contract for work and labor are not waived). If the contractor is unable to achieve performance as contractually agreed, thereby culpably violating a performance obligation, the contractor legally has to put the client into the same position that the client would have been in, if the contractor had met its service performance obligations according to the contract. This can have very unfavorable economic consequences for the contractor. In addition to the planned, additional costs to create the work (such as rectification, costs for replacement) or the (also entire) waiving of compensation (abatement, withdrawal), additional

	Fixed price	Time and materials
Service contract		
Contract for work and labor		

Fig. 12.1 Contract types in legal and commercial dimensions

consequential damages due to defects or delays and even lost profits may have to be paid. The economic risks of meeting the specified deadline, and therefore the responsibility for the success of the projects, are therefore borne solely by the contractor under a contract for work and labor.

In case of an (IT) service contract on the other hand, the contractor owes (independent) services, which means purely an activity and therefore effort but not certain results. The contractor has to ensure that the activity is performed within the specified time frame, that the personnel which is deployed has the necessary (and/or contractual) qualifications, that the activity is performed as agreed and at least average in terms of quality and efficiency. The legal consequences of culpable defective performance are regulated in much less detail by law compared to the contract for work and labor. Due to the reduced responsibility of the provider to the customer, these are correspondingly limited. Under a service contract, the activity itself and not the success of the project is warranted. This means the consequences in practice are essentially limited to rectification (performing the activity) and a reduction of compensation. Both the risk of violating the performance obligations and the economic consequences are much less severe for the contractor under a service contract compared to a contract for work and labor.

A straight service contract often fails to meet the economic requirements for the distribution of responsibilities between the contracting parties. As a result, it is rarely used for software development IT projects. The economic dependency of the client on the contractor, usually with dominant business knowledge, would be too great. Conversely, the choice of a (straight) contract for work and labor demands that (all) requirements for the work have to be defined in advance. Otherwise, the already high risk of the contractor significantly increases even further. However, (fully) establishing the requirements in advance is not always possible or desirable in practice. The contractor would compensate for this circumstance by adding uneconomical risk surcharges to the offer.

In practice, fairly and equitably sharing responsibility between the client and contractor can only be achieved with suitable mixed contract forms. In the following, we will largely distance ourselves from the question of the contract type in this legal dimension since we are mainly interested in the commercial basic conditions for contracts in agile project situations. As already hinted at in Fig. 12.1, we are going to introduce the adVANTAGE model as a contract template that lies somewhere in the middle on the spectrum between a fixed price and compensation on a time and materials basis. First, we will examine the two ends of the spectrum in regard to how they can be applied in agile project situations.

12.1   Fixed Price

The world used to be quite simple when it was usual for custom software projects under the external service provider model to be strictly plan-driven: The client put a lot of effort into a product brief, describing what was needed in the greatest possible detail. The contractor was able to calculate its effort on this basis and the detailed specification was jointly developed—usually after the contract was awarded. Then the world either still looked similar to what the product brief said, so everything was good, or changes were required that led to additional demands. Based on the specifications, communication about these demands was usually quite good. Fixed prices and corresponding plan-based contracts were the means of choice in this world. Since extensive descriptions of the delivery object at various levels of detail were on hand, the contractor felt confident because the development goals were clear. The only commercial risks were the general risks of software development briefly mentioned above, such as poorly qualified or unproductive personnel, technological complexity or remaining, minor leeway for interpretation. A risk surcharge was included in the calculation to cover these "residual risks."

Naturally, such situations still occur today and nothing speaks against approaching them on the basis of a fixed price contract. The commercial risk for the client—assuming corresponding creditworthiness of the contractor—can be practically disregarded, which is precisely why this contract type is so popular. For the contractor, commercial success largely depends on the accuracy of the estimated effort, which we will not explore further here. A good overview is found for example in Boehm et al. (2000).

The contract provisions for a fixed price project are often agreed on the basis of work packages, although this does not have to be the case, as illustrated above. Not too much needs to be defined in terms of the compensation model: The software corresponding to the respective document referenced in the contract, such as a product brief or specification, has to be supplied by the contractor before a certain date and the client has to pay a fixed price for it.

Leeway for adjusting the established fixed price is essentially found at exactly one point—during the project, when late requirements become known that are clearly outside the previously specified context, which means they could not be included in the original calculation. Handling such change requests has to be covered by the contract provisions, otherwise there is potential for conflict. On the one hand, the contractor has to be protected against the excessive expansion of the delivery object resulting from overly client-friendly interpretation. When it comes to the question of whether a certain feature was included in the product brief, only not in as much detail, smart clients like to point to the cornucopia of subsequent orders one would naturally prefer to award to a cooperative partner who already knows the ropes. The extent to which this leverage, which is clearly applied outside the letter of the contract, leads to success ultimately depends on the supplier's tactic and of course its arguments with regard to content.

If one agrees that a certain change request is exactly that, rather than stating a specified feature in concrete terms, the client in turn now has to be protected—against an overly ample estimate of the required implementation effort and the resulting (fixed) price payable for the change request. This in fact often constitutes a back door in practice for a supplier who may have had to offer the project at a cut price in order to win the contract. It does not even have to occur with dishonest intent. In certain market contexts, it is common to offer large work packages at low base prices and make money through subsequent change requests or even later in the maintenance phase.

Unfortunately, contract provisions do not prevent the inherent back and forth in the negotiation of change requests. If one could clearly define whether a feature constitutes a change request or not, it would probably have been included in the product brief. This is exactly where disputes arise in case of doubt. Once the question is resolved, the consequence is clear: Payment is either required or not. Then the amount can also be disputed, which is another problem that is difficult to handle contractually. While daily rates as the calculation basis can be established, this does not solve the problem of estimating the required effort. Ultimately, this gap can only be filled through negotiation, which should be successful as long as no party to the contract exaggerates.

So much for the theory. In practice, it has been shown that fixed price projects often create a false sense of certainty that does not exist in reality. On the client side, the wolf of uncertainty is disguised in the sheep's clothing of the product brief. The assumption that socio-technical systems can be described on paper is also false as a rule. A product brief is an appealing document that can provide a high-level statement of intent. It normally fails to describe the subsequent system. We have described why this is in detail in Sect. 2.1, so that we are simply acknowledging here that change request processes—other than by skillful or insidious suppliers— are mainly caused by the fact that late requirements are quite simply normal and of course increase the total price for the software. Experienced project managers on the client side plan corresponding budgets for this purpose. This is where the uncertainty inherent in a project is uncovered—how high should such a budget reasonably be? If a halfway reasonable estimate were possible, the product brief (or any other contractually relevant estimating basis) would define what needs to be developed for this amount.

Because this cannot be accomplished, agile methods have been developed that do not assume in the first place that a reliable estimating basis can be defined in advance. Not only because late requirements are just a fact of life, but because everything ultimately depends on an unpredictable moment: The moment when the originator of the requirements sees the result for the first time—the finished software, or parts of it. Often this is the moment that ends with the words: "That's not what I meant, of course I meant something quite different." The later this moment arrives, the more expensive it gets. This is why agile methods strive to avoid a lot of specification in the first place, focusing instead on creating software as quickly as possible so the discussion is not about paper but about the result. But eliminating the basis of estimation disturbs the contractually established balance of power between the client and contractor. A fixed price in the literal sense would mean that the contractor would have to implement anything and everything at a fixed price— an option no reasonable supplier will agree to. Or that the price may be fixed, but the client does not know what will be delivered in return for the budget—hardly a satisfying prospect for the user.

12.2 Time and Materials

Time and materials (T&M) contracts lie at the opposite end of the spectrum for commercial models in custom software development by an external service provider. They are often but not necessarily used in service contexts, that is, in situations where project success is by and large not legally owed. Naturally, the compensation under a T&M contract can in principle also be negotiated in case of a work package. One way or another, payment by the client is based on the personnel and material actually deployed and used, with the former naturally accounting for the largest share by far in case of software development. Therefore, this is a relatively simple compensation model where the contractor assumes virtually no risk because it is compensated for its actual effort, unless any restrictive rules are specified. When corresponding daily rates are agreed, the profit margin is fixed and not subject to any fluctuations. Contingency agreements are often negotiated, specifying that a minimum number of person-days will be used within a certain period of time. This eliminates the risk of short-term unemployment for the supplier in case of a sudden project stop. In exchange, the contractor assures the availability of qualified and trained personnel, along with fixed prices for the duration of the contingency agreement. If there are no contingency agreements, the contractual obligations of the partners are significantly less compared to classic fixed price contexts and can usually be revoked at short notice. However, this does not apply in case of a contract for work and labor with T&M compensation. All obligations including a corresponding warranty that typically define a work package apply here.

In case of plan-driven software development methods, not much speaks for a T&M-based compensation model for the client as a rule. If work has already been invested in preparing a product brief or when this is part of the project anyway, the client will be very interested in agreeing on a fixed price in case of doubt. Otherwise, the client would bear all risks—in T&M projects, the client not only bears the risk of late requirements, but usually also the general risks such as a lack of qualifications or technical complexity. Nevertheless, it occurs more often than one would expect that even projects with existing artifacts that can be estimated are implemented on a T&M basis. This happens for instance when successful cooperation with the supplier has been proven over many years, so that confidence in the supplier's performance and understanding of the business domain is high. The client's underlying motive may simply be to eliminate the risk surcharge which the supplier would include in a fixed price project. Comparatively straightforward and rapid contract design can be a good argument in favor of T&M compensation for plan-driven methods in certain cases as well.

In agile projects, there often appears to be no alternative to settlement on a time and materials basis. As outlined above, balancing the interests of the client and contractor is difficult on the basis of a fixed price in agile projects. This is mainly due to the unequal distribution of risk in one or the other direction, depending on how the fixed price is defined. Then the easy way out often lies in applying a T&M

model. If there is no basis for estimating then an estimate is just not possible, and without an estimate, there is also no assumption of risk by the supplier. As we will see later, more creative and differentiated models exist to shift the risk somewhat in the direction of the contractor even in agile situations. With pure T&M models on the other hand, the client has no choice but to pay for the music that was ordered, even if it is played badly.

In choosing between fixed price and T&M contracts for agile projects, the following assessment of risk distribution serves as an interim conclusion and rough abstraction: The fundamental problem in the agile context is that there is no sufficiently detailed basis for a halfway reliable estimation of effort. If we disregard the general software development risks (which are not specific to agile projects), the risk is that the development effort for the implementation of the target system is not foreseeable. To put it briefly: One (only) has a high-level vision of what is going to be built and no idea how much work (money) this is going to take. When a contractor offering a fixed price finds itself in this situation, it thereby assumes the full risk. In case of a T&M contract on the other hand, the full risk is borne by the client. Both are unappealing risk distributions because they are unbalanced.

Resourceful clients therefore develop supposedly more balanced mixed forms with titles like "T&M with cap" or "T&M with cost ceiling." For the contractor, these are nothing more than the worst of both worlds. Yet it sounds so fair: The contractor is paid on a T&M basis, which means the incurred effort is compensated, but accepts an upper limit to limit the risk of the client. In reality, even a pure fixed price project would be better for the contractor, since it would have the chance of staying below the calculated budget and making a profit. The contractor does not have that chance in a "T&M with cap" model, since it is paid exactly for the expended person-days if it stays below the budget. If the budget is exceeded, the contractor does not get a cent more and therefore bears the full risk without having the corresponding opportunity. This compensation model does not constitute a good solution for anything. There are better solutions for agile projects.

12.3   Pay Per Use

Paying for software according to actual use is not a particularly new model. Usage-based contract models are especially common in software-as-a-service (SaaS) models, where the application system is operated by an external contractor (and not the user). Settlement is usually either according to units of time or the number of transactions, and various scopes of functionality can be booked in addition in some cases. SaaS models became fashionable as the acceptance of cloud applications increased, especially in case of standard software such as Office 365 from Microsoft or the offerings of Salesforce.com.

While SaaS models remain uncommon in custom software development under the external service provider model examined here, they can constitute a reasonable alternative for certain project situations. In this case, we refer to pay-per-use contracts, because the term SaaS implies that the application is operated by the contractor which is not necessarily the case in our context. On the contrary, where the application is operated is initially irrelevant for the compensation model. The fundamental idea is to calculate part of the compensation for the software being developed depending on actual use. Only in very rare cases will this proportion be 100 % for custom software development by an external provider, since that would unreasonably shift the risk sharing profile in one direction as illustrated by the following discussion.

Applying the model of a usage-based price adds another risk component to our previous examination. Once again disregarding the general risks of software development, we previously dealt primarily with the risk of realization effort which is difficult to estimate. Differently put, the risk which has to be fairly shared between the client and contractor arose from the question "how expensive will it be to build the software?" Depending on the classic compensation model that was chosen (fixed price or T&M), the risk was borne either by the client or contractor.

Now we are adding another question which can result in new risk: "To what extent is the software going to be used?" Naturally, this question existed previously as well, but it was always assumed that the risk of developing software that would subsequently be used less than planned or not at all is borne by the client. Of late this assumption is being overturned here and there, which is due to the changed role of contractors in the New School of IT (Sect. 1.1). In the context of our examination of agile projects under the external service provider model, a fully usage-dependent price (a pure pay-per-use contract) is usually out of the question, since it shifts the risk even more in the direction of the contractor than an already unbalanced fixed price model does. The contractor would not only bear the risk that development, which cannot be estimated realistically, gets significantly more expensive, but also the risk that the software is ultimately used little or not at all. On the other hand, a combination of both (fixed price and pay per use) can constitute a fair alternative. For example, the contractor could bear the fixed price risk (in case of doubt, requiring more effort for developing the finished application than initially "guessed") but gain the opportunity to generate profitable business over the period of use. Such a mixed model is attractive for the client as well, since it has the certainty of a fixed price (which is rather unusual in case of an agile model) and subsequently pays a fee for actual use (which should not be a problem if the fee is reasonable).

Comparatively good experiences have been made with such models in some past cases, mainly in situations where the way an application has to be designed in order to be successful is not entirely clear (so they call for agility), and where potential clients are therefore uncertain in regard to the resulting cost risks. The *drebis* platform is an example (adesso 2013). It handles the exchange of information between law offices and defense insurance providers based on meaningfully structured business documents and information components, which therefore serve to optimize and automate the processes between the stakeholders. The exact design of the processes and structure of the business documents was unclear at the outset, but it was foreseeable that the processes to be supported could be handled much more efficiently with the use of a central portal in any case. Therefore, the contractor adesso assumed the realization of the system in an agile process for a fixed price (thereby accepting the risk of an uneconomical project at the time of go-live). On the other hand, the legal defense insurers originally involved were able to share the costs established in advance so they did not have to assume risk. Now they pay an amount per case actually processed through the platform under a pay-per-use model which is below the cost savings. The contractor generates a return on the fixed price risk it assumed.

This model can be considered an example for a trend in the IT service sector. Table 12.1 shows maturity levels of contractors, which they can reach in the course of their company history by accumulating experience and through purposeful business development. While technical expertise, later combined with business expertise, in the form of employees with corresponding experience largely determines the service portfolio in the first two maturity levels, more complex projects can be implemented under personal responsibility in higher maturity levels (maturity levels 3 and 4).

When a contractor reaches a higher maturity level (far right in Table 12.1), it is able to handle complex client processes, which is usually done on the basis of a pay-per-use contract. In addition to technical and business expertise, this requires

Table 12.1 Maturity levels of contractors

	1. Technology sourcing	2. Technology sourcing with business knowledge	3. Work packages	4. Agile work packages	5. Business process outsourcing
Technical expertise	X	X	X	X	X
Method expertise	X	X	X	X	X
Process expertise		X	X	X	X
Business expertise			X	X	X
Scope expertise				X	X
Optimization expertise					X
Operations expertise					X
Contract model	Time and materials	Time and materials	Fixed price	Risk sharing with fixed price components	Transaction based

optimization expertise and—if the corresponding application system is operated by the contractor—hosting and application management expertise. The more of the client's requirements for expertise the contractor can cover, the more willing it will be to assume risk, and the greater is the contractor's chance to generate corresponding revenue through transaction-based billing models according to the pay-per-use contract model in exchange for the assumed risk.

12.4   Summary

Before exploring contract types for agile contexts in the following chapter, let us briefly summarize the traditional approaches for contract models described above, based on two simple questions and an equally simple classification (Fig. 12.2).

We differentiate the contract types according to the variability of the two contract parameters "scope" and "price" (deliberately ignoring the existence of the typical third parameter "time," in part because it typically offers the least leeway for contract design). Furthermore, we want to differentiate the three traditional contract types based on the distribution of risk between the client and contractor. Here we limit ourselves to two core questions that are relevant in this context:

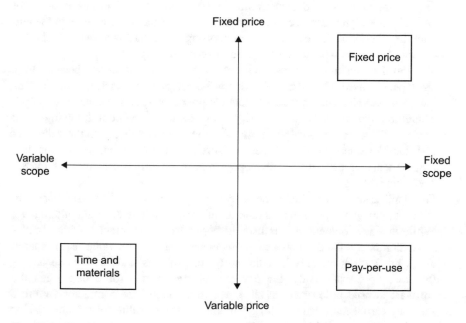

Fig. 12.2 Classification of traditional contract types, based on Opelt et al. (2013)

- First, who bears the risk whether the *right software* is built? This refers to the risk that the resulting software in the end provides the features and interfaces that are "needed," i.e., that have business value. Therefore, we call this the **value risk**.
- Second, who bears the risk whether the *software is built correctly*? This in turn means the risk whether the software is developed in an economically efficient manner. It includes the general software development risks addressed above, which is why we speak of **development risk**.

The three contract models discussed so far are evaluated in the three dimensions as follows:

- As the name implies, the price in the **fixed price contract** is established in advance, which also makes it especially well-suited for situations in which the scope is established as well. Typically, the latter is achieved by preparing a somewhat reliable basis for estimation before the contract is concluded, describing the scope of the project. Accordingly, the value risk is generally borne by the client, who according to the fixed price contract concept has to ensure that the requirements with a sufficient business value are described in advance, and that useless or low-value requirements are eliminated. The contractor has little interest in this. On the other hand, the contractor has to assume the development risk under this contract model, since the client in turn does not care whether higher costs are incurred to implement the requirements in the end than the amount paid. Cost forward progressing (Sect. 8.6) is a useful method to at least determine whether costs will be exceeded early on.
- **Time and material contracts** are found in the opposite quadrant because they are typically used when the scope cannot be established exactly, which means the business value can only be estimated approximately in advance or not at all. Therefore, the client pays for every hour of work, without knowing what business value will be obtained in the end, thereby assuming both the value risk and the development risk. Whether increased effort is caused by unclear requirements or unqualified developers makes no difference under a classic T&M contract.
- For application cases where the scope can be more or less established in advance, **pay-per-use contracts** offer an interesting risk distribution alternative: While the development risk is usually borne by the contractor (since implementation is at a fixed price or not compensated at all), the value risk is shared albeit not entirely balanced. If the software provides a desired value and is therefore used extensively, the payment is higher than for a flop when the software is used little or not at all. Under this model, the contractor therefore assumes partial responsibility for generating business value for the client. This may be a template for agile contract models.

References

adesso AG (2013) drebis – Claims Management System. https://www.adesso.de/en/leistungen/loesungen_sub_leistungen/drebis/index.html. Accessed 1 Mar 2016

Boehm B, Abts C, Chulani S (2000) Software development cost estimation approaches – A survey. J Annals of Software Engineering 10(1–4):177–205. doi:10.1023/A:1018991717352

Opelt A et al (2013) Agile contracts: Creating and managing successful projects with Scrum. Wiley

Agile Contract Models

13

Various suggestions have been made in the past with the objective of better balancing the interests of clients and contractors in agile software projects. We are going to present some of these as examples in this chapter, briefly discussing them based on the three dimensions that we introduced earlier (variability of price and scope as well as risk sharing). One should keep in mind that an unlimited number of mixed forms is not merely conceivable but actually occurs in practice. The examples that follow are sufficient for our purpose, which is to determine the criteria that a fair model should meet.

13.1 Fixed Price per Iteration

When one thinks about agile software development and the challenging basic conditions of the business environment, one might think that nothing is fixed. Naturally this is particularly true of the scope. If we were able to describe it with sufficient accuracy in advance, then we probably would not consider anything other than a fixed price contract anyway. That is why compensation models that appear to take this initial situation into account—by making the price variable as well; T&M models in other words—seem to suggest themselves as an initial approach. But there are problems. Not only is the distribution of risk unfair, as illustrated above (because there is no risk distribution; the full risk is borne by the client)—another imbalance is built in as well: The contractor has an incentive to expend as much effort as possible, regardless of the result that is achieved, because it is paid for every person-day expended. It may be very late in the game before the client suspects that the supplier's team is rather inefficient. But by that time, it is usually too late to engage in discussions about efficiency. Such a contract model trains the supplier to develop an interest in bloated software.

© Springer International Publishing Switzerland 2016
M. Book et al., *Tamed Agility*, DOI 10.1007/978-3-319-41478-2_13

Fortunately, one of the characteristics of agile software projects is that they work with iterations, i.e. sub-projects providing results within defined time periods. This forms the basis of a rather simple contract design model—contracts according to the principle of a fixed price per iteration. The idea is simple: A fixed price is paid per iteration, the basic assumption being that every iteration takes the same amount of time and the development team is kept constant. Let us assume the team consists of five developers and a project manager. A rate of 800 € per person-day was agreed. This means a two-week iteration (or sprint) costs 10 working days × 5 persons × 800 €, which equals 48,000 €. Based on this calculation, one might think this is no different from a simple T&M model. Superficially and from a purely contractual perspective, this may be true, since the supplier makes no commitment about the attainable scope with this model, so both the value risk and development risk are borne by the client.

However, commercial reality often lies outside the legal construct. In this case, the simple fact is that the existence of iterations with defined time limits permits the frequent verification of success and promotes quick reviews and evaluations. The shorter the iteration and the smaller the team, the clearer the objective of the iteration is going to be before the start of the sprint. This means the client will be that much more disappointed if this objective is not achieved. Maybe not after the first, but most likely after the second and definitely after the third iteration, the discussion will not only turn to underestimated complexity in this scenario but also to the efficiency of the team. While the risks formally remain on the client side, the contractor will develop a vital interest in measures that improve efficiency and quality—especially when the client not only looks disappointed but angry as well. Certainly it becomes more difficult for the client to change suppliers the further the project has progressed (which is the actual threat and therefore the motivator for the contractor). However, the contract model with a fixed price per iteration [also known as "progressive contracts" (Larman and Vodde 2010)] ensures that it is unlikely to be "too late" to change suppliers, because early escalation is built into the model. Insofar as this mechanism lying outside the legal framework works, it will ensure that at least some of the development risk is shifted to the contractor side, and perhaps even some of the value risk.

13.2 Fixed Price per (Whatever) Point

Under the fixed price per iteration model, we have a discrepancy between the formal contract provisions and the resulting commercial behavior of the parties to the contract. Ultimately this can lead to the desired effect of shifting part of the risk to the contractor. Therefore, would it not make sense to find a more direct way of accomplishing this, putting into place contract provisions to ensure that the contractor earns less if it builds software of lesser quality, and more if it delivers better software? (Or, since "worse quality" and "better quality" are difficult to define clearly in a contract, if the supplier achieves a greater or lesser scope per iteration?)

However, this too is more difficult to measure than one might think. Surely, giving the contractor an incentive (with whatever contractual provisions) to produce many lines of code cannot be a sensible construct. What we really want is a model that rewards efficiency or cost-effectiveness, that is to say the ratio between the invested effort and the resulting output. This has led to contract models that attempt to evaluate the output produced in an iteration (while the effort is already well defined with the fixed price per iteration), and to establish commercial provisions on this basis.

While this is a nice idea, it poses a virtually unsolvable problem. One might think of using function points as a measure of the output produced in an iteration. If this were a meaningful measurement, we would have found an excellent compensation model in the form of a "price per function point" (or a hundred or thousand function points), regardless of the effort that was required in the iteration to realize this scope of functionality. The function point method is after all standardized. There are certified function point analysts and one could shift the development risk to the supplier fairly according to the completed function points. The supplier is only paid for the scope actually delivered and is therefore very much interested in working efficiently. Such models are in fact used, but they do not constitute an elegant solution. This is because nobody needs function points. What one really needs in order to distribute the second risk fairly as well is business value, but that is even more difficult to measure. Constructs such as story points or feature points (or generally "units of work") are supposed to relativize this, but often turn out to be measurements of effort rather than value in practice (Larman and Vodde 2010).

With the Interaction Room and value annotations, however, we have an instrument available to determine the value of a feature, a process or an application in a structured manner, at least within the stakeholders' frame of reference (Sect. 3.3). Ultimately this does not yet provide us with a usable unit for a contract provision, since the Interaction Room does not supply a value in euros either. If it did, determining a fair price per "unit of work" would be easy, since it would already be established and the contractor could consider whether it can realize this unit of work at the specified price. Nevertheless, the value annotations from the Interaction Room provide us with indications of value relationships between features, processes or applications within the given frame of reference for the project. This will form the basis for deriving the adVANTAGE model in Chap. 15.

13.3   Money for Nothing, Change for Free

The model "money for nothing, change for free" (Sutherland 2008) also belongs in the category of contract models that have more of a fixed price character, but are designed to shift part of the risk to the contractor. Aside from the agreeable name, this model actually has a certain charm and interesting background mechanisms. It is based on the fixed price per iteration model (Sect. 13.1), adding two simple rules.

Once again the starting point is the assumption that the implementation team is stable, the length of the iterations stays more or less the same and—in addition—there is a list of features (or user stories, or some other kind of work and value units). These also have to be planned for iterations in a product backlog at a very high level.

Now the client can exchange features between two iterations at any time, similar to our requirements exchange (Sect. 8.3). Based on the assumption that features have approximately the same magnitude (and therefore similar development effort), the client can perform such exchanges without changing the price (change for free). The idea behind this rule is comparatively simple: From iteration to iteration, the client keeps gaining a better feeling for the value of individual features thanks to actual user feedback. This is because an actual working version of the software realized thus far is available after each iteration in the best agile sense. Therefore, the client will shift the features for which the highest business value is expected to early versions of the software.

Eventually a point is reached where only features with a low business value remain in the backlog. Now the client can decide at any time to terminate development because additional effort (in the form of the fixed price per iteration) will no longer generate a lot of additional business value. The fundamental mechanism of this model is that the contractor is interested in this as well, since it gets a termination premium corresponding to 20 % of the saved effort without having to continue working (money for nothing). Of course, this is particularly attractive when the developers can be subsequently deployed in a new project without idle time.

When the typical margins of third-party software providers in the custom development business are taken into account, terminating such a project is in fact lucrative which means the interest of the client and contractor is aligned. Both are very much interested in creating business value as quickly as possible (and they share the value risk if this is not accomplished). Just like with the fixed price per iteration model, the development risk is contractually/formally borne by the client. However, the supplier too will strive to work as efficiently as possible here, since this leads to the desired project termination by the client that much sooner. Certainly the idea of considering the termination of a project by the client a success takes some getting used to. But that does not change the charm of this contract model. Admittedly the assumption that features have approximately the same magnitude is a weak point of this model, which is why we will come back to it when discussing the adVANTAGE model later on.

13.4   Shared Pain/Shared Gain

The goal to share risk in case a project gets more expensive than planned (in the form of value risk or development risk) can generally be achieved in two ways. One can put the greatest possible value on a fixed price and then either build variable elements directly into the contract or select contractual constructs that provide incentives for corresponding behavior of the provider. Or one approaches the problem by choosing the T&M model (which fundamentally increases risk on the client side) and then builds in elements intended to prevent the contractor from having an elevated interest in expending as much effort as possible, regardless of what the result is. The shared pain/shared gain model falls into this category. It is a mix of a pure T&M approach and a model incorporating the realization of a certain number of "points" (with all the resulting problems, as described in Sect. 13.2). Since it was proposed by Martin (2004), it is also referred to as "Bob Martin's idea".

The model is based on the initial evaluation of the software being developed, in two dimensions—first in points (such as function points) to assess the output produced, and second in person-days as the usual way to measure the effort expected to be expended in order to produce the intended output. Let us assume the desired result is software with a scope of complexity of 10,000 points, and the estimated implementation effort is 1000 person-days. If we also assume an agreed daily rate of 1000 € per person-day, the theoretical fixed price for the project would be 1 million €. Since we are in a T&M-based context here, this means nothing other than the payment of 1 million € if the team delivers a perfect result. In this idealized world where we are not only able to estimate the effort but the software can also be evaluated in points, one could, however, also say that the price per point is 100 €. If the team builds the desired features exactly in the end (reaching precisely 10,000 points), 1 million € would also be payable under a fixed price per point model (Sect. 13.2).

Let us briefly stay with the T&M example. In this case, reduced effort by, say, 20 % would cause the price to drop to 800,000 €. Increased effort by the same percentage would lead to a price of 1.2 million €. Simple so far. The idea of shared pain/shared gain is to mitigate the effects of increased or reduced effort, giving the contractor an incentive to develop as efficiently as possible. This is where the points come into play along with a discount on both the daily rate and the fixed price per point. According to the model, not only the effort but the actual output also plays a role in pricing, for example by paying 500 € instead of 1000 € per person-day but then adding a premium of 50 € per point earned (instead of the arithmetical 100 €). In case of perfect performance, this means that the price stays exactly the same at 1 million €   (1000 person-days × 500 € + 10,000 points × 50 €). If the team requires 20 % less effort (with the same output), the resulting price is 900,000 € while the price increases to 1.1 million € if the effort is exceeded by 20 %. As a result, the contractor is interested in the most efficient possible development since this leads to a higher yield.

The problem with this model is readily apparent—evaluating the software in points (however, they may be defined), both ex ante and ex post—a difficult problem that cannot even be handled identically before and after the project.

13.5 Multi-stage Contract Models

So far we have placed a lot of emphasis on the "fair" distribution of risks in the discussion of various contract types for agile software projects. Different contract models make it possible to handle risk distribution in various ways—that is to say, dealing with the question of who incurs what costs in the end, which is open at the outset. Clearly an essential aspect plays into managing such risk positions, which means dealing with uncertainty: trust. If there was unlimited trust between the parties to the contract, we might not need contracts at all. At the very least, we would have to give far less thought to the ultimate distribution of the costs and risks resulting from uncertainty. Clearly and for understandable reasons, however, the trust between companies in a client/supplier relationship is anything but unlimited, and that is why simple models such as pure fixed price or T&M contracts are not suitable. No rational contractor will agree to a fixed price in case of great uncertainty regarding the system scope to be realized, since this would require maximum trust in the client. Otherwise the client could expand the scope endlessly and the supplier would have to include all those many ideas in the software at the fixed price. Conversely many clients shy away from pure T&M situations since they cannot trust the contractor not to exploit the situation, filling gaps in the specifications with unnecessary features in more and more person-days.

Some of the contract models described above are already quite well suited for handling such entirely normal trust deficits. Mixed forms that address this issue even better have in some cases already been developed from these in practice and in the literature. Multi-stage contract models or multi-phase contract models are one such category (Larman and Vodde 2010). These are forms of cooperation that stagger different contract types over time in order to account for the fact that uncertainty is usually greater at the outset than in the middle of a project. The client and contractor also get to know each other better in the course of a project, gradually building trust, which may justify a change in the contract model during the project term.

This game can be played in entirely different directions depending on the negotiating power, trust position and experience of the partners involved, as well as the degree of uncertainty and the type of project. Let us examine two examples:

- If both partners agree that the scope is largely open, the fixed price per iteration model is suitable for the first phase. This allows the parties to jointly learn through experience what the true scope of the project is during the initial iterations. In this first phase, the client is advancing trust by financing a few iterations at fixed prices without knowing the result that will be delivered. Then the model is turned around after a while, once the parties are sufficiently familiar with each other, trust has been established and the understanding of what is actually supposed to be built is much better. If a backlog that can be planned and estimated has been developed in the meantime, the second half of the project could be implemented using the fixed price per feature model. Now the contractor advances trust by assuming that the client will not subsequently inflate the scope in detail.

- If at least specific features out of the overall scope can be adequately evaluated, the client can also argue that the contractor should prove its performance in the first few releases. Typical fixed prices per feature would then be in order during the initial phase. In this case, the supplier advances trust, delivers the desired features at a fixed price and makes the actual effort transparent. The client gains trust in the contractor's ability to perform, and the less clear features can be implemented based on a T&M order or fixed price per iteration in a second phase.

Strictly speaking, multi-stage contract models cannot be viewed as a separate contract type but as a combination of "simple" contract types in a series over time. They make it possible to manage risks and build trust over a period of time and are an option in particular when the client and contractor want to work together for a longer period of time or at least intend to implement a larger scope together. Whether the design of the second phase is described in detail at the outset, contractually defined or merely discussed as a possible option is solely at the discretion of the parties to the contract.

13.6 Summary

In Fig. 13.1 we arranged the agile contract types discussed so far in the schema from Fig. 12.2. It is based on the high-level differentiation that agile contract types either tend to have a fixed price orientation with the integration of variable elements, or follow the concept of T&M contracts with the addition of elements to reduce costs. The second group includes the shared pain/shared gain model in particular, which is why it is found in the bottom left quadrant of Fig. 13.1.

Weakening the pure T&M model, the shared pain/shared gain approach has elements that "tame" variability both in regards to the scope and the price. The latter is obviously less variable, since that is precisely what the settlement model intends. If the supplier exceeds the effort, the price per unit of performance drops. Due to the fact that evaluating the scope is mandatory with this model in the form of "points" (of whatever type), which means the scope is discussed in detail early on, somewhat less uncertainty can generally be expected.

Among the contract types more akin to the fixed price world, the fixed price per iteration model is surely the one that most clearly represents the top left quadrant which previously remained open. The client has price certainty since the cost of an iteration is precisely defined, but the scope is largely open since there is no guarantee what features will actually be implemented and therefore what business value will be generated. In order to mitigate precisely this, the fixed price per point model and the "money for nothing, change for free" model were developed. Since the latter approach offers somewhat more content flexibility because the scope can be

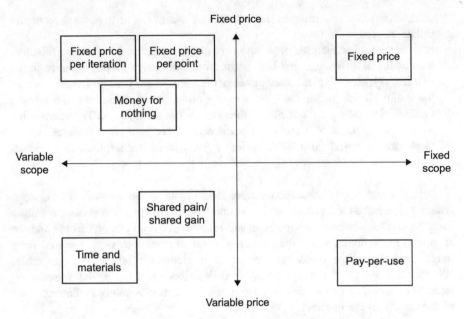

Fig. 13.1 Classification of traditional and agile contract types, based on Opelt et al. (2013)

changed at no cost, it was placed slightly more in the variable scope direction in Fig. 13.1 and, due to the possibility of terminating the project at any time, further away from the fixed price.

With the contract types that were discussed, we therefore have a rather broad spectrum of possibilities for designing the legal and economic relationships between the partners in agile software projects. Some of them, like the fixed price per iteration model, are practical, easy to implement and proven many times, but offer little certainty for the client and fail to achieve balanced risk participation by the contractor. Others like the shared pain/shared gain model share the risk far better, but experience has shown that they lack practicality since they are based on difficult-to-capture "points". With the adVANTAGE model, we will next present an additional alternative that shares the risk fairly, is easy to use and enables good control by the client. Obviously such an alternative can only be realized on the basis of more trust.

References

Larman C, Vodde B (2010) Practices for scaling lean & agile development: Large, multisite, and offshore product development with large-scale Scrum. Addison Wesley

Martin R (2004) Estimating costs up front. Post in comp.software.extreme-programming, https://groups.google.com/d/msg/comp.software.extreme-programming/egY-zCgthSo/Y9Pzha0_IJoJ. Accessed 1 Mar 2016

Opelt A et al (2013) Agile contracts: Creating and managing successful projects with Scrum. Wiley

Sutherland J (2008) Agile 2008 – Money for nothing. https://www.scruminc.com/agile-2008-money-for-nothing-2/. Accessed 1 Mar 2016

Key adVANTAGE Principles

14

In this chapter, we introduce the adVANTAGE contract model that can serve as a framework for agile software projects undertaken by external contractors. In this name, "ad" stands for "agile development", and the whole term aims to indicate that both parties to the contract should gain an advantage compared with conventional approaches and the contract models they typically involve. This advantage can take many forms. It depends on:

- the application of an agile method (fast start of development activity, omission of costly advance specifications, fast availability of software that can be demonstrated, close collaboration between users and developers, flexible adaptation of requirements, acceptance of late requirements, etc.), and
- the application of a fair contract model that represents the agile method (eliminating inflated costs for specification work, billing according to features actually delivered, fair distribution of risks, fair distribution of opportunities).

From a high-level perspective, adVANTAGE consists of three elements: a price model, a contract model, and procedures that can be applied in the Interaction Room. In short, adVANTAGE = price + contract + procedures. Like the Interaction Room, adVANTAGE is shaped by the recognition that custom software development by an external contractor model always involves considerable uncertainty. The exact result of the project is not known in advance, there are many ways that the product could be built, and nobody can predict exactly how expensive the whole project be in the end. Accepting this is the core idea behind adVANTAGE. The model has been tested and adapted many times in practice, resulting in a framework for pragmatically handling the economic aspects which can (and should) be adapted to the individual situation of every new project.

The adVANTAGE model supplies general provisions for the legal and commercial aspects that have to be regulated between the client and contractor in an agile custom development project. Accordingly, Appendix C.1 provides a concrete template for an actual contract document. However, it is much more important to illuminate the

© Springer International Publishing Switzerland 2016
M. Book et al., *Tamed Agility*, DOI 10.1007/978-3-319-41478-2_14

fundamental principles underlying the adVANTAGE model. For one thing, we recommend adaptation to concrete project situations, and for another, we believe that it is far more important to develop a good feeling for the compatibility of cultures of the client and contractor than to establish legal certainty down to every detail.

While the adVANTAGE model is a very good fit for some project types, it may not be suitable for others. This chapter therefore introduces some general principles underlying adVANTAGE and discusses whether the application of adVANTAGE is suitable for a certain project constellation. These principles are a willingness of the supplier to assume risk, mutual trust, budget certainty, shared pain, rewarding efficiency, and of course agility. If the organizational cultures of the partners in a project match these principles (discussed in more detail in the following sections), the adVANTAGE model should be considered. When a partner's culture clashes with some of the principles, the model is better not used.

For example, we will see that the adVANTAGE model would lose its foundation without the supplier's willingness to assume a certain measure of financial risk (which is not solely within the supplier's control). There are however contractors in the IT sector whose risk management policies are so strict that getting them to sign an adVANTAGE contract would be simply impossible. This may be desirable if company policy demands a choice of one of the less risky contract types described above.

14.1   Commitment to Agility

Making agility a core principle of a contract model for agile projects may sound very much like a tautology. However, one should actually seriously consider whether the project for which one is seeking a legal-commercial framework can truly be realized best using an agile approach. If a detailed specification that supports estimates is already available for example, with a lot of groundwork having been done and leaving little uncertainty regarding the characteristics of the development results, then why not use a classic plan-driven development approach and agree on a fixed price? But perhaps all stakeholders agree that they want to be as free as possible, deciding again from iteration to iteration on how to continue— these are indications in favor of an agile method.

Deciding in favor of agility in the partnership between a client and contractor does not however mean establishing an agile process model such as Scrum. It mainly assumes the readiness to accept uncertainty—not just uncertainty regarding the resulting software product, but also regarding

- the number of iterations required to achieve an adequate, acceptable, or desirable result,
- the capabilities of the chosen technology and the resulting technology risk,
- the productivity of the development team and its progression over time, possibly through numerous iterations,

- the obtainable quality measured by the number and severity of errors that occur, and the work required to identify and eliminate them,
- the effort per iteration, including overhead such as project management and communication,
- the total effort for the project as a whole,

and other circumstances that cannot be estimated exactly or at all in advance. The decision in favor of agility means that such uncertainty is not only acknowledged, not only accepted, but understood as an essential characteristic of this concrete impending project. This applies to other areas as well. At least in an external service provider context, agility not only affects the development team, but the entire organization: A new way of thinking is required from Purchasing to Legal to Controlling. Agility in this context is the answer to uncertainty. But this does not mean that agility makes uncertainty go away—it merely forces all stakeholders to deal with it consciously and based on clear rules. But since rules always leave loopholes for egoistic action, mutual trust is essential.

14.2 Mutual Trust

Mutual trust between a client and contractor, i.e., between legally and economically independent organizations that each serve their own goals—is that possible? Is trust not more of a human affair? Yes and no. For one thing, all organizations, including the contractual partners in software projects, consist of people. For another, economic science does in fact define the term of inter-organizational trust (Lane and Bachmann 2000) as the concept of a company fundamentally assuming fairness in the actions of another company or its staff. In agile software projects under the adVANTAGE model, this is absolutely essential. Unlike some of the contract models outlined above, the adVANTAGE model leaves some leeway and flexibility for responding to specific project situations, which always means freedom to negotiate on a small scale as well—that is to say, within the framework of a signed contract. This becomes obvious for example with the question of whether a certain feature is "done." In the description of the adVANTAGE procedures that follows (Chap. 15), a lot will depend on whether the implementation of a feature X planned for a sprint has been concluded (whether the feature is "done"). Depending on how this question is answered, other mechanisms apply for planning the next sprint but also for the settlement of the sprint that has just ended. As we will see, "done" can mean various things ranging from "a feature that could be called X exists as a result of the sprint" to "a feature exists which more than adequately represents X, takes all exceptions and special cases into account, has been tested, and is free of defects as far as discernible."

We have purposely left the Definition of Done (DoD) open in the adVANTAGE model. In doing so, we have built in the risk that the parties to the contract will not be able to agree, or only after protracted discussions, whether a feature in a specific case is done or completed so that money is owed. There are two reasons for this:

- The attempt to establish a DoD that is comprehensible and as detailed as possible, and therefore preferably a degree of completion that can be determined by an algorithm, appears diametrically opposite to the agile philosophy. Those who choose an agile software development method because they accept uncertainty should also tolerate the fact that common sense has to decide on what is "done" in specific cases. If this is not acceptable, one should decide whether writing a detailed specification first is perhaps preferable after all. That is not to say that there should be no DoD. It should exist, but one should not fall victim to the illusion of having established an unambiguous decision-making basis.
- If the contractual partners suspect that the risk of leaving the DoD open will lead to disagreements, or even legal disputes, then working together in an agile project is not recommended in the first place. When one doubts one's own willingness to compromise, or fears the other side cheat when given a chance, trust is lacking either way.

The problem with the DoD is just one of many examples of the need for trust in agile projects. Of course, there would be numerous reasons not to trust each other in agile software projects. The client could accuse the contractor of

- tending to deploy the second-rate software developers for the project while reserving the best for the risky fixed-price projects,
- sticking as closely as possible to the letter of the features in the backlog, implementing them without attempting to generate business value,
- actually focusing on optimizing his own capacity utilization even though a certain price risk is assumed,

and much more. Conversely, the contractor could accuse the client of

- dragging its feet when it comes to the client's duties to cooperate, because business operations always take priority,
- attempting to stuff as much functionality as possible into every little feature, which may only be outlined in broad strokes, or
- deliberately delaying acceptance procedures and approval of the next sprint in order to get more performance.

All of that can happen, since the project participants are after all employed either by the client or by the contractor. Yet all these cases merely represent a very short-sighted view of optimizing personal benefits. In most cases, both sides should have a vital interest in long-term cooperation. The closer a client/supplier relationship in custom software development is and the longer it lasts, the more efficient it becomes. Not only do the teams develop a shared understanding of the business relationships in the course of time, they also use the same vocabulary, have shared experiences and learned from them, and have experienced success and worked out the crucial reasons for that success in retrospect. In short, the longer teams work together in such a relationship, the less room there is for misunderstandings and other effects that reduce efficiency.

14.3   Contractor's Willingness to Assume Risk

In Table 12.1, we illustrated the various maturity levels of contractors in the IT sector and discussed these in the context of pay-per-use models. The central theory was that contractors with a high maturity level (and the associated in-depth, broad-based business experience) tend to be more willing to accept transaction-based business models. With such models, compensation for software development is not determined as a fixed price or depending on the effort expended for realization, but depends solely on the actual use of the system. Highly mature contractors are generally more willing to accept risk in such a relationship because they are in a good position to assess the business value of the software. This is similar when it comes to the willingness to assume the risk associated with the adVANTAGE model.

A key element of the willingness to assume risk based on experience is the absence of knowledge gaps in business contexts. When a contractor has been active in a certain business domain for years, it will have numerous business experts among its employees who know exactly how a medical risk assessment for the reinsurance of life insurance contracts has to be implemented, or what the detailed process for central profit determination in a lottery has to look like. The more experience, the less uncertainty. This is why the maturity of a contractor often enables its willingness to assume risk. Of course, there are exceptions as well, namely contractors that have developed increasingly efficient risk management processes in the course of their evolution, and are hardly willing to accept imponderabilities without T&M protection.

The willingness of the contractor to assume risk is essential for the adVAN-TAGE model. A vital element of the model is to share the risk arising from uncertainty between the two sides. This means part of the risk always lands on the supplier's side. Those unable to accept this risk should not consider entering into an adVANTAGE contract with a client. Those who have some courage on the other hand may find that adVANTAGE is a construct that can be used to win clients with the argument that the contractor assumes part of the general risk. Aside from extensive experience in the business domain relevant for the project, the following points can promote the supplier's willingness to assume risk:

- A company culture that generally recognizes opportunities in addition to risks and takes a long-term view
- The availability of teams that are stable over the long term, have already implemented numerous projects together, and work smoothly together

- Extensive expertise in the various technical domains in order to minimize technology risks
- Previous good experience with the client, as a foundation for a high level of trust.

14.4   Budget Security

In discussing the various contract types for agile projects, we have already noted that absolute budget security does not exist—certainly not with T&M-oriented approaches—and residual uncertainty remains even with fixed-price constructs. One way or another, features can be forgotten or described with clearly insufficient complexity. Any resourceful supplier will quickly open a change request in such cases, so the original budget immediately goes out the window. So if absolute budget certainty does not exist, we should at least implement mechanisms that make it likely that the budget will not be exceeded to an intolerable extent. The adVANTAGE model uses various constructs to achieve this. One of them is the adoption of cost forward progressing (Sect. 8.6), and another is the use of the risk map (Sect. 8.4). A third element is daily rates at which the supplier actually does not really want to work, as discussed in the following section.

14.5   Shared Pain

A central element, if not *the* central element of the adVANTAGE model, is shared pain. In brief, this means that the contractor suffers (almost) as much as the client from the risks that materialize in the project.

In classic software development contract models—as shown above—some effort is made to clearly assign the two general risks to one of the two parties. The value risk, i.e., the risk whether the desired business value is achieved and at what cost, is preferably (mostly) handed to the client. This is where one expects the greatest business expertise and responsibility for a reasonable description of what needs to be built. The development risk, on the other hand, is (mostly) handed to the contractor in most models, since it can be assumed that the contractor is responsible for the hiring of competent employees, conducting adequate and accurate tests, and mastering the technology.

The core problem with this assignment of risks and the related costs is the fact that, if the risks materialize, each side attempts to keep *its own* risks in check. The risks of the other partner are of very little interest. In case of doubt, worsening the risk position of the other side is accepted if this improves one's own position. The greatest benefit would however be achieved if both parties focused on avoiding a project disaster, which costs both sides a lot of money, effort, and aggravation. But as long as both sides are busy keeping a close eye on their own risks, there is no room for cooperative disaster avoidance. The adVANTAGE model attempts to solve this problem by imposing all risks equally on both parties. It simply does not differentiate whether the additional effort for realizing a certain feature or an entire iteration results from lack of developer skills or imprecise functional specification. All discussions of this kind simply do not take place under the adVANTAGE model. Not only does this save a lot of work and is easier on the nerves, it also encourages reasonable behavior. But how? The simple mechanism that enables this consists of two daily rates for calculating the price to be paid, combined with a calculation procedure that is established at the start of the project and then left unchanged.

Chapter 15 describes this process in detail. For an understanding of shared pain, this much can be said here in advance: Based on a list of features (mostly just named but not described in detail), the estimated effort for each feature is negotiated at the start of the project. Methods such as planning poker can be used to make an initial estimate that is obviously subject to uncertainty. Both parties know that excessive, petty haggling about this estimate is not only meaningless but appears downright ridiculous due to the uncertainty—this has been agreed on, otherwise an adVANTAGE project would not be carried out. These initial (highly uncertain) estimates per feature are never touched again. New estimates are only made in case of entirely new features that crop up during the project. Two different daily rates are negotiated next. One is the "regular" daily rate and should be in line with the market, including a profit margin. The second, "reduced" daily rate should be set to a "painful" level so it does not ruin the supplier, but also so the supplier is not interested in working for this daily rate. In practice, this second daily rate will be somewhere close to the cost of production. Fine-tuning it is important for the success of the model. Once these parameters have been negotiated, between the client and contractor, the project can proceed. At the end of each iteration, the effort estimated in advance is billed at the "normal" daily rate. Effort that exceeds the previously negotiated effort for a feature (or the iteration) is billed at the "painful" daily rate. There is no discussion, especially regarding the cause of exceeding the budget, since the pain is shared: The client has to pay, but the supplier is not making a profit. The client and supplier share a common destiny; they do not discuss the past and both have exactly the same interest: meeting the estimated effort.

14.6   Efficiency Incentives

The principle of shared pain establishes an important mechanism to encourage aligned behavior. To further boost this effect (and to add vocabulary with a positive connotation), a gain can also be shared under the adVANTAGE model (or at least allocated fairly). A gain in a software project always results from a budget excess at the end of an iteration. Various ways of handling the reduction in effort and therefore the monetary savings are conceivable here. An agreement should be reached at the start of the project or during the contract negotiations. An iteration could be billed at the planned budget as a minimum, regardless of whether it was actually used up. This encourages the contractor to achieve the greatest possible budget savings. It does nothing for the client. Therefore, the client will likely want the cost savings to be fairly distributed. For example, half of the amount could be paid out as a bonus to the contractor, and the other half could be saved by the client.

It is also conceivable (and sometimes practiced) to relate such bonuses to the total effort for the project rather than individual features or iterations. This assumes that the bonus was negotiated in advance or is simply determined as the sum of the budgets for individual features. While it does not change a lot on the bottom line, it encourages looking at the big picture. That is after all the aim of the adVANTAGE model: For both partners to have their eye on the same goal.

Reference

Lane C, Bachmann R (eds) (2000) Trust within and between organizations: Conceptual issues and empirical applications. Oxford University Press

adVANTAGE Procedures

15

In this chapter, we provide a detailed description of the adVANTAGE model for the cooperation between contractual partners in agile custom development projects. The following sections cover the individual project phases from project initiation via development to project completion and take a particularly close look at how the individual development iterations are planned, monitored, and billed.

15.1 Initial Requirements Collection and Budget Estimate

In many cases, not much more than an idea exists in the earliest stage of the project (as in the example in Sect. 16.1). The first step in an agile software project therefore is to determine the initial requirements and describe them in a list of features. This step is well supported by the IR:scope and IR:agile, since they promote the discussion and evaluation of features and their assignment to sprints over the entire course of the project. We have described the initial preparation of a feature canvas in Sect. 5.2, which now becomes the basis for the first activity described by the adVANTAGE contract model: the initial budget estimate. During the transition from the feature canvas to the product backlog (Sect. 8.1), we estimated efforts for the individual features in person-days. These are our initial estimates (IE) of the pure development effort. This restriction is important, since the adVANTAGE model differentiates between two different types of effort that are handled differently:

- The **pure development effort** is the number of person-days expended by the developers and architects for implementing and testing a feature within a sprint.
- This is distinct from the **overhead** for planning the sprints, the work of the scrum master, the daily scrum meetings, and other activities not associated directly with implementation.

© Springer International Publishing Switzerland 2016
M. Book et al., *Tamed Agility*, DOI 10.1007/978-3-319-41478-2_15

This differentiation is important for the adVANTAGE model because the second effort category is billed at a base rate which is fixed per sprint and negotiated at the start of the project. This constitutes a fixed price component within the commercial model. The following costs of the contractor are intended to be covered by the base rate (BR):

- **All effort for planning a sprint**. This includes prioritizing the features and establishing the extent and scope of the sprint. Generally, this is done in a workshop with the client.
- **Effort for the work of the scrum master**. This role's activities should be deliberately kept out of the T&M-based settlement component because the scrum master is responsible for establishing and enforcing the agile framework, rather than directly adding value in development. Depending on the size of the project, a full-time scrum master is not always necessary, especially with experienced teams.
- **Effort for attending regular meetings**. This primarily refers to the daily scrum and other regular meetings. Billing this effort through the base rate mainly aims to prevent discussions about the meetings' necessity at the end of a sprint. Either we believe that these meetings are important or not, in which case they should be omitted (although we strongly advise against this).
- **Warranty effort**. While a certain percentage surcharge on the total price is normally applied in classic fixed price projects (between five and 15 %, depending on risk and complexity based on experience), the warranty in T&M-based models is somewhat more difficult to handle. Adding a percentage surcharge to the actual effort expended means a significant uncertainty risk for the client on the one hand and is not necessarily reasonable on the other hand. Just because more effort was expended on development, this does not necessarily result in more warranty cases. The opposite is possible as well. Therefore, the adVANTAGE model calls for including warranty provisions in the base rate. Since the size of the development team and the duration of the sprints are known, an experienced estimator can determine an amount that is adequate for the company's risk policy. After all, warranty provisions are no more than qualified guesswork on the basis of empirical knowledge anyway.

Once the base rate has been negotiated between the parties to the contract at the start of the project, it remains fixed and is not touched or discussed again—unless there are significant changes to the project setup. A major change in the sprint volume, for example, by adjusting the sprint duration or altering the size of the team, can constitute such an exception. However, one should resist the temptation to start a debate about the base rate with every small change. This would not promote trust, which we have already argued to be the most valuable asset in an adVANTAGE project.

As part of our initial budget estimate, we now have to multiply the base rate by the number of expected sprints. If the N features f_i in the product backlog have an initial estimate $IE(f_i)$ and we know the planned team size and sprint duration, the number of sprints S results in an initial approximation by simple division. Then, the initial budget IB is quite simple to determine:

$$IB = \sum_{1 \leq i \leq N} IE(f_i) \times DR_1 + S \times BR$$

Here, DR_1 is the "normal" daily rate agreed between the client and contractor in case of meeting the budget (Sect. 14.5). Whether and to what extent this initial budget can already serve as a benchmark for incentives is discussed in Sect. 14.6. Initially, it is just a value assumed by the client and contractor to approximately equal the effort required to realize the project. Neither side has forgotten that this is subject to great uncertainty and that things may develop differently than planned. At first though, the parties to the contract reach an agreement that contains the following provisions (a concrete draft contract can be found in Appendix C.1):

- An agile custom development project is carried out in a client/supplier relationship. The approach, roles, and obligations to cooperate as well as the respective tasks are agreed and regulated.
- Both parties assume that S sprints will be carried out to realize the target system. The initial team size and therefore the numeric scope of an average sprint are established.
- The base rate BR is defined and established as a fixed price per sprint. Two daily rates DR are agreed on as well, with DR_1 applying to effort expended within the calculated budget per feature, and DR_2 applying to effort required in addition. There is no differentiation between the realization of value risk or development risk as the cause for the additional effort.
- Each sprint is planned jointly and the scope is established based on a product backlog, i.e., a sorted list of features that is prioritized by the client. An effort has been estimated for each feature.
- Settlement takes place at the end of a sprint (more details below), also in the literal sense—an invoice is issued and paid. The acceptance of the corresponding features is a prerequisite. After the sprint, the client can reprioritize and establish the scope of the next sprint (the sprint backlog) or terminate/end the project.

These are the basic rules of the adVANTAGE model. The details are described in the following sections.

15.2   Feature Prioritization and Sprint Definition

After a well-filled product backlog has been collected in the IR:agile, with an estimated pure development effort assigned to each feature, and after the client and contractor have agreed on the base amount, the number and extent of the sprints, and therefore the overall budget, the features have to be prioritized and the scope of the first sprint (i.e., the sprint backlog) has to be established. The annotations placed on the canvases of the IR:agile are an important tool in this process. A cluster of these annotations (which we have summarized into two categories in the following) should ensure that a high priority is assigned to a feature so that it is implemented in an early sprint.

- **Value (business value/user value)**: Annotations from this category mark features that promise increased value creation if they are implemented. The strategy behind this principle is to quickly create value that is recognized as such by all stakeholders. Not only does this improve project acceptance and therefore the probability of success, it can even reduce costs. This is because the features that accumulate at the bottom end of the sorted list do not add any particular value, and may not need to be implemented at all in the end. More about this is explained in Sect. 15.6.
- **Risk (complexity/uncertainty)**: Annotations from this category indicate a high level of risk, which results in greater effort if it materializes or makes implementation impossible in the worst case. This may be due to technical or business reasons. As the case may be, development teams tend to put such features on the back burner and hope for the usual miracle at the end of the project—"don't worry, it will be ok." Since things do not usually work out that way, identifying such risks early on is a good idea. Therefore, high-risk features should be included in early sprints as well, if only either to eliminate the risk or to understand it precisely and manage it.

Based on the annotations, a moderated discussion process for prioritization follows. The goal is to bring all features into a linear sequence. Features with the corresponding value and risk annotations are candidates for a high priority. Low-priority candidates are those which are not necessarily required in the first release in order to put the system into operation. There are often more of these features than one might think, and it is a good idea to be very critical in reviewing whether a feature belongs in the initial-release category after all. Features applying only to a small number of exotic business scenarios can be bumped to a later release, and sometimes remain in that limbo forever—which is a good thing.

The IR coaches play a special role in the feature prioritization phase. They have to ensure that the argumentation for a production release is strictly based on value, risk and requirements. On the other hand, they have to make sure nobody suffers too much because none of their favorite features are assigned a high priority. This is no easy task depending on the mix of stakeholders. The negotiation process ends with a sorted list of features (the prioritized product backlog), which is shown schematically in Fig. 15.1.

Simple addition is sufficient to get a suggestion for the scope of the first sprint. The first n requirements for which the sum of the effort estimates is just barely less than or equal to the specified sprint scope are planned for the release. The sprint scope is simply the sprint duration times the number of developers.

Fig. 15.1 Initial prioritized
product backlog

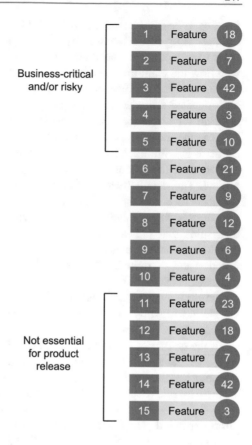

Business-critical
and/or risky

Not essential
for product
release

1	Feature	18
2	Feature	7
3	Feature	42
4	Feature	3
5	Feature	10
6	Feature	21
7	Feature	9
8	Feature	12
9	Feature	6
10	Feature	4
11	Feature	23
12	Feature	18
13	Feature	7
14	Feature	42
15	Feature	3

For example, if our team had four developers and the sprint duration was four weeks, the sprint scope would be 80 person-days and the first five requirements from Fig. 15.1 could be implemented in an initial sprint—provided the team agrees on exactly this scope (the sprint backlog is the result of a moderated negotiation, although compromise is generally promoted by the methodology). Let us further assume the daily rate DR_1 is 1000 € and the agreed base rate BR is 22,000 €. This makes the initial budget for the first sprint according to the above formula

$$IB_1 = (18 + 7 + 42 + 3 + 10) \times 1000\,\text{€} + 22{,}000\,\text{€} = 102{,}000\,\text{€}.$$

15.3 Sprint Implementation and Controlling

Now comes the implementation. The developers go to work, so does the product owner, and the scrum master makes sure everything happens within the specified organizational framework. But before the coding begins, the effort for the individual features to be implemented in the sprint is estimated in detail. The method for this estimate is up to the team—they may prepare a detailed specification first or continue to accept some uncertainty. From the commercial perspective, it is not relevant how the team prepares the detailed estimate, but that it does make an effort to refine the initial estimates on a sprint-by-sprint basis.

A detailed estimate is made for each feature in the sprint backlog, so that we now have an initial estimate $IE(f_i)$ and a detailed estimate $DE(f_i)$ for each feature f_i. What is the meaning of any difference between these two values? Only the initial estimate is commercially relevant for the settlement between the client and contractor, since the parties to the contract agreed to this budget at the beginning of the project. The detailed estimate on the other hand is made far later in the project, possibly in a late sprint, and is therefore based on far more experience and knowledge of the project and the underlying business relationships. There is reason to assume that this figure is more accurate and closer to the actual effort. The detailed estimates are therefore used for sprint planning. They also have a statistical function and are quite likely to offer additional insights in the course of cost forward progressing (Sect. 8.6). This is the case, for example, when we note that the average difference between $IE(f_i)$ and $DE(f_i)$ grows from sprint to sprint. If this is the case, we should urgently take a look at the risk map (Sect. 8.4) to see what may be sources of the problem.

In the course of implementation, all stakeholders also record their actual effort $AE(f_i)$ per feature f_i. In addition to working on the features however, we also need to complete some tasks that cannot be assigned to concrete features but are covered by the base rate (Sect. 15.1). It is of great interest for controlling (not for settlement) to establish an effort budget for the base rate as well and to determine the actual effort expended. The latter is straightforward and results in the value $AE(BR)$. But what is the initially estimated budget $IE(BR)$ of the base rate activities? In order to establish this, we need to take a look at the calculation documents used to establish the base rate. This is usually accomplished with assumptions about the frequency of meetings, the extent of availability for a scrum master (e.g., 0.5 full-time equivalents in smaller projects), and so on. Explicitly excluding the warranty provision, this results in a calculated value for $IE(BR)$ in person-days (PD), so that we can perform pragmatic controlling for these activities as well.

Project controlling now becomes very simple. As long as all team members keep daily records (although weekly recording is often sufficient as well), we can determine the economic position of our project at any time. Figure 15.2 shows a diagram that can be used to determine the current effort situation during a sprint.

The bars are read as follows: An initial budget of $IE(BR) = 22$ PD was estimated for the base rate; 12 PD have already been expended to date. Feature f_2 already went into overspend (OS), since the initially estimated budget $IE(f_2) = 7$ PD has already been exceeded by 2 PD. The other features are still in underspend, since the actual effort of, e.g., $AE(f_3) = 36$ PD is still below the initial estimate $IE(f_3) = 42$ PD.

Fig. 15.2 Determination of effort in a sprint with five features

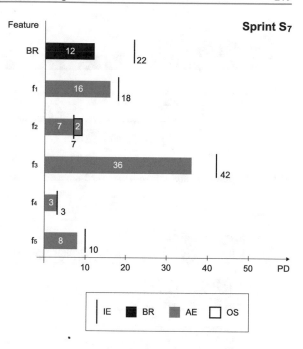

In the course of a properly conducted earned value analysis (Cabri and Griffiths 2006), another value is now recorded for each feature at least on a weekly basis: the estimated remaining effort $RE(f_i)$. To obtain this, the developers are asked how much work they estimate they will still have to put into each feature in order to complete it. Added up across all features in a sprint, this may, for example, result in the picture shown in Fig. 15.3.

The sum of all initial feature estimates in this sprint is 80 PD. A total of 70 PD have already been expended, and the sum of the estimated remaining effort for all features is 15 PD. This means an overspend of 5 PD is predicted. Meanwhile, we see that the project manager expects an underspend (US) of 3 PD on the base rate activities, since only 12 PD of the initially estimated 22 PD have been expended so far, and only 7 PD will likely remain.

We should emphasize that these figures constitute an internal review by the contractor; i.e., they are used for project controlling. Whether and to what extent these figures—beyond the information required for invoicing—are made transparent for the client depends on the corresponding agreements. For example, whether overspending and underspending on the base rate is disclosed to the client is up to the contractor. After all, this is a fixed price component, and the risk is borne entirely by the contractor. On the other hand, greater transparency increases trust, which we like to encourage in adVANTAGE projects.

A possible example of project controlling at the end of a project is shown in Fig. 15.4.

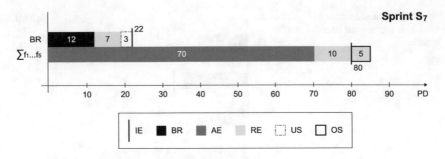

Fig. 15.3 Project controlling with estimated remaining effort during a sprint

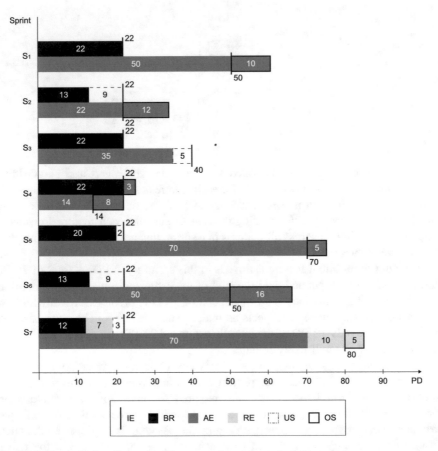

Fig. 15.4 Example for effort controlling per sprint at the end of the project

The last sprint S_7 is still going on in this example and will likely end in an overspend, just like most previous sprints. On the other hand, the base rate appears to be rather generously estimated since initially estimated effort is often not needed, resulting in underspends there.

15.4 Sprint Inspection and Billing

For the client, the project controlling figures from Fig. 15.4 would be presented as shown in Fig. 15.5.

The solid black bars show the fixed compensation of the base rate, which is 22,000 € per sprint in this example. The dark gray bars show compensation for work that is within the respective agreed budget $IE(f_i)$ for the individual features and therefore completed at the regular daily rate DR_1 (here, 1000 €), i.e., $IE(f_i) \times DR_1$ for each feature. Bars with a solid outline represent amounts for work completed at the reduced daily rate DR_2 (here, 600 €), i.e., $(AE(f_i) - IE(f_i)) \times DR_2$ for each feature that went into overspend. This presentation for the client does not reveal whether the fixed price for the base rate was sufficient or not.

So how is the settlement of individual sprints accomplished? This depends on the progress achieved in each sprint, as the following sections show.

15.4.1 Full Completion of Sprint

Let us start by examining the straightforward case where the sprint was finished completely. This means all features planned for the sprint have been realized, tested, and accepted. The adVANTAGE model in fact assumes the acceptance of

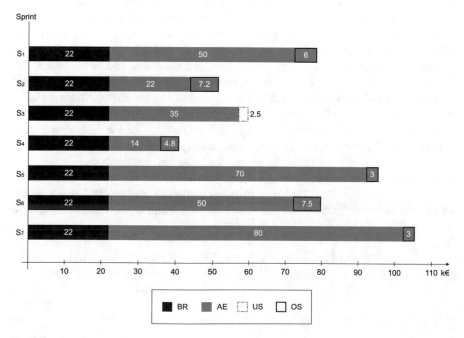

Fig. 15.5 Example of commercial billing of sprints

individual features at the end of a sprint. However, the definition of acceptance is not necessarily equivalent to the legal meaning under a contract for work and labor. In the adVANTAGE model, acceptance of a feature means that the client confirms that the desired feature has been realized, that it is complete in terms of content (that the scope of the feature meets expectations; i.e., the feature is "done"), and that it is of sufficient quality. The final point is important and requires explanation. With the acceptance of a feature at the end of a sprint under the adVANTAGE model, the client is not confirming freedom from defects but completeness in terms of content. This is important for differentiating between billable and non-billable rework in the future:

- If it turns out in the future that an accepted feature should have been implemented differently or that something is missing, a change request is created, which means a new feature is added to the product backlog. The implementation is billed as a new feature according to the adVANTAGE model (which means the client will pay for it).
- If it turns out in the future that an accepted feature is defective with regard to the given specification, which means it was not implemented correctly, the defect has to be rectified free of charge. This means the costs are borne by the contractor.

Of course, a gray area remains between a change request and the rectification of defects, as it does in other software projects as well. This is one of the reasons we talked about trust as a basic requirement in Sect. 14.2. The adVANTAGE model does not offer a solution for this gray area. However, it clearly regulates the transfer of responsibility and the risk of warranty cases in agile development projects. It therefore accomplishes the differentiation between value risk and development risk introduced in Sect. 12.4. The former is about the question of whether the correct software was built (this risk should be borne primarily by the client), while the latter is about the question of whether the software was built correctly (free of defects). This risk should be borne primarily by the contractor. Once a feature has been accepted, the subsequent risk is distributed exactly according to this requirement.

In case of full delivery of the sprint, the settlement procedure is as follows. If all features have been realized and accepted, the budget is compared to the actual effort. In the example from Fig. 15.1, the total budget IB was 102,000 €, composed of the base rate of 22,000 € and the monetary equivalent of the initial estimate for the five planned features:

$$IE(f_1) = 18 \text{ PD}; \ IE(f_2) = 7 \text{ PD}; \ IE(f_3) = 42 \text{ PD}; \ IE(f_4) = 3 \text{ PD}; \ IE(f_5) = 10 \text{ PD}$$

This adds up to an initial effort estimate of 80 PD at an agreed regular daily rate DR_1 of 1000 €, which corresponds to a budget of 80,000 €. Let us further assume that the actually expended effort is as follows:

$$AE(f_1) = 18 \text{ PD}; \; AE(f_2) = 14 \text{ PD}; \; AE(f_3) = 40 \text{ PD}; \; AE(f_4) = 3 \text{ PD}; \; AE(f_5) = 10 \text{ PD}$$

This means feature f_2 was significantly overspent, feature f_3 slightly underspent, and the other features were realized exactly on budget. The total actual effort is $\sum_{i=1...5} AE(f_i) = 85$ PD. Under the assumption that the reduced daily rate DR_2 is 600 €, the amount invoiced for sprint S_1 is:

$$\text{Inv} \, (S_1) = BR + \sum_{1 \leq i \leq 5} IE(f_i) \times DR_1 + \left(\sum_{1 \leq i \leq 5} AE(f_i) - \sum_{1 \leq i \leq 5} IE(f_i) \right) \times DR_2$$
$$= 22{,}000 \, € + 80 \times 1000 \, € + (85 - 80) \times 600 \, € = 105{,}000 \, €$$

This calculation applies for overspending. The principle of shared pain established in Sect. 14.5 is implemented by the reduced daily rate for work on features that ran into overspend. This example uses 600 €—the parties should negotiate a reduced daily rate at which the contractor would prefer not to work (since this manpower could be used more profitably in other projects at the full daily rate), but that at least covers all or part of the costs.

The principle of shared gain manifests itself in efficiency incentives (Sect. 14.6) that apply in an underspending situation, i.e., when $\sum AE(f_i) < \sum IE(f_i)$. This could be the case, e.g., in the following situation:

$$AE(f_1) = 14 \text{ PD}; \; AE(f_2) = 10 \text{ PD}; \; AE(f_3) = 34 \text{ PD}; \; AE(f_4) = 3 \text{ PD}; \; AE(f_5) = 9 \text{ PD}$$

The handling of this situation depends on what the parties agreed on for sharing any budget savings. In general, the invoice amount is determined by

$$\text{Inv} \, (S_1) = BR + \sum_{1 \leq i \leq 5} AE(f_i) \times DR_1 + \left(\sum_{1 \leq i \leq 5} IE(f_i) - \sum_{1 \leq i \leq 5} AE(f_i) \right) \times DR_1 \times EI$$

where the efficiency incentive EI is the ratio of sharing the savings, which can be any value between 0 and 1. If the effort actually expended for the release was 70 PD in our example, and the client and contractor had parameterized the adVANTAGE model so cost savings were shared equally by both parties (i.e., $EI = 0.5$), the resulting invoice amount would be

$$\text{Inv} \, (S_1) = 22{,}000 \, € + 70 \times 1000 \, € + (80 - 70) \times 1000 \, € \times 0.5 = 97{,}000 \, €.$$

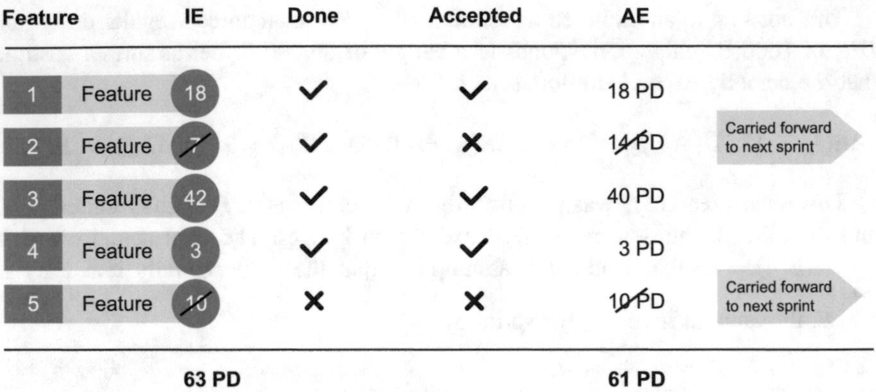

Feature	IE	Done	Accepted	AE
1 Feature 18		✓	✓	18 PD	
2 Feature ~~7~~		✓	✗	14 PD	Carried forward to next sprint
3 Feature 42		✓	✓	40 PD	
4 Feature 3		✓	✓	3 PD	
5 Feature ~~10~~		✗	✗	10 PD	Carried forward to next sprint

| **63 PD** | | | **61 PD** |

Fig. 15.6 Example of incomplete sprint results

15.4.2   Partial Completion of Sprint

The more complex case of settlement for a sprint occurs when the results are incomplete. Possible reasons for this could be that not all features could be (fully) realized within the sprint's time box, or that some features were delivered but not accepted by the customer.

Figure 15.6 shows a schematic of such a mixed outcome.

Feature 5 was not delivered, and feature 2 was delivered but not accepted by the client. Both features are removed from the examination and settlement of the current sprint and carried forward to a subsequent sprint (i.e., they are put back into the product backlog, with the effort already expended being noted). Now only features 1, 3, and 4 are relevant for the settlement. The sum of actual effort (*AE*) expended for these features is 61 person-days, which represents a slight under-spending since the initial estimates (*IE*) for the three accepted features totaled 63 person-days. If we once again assume that cost savings are shared equally, the resulting settlement for the sprint is:

$$\text{Inv}\,(S_1) = 22{,}000\,\text{€} + 61 \times 1000\,\text{€} + (63 - 61) \times 1000\,\text{€} \times 0.5 = 84{,}000\,\text{€}.$$

15.5   Planning the Next Sprint

Once a sprint has been properly settled, the product backlog has to be re-sorted and the next sprint needs to be prepared. Figure 15.7 shows the situation at the end of the sprint in our example of partial acceptance.

The first column contains the features 1, 3, and 4 which are done and settled. They are no longer relevant for planning the next sprint. The second column contains features 2 and 5, which were not completed or accepted in the previous

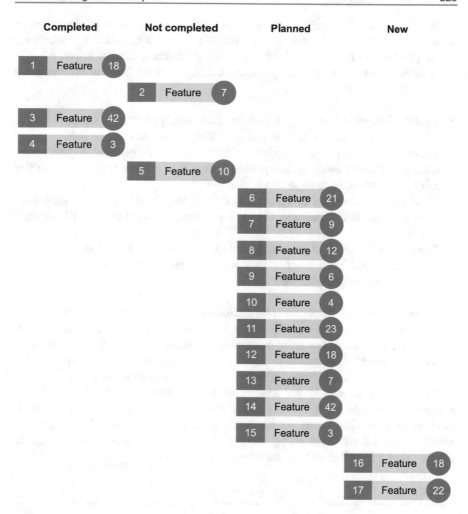

Fig. 15.7 Example of a feature canvas after the completion of a sprint

sprint. They are candidates for continued implementation. The first two columns together constitute the sprint backlog of the sprint that was just completed. The third column lists the features that were planned initially but have not yet been realized. Finally, the last column lists two new features that were added during the last sprint. As we have emphasized several times, late requirements are no accident but a normal occurrence in agile projects. These may constitute entirely new features or also changes to the content of older features, which are treated as change requests and therefore appear as new features. Initial estimates have already been assigned to the two new features in this example. As long as no features are eliminated, columns 2, 3, and 4 constitute the current product backlog.

Now another prioritization workshop is held in the IR:agile as described in Sect. 8.2, in order to plan the next sprint. This can be preceded by a backlog reprioritization with the client, using the requirements exchange (Sect. 8.3). In determining a newly prioritized product backlog, various courses of action are possible on this basis:

- Features left over from the previous product backlog (the third column) can be reprioritized, for example, to reflect new insights about value or risk.
- Features from the previous product backlog can also be eliminated entirely, for example, if they have proven superfluous or if their content has changed so that they are replaced by new features.
- New features with an initial estimate may be added. They are prioritized according to their value and risk and positioned accordingly in the product backlog.
- Features left over from preceding sprints can be assigned a detailed estimate according to the latest insights; they are prioritized and positioned accordingly in the product backlog as well.

At the end of this discussion and exchange process, there should be a newly sorted product backlog—a sorted list of prioritized features. The candidates for the next sprint backlog are once again quite simply determined as the first n features for which the total effort is equal to or just less than the sprint scope. It is important to note that starting with the second sprint, we not only have an initial effort $IE(f_i)$ and a detailed estimate $DE(f_i)$ per feature f_i, but the actual efforts $AE(f_i)$ already expended for not-yet-accepted features are also known. These are transferred to the next spring as starting values for the features' actual effort counts. In the example above, features 2 and 5 are going into the next sprint and their already expended efforts of 14 PD and 10 PD are transferred accordingly.

15.6   Project Termination

An important objective of the adVANTAGE model is to generate economic benefits for both sides (i.e., for the client and the contractor), in contrast to plan-driven and fixed price models. A key aspect is that an agile project can be terminated at the end of each sprint. There are generally two possible reasons for this. For one, terminating the project may become necessary because the goal proves to be unattainable. The economically reasonable continuation of the project may be impossible for technical or other reasons. If features are prioritized by value and (in particular) the expected risk of realization, the probability of project termination in late sprints should be minimized since the greatest risks ought to materialize early on.

The more pleasant reason for project termination is reaching an adequate business value, thereby accomplishing the project objective. Whether this goal has been reached needs to be discussed after each sprint, based on the results achieved so far.

If prioritization was effective, sometime during the project a point will be reached where all the remaining features in the product backlog only promise a very low additional value. Ideally, the software produced thus far is already being used in production at this point, and the users have learned to value the benefits of the new system. It is even better if nobody is bothered by the fact that the final 10 % of features do not exist yet. This effect can be observed in many agile projects: While the laboriously developed detailed specification is also implemented down to the details in plan-driven projects, production software is produced more quickly using agile methods. Cases where nobody needs the final features from the product backlog anymore, or a decision is made not to invest the additional effort to build them, are quite realistic here.

The benefit for the client is apparent. When future sprints do not have to be realized anymore, the costs are lower as well. In keeping with the efficiency incentive principle however, a construct should exist to also make it appealing for the contractor to generate sufficient business value early on so the project can be ended accordingly. An elegant way to accomplish this is to pay a premium for budget savings compared to the total initial budget (*IB*). For example, paying *x* percent of the budget savings as a completion premium could be agreed. This means the contractor will not be upset about a termination, since it receives a payment without incurring additional costs (at least starting at the time when the development team can be assigned to a new project). In practice, *x* will be significantly below 50 % as a rule.

15.7 Summary

The adVANTAGE model is intended as a framework for legal and commercial rules that support the successful realization of agile software projects. How "successful" is defined on a case-by-case basis clearly depends on the respective project. If an agile method is chosen, much speaks in favor of generating a certain business value as quickly as possible with the least possible effort, relinquishing certainty in exchange for getting assessable results instead of paper early on. The parties involved should reap a benefit compared to conventional methods. Agility is represented by the adVANTAGE model insofar as

- the entire body of rules is tailored to the processes of typical agile methods such as Scrum,
- late and changing requirements are considered normal,
- the work is performed in iterations, which keep being adapted to the latest insights, and
- settlement is closely corresponding to the actual generation of business value.

The method is based on mutual trust at a crucial point—the question of whether the functionality intended for a sprint (i.e., a feature) is "done" in the sense of being complete but perhaps not free of defects. Subsequent progress, the commercial settlement, and therefore the success of the project depend on how this question is answered (the model deliberately does not provide any additional assistance here). If both parties live up to the trust placed in them, the model is economically attractive for both sides due to its principles of shared pain and efficiency incentives. In addition, the client's risk is limited by the principle of two daily rates and settlement based on the actually produced business value. It gives the contractor an incentive to accept a more risky approach—compared to plan-driven methods—since the contractor is reimbursed at least for its costs (or part of them). The possibility of participating in reduced effort without incurring additional costs provides an added incentive to work as efficiently as possible. This in turn improves budget certainty for the client, since it can rely on the fact that none of the stakeholders are interested in generating increased effort.

The attentive reader will of course have noted that the construction of the adVANTAGE model is by no means rocket science. But that applies to agility in general. A few principles, which are followed all the more strictly, and trust that the persons and organizations will behave reasonably, form the basis of agile process models as well as the proposed commercial model.

Reference

Cabri A, Griffiths M (2006) Earned value and agile reporting. In: Maurer F, Melnik G (eds) AGILE 2006: Agile Conference, pp 17–22. doi:10.1109/AGILE.2006.21

adVANTAGE in Practice

16

The description of the adVANTAGE model in the preceding chapter was based on the typical, iterative approach in agile projects. A few sample parameters were chosen, and a prototypical process was assumed. Highly specific situations often arise in practice, so that answers which deviate from the prototypical process have to be found. We will therefore discuss some practical aspects for the application of the adVANTAGE model in this chapter. These include for example establishing the model parameters, but also a fundamental discussion of the model with a potential client.

16.1 Case Study: The BERGFÜRST Crowd Investing Platform

We will start by outlining a case study from an actual project. The client was the start-up company BERGFÜRST, which intended to establish a new business model based on crowd-funding in the market. Crowd-funding is the procurement of equity or financial means similar to equity from numerous small investors, each of whom acquires a (usually silent) share in the company being financed (Ordanini et al. 2011). In addition to companies, social or art projects can be financed as well. In order to establish contact between these projects or companies and potential investors, platforms similar to a marketplace are usually operated the way they are also used in e-business. The fundamental idea behind the crowd-funding model is that projects can be financed for which an individual investor would not likely be found because the risk is too high, or because the business model cannot (yet) be described in as structured and reliable a manner as expected by conventional venture capitalists. On the other hand, the risk in crowd-funding is manageable for the individual investor due to the limited investment. Often, there is an additional incentive that goes beyond the investment calculation as such. For example,

© Springer International Publishing Switzerland 2016
M. Book et al., *Tamed Agility*, DOI 10.1007/978-3-319-41478-2_16

investors may want to support a project because they find the idea personally attractive and want to see it implemented.

In our case study, since trust in the capability of the contractor had been established through personal contact, since a lot of positive experiences had been made with agile software projects, and since the geographical proximity at the Berlin site promised close collaboration, the IT service provider adesso was chosen as the contractor for the realization of the BERGFÜRST crowd investing platform. The decision in favor of an agile process model was apparent from the outset. There was no exact description of a business model, nor a concept of the individual processes and features needed for the platform. This ruled out a plan-driven method based on a specification prepared in advance, if one did not want to lose precious time before the development team could start working. However, a fast start to development was essential since a short time to market was desired. This was a classic situation calling for an agile method: unclear requirements, little time before the start of development, and a client who wants to evaluate real software as quickly as possible.

After a detailed presentation of the model and after reaching a fundamental agreement regarding the project objectives, the parties agreed on the adVANTAGE contract model. What mattered most was the model characteristics that align the interests of both parties with the same goal: generating business value quickly while keeping the development effort as low as possible. The desired business value could only be outlined as a high-level vision at first. A platform should exist where companies and investors could find each other, and that would handle all processes required for financing. After the adVANTAGE parameters were established in the course of a negotiation session and a corresponding contract was concluded based on the sample contract described in Appendix C.1, the first workshop was carried out in the IR:scope. The goal was to prepare a feature canvas to obtain an initial overview of the stakeholders for the planned platform. Figure 16.1 shows an example from the IR:scope and a section of the first context model.

In addition to the context model, a system of targets influencing the course of the project was established. An excerpt from this target system is shown in Table 16.1.

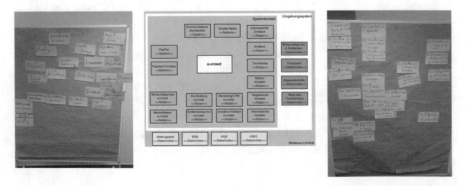

Fig. 16.1 Interaction Room with context model and feature canvas for the BERGFÜRST project

Table 16.1 An excerpt from the BERGFÜRST target system

Target 1: Companies (issuers) want to offer shares as own issues to obtain capital	
Target 1.1	The book building method is to be used for the issue
Target 1.2	The issuer wants to generate predefined minimum proceeds
Target 1.3	The number of shares issued is to be established before the issue
Target 1.4	The price range for a share is to be established before the issue
Target 1.5	The issuer wants to issue a minimum volume of shares
Target 1.6	The issue process is to be confirmed by an auditor
Target 1.7	Only one issue process is to be carried out at one time

Based on the target system and context model, a list of about 65 features was then derived, put through the initial estimation process described previously and prioritized. Various estimating methods such as expert estimation, planning poker, and relativizing estimates were combined due to the high level of uncertainty. The sum of the initial estimates for all features (the entire product backlog) was over 500 person-days at the end of this process. Eight sprints with a duration of three weeks each were planned. The initial team consisted of three developers, a scrum master assigned to the project half-time and a proxy product owner who, together with the product owner on the client side, assumed responsibility for the product backlog maintained in the IR:agile and for acceptance of the completed features.

Only a few weeks elapsed between the fundamental agreement on the contract model and the start of development. The team was able to begin with the production of presentable and usable software quickly. As previously noted, the basic conditions were anything but stable. The exact business model was not established until halfway through the project. While the focus was exclusively on company financing at the outset, support for financing real estate funds was to be enabled as well in a later phase. Changes were also made repeatedly to the features at the detailed level. For example, it was not clear at the outset how to handle the reservation of payments: As long as a crowd-funding project has not found the minimum number of investors, whether it will be realized at all remains uncertain. Once this threshold is exceeded, one needs to ensure that all investors actually make their financing contribution. However, reserving funds through a variety of payment methods is a process that can require a banking license in certain cases. Such uncertainty needed to be resolved, and decisions had to be made in the course of the project while software development proceeded at top speed. Imponderables also existed at the technical level. The first version of the portal ran in the cloud under Amazon Web Services to enable the fastest and especially most flexible possible response to future requirements for the production environment. Later, it turned out in the course of discussions with the BaFin (the German Federal Financial Supervisory Authority) that this does not comply with the applicable security regulations in regard to processing certain financial transactions.

In short: BERGFÜRST was a truly agile project with uncertainties from many perspectives. This made adVANTAGE downright ideal as a contract model, and the corresponding requirements were met as well, with mutual trust between the partners being first and foremost. Both sides noted that this trust was justified after just a few sprints: The contractor dealt reasonably with change requests, while the client displayed understanding for less than optimal productivity at the outset due to the uncertainties and rapid changes. In parameterizing the adVANTAGE model, besides the regular and reduced daily rates DR_1 and DR_2, a special daily rate DR_{PO} was agreed for the work of the proxy product owner. The base rate BR was initially set quite low and not raised later even when the team was expanded, since it turned out that the overhead in the closely cooperating team of the two contractual partners was extremely (and favorably) low, and because the sprint duration was shortened to two weeks in return. An efficiency incentive was not defined.

The adaptations of the business model during the course of the project and the resulting changes and additional features in the product backlog ultimately led to 13 sprints instead of the eight calculated originally. Instead of slightly over 500 person-days calculated from the initial estimate, a total of approximately 650 person-days of actual effort was recorded. One particularity was the composition of the team over time. While all software experts were originally from the contractor adesso, developers from the client's team were gradually added. This was therefore a cooperative performance structure in the sense of Fig. 11.1. These employees initially operated outside the budget and, after corresponding training, were treated like developers of the supplier except that their work did not appear on the invoice

Fig. 16.2 The BERGFÜRST crowd investing platform

in the end. Enabling long-term further development and maintenance by the client was the goal, which has also been fully implemented in the meantime. The resulting portal (Fig. 16.2) is being further developed and maintained by BERGFÜRST under its sole responsibility today.

16.2   Fine-Tuning adVANTAGE Parameters

In the presentation of the general adVANTAGE model and the preceding description of the example, the values for the typical parameters of the settlement model were not discussed in detail. However, the exact parameterization of the model is anything but unimportant in a practical project context. We are talking about the following variables in particular:

- Sprint scope,
- Sprint duration,
- Base rate,
- Regular daily rate,
- Reduced daily rate, and
- Efficiency incentive.

The first two parameters, sprint scope and sprint duration, will not be influenced to a significant extent by commercial aspects of the adVANTAGE model in practice. Rather, they will be determined according to practical considerations based on comparable projects. The **sprint scope** is the maximum number of person-days that can be used in a sprint for the implementation of features. It is roughly determined by multiplying the number of developers by the sprint duration in working days. But since the developers cannot spend 100 percent of their time programming features, but also have to perform overhead tasks paid by the base rate, the product has to be multiplied by a productivity factor (such as 85 percent depending on empirical values) to determine the actual, realistic sprint scope. Regarding a sensible team size, i.e., the number of developers that can collaborate efficiently on an agile project, we refer e.g. to Lindvall et al. (2002).

The **sprint duration** not only affects the sprint scope for a given team size, but also has a direct impact on the base rate. Insofar, it clearly has commercial effects. But as long as we assume that sprints in agile development processes should not be longer or shorter than a few weeks, the commercial effects become rather blurred. This is why choosing the sprint duration should be guided less by economic and more by practical empirical values. One should not be afraid to change the sprint duration either (in the course of the project, not during a sprint)—of course this means adjusting the base rate if applicable.

We listed the essential components of the **base rate** in Sect. 15.1. They are also the cost drivers that form the basis of a corresponding calculation. Ultimately, this is the estimated effort for the scrum master, regular meetings, and planning tasks multiplied by a daily rate as the calculation base, as well as the establishment of a warranty surcharge that can be estimated as a percentage of the sprint budget. Here, a supplier should calculate soundly but also not be too fearful. By far, the greater share of the settlement, which therefore has more leverage, will consist of the effort for realizing the features.

Agreeing on the regular and reduced daily rates is therefore of vital importance. The simplest case is when the contractor and client have already worked together successfully in other projects on a T&M basis. A **regular daily rate** that considers the expectations and pain thresholds of both parties has already been established in this case. The **reduced daily rate** on the other hand is more difficult to determine. It needs to be set so that the supplier does not really want to work at that daily rate, but does not suffer an economic disaster either. A price that is close to the cost of production for the work has repeatedly proven itself as negotiable in practice. Fine-tuning will be largely limited to a range of a few percentage points above or below this threshold. The client may be very interested in seeing the contractor "suffer" if the budget per feature is exceeded. However, the client should consider that every percentage point below the cost of production not only increases the inclination to inflate the estimated effort, which leads to more discussion in the project, but also that the supplier will demand a higher efficiency incentive in return as well.

The **efficiency incentive** in the standard model represents a share of the reduced effort for implementing the respective feature compared to the initial estimate. If the contractor remains below the agreed budget, it can bill a percentage of the difference anyway. As usual, the higher the risk, the greater the opportunity—as long as the parties deal fairly with each other. In practice, the rate is between 10 and 50 %, depending on the values of the remaining parameters since an overall package is negotiated.

References

Lindvall M et al (2002) Empirical findings in agile methods. In: Wells D, Williams L (eds) Proc 2nd XP Universe and 1st Agile Universe Conf on Extreme Programming and Agile Methods. Lecture Notes in Computer Science, vol 2418. Springer, pp 197–207. doi:10.1007/3-540-45672-4_19

Ordanini A et al (2011) Crowd-funding: Transforming customers into investors through innovative service platforms. J Service Management 22(4):443–470. doi:10.1108/09564231111155079

Summary

17

A sample contract for adVANTAGE projects is found in Appendix C.1. It is intended to outline the basic legal conditions for a project where the two parties to the contract have decided on a very special cooperation model—a model that accepts uncertainty as given and distributes the opportunities and risks fairly on this basis. However, the most important principle cannot be guaranteed, even by contracts that are negotiated in detail and cleverly phrased: trust. This is why we postulated that mutual trust is an essential, core principle of adVANTAGE in Sect. 14.2. Trust is so important because both parties assume risks in the course of an agile project that result from inherent uncertainty. This uncertainty refers to the fact that estimated effort always remains an estimate, as much as validation is desired. However, the adVANTAGE contract model is an instrument to align the economic interests of the contractual partners with the same objective, which is to adhere as closely as possible to a cost budget agreed in advance.

However, this contractual (legal and/or commercial) aspect is only one side of the coin. The other is derived from the methodic framework which is provided by the Interaction Room, and especially its IR:scope and IR:agile variants. In the IR:scope, the two parties to the contract find an opportunity to discuss and establish the scope for the intended project. On this basis, the IR:agile then makes it possible to repeatedly review the intrinsic value of the agile development project across all phases. It therefore provides the tools for managing the entire life cycle. Managing uncertainty is supported by the division into manageable sprints as well as feature-based controlling and settlement. Insofar the concepts of the Interaction Room and the adVANTAGE contract model go hand in hand.

Whether and when adVANTAGE is the right model for cooperation between two contractual partners can be discussed on a case-by-case basis. Figure 17.1 illustrates the dimensions relevant for such a discussion.

The dimensions of interface intensity and likelihood of manifold late requirements were already discussed previously in Chap. 10. The following dimensions are added in the context of the adVANTAGE model:

© Springer International Publishing Switzerland 2016
M. Book et al., *Tamed Agility*, DOI 10.1007/978-3-319-41478-2_17

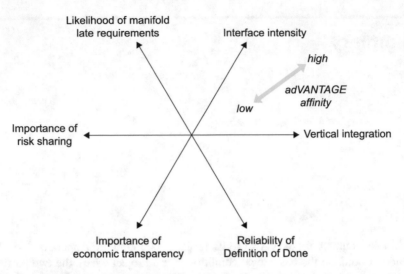

Fig. 17.1 Suitability of adVANTAGE for a concrete project

- **Vertical integration:** adVANTAGE is based on the assumption of continuous management of changing requirements, making it especially well suited when such flexibility is permitted. This makes it unsuitable when, for example, large work packages are to be developed externally at fixed prices or off-shoring models are to be applied.
- **Reliability of Definition of Done:** adVANTAGE is based on the continuous reprioritization of features and the completion of individual features in the shortest possible realization cycles. Both make sense, provided it is clear when a feature is considered done. Why we accept that a formally determinable DoD does not exist in the adVANTAGE model was discussed in Sect. 14.2. Nevertheless, the parties to the contract should have compatible expectations to mutually support an assessment of the state of completion with reasonable reliability.
- **Importance of economic transparency:** adVANTAGE is intended to benefit both parties to the contract, also economically. The observation of economic efficiency is therefore an essential means to check whether the initial goals can still be reached or have been reached already. However, the level of detail required for information about the economic efficiency of an ongoing project can vary widely. It can range from a general prediction ("everything is looking fine, we are within the cost budget") to current forecasts and projections on a feature basis. Cost and budget transparency should be granted to those who exchange and re-prioritize requirements in projects according to the adVANTAGE model, since this is the only way they can evaluate the economic effects of their own actions.
- **Importance of risk sharing:** A key characteristic of the adVANTAGE model is the special approach to the management of software development risks.

The contract model supports a fair distribution and sharing of these risks. The more important the issue of risk sharing is for the parties to the contract, the more suitable the adVANTAGE model.

In Chap. 14, we introduced the brief adVANTAGE formula "price + contract + procedures." Compared to the contract models for agile software projects discussed in Chap. 13, adVANTAGE in combination with the Interaction Room offers a comprehensive framework—consisting of commercially (price) and legally (contract) effective elements as well as concrete methodology support for project activities (procedures). How this can look like in concrete terms will be illustrated by the example in the following part.

Part IV
A Sample Project

Case Study: The Cura Health Insurance Benefit System

18

To put the methods we presented in the previous chapters into a larger context, and give an idea of an appropriate modeling volume and level of abstraction as the project progresses from its initial setup to operations, we present a visual documentation of the models that evolved in the Interaction Room over the course of an actual project. After a brief introduction to the project, the examples from the project scoping phase using the IR:scope are provided with commentary explaining both the project domain and the IR coaches' choices, as well as references to preceding chapters for a more detailed description of the respective modeling techniques. We then explain the process of monitoring the project with the help of the IR:agile and present lessons that could be learned from the application of the IR: scope and IR:agile in this project.

The example we are using to demonstrate the IR:scope, IR:agile, and their interplay is the development of a private health insurance benefit system (HIB). Such a system supports all processes related to serving policyholders as briefly outlined below.

Prior to the treatment by a doctor which may lead to insurance benefits (i.e., the reimbursement of costs to the policyholder), prequalification may occur (e.g., prequalification to determine whether and what proportion of certain dental treatments that could also be due to cosmetic reasons would be reimbursed). Therapy plans may be the subject of prequalification as well. These are used in case of certain diagnoses to commission dedicated Personal Injury Managers for monitoring, controlling, and intervention. The actual granting of insurance benefits then follows the treatment based on invoices and receipts that are submitted. All sorts of investigations are conducted prior to the actual granting of benefits. These pertain among other things to violations of disclosure requirements before the contract was concluded, insurance exclusions, and the appropriateness of the services provided based on type, scope, and fees. All communication related to benefits must be recorded in order to avoid future misunderstandings and so that disputes can be examined in the overall context.

© Springer International Publishing Switzerland 2016
M. Book et al., *Tamed Agility*, DOI 10.1007/978-3-319-41478-2_18

On the one hand, all of this needs to be done quickly and in a user-friendly manner in modern benefit systems such as the HIB system described here, so that customer dissatisfaction is avoided. On the other hand, there should be no payment of benefits that are not required according to the contract. All of this should happen reliably and, in view of the challenging economic situation faced by health insurers, with as much automation as possible. Intervention by administrators shall only take place when their technical expertise is required.

The HIB system was developed in close coordination of the private health insurer Cura AG[1] and the contractor adesso. The health insurer assumed the role of the requirements originator and participated in development with its own personnel. Most of the development work was to be handled by adesso. The software system being developed was to be integrated into Cura's application landscape and would be operated by Cura. It was clear to the stakeholders that the new development of a benefit system is subject to the risk of simply replicating the existing production system, without taking advantage of the opportunity for functional optimization and innovations. They wanted to avoid this risk. The stakeholders were aware that there would be late requirements and agreed to omit the preparation of the most complete possible specification. Instead, they intended to compile the functionality and describe it as concisely as possible. Only functionality with a high potential for misunderstandings was to be described in more detail. Even though the initial descriptions would largely be brief, the effort was to be estimated at the feature level. The two companies used the IR:scope to establish the scope of the system being developed. They agreed to establish a requirements exchange in order to continuously swap late requirements for early ones, to regularly use the risk map and to apply adVANTAGE in order to share risks between Cura and adesso.

---

[1]The company and stakeholder names have been changed to protect the client's anonymity.

Initial Project Scoping with the IR:scope

19

This chapter describes the initial population of the IR:scope in the HIB project. Beside the models on the IR canvases, a few additional artifacts played a role in the preparation and follow-up of the IR population.

19.1 Project Vision

In order to describe the target state of the project, the stakeholders in the IR:scope initially prepared the fictitious "press release" shown below, as recommended in Sect. 3.6:

Cura insurance introduces new benefit system

Massively improving service for policyholders while reducing costs

Cura AG has introduced a new benefit system for private health insurance, supporting a high level of automation and simultaneously making a contribution to providing much better service to the policyholders. Benefits will be settled within 36 h in cases where there are no inquiries. Clients will be able to contact the insurer through mobile apps, social media, e-mail or regular mail. This is made possible by the introduction of the new HIB system, which provides optimum support today for the digital transformation that has begun. That means media breaks are eliminated as early as possible and the entire process is fully supported electronically. Operation of the system is largely automated in the background; 75 % automatic processing is the goal for future system operation. The fact that minor individual cases will be settled with no manual review is deliberately accepted, achieving high overall efficiency as a result. This results in great simplification for the policyholders and the administrators at Cura. The new system supports benefits for full health insurance and supplementary insurance. It is flexible in regards to future new and innovative health insurance products in the broadest sense. Benefit management processes can easily be

© Springer International Publishing Switzerland 2016
M. Book et al., *Tamed Agility*, DOI 10.1007/978-3-319-41478-2_19

added later, without having to fundamentally alter the system structure. "With the new system, our clerks can handle standard cases independently, mostly closing them, without extended training periods," says Cura IT director Dirk Kalker. Full integration with related systems has also been considered, making it possible to support automated business processes across system boundaries. Company-specific rules can be stored and used through parameterization. Kalker: "I'm so happy."

19.2   Identification of Stakeholders and Objectives

According to the recommendations in Sect. 5.1, the following roles were identified as stakeholders in the IR:scope on the side of the health insurer:

- Project manager,
- Benefits business expert,
- Clerks (two),
- Benefits department manager A-K and benefits department manager L-Z,
- Director of patients/benefits,
- Software architect, and
- Operations officer.

The following stakeholder roles were identified on the side of the contractor adesso:

- Project manager,
- Head developer, and
- Software architect.

Twelve persons were identified to represent the three most important stakeholder groups: business, development, and operations. They were at various levels of the hierarchy. Eight future users and the process owner were included. The ratio was balanced along the client/contractor axis as well.

The following were identified as explicit goals of the leading stakeholders:

- The director of benefits wants to be able to exchange benefit administrators between the divisions depending on the workload.
- The director of IT wants to drive digitalization of the company under the umbrella of the project.
- The clerks want to automate data capture processes with a high number of repetitions.

- The clerks want access to all relevant information at a glance for difficult cases under review.
- The enterprise IT wants to demonstrate that using agile techniques leads to suitable software which can be deployed automatically.

Notwithstanding these individual goals, all stakeholders were able to agree on the higher-level objective described in the "press release."

19.3 Feature Canvas

19.3.1 Feature Identification and Canvas Population

In the course of the initial population of the IR:scope, the feature canvas shown in Fig. 19.1 was developed as described in Sect. 5.2.1.

19.3.2 Annotation and Analysis

Following the collection of the features, the feature canvas was annotated, using all annotations from the set of feature canvas annotations (Sect. 5.2.2). Figure 19.2 shows the feature canvas including the annotations.

Several circumstances were noted regarding the annotations on the feature canvas:

- The features related to quotation preparation were thinly annotated. Together with the straightforward identification of these features, this was cause to suspect that these features existed in a very similar form (or were at least known from other systems). By and large, it seemed that these features were expected as basic functionality without assigning a special benefit for the user or company to them. Conversely, it could be assumed that their lack would be perceived as a substantial defect. The existing quotation system was examined in more detail as a result. The users were asked about potential for improvements.
- The features in the context of personal injury management were annotated much more densely. Here, the mix of annotations was very lively. Multiple user and business value annotations appeared on the one hand and combined with complexity and uncertainty annotations on the other hand. This mix is typical for new functionality, which is initially associated with vague expectations. As a result of this mix, the personal injury management processes were examined more intensively and some circumstances were studied in greater detail so that expectations could be stated in concrete terms.
- The feature "determination of similar healing/therapy plans" in particular was assigned a variety of annotations. Here, the annotations user value, business value, complexity, and uncertainty were applied. This was a clear indication that imaginative expectations could encounter significant realization difficulties. In fact, the

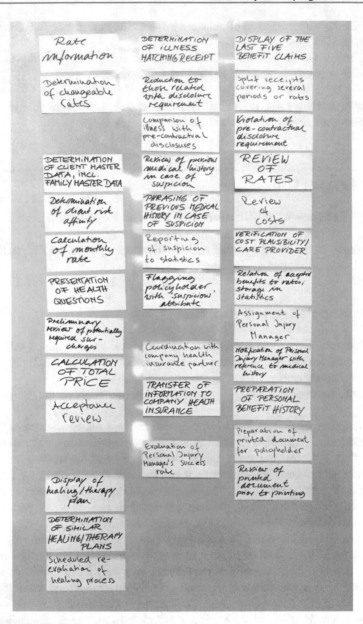

Fig. 19.1 Initial feature canvas of the HIB system

word "similar" harbored major interpretation potential. Ultimately, the relation "similar" for healing and therapy plans had to be defined, which in turn only succeeded after the object type "healing/therapy plan" was defined in concrete terms.

Fig. 19.2 Feature canvas with annotations

- As an individual feature, "review of previous medical history in case of sus-picion" was especially dubious, receiving fully three uncertainty annotations. Following a more detailed analysis, it turned out that the stakeholders did in fact have a compatible concept of what the feature was supposed to do, but no idea whatsoever regarding the question of how it could be realized. This example shows that the complexity and uncertainty annotations are not always used with specific appropriateness. Apparently, there was a tendency toward complexity when the person proposing the annotation had an idea of how this could be realized (where this had nothing to do with whether this usually vague idea would somehow assert itself). If such an idea was lacking, the stakeholders tended to use the uncertainty annotation instead.
- The fact that the feature "preparation of printed document for policyholder," which appears simple at first glance, was assigned double complexity is striking. This annotation became comprehensible later when it turned out during the population of the integration canvas that the printing system was being replaced at the same time. This in turn was urgently required due to recurring problems with mass printing. Therefore, the feature was assessed as complex because the printing system being used, which was used as a mental point of reference, was perceived as cumbersome.

The Kano classification which was carried out as a refinement of the user value annotations is not reproduced here, since it had no particular influence on the prioritization and grouping of features for sprints.

19.4   Process Canvas

19.4.1   Identification and Prioritization of Business Processes

The most important business processes were identified based on the feature canvas and its annotations. Here, the approach was largely heuristic. While it could be assumed on the one hand that most of the features identified as important could also be assigned to the important business processes, some important features were in fact not covered by the most important business processes. The next step on the way to the important business processes was clustering the features (grouping the features having a business relationship). On the basis of such a clustering, the following business processes were identified as especially important:

- Mailing classification,
- Receipt identification,
- Review for violation of precontractual disclosure requirement,
- Benefit review,
- Granting of benefit,

- Rejection,
- Fraud detection,
- Rate statistics,
- Determination of sales potential,
- Determination of information for product engineering,
- Personal injury management,
- Consulting, and
- Receipt splitting.

Prior to detailed modeling, these processes were initially described according to their high-level input/output behavior, their purpose, and by assigning a name. Examples of such an abstract description are presented below:

- Mailing classification

    - Purpose: A random incoming document is classified by type. Possible document types are cost plan, healing plan, receipt, drug, and device settlement.
    - Inputs: Document in electronic form (PDF).
    - Outputs: Document in electronic form (PDF), tagged as a document type.

- Receipt identification

    - Purpose: A submitted receipt is classified automatically. Achieving a high level of automation is the goal. In case of classification peculiarities, the result is transferred to manual post-processing.
    - Inputs: A document identified as a receipt is transferred to an automated identification process.
    - Outputs: Structured information, at least with the characteristics "name of policyholder," "date," "policy number," and "ICD classification."

- Receipt splitting

    - Purpose: A receipt can apply to more than one settlement period. For proper cost allocation, it needs to be split into more than one receipt for unique assignment to a settlement period.
    - Input: Receipt.
    - Output: Two or more logically related subreceipts.

- Review of receipt for violation of precontractual disclosure requirement

    - Purpose: Incoming receipts are examined in view of the question whether they give grounds for suspicion that the policyholder failed to truthfully answer all risk questions in the course of the application process.

- Input: Receipt.
- Output: Suspicion: yes/no; if yes, notification that a manual review is required.

- Consulting

  - Purpose: Consulting for a lead, and presenting and pricing suitable products.
  - Input: Client lead, identification of the sales channel through which the lead was generated.
  - Output: Quotation.

19.4.2 Canvas Population

A maximum of 15 activities were identified for each identified business process during the population of the process canvas (Sect. 5.3). Often the features identified on the feature canvas appeared as activities, but it was also permitted to introduce activities in the course of modeling that had not appeared as features. This was essential; otherwise, an arduous back and forth between the feature and process canvases would have resulted, which would have been good for nothing other than syntactic consistency between the two canvases. Conversely, some features that were previously identified did not appear in the process models. This could be meaningful, if only because the appearance of new activities during process modeling and the quantity restriction caused features to fall victim to abstraction. In such cases, the annotations of the features were examined to ensure there was no unreasonable loss of information. If such a case occurred, the features were marked on the feature canvas and examined again later. In case significantly more than 15 features were identified, the quantity restriction came into force, which led to focusing on those activities occurring in the normal process (not dominated by handling exceptions). Here, the features were referenced wherever possible. The activities of a process were arranged by means of the data and control flow. In case of the data flow, the types of exchanged objects/documents/information were named and transferred to the candidate list for the object canvas.

Figures 19.3, 19.4, 19.5, and 19.6 show the initial models of the processes "consulting," "review for violation of precontractual disclosure requirement," "benefits review," and "personal injury management." Some syntax questions arose: For example, the activity "monitoring healing/therapy plan" occurred in the personal injury management process model with three different inputs. The process sequence makes it seem likely that the activity can be started as soon as a start is triggered by one of the incoming control flows. In fact, this is how it was intended. Here, the syntax would have required a merge connecting node, which was not forced due to the concrete modeling dynamics. Such carelessness was rectified in the course of documentation post-processing.

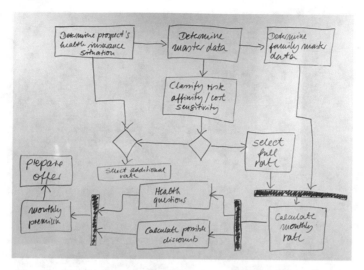

Fig. 19.3 Process canvas with process model "consulting"

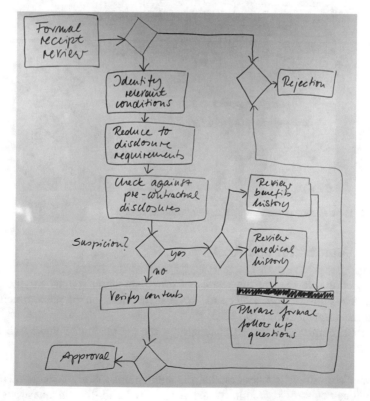

Fig. 19.4 Process canvas with process model "review for violation of precontractual disclosure requirement"

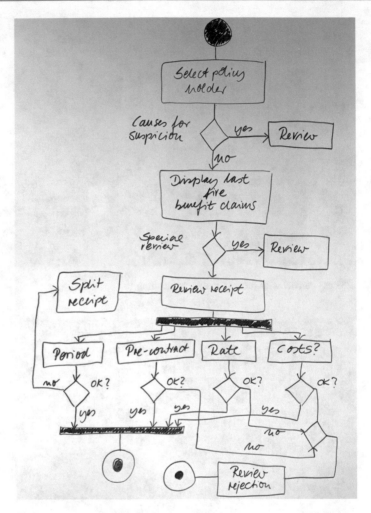

Fig. 19.5 Process canvas with process model "benefits review"

19.4.3   Annotation and Analysis

In this section, we present the results of four annotation rounds for the process models "consulting" (Fig. 19.7) and "review for violation of precontractual disclosure requirement" (Fig. 19.8).

A few circumstances stand out regarding the annotation of these two process models:

- In the "consulting" process model, the annotations mainly concentrated on the activities "classify risk affinity/cost sensitivity" and "health questions," Both were annotated at least three times. There were two uncertainty annotations in

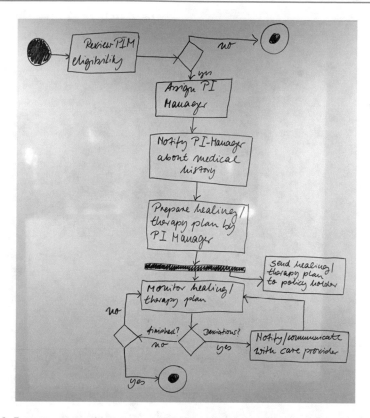

Fig. 19.6 Process canvas with process model "personal injury management"

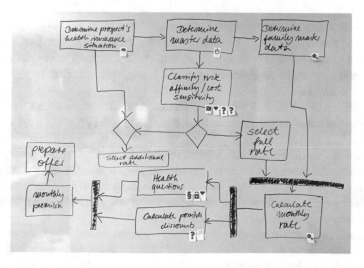

Fig. 19.7 Annotated process model "consulting"

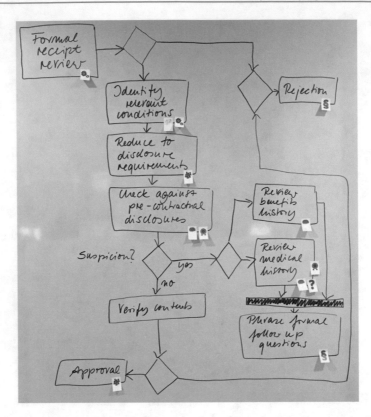

Fig. 19.8 Annotated process model "review for violation of precontractual disclosure requirement"

the first case, indicating that things were unclear regarding the realization possibilities. Regarding the activity "health questions," the business value, security, and policy constraint annotation mix indicated a certain sensitivity regarding the basic legal conditions, which was also reflected by security concerns in the concrete case.

- A number of additional weakly annotated activities were found in the "consulting" process model. This indicated that while they were necessary for the consulting process, the success or acceptance of the overall process did not depend on them. For the subsequent realization, this information was relevant insofar as the focus was on activities with extensive annotations. Ultimately, this proved reasonable although the activity "quotation preparation" would have deserved more attention than indicated based on examining the annotations. This was only determined after a few sprints.
- Two activities occurred in the "consulting" process model where the automation annotation appeared surprising at first glance, since they would have been automated in readily apparent ways. The explicit automation annotation was due

to the fact that the predecessor system exhibited automation gaps at precisely this point. Since these gaps were previously perceived as bothersome, the desired automation was made explicit with the annotation.

- In the process model "review for violation of precontractual disclosure requirement," some policy constraint and accuracy annotations occurred at the interface to the policyholder. It turned out in the course of detailed documentation of these annotations that there had been problems in the past with the proper legal phrasing of notices and inquiries. The annotations in question were aimed at precisely this problem, which was easy to address by involving a legal specialist in drafting the documents in question. In addition to the immediate benefit on the factual level, this was particularly beneficial since it helped eliminate vague reservations and worries.

19.5   Object Canvas

19.5.1   Canvas Population

Some of the object types recorded on the object canvas were already identified in the preceding step based on the business processes: The inputs and outputs of the business processes were fully reflected on the object canvas. This also applied for the inputs and outputs of the important features and the activities of the important business processes. Still, it was meaningful and possible to identify the additional important object types as described in Sect. 5.4.1 in the business context of the previously identified entries on the object canvas. Numerous other measures for identification of the relevant objects are of course possible as well. Suitable measures include examining existing systems, studying specifications, and interviewing experts. However, such measures were not applied in this example.

Figure 19.9 shows the object canvas for the process models that were discussed.

19.5.2   Annotation and Analysis

The part of the object canvas shown in the previous section was annotated in two rounds, as described in Sect. 5.4.2. Figure 19.10 shows the object model that forms the basis of the process models discussed. In the analysis of this model, it turned out that the object model was initially too coarse-grained and required ongoing refinement in order to serve as the basis for feature realization planning. This was noted in the course of preparing for realization, since large numbers of characteristics were identified per object type. That was viewed as a clear indication that extensive refinement was required for the meaningful specification of data handling by specific features or business processes.

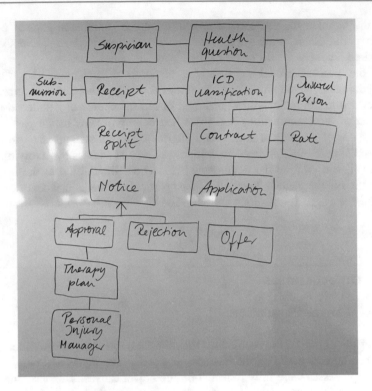

Fig. 19.9 Object canvas of the HIB system

Analyzing the annotations on the object canvas resulted in the following circumstances that called for further inquiry:

- A cluster of annotations was seen around the quotation/application/contract trio.
  There were a few user value annotations on the one hand, and the correctness of
  quotations and contracts played an important role on the other hand. The
  mobilization of quotations was desired as well. This cluster indicates that
  in-depth consideration is required here in order to determine what could and had
  to be expected of the user, with what degree of completeness and consistency.
  Too high a level of consistency and completeness could act as a deterrent since
  too much data would have to be collected in advance. Too low a level could
  contradict the desired level of precision and correctness. In fact, it was observed
  in the subsequent course of the project that intensive discussions regarding the
  desired level of usability kept recurring at exactly this point and that user
  interfaces were frequently adapted.
- The relationship between the therapy plan and personal injury manager (in
  combination with the annotations that were applied) indicated from the start of
  the project that preparing the therapy plan would be a critical activity. On the
  one hand, the therapy plan was important in regard to user value, and on the

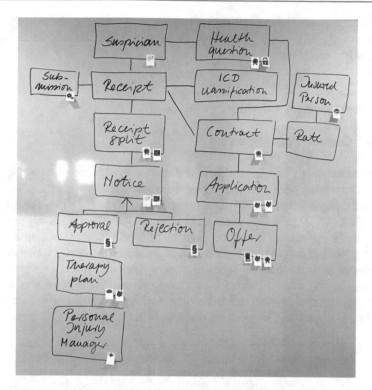

Fig. 19.10 Annotated object canvas of the HIB system

other hand, it required manual intervention and an external Personal Injury
Manager was involved as well. In fact, it was precisely at this point that one of
the fundamental and structural innovations came into play, which remained
poorly defined for a very long time. This could only be corrected by defining the
therapy plan in concrete terms and establishing the algorithmic elements for
generating it. The combination of annotations indicated this need from the
outset.

- The combination of the accuracy and complexity annotations indicated an
  impending disaster in the sense of having to expend a lot of effort. This combination can be seen on the model element "receipt split" in Fig. 19.10. Correctly splitting receipt was essential to avoid excess benefits or large numbers of
  complaints. The perceived complexity was based on the assumption that the
  combination of various triggers for splitting a receipt (more than one period,
  more than one benefit type, relationships with more than one contract) would
  lead to significant diversity and a whole series of special cases. Splitting receipt
  was in fact difficult, but ultimately, it would be well managed following a

systematic examination of all trigger combinations. Analyzing the combinations here put the focus on a potential problem, which was solved reliably through intensive examination.

19.6 Integration Canvas

19.6.1 Canvas Population

Systems to be integrated appeared here and there during preparation of the process canvas. Candidate systems for integration were also found during the population of the object canvas. These candidates were collected and entered on the integration canvas (Sect. 5.5). The stakeholders also had additional ideas regarding the systems that had to be considered during the population of the integration canvas.

Figure 19.11 shows the integration canvas for the HIB system, which comprises a number of systems that are logically closely related. Typical examples are the portfolio, clearing center, products, and associations. There were also numerous interdisciplinary systems that had to be integrated with virtually all central systems. These included partners, e-mail, and disbursements.

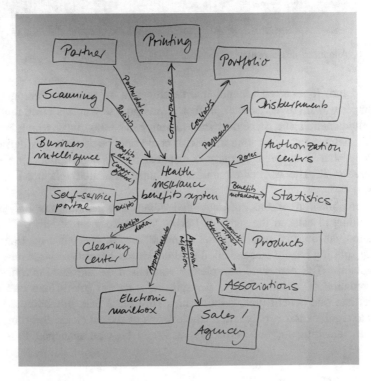

Fig. 19.11 Integration canvas of the HIB system

19.6.2   Annotation and Analysis

Figure 19.12 shows the integration canvas after the annotation process. Two of the interfaces that needed to be considered were considered unmodifiable (associations, statistics). While the interface to "associations" did in fact turn out to be entirely unchangeable (since it is an external interface that requires strict compliance), the assessment of the interface to statistics as supposedly unmodifiable turned out to be a—understandable—misinterpretation. The architects and developers responsible for the statistics system did in fact actively defend against any kind of changes to "their" interface. This created the impression that it was unmodifiable. In actuality, however, essential changes were in fact pushed through successfully. Figure 19.12 also illustrates a number of interfaces considered critical in terms of security, as well as a system in the process of being replaced—the printing system. There was uncertainty regarding the integration with the business intelligence system. An especially complex interface existed to the health insurance portfolio system, which was readily comprehensible due to the close dependency of content and the interdisciplinary business processes between benefits and the portfolio.

To manage the integration risk between the HIB and the portfolio system, a decision was made to promptly realize a technical spike prototype in order to collect experience with the system interface. This spike prototype did in fact turn out to be

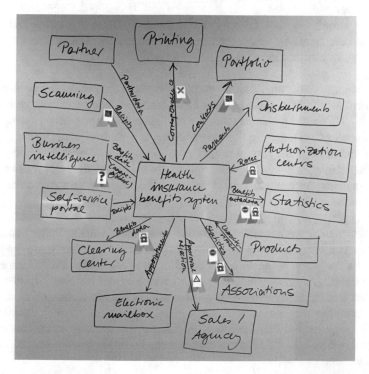

Fig. 19.12 Annotated integration canvas of the HIB system

extremely useful in order to illuminate the problems of technical communication between the two systems. Furthermore, it was examined in advance whether the delineation of the two systems was consistent and clear for both sides. Here, it was revealed that the features "benefit confirmation" and "benefit exclusions" were required by both systems but not considered for realization in either.

The uncertainty annotation on interface to the business intelligence system was clarified early on. This was done by using the business processes from the process canvas to act out what data was to be exchanged at what time over the "uncertain" interface. At least the first expansion stage of communication with the business intelligence system was clarified in this way.

19.7 Cross-Canvas Annotation Analysis

Analyzing the individual canvases indicated potential discrepancies and suspicious facts related to the model elements and annotations on a canvas. The model elements of the feature canvas, process canvas, object canvas, and integration canvas, however, also related to each other (Sect. 5.6). Activities in business processes, for example, resulted in objects of types that occurred on the object canvas. Types of objects appeared as the labels of interfaces on the integration canvas. Numerous discrepancies were noted in the IR:scope itself because the canvases could be examined simply by looking around the room. Further suspicious facts across canvases were found by analyzing the annotations of all canvases in the IR. The corresponding analysis led to the following results:

- The object types "application" and "offer" each had at least one user value annotation. Objects of these types came from the sales/agency system among others. This system was annotated with "need for improvement." Due to this combination, the question arose whether the desired user value could be achieved through the current project or whether an accompanying improvement to the sales/agency system was required. In this case, the improvement to the sales/agency system was considered essential in order to achieve the desired user value.
- The object type "offer" and the activity "prepare offer" in the "consulting" process model were marked with user value and business value annotations. This was a good indication of an actual opportunity to create value for the user and the company. Whether quote preparation was to be mobilized appeared to be unclear. A corresponding annotation was lacking, but mobility of the quotations was explicitly required. This was not necessarily a contradiction, since it was possible that the activity was exclusively stationary, with mobile availability required only for the result. Whether it was actually meant this way had to be examined. In the concrete case, it turned out that quote preparation was to be mobilized as well.

- Numerous annotations (business value, complexity, and twice uncertainty) were applied to the activity "classify risk affinity/cost sensitivity" in the annotated "consulting" process model. These annotations were not reflected in the corresponding object types "application" and "offer." The question of what criteria to use in order to select the applicable rate was therefore not considered equally difficult from all perspectives.
- The activity "review medical history" in the annotated process model "review for violation of precontractual disclosure requirement" had numerous annotations (manual processing, uncertainty, accuracy). The term "medical history" appeared neither on the integration canvas nor in the process model. In the course of the project, this incongruence led to the addition of the "benefit history" and its refinement "medical history" to the object model.
- On the feature canvas, the entry "preparation of printed document for policy-holder" bore a double complexity annotation. The interface to the printing system was identified on the integration canvas as being replaced. This led to the question of whether the feature was as complex as it was perceived to be such, or whether it merely appeared complex because the current interface was difficult to use (which after all could have been the reason why it was being replaced). In the course of the project, it turned out that most of the difficulties with the current printing system could be eliminated by the replacement. On the other hand, the parallel introduction of a printing system and health insurance benefit system meant extensive effort was required for testing related to this interface.

19.8 Documentation and Follow-up Activities

After the initial population, all canvases were drawn again cleanly on the whiteboard for documentation purposes. This documentation (which was also the source of the translated figures in the preceding sections) formed the starting point for a context and system specification subject to further development throughout the course of the project. The annotations were recorded in detail using the form in Fig. B.4. These descriptions were used frequently in the course of the project in order to look up the reasons for using a specific annotation. The results of analyzing the individual canvases and the cross-canvas analysis were also documented and addressed over the course of the project.

Project Monitoring with the IR:agile

20

This chapter relates the core activities undertaken in the HIB project during the transition from the IR:scope to the IR:agile. First, the effort for the features in the backlog was estimated, then the risk map was filled and the first sprint was outlined. After completion of the first sprint, settlement occurred according to the adVAN-TAGE model. Cost forward progressing was first employed after the first sprint, and the requirements exchange after the second sprint, as discussed in the following sections.

20.1   From Feature Canvas to Product Backlog

The product backlog was initially derived from the feature canvas of the IR:scope, as described in Sect. 8.1. Some features were added in this process and others were omitted since they had been identified as superfluous in the course of working in the IR:scope.

An initial estimate for all features was obtained through expert estimates using the planning poker method. There were only a few very large deviations in the estimated realization effort of individual features by the experts. An estimated value was quickly agreed on for most features. The remaining features were discussed again in detail until all estimators had a good impression of the complexity and business content of the feature. This procedure made it possible to quickly establish a product backlog with a broadly accepted estimate of the realization effort for each feature. In case an initial estimate was not possible after all, the reason was noted for future refinement. Table 20.1 shows the items of the resulting product backlog.

© Springer International Publishing Switzerland 2016
M. Book et al., *Tamed Agility*, DOI 10.1007/978-3-319-41478-2_20

Table 20.1 Product backlog of the HIB system with initial estimates

Product backlog item	Initial estimate [person-days]
Rate information	8
Determination of changeable rates	12
Determination of client master data, including family master data	5
Determination of client risk affinity	10
Calculation of the monthly rate	4
Presentation of the health questions	12
Preliminary review of potentially required surcharges	5
Calculation of the total price	5
Acceptance review	3
Display of healing/therapy plan	3
Determination of similar healing/therapy plans	25
Resubmission, control of healing progress by the deadline	5
Determination of illnesses matching the receipt	? (Little effort expected, but it is possible that algorithms similar to an expert system are expected, which can get quite complicated)
Reduction to illnesses having to do with the disclosure requirement	6
If any are left over: reconciliation with precontractual information	8
In case of suspicious facts: review of previous medical history	? (Annotations indicate there is no clear concept of this. The ideas fluctuate between a complete review and analysis of the medical history to merely displaying previous illnesses)
If suspicious facts are confirmed: phrasing the inquiry	8
Flagging the policyholder as "suspicious"	4
Transfer of information to company health insurance	? (The company health insurance interface to be used for integration is entirely unclear)
Display of last five benefit claims	12
Receipts that extend over more than one period or rate shall be split	20
Review for violation of precontractual disclosure obligation	18
Review of the rates	10
Review of the costs	25

(continued)

Table 20.1 (continued)

Product backlog item	Initial estimate [person-days]
Assignment of each accepted benefit to a rate, storage in statistics	12
Prognosis of policyholder benefit class	4
Review of suitability for personal injury management	2
Assignment to personal injury manager	2
Message to personal injury manager referencing medical history	2
Notice to care provider in case of repeated expensive benefit	2
Preparation of the personal benefit history	10
Preparation of printed document for policyholder	25
Review of printed document on a sampling basis prior to printing	2
Evaluation of success rate of personal injury manager	20

20.2 Risk Map

Figure 20.1 shows the risk map after initial population in the IR:scope (Sect. 8.4). It was apparent that the question of integrating the system being developed with the systems related to it and the issue of estimating the required effort were considered particular disaster indicators. The sum of 75 disaster points indicates some problems in the project setup. The highly valued disaster indicators were examined in particular detail and discussed with the stakeholders, which led to the definition of the countermeasures and also allowed them to be verified.

Figure 20.2 shows a later risk map (after the first eight sprints). We can see that most disaster indicators have developed in the right direction (the risk of disaster is considered lower compared to the start of the project). It is also apparent that the cost side of the project could have become a relevant problem, since convergence did not occur in the predictions of the cost forward progressing even after eight sprints, so that a serious problem could be suspected here.

Figure 20.3 shows the development of the disaster points over time. Each assessment was obtained after concluding the planning of a sprint.

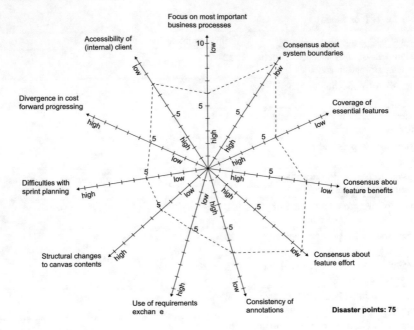

Fig. 20.1 Initial risk map for the HIB project

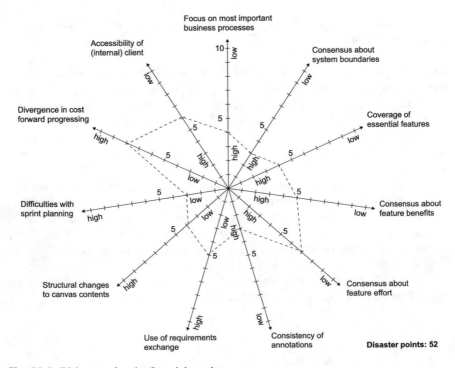

Fig. 20.2 Risk map after the first eight sprints

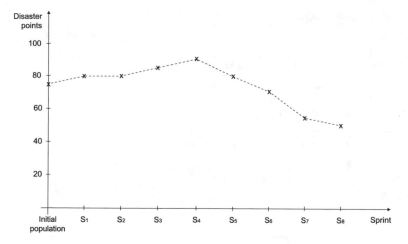

Fig. 20.3 Development of disaster points over time

20.3   The First Sprint

20.3.1   Planning the First Sprint

Planning of the first sprint was based on the initial version of the product backlog presented in Sect. 20.1, under consideration of the previously added annotations.

The maximum sprint scope in was determined as follows: A sprint duration of three weeks was agreed with the client. The core development team (excluding the scrum master and product owner) comprised seven persons who were included in the calculation with an average of 70 % pure development effort. This meant a total of approximately 75 person-days in development capacity was available for the first sprint.

After some discussion, the features listed in Table 20.2 were committed to for the first sprint, and more detailed effort estimates were prepared for them. The feature "determination of similar healing/therapy plans" in particular led to a lively discussion and was ultimately accepted into the sprint with the argument that, while it added little value, this would allow a comparatively high-risk feature to be implemented right away in order to quickly develop a feeling for the complexity.

20.3.2   Results of the First Sprint

Three weeks later, at the end of the first sprint, the results of the work appeared as shown in Table 20.3.

Most features were delivered, passed an acceptance test by the client, and were accepted. Previously, the client and supplier had agreed on a pragmatic Definition

Table 20.2 Sprint backlog for first sprint with detailed estimates

Sprint #1 backlog item	Detailed estimate [person-days]
Determination of client master data, including family master data	5
Determination of client risk affinity	10
Calculation of the monthly rate	4
Presentation of the health questions	21
Preliminary review of potentially required surcharges	3
Calculation of the total price	.5
Determination of similar healing/therapy plans	23
Total effort	**71**

Table 20.3 Results of first sprint

Sprint #1 backlog item	Detailed estimate [person-days]	Actual effort [person-days]	Accepted by client
Determination of client master data, including family master data	5	7	Yes
Determination of client risk affinity	10	13	Yes
Calculation of the monthly rate	4	6	Yes
Presentation of the health questions	21	20	Yes
Preliminary review of potential surcharges	3	6	Yes
Calculation of the total price	5	8	Yes
Total effort (accepted items)	**48**	**60**	
Determination of similar healing/therapy plans	23	15	No
Total effort (all items)	**71**	**75**	

of Done which roughly corresponded to that in Sect. 15.4.1. Accordingly to this, a feature is accepted when it exists with its full functionality and works correctly aside from small cosmetic flaws.

The feature "determination of similar healing/therapy plans" failed to meet this definition, since its realization was only rudimentary. There were two crucial reasons for this: Other features had taken more effort than planned, so that less effort within the available time box could be expended on this feature. The previously suspected complexity had materialized as well and the corresponding risk was realized. For these two reasons, only an approximation of the feature was delivered and therefore it could not be accepted. The effort of 15 person-days already expended was documented.

The remaining functionality from the sprint backlog was completed to the client's satisfaction, but somewhat more expensively than planned. Instead of the 48 person-days estimated for the first six features, 60 person-days were needed for them, which corresponded to statistical overspending of 25 %. While this sounded high at first glance, it was clear to all stakeholders that a learning curve had to be expected. For the settlement of the first sprint, 48 person-days were therefore billed at the regular daily rate and 12 person-days at the reduced daily rate. The agreed base rate was added. The feature "determination of similar healing/therapy plans" was not delivered in its final version until the third sprint and ultimately required an effort of 35 person-days. However, the assessment of all stakeholders agreed that the early realization of this feature helped overcome complexity and favored more accurate sprint planning in later iterations.

20.4   Settlement Using adVANTAGE

At the commercial–contractual level, the HIB project was managed quite closely along the lines of the adVANTAGE model described in Chap. 15. A few particularities are worth mentioning:

- Gauging the effort compensated by the base rate turned out to be more difficult than expected, since the scrum master's and product owner's work, as well as the time invested into the meetings, initially fluctuated widely from sprint to sprint. However, the effort appeared to settle at a mean value after a few iterations, and the client was willing to increase the base rate by approximately 20 %.
- The accuracy of the detailed estimates for specific features obtained at the start of each sprint improved steadily and continuously. While the initial budget estimated at the start of the project was exceeded, controlling improved in the course of time since the accuracy of estimating the realistic content of individual sprints kept improving.
- One reason for modestly exceeding the initial budget was the fact that entirely new requirements (partly due to legal constraints) were added in the course of the project. While a few lower-priority features were ultimately not implemented, saving some effort, this effect did not balance out the additional features.
- Since the composition of the team could be kept stable and the estimates kept getting more accurate, it was decided about halfway through the project to moderately increase the staffing in order to gain development speed. While a linear increase in productivity could not be achieved, the scope per release was boosted significantly while maintaining the level of quality.

Both parties to the contract drew satisfactory conclusions at the end of the realization phase. The project was a success from the user perspective. While the initial budget was exceeded, the magnitude of the overspending clearly within the accepted tolerance range for projects of this size, not to mention that requirements added in the course of the project were covered as well.

20.5   Cost Forward Progressing

After the first sprint, it turned out that 60 person-days had actually been needed for realizing the accepted features, as opposed to the estimate of 48 person-days. 60 instead of 48 person-days for the realization of the first sprint does not sound all that alarming at first glance, although a factor of 1.25 on the detailed estimate was of a magnitude that had to be summarily taken into account. The precise ΔDE deviation in the sense of cost forward progressing (Sect. 8.6) does not calculate the deviation of actual effort from the detailed estimates as a quotient of the sum of actual effort and detailed effort estimates, but as the mean of the feature-specific deviations. The value of the ΔDE deviation for the first sprint was 1.45. In the "computer scientist's forecast", the 12 additional person-days of effort expended were disregarded entirely. The "statistician's extrapolation" appeared less promising due to its consideration of the ΔDE deviation though. Since this was the first sprint which is typically encumbered by a certain orientation effort, an effect that is alleviated in subsequent sprints, this value did not need to be overemphasized but did provide cause for further observation.

The situation surrounding the feature "determination of similar healing/therapy plans" at the end of the first sprint was more interesting. Fully 15 person-days compared to a detailed estimate of 23 person-days were expended here without leading to acceptance of the feature. This could be entirely unsuspicious, especially since the estimated remaining effort for this feature did not exceed eight person-days. Even if the estimated remaining effort had been between 8 and $0.45 \times 23 + 8 \approx 18$ person-days, this would still be unsuspicious since a ΔDE deviation of 1.45 means that the effort according to the currently applicable calculations was exceeded by a factor of 0.45. An even higher estimate of remaining effort on the other hand would have had to be considered suspicious. For example, an estimated remaining effort for this feature in the magnitude of 23 person-days would have meant that 15 person-days had already been expended without coming closer to acceptance at all.

20.6   Using the Requirements Exchange

The requirements exchange was first used after the second sprint, with the addition of the following new features:

- **Personal injury manager clustering** (initial estimate: five person-days)

  - Motivation: A cluster of personal injury managers was to be formed for each type of personal injury and assigned to exactly this type of injury. This would support the optimum selection of suitable personal injury managers.

- **Updating personal injury types based on annual personal injury management statistics** (initial estimate: eight person-days)

  - Motivation: The initial clustering based on types of personal injuries was basically just a guess. Therefore, it was not certain whether the assumed clusters were meaningful. An annual review was to be performed to determine which types of personal injuries occur with what frequency, and the clustering structure was to be adapted.

Removal of the feature "evaluation of success rate, personal injury manager" from the product backlog was proposed as financing for the new features. Initially, the product manager responsible for the HIB system had major concerns, since he considered the personal success rates of the personal injury managers a key indicator relevant for controlling. After some discussion, it turned out that the procedures for determining and quantifying personal rates were comparatively unclear, leading to an agreement to exchange the two new features for the success rate feature. This exchange left a certain aftertaste, since it created the impression that the success rate feature was (and remained) fundamentally desired and that it was only omitted because it was unclear on the one hand and a convenient replacement candidate on the other hand. In fact, this feature was subsequently discussed again several times, but was not added back into the feature backlog.

With this exchange, the 20 person-days initially estimated for the success rate feature was offset against the 13 person-days initially estimated for the two new features. The calculated reduction of seven person-days had no relevant effect— even at a ΔIE deviation of 1.15 applicable at the time and a ΔDE deviation of 1.2 (which mathematically results in a reduction of the estimated effort by nearly ten person-days for the seven days).

Lessons Learned

Based on the experiences described above, we can reflect on the lessons learned by the client's and supplier's team members in the course of applying the Interaction Room and adVANTAGE model in practice. Specifically, we review the learning curve experienced by the team members, courses of action that did not work out, compromises that had to be made in adopting these methods, and the observed benefits and drawbacks.

In addition to the reflections based on the example of the HIB project, we also make observations based on numerous other applications of the Interaction Room.

- **Problems with incompleteness and uncertainty**: The underlying philosophy of the Interaction Room, i.e., the acceptance of incomplete information (especially at the beginning of a project) and the explicit identification of uncertainty, can be hard to accept for some stakeholders in the course of IR workshops. This is particularly true for stakeholders who, due to insufficient experience with software projects, still believe that software can be described completely in advance. Yet other stakeholders are sometimes not comfortable with explicitly "admitting" uncertainty. In such situations, the IR coaches have no choice but to repeatedly emphasize the unavoidability of initial incompleteness and the opportunities of explicitly identifying uncertainty.
- **Benefits of focusing on business aspects**: The benefits of initially focusing on business aspects are usually clear to all stakeholders in IR workshops. Nevertheless, sticking to the business level is difficult on occasion. This is understandable, since it does make sense to discuss solution-related requirements as well. From there, moving to the discussion of solution details is only a small step. But such discussions must not be permitted to dominate; otherwise, the business aspects fade too far into the background. This risk appears to be especially high when the business representatives have IT knowledge, even if they merely understand (or think they understand) the current implementation in its structure or technical details. The IR coaches can counteract this tendency by

suppressing discussions that stray too far from the business aspects, consistently steering the discussion back to business matters.

- **Usefulness of the integration canvas**: The usefulness of the integration canvas is questioned regularly. It is created with significantly less effort than virtually any other canvas, changes rarely during development, and also appears less closely integrated with the other canvases at first glance than they are integrated with each other. Yet the integration canvas plays an important role—illustrating the purely technical complexity of the project. This complexity results from the set of systems that have to be integrated and the interfaces that have to be satisfied. Omitting this view entirely causes the stakeholders to lose sight of a significant part of the required effort, and the relevant risks cannot be anchored on the canvases. Therefore, the IR coaches should consistently assert their methodology authority and insist on the population of the integration canvas.

- **Difficulties compiling the feature canvas**: Problems repeatedly arise during the population of the feature canvas in regard to the desired level of abstraction. Surprisingly however, the trend here is not clearly in the direction of wanting to note too many details (as is usually the case on the object canvas and process canvas). Rather, there is an equal trend toward excessive abstraction on the feature canvas. In fact, population of the feature canvas often starts out with too much detail, and pointing out the volume restriction (a few dozen features) then causes only the very highest level requirements to be named (tending to be at the level of the business processes that have to be supported). In this yo-yo situation, the IR coaches have to keep pushing for a suitable balance in the level of abstraction.

- **Desire to record more information on the object canvas**: The object canvas is perceived as the simplest element for anyone who has been involved in modeling before. The volume restriction is easy to explain and so is the focus on business relationships. Once the most important object types have been recorded, there is often a desire to consider cardinalities, association types, and the optionality of relationships. Experience has shown that such considerations in the early phases of the IR:scope tend to be unreliable; i.e., they do not result in a relevant gain of information. Yet rigorously suppressing this discussion is not always expedient. Sometimes, it needs to be given a bit of room, if only to ensure that all stakeholders remain mentally involved. However, the IR coaches have to consistently avoid distraction from the business relationships.

- **Difficulties preparing the partner canvas**: While many of the canvases are familiar from other modeling situations, the partner canvas is usually new for the stakeholders in an IR population. Determining the input/output relationships at the company level and naming the types of information exchanged and the real objects involved can be quite challenging. Here, the IR coaches have to offer methodology support and name the first interfaces themselves. If this is not sufficient, it may be useful to link the preparation of the partner canvas and physical object canvas. Then, it becomes clear to the stakeholders sooner how the results of the partner canvas will be subsequently used.

- **Inconvenience of the OoI descriptions on the physical object canvas**: In many cases, the stakeholders only see the benefits of describing the details of objects of interest (OoIs) in the course of preparing the physical object canvas once they recognize what those details are used for. They are used in the course of the discussion of how an OoI can send information to ongoing business processes or be controlled by ongoing business processes. Without this context, preparing the physical object canvas often appears technocratic and is frequently performed halfheartedly. So if the interdependency is not apparent at the outset, the IR coaches should specify a particularly suitable OoI from the project in question at a high level and use it as an example to demonstrate how the information can be used.

- **Inaccuracy of the touchpoint canvas**: During the population of the touchpoint canvas, situations are frequently encountered where the weakly defined specifications for the syntax and semantics encounter their limits. The stakeholders want to express certain circumstances and have the impression that this cannot succeed with the simple model elements of the touchpoint canvas. This impression is may be comprehensible, even though it is often questionable whether the specific circumstances that the stakeholders wish to express have to be noted necessarily. This is where the IR coaches need to proceed with particular tact: Sometimes, it makes sense to introduce additional symbols; sometimes, it makes sense to note details with text labels on model elements; and sometimes, the details being examined are not relevant and should be left out. Generally however, it must be noted that the population of the touchpoint canvas tends toward a more individual syntax than the population of all the other canvases.

- **Excessive annotation precision**: It is usually easy to explain the fundamental benefits of the various annotation rounds. The precise meaning of the annotations, on the other hand, can often lead to discussions. Terms such as "security" and "reliability" in particular can have various meanings and are understood in different ways. The attempt to define differences in understanding often leads to a desire for creating additional annotations. Introducing additional annotations should however be prevented in order not to overwhelm stakeholders. The existing set of annotations has proven sufficient so far. Possible semantic differences or special meanings can be documented in the individual descriptions of the symbols applied to the model elements. Even though the use of annotations is systematic, it must remain clear that the interactive annotation process is prone to error. An annotation that has been attached to a model element is not normative; it can also be removed again. Discussing the annotations can lead to new insights. This means annotations are always qualitative references as well, and a strictly quantitative perspective to evaluating them is rarely appropriate.

- **Using the volume rules to prevent the population process from getting out of hand**: The volume rules of how many model elements are allowed on each canvas are usually not plausible for most stakeholders at first glance. They want to quickly, completely, and precisely document their knowledge and ideas about the software system being developed, making sure they do not forget anything and that no gaps remain. Rules imposed on the upper limit of model elements interfere with that. Therefore, the IR coaches are well advised to explain and enforce the volume rules and to point out from the outset that they will do so. Otherwise, too much information and especially excessive, initially unimportant details are virtually impossible to avoid.

- **Transition to the concrete specification**: We described an immediate transition from the IR:scope to the IR:agile in the example of the HIB project. Often however, established software process models require the preparation of additional artifacts, such as a specification document. The results of the IR:scope can in principle be transferred to such artifacts without losses. Dealing with the deliberate incompleteness of the IR:scope results however remains awkward. It makes little sense to transfer the explicitly incomplete knowledge after the end of the IR:scope to a specification format which is basically geared toward completeness and invariability. Difficulties are regularly encountered at this point, since amendments are desired that are aimed at closing the gaps identified in the IR. Managing the process of closing these gaps is not the responsibility of the IR coach anymore, but of a selected team of business and technology experts.

- **Estimates required for the transition from the IR:scope to the IR:agile**: During the transition from the IR:scope to the IR:agile, the individual features have to be estimated in person-days. Quantitatively estimating the features at this point is often difficult however, and many stakeholders feel more comfortable with a classification into "small," "medium," and "large" categories. In fact, it is often understandable that the estimate in person-days is challenging. Yet this should be done, since estimating all features is essential for the requirements exchange on the one hand and to assess the overall scope on the other hand. In case of great vagueness, a workshop to define groups of logically related features more precisely can help establish a basis for estimation.

- **Corridor between the "computer scientist's forecast" and the "statistician's extrapolation"**: The significance of the "computer scientist's forecast" and the "statistician's extrapolation" obtained through cost forward progressing is frequently discussed in projects. While the extrapolation makes a more reasoned impression overall, there are also situations (e.g., when a specific feature was incorrectly estimated due to a wrong assumption) where the forecast provides the better indication of the effort actually required. Generally, both values should be understood as what they are: indications of the effort expected to be required that change over time. Like all values determined solely by algorithms, they have to be interpreted in the larger project context.

- **Desire for a differentiated extrapolation of the estimate deviations**: Cost forward progressing develops extrapolations by applying the deviations to date to all estimated values. The desire for better differentiation has often been expressed in this context. A typical line of thinking, e.g., is "these concrete deviations are related to the development of interfaces, so only the effort that has to do with interface development should be extrapolated." While this desire is comprehensible, its consistent application leads to individual decision making for every deviation regarding the extent to which it is extrapolated and suggests a higher level of precision than the approach can actually provide. The more straightforward high-level extrapolation and forecast as described in Sect. 8.6 should therefore remain unchanged (with full awareness that it does not deliver the most precise values). When there is an urgent need, this can be supplemented with calculations that have to be justified on a case-by-case basis. This ensures that a high-level orientation based on the values of cost forward progressing which are always determined the same way remains possible at all times.

- **Overestimating the requirements exchange**: The requirements exchange is frequently the object of suggestions for greater precision. Perhaps the idea is to carry minor differences forward for future financing (e.g., "if a new requirement with an effort of 20 person-days is exchanged for an old requirement with a scope of 22 person-days, the two "saved" person-days should be noted for future exchanges"). Or perhaps the deviations that arise for new requirements in the future should be separately recorded in order to measure whether the desire for suitable financing leads to corrupt estimations of effort. Or perhaps groups of requirements should be formed, where exchanges within these groups do not constitute a problem, while exchanges between groups are supposed to balance out over defined periods of time. While these and some other suggestions all appear reasonable and well-intended, they overestimate the algorithmic effect of the requirements exchange. The purpose of the requirements exchange is to prevent the bloating of software and anchor the concept of elimination in the minds of the stakeholders. However, its algorithmic institutionalization and regulation must not be taken too far. In the end, the actors have to make a qualitative decision, determining which requirements are actually indispensable. It is precisely this responsibility for lean software that cannot be delegated to rules and algorithms.
- **Usefulness of the requirements exchange**: After a brief acclimatization period, the requirements exchange has proven itself as an important instrument to put the emphasis on lean software in virtually all application situations. Most stakeholders quickly grasped that some requirements can safely be eliminated, and that a lean implementation is worth striving for. Often, this went so far (especially in the HIB project) that business representatives supported an implementation that afforded somewhat reduced convenience but could be realized with significantly less effort. The focus on software that is "good enough" has turned out to be a major cost control factor.
- **Usefulness of the risk map**: The informative value of quantitative disaster points determined by populating the risk map is limited, since they depend on personal estimates and do not correspond directly to quantifiable cost or effort. Two considerations are useful in interpreting the risk map however:

  - Taking into account the reasons of the stakeholders in assessing the risk dimensions.
  - Determining the disaster points periodically and observing their development over time.

Suggestions for the more precise assignment of disaster points per dimension have been frequently discarded since the situation is different for each project. This makes it impossible to compare disaster points between projects, but they are useful as a relative measure of the evolution of risk within a project. Usually, the risk map values tend to change very little once the project has reached a certain maturity. When this is the case, updating the risk map can stop, with full awareness that exogenous events may still lead to a need to re-evaluate the risks.

Applicability of adVANTAGE: adVANTAGE often appears complex at the start of an IR:agile. This impression has evaporated after the second sprint in every single application situation. On the other hand, the desire for refinement in regard to several special situations often develops (e.g., the handling of features that are reported as ready for acceptance while the client does not want to test them until later, warranty on accepted features, combining features from different sprints into releases, and so on). All of these discussions need to be permitted, and some refinements actually make sense for specific projects. In general, it has proven useful to maintain the simplicity of adVANTAGE.

Part V
Conclusion

The Big Picture

In the preceding chapters, we explored the novel role of enterprise IT as the enabler and designer of new business models, the resulting requirements for the domain expertise, communication skills, value orientation and flexibility of enterprise IT, and methodical and contractual instruments that can help to complete such projects pragmatically and effectively.

To conclude, we finally discuss the experiences with the different versions of the Interaction Room in the larger context of the New School of IT discussed at the outset. For this purpose, we first summarize the insights we were able to gain about the Interaction Room so far. In order to implement the New School of IT with the extensive support of the Interaction Room in practice, the acting persons must have qualifications they may not have needed in the established world of enterprise IT. These are discussed in Chap. 23. They range from general software engineering and methodology requirements to essential domain and process knowledge and the requirements of the New School of IT (mobility, agility, and flexibility). Chapter 24 then closes with an outlook on the impact of the New School of IT, concisely expressed in 12 hypotheses.

Three topics kept coming up in the preceding discussions: complexity of the business domain, business and user value orientation, and awareness of unavoidable uncertainty. None of these aspects are revolutionary—Curtis et al. already lamented the "thin spread of application domain knowledge" in 1988, Lehman formulated his "uncertainty principle for computer application" in 1989, and Boehm has been advocating value orientation in software development since 1981.

Plan-driven and agile software process models approach this challenge with different philosophies—on the one hand, by attempting to understand and describe the system and context as completely as possible at the outset, and on the other hand, by following a step-by-step approach where smaller individual problems are resolved ad hoc. Both approaches have their strengths and weaknesses. Therefore, it is no surprise that the key is finding a suitable middle ground between the exccessively dogmatic interpretations of both sides.

© Springer International Publishing Switzerland 2016
M. Book et al., *Tamed Agility*, DOI 10.1007/978-3-319-41478-2_22

But finding this middle ground is not easy—using common sense is easy to say but not a reliable methodology. Therefore, the instruments introduced in the preceding chapters offer a pragmatic way to find this middle ground in practice.

The Interaction Room provides an environment where the stakeholders, in keeping with the agile credo, can communicate face-to-face and without a heavy methodology or formal superstructure. At the same time, however, it also offers the permanence and structure that provides for the appeal of the plan-driven approach. As an additional benefit offered neither by plan-driven nor agile approaches alone, an Interaction Room yields insights about "soft" factors such as complexity, basic conditions, value drivers, and uncertainty. In contrast to other software models, the stakeholders can explicitly record these on the IR canvases with annotations.

The adVANTAGE contract model ensures that an agile approach—based on the insights gained from the Interaction Room—can be actually put into practice in the course of the project and that its flexibility is not destroyed by excessively rigid contract structures. The contractor and client have the flexibility to respond to new requirements and new value assessments without having to argue about the distribution of effort or cost risks, and without needing to be concerned about the initial time and budget specifications getting entirely out of control.

This prepares projects for a value-oriented, pragmatic approach to complex business aspects that only become apparent piece by piece—and especially for the novel understanding of roles required from enterprise IT by the New School of IT.

References

Boehm B (1981) Software engineering economics. Prentice-Hall
Curtis B, Krasner H, Iscoe N (1988) A field study of the software design process for large systems. Comm ACM 31(11):1268–1287. doi:10.1145/50087.50089
Lehman MM (1989) Uncertainty in computer application and its control through the engineering of software. J Software Maintenance 1(1):3–27. doi:10.1002/smr.4360010103

A New Skill Set

23

To operate in the world of tamed agility, establish the correct extent of agility depending on the basic conditions for the project and also to effectively use the instruments presented in this book, enterprise IT needs a number of skills.

23.1 General Software Technology and Methodology Skills

Enterprise IT in the New School of IT obviously needs a number of software technology skills. These include:

- **Requirements management**: Dynamic requirements management plays a particularly important role in software development using tamed agility (especially for the development of software in the context of mobilization and digitalization). In addition to the technical skills [e.g., according to IREB (2016)], the ability to differentiate between essential and non-essential requirements is especially important.
- **Business analysis and modeling**: Most software systems are intended to provide commercial benefits. This means it is essential that enterprise IT understands business relationships, is able to structure them, and documents them at a suitable abstraction level. These descriptions must abstain from making any technical decisions. From a methodology perspective, this requires process and object modeling knowledge. A command of corresponding modeling languages is needed.
- **Architecture management**: The management of enterprise architectures (the architectures of entire application landscapes) is a classic component of enterprise IT. However, emergent architectures are often encountered in the context of mobile applications and the digitalization of business processes. They are difficult to plan but have to be integrated into the application landscape anyway.

© Springer International Publishing Switzerland 2016
M. Book et al., *Tamed Agility*, DOI 10.1007/978-3-319-41478-2_23

This is challenging at interfaces. Even though classic architecture management models and processes that tend to count on plannability and long-term further development are not made for this, the emergent architectures nevertheless have to be managed and their further development must be planned and realized. This requires knowledge of traditional architecture management on the one hand (models, languages, processes) and, on the other hand, the insight that certain systems have to be integrated in spite of characteristics that do not "fit."

- **Automation and digitalization techniques**: Ultimately, many IT projects are about automating processes or supporting manual activities in order to boost productivity. Numerous techniques and methods are used here, which are subject to technology changes. Knowledge of these techniques is essential. Detailed knowledge of specific techniques is required along with assessing the lifecycle of related technologies. Techniques for the synchronous and asynchronous linking of heterogeneous systems, bus systems, various types of middleware systems, and protocols to connect distributed and mobile systems are currently part of the dominant technology canon.

23.2 New School of IT Skills: Mobility

While the mobility of data and applications is only one dimension defining the New School of IT, it plays an important role—if only because mobility cannot be abstracted away. Development methods and instruments that encapsulate the mobility of data and applications in a layer, so that classic, non-mobile programming models are maintained, simply do not exist yet—and neither is such a solution foreseeable. Applications have to be mobile-friendly. The architect has to decide in the course of designing applications what parts of them have to be available on mobile devices, and developers have to take into account in the course of development that telecommunication connections are unreliable in practice. But this is not the only reason the mobility dimension is relevant. Mobile applications are also operated in various usage contexts and potentially have to run on many different devices, and testing mobile systems poses a number of specific challenges. In the following, we discuss the skills of enterprise IT that are required due to the increasing demand for data and application mobility.

- **Usability engineering and user experience design**: Users are familiar with mobile systems. By and large, they are accustomed to appealing and easy to use interfaces. Their experiences define their expectations of everything mobile. Appealing applications that can be learned without effort are intuitive to use and efficient are expected. This alone means the requirements for the usability of mobile applications are extremely high. But making things nice and colorful is not sufficient for usability. Usability engineering needs to be taken into account systematically in the development process. This requires usability engineers who know what usability is, how the interfaces on the various platforms have to be designed, and how usability is measured and evaluated. Usability engineering is not limited to usability in the narrower sense. Integrated usability engineering goes beyond that, not only evaluating the usability of an application against usability criteria but also including the usage context of the user. Fundamentally, good usability may not be sufficient for a positive user experience if the user interacts with the application under a high cognitive load. On the other hand, technically poor usability may actually be sufficient if the user can complete a bothersome process quickly and reliably. And perhaps the entire user experience does not depend on usability alone, but on the context, annoyance factor of the process being handled and cross-application characteristics. Enterprise IT should include experts who have mastered usability engineering in the details and at a high level and who evaluate applications strictly from a client perspective.

- **Interface technologies**: Nothing changes as often and fundamentally as interface technologies. This happens in a recurring cycle with the increased or reduced centrality of software systems. The issue of what can be handled decentrally and how much server-side control is required changes over time, simply because both ends of the spectrum appear plausible. Central systems have the advantage that they can be centrally controlled and monitored. Dependencies on decentralized devices are eliminated. These benefits were already realized during the era of mainframe computers and in times when the browser was the only decentralized software. But the disadvantage of centrality is that local input on the decentralized device has to be sent to the server, where it must be validated and processed. This means a decentralized architecture has advantages as well: A lot of local processing by devices is possible and their performance can reduce the load on central infrastructures. Much of the communication between clients and servers is eliminated as well. Another appeal of native apps on mobile devices is that they are easily made available through app stores and marketplaces, and can be updated virtually as desired. But then there is the question of integration with the local sensor technology, which is not standardized—so that decentralized testing is required again after all. The back and forth continues. With this back and forth, the question of how decentralized interfaces can be realized changes. Pure HTML? Or better JavaScript too? Perhaps not such lean clients after all? Or angular? Here, the world remains colorful and unsorted, and can be expected to remain that way for some time. As long as this is the case, enterprise IT has to have knowledge of common interface techniques and their lifecycles.
- **Telecommunication protocols**: Mobile data and applications require communication between application components. This takes place based on the connections between these components and telecommunication protocols that establish the technical level on which communication takes place. Different telecommunication protocols are associated with various bandwidths, service

levels, and costs. Which of these protocols will be used in what application is of central importance for system acceptance. Some applications only exchange low volumes of data but have to do so with absolute reliability. Others are more talkative. Others again may be non-critical, which means the user is not that concerned if the connection should fail at times. Perhaps the user even wants to decide: large bandwidth and high reliability in exchange for additional costs. Both the question of which data and applications must be available offline and the question of what telecommunication integration is required demands knowledge of the applicable situation on the one hand and of the possible telecommunication protocols and their integration in software on the other hand.

- **Knowledge of important device classes and their management possibilities**: In some situations, the mobile devices that will be used can simply be prescribed. This occurs as a rule when the user operates in a self-contained context or the devices are centrally procured and financed. In such situations, the mobile devices often have to be centrally managed as well: What software (in which version) is running on which device? Where is the device? What user has which usage rights? Is there a need to centrally block specific devices? When is that supposed to happen? How are software and hardware exchanged? However, such tight management is not possible in many other situations. This is obvious as soon as end customers come into play, but a heterogeneous device landscape is unavoidable in case of mixed partner landscapes as well. Explicitly establishing the device classes to support is mandatory for mobile applications as a result. Enterprise IT therefore has to be familiar with the common device classes and types.

- **Platforms and corresponding processes**: Depending on the chosen platform (e.g., iOS or Android), the rigidity of processes offered by the application delivery platform for validation, security, and advance verification differs. These mechanisms and processes must be known to enterprise IT, since they influence testability, release cycles, and possible monetization.

- **Implementation strategies**: Whether web-based mobile systems or native apps are going to dominate the mobile experience is still undecided. The trend appears to be heading in the direction of hybrid systems. Questions about the role of cross-platform approaches, of generated and interpretive approaches, also fall into this context. As long as a de facto standard has not been established here, enterprise IT should know the advantages and disadvantages of the different realization versions.

- **Security**: Security plays a greater role in distributed systems than central ones, and a greater role in mobile systems than in distributed ones. Techniques for the secure transmission of data and protection against unauthorized access and falsification are basic elements of mobile systems. In addition, security requirements are tending to gain importance but are also subject to social change. Accordingly, enterprise IT has to be familiar with the solutions to common security problems, if only to effectively counter the use of security as a killer argument against process innovations.

- **Test automation**: Stationary information systems are rarely tested in full in the sense of source code coverage. With the increasing spread of test automation techniques and the management of suitable test case sets however, stationary testing has become managcable in the meantime. Testing mobile systems remains a different matter. Input vectors explode because location data and the use of different telecommunication protocols and providers are added (Griebe and Gruhn 2014). In general, every sensor used to exchange data with the environment has to be included in testing. This quickly becomes too much to handle manually. Furthermore, there are annoying differences between actual systems and sensor emulations. As a result, testing mobile systems is not highly systematic yet. Yet a lot can be gained in this area. Those who can reliably test mobile applications more quickly gain leeway in the market by being able to deliver new features sooner. This means it is unavoidable for enterprise IT deal with this area as well.

23.3   New School of IT Skills: Agility

Agility affects the whole company and not just the application developers. Purchasers, controllers, and legal practitioners are affected by agile development, at least when suppliers and contractors have to be integrated. Since agility originates in technology, enterprise IT must be familiar with the fundamental concepts of agility because this is the only way it can formulate the requirements for the other functional units. This knowledge is of course essential to apply tamed agility. The required knowledge includes:

- **Principles and measures of agility**: Agile development techniques encompass numerous reasonable elements but also some ideological ones. They have to be applied according to the project situation. In the New School of IT, it is necessary to determine at the outset how agile the approach will be and which agile best practices are going to be applied. This can only work if those making these choices are familiar with the canon of agile best practices and able to assess the techniques. Knowledge of Scrum and Kanban is indispensable, and field reports on their benefits and risks should be known. The techniques of the more plan-driven process models should be known as well, since both practices from both worlds likely have to be combined.
- **Techniques of continuous delivery/integration**: Agility does not stop at the limits of application development but affects all of enterprise IT. This means enterprise IT has to be familiar with the concepts and architectures of continuous delivery and integration (Duval et al. 2007), since ultimately it is not enough to deliver software in foreseeable increments. It also has to be made available for production as early and as often as possible.

23.4   New School of IT Skills: Flexibility

Flexible infrastructures, data outsourcing, and application management are buzzwords associated with significant benefits and potential savings. Whether and when what shift and scaling is applied depends to a large extent on the specific case, whether data protection and autonomy play a special role, and also how often changing the basic conditions quickly has to be possible. In order to assess the potential of scalable infrastructures and the risks and opportunities of using certain technologies, enterprise IT should have knowledge of the following technologies:

- **Cloud technologies**: Whether infrastructures and applications are shifted to public clouds or not depends on numerous regulatory conditions and risk assessments. But even when this is not done, using cloud-like structures and mechanisms can make sense in order to meet the requirements of flexible scaling. Whether this is a full-blown private cloud or merely the implementation of automated delivery processes does not play a role. Enterprise IT must be familiar with corresponding mechanisms and has to be able to generate and operate suitable structures.
- **Big data technologies**: Big data technologies in the broadest sense are a driver of flexible infrastructures. We are talking about collecting, summarizing, and storing large volumes of data in different formats and of various origins. In order to be able to do that, enterprise IT requires knowledge of digitalization techniques. It has to master the handling and inclusion of real objects and their more or less continuous delivery of data. It must be familiar with various persistence techniques since all the incoming data, which may be differently structured, cannot be processed in relational structures quickly enough and in a meaningful manner (both regarding its storage and its evaluation).
- **Statistics**: Large volumes of data have to be evaluated. This always has to happen at runtime, since the detour using extraction, transformation, and loading processes only delivers results after days or even weeks in many cases—often too late for business processes with customer contact. The fast evaluation of large data volumes and immediate feedback to operational business processes means that patterns have to be recognized in data, the data must be summarized, and relationships relevant for business need to be identified. In order to accomplish this, enterprise IT requires statistics know-how and has to fill the role of the data scientist (Davenport and Patil 2012).

Rapid further development is taking place in all of these areas, so that it is not sufficient for enterprise IT to develop the right competencies at a given moment. Even more so than in other fields, the flexibility dimension requires the continuous observation of market trends and technology developments along with the evaluation of their potential.

23.5   Business Development and Domain Knowledge

The content of a largely stable software system, subject only to gradual and continuous further development and based on stable technology, can be driven by users. This is true for most systems of records. The situation is different when it comes to a new software system. Here, "new" means "structurally new." We are not talking about the exact replacement of legacy systems with new systems. Structurally new systems are developed for new business models or when novel technologies enable entirely new solutions.

The availability of reliable, ubiquitous telecommunications, for example, led to entirely new, partly mobile business processes and corresponding software systems. Which mobile solutions make sense can only be evaluated when one understands the potential of mobile technologies. This cannot be assessed without specialized IT knowledge. Of course, this knowledge gradually becomes mainstream; until at some point, the potential of a technology is also clear to the users so that they can develop new application ideas based on their domain knowledge. But by then, the technology is no longer new and disruptive. In short, the future business potential of new technologies can only be assessed with expert IT knowledge.

The convergence of systems of records with systems of engagement is leading to entirely new technology mixes. As long as this is the case, business development also has to take place in IT departments. This means IT is no longer just a service provider but actively participates in the product design. The more domain knowledge is available in the IT department, and the more effectively IT and users are engaged in productive discussions, the better this role can be filled. The phenomenon that the performance of traditional enterprise IT in view of digital transformation in companies is often considered low, so that parallel organizations are set up, is described by Westerman et al. (2014). It goes on to discuss that companies known as digital masters (i.e., companies with a high level of leadership capability and digital capability) refrain from doing exactly that. Instead they ensure their enterprise IT obtains the necessary qualifications and bring it close to business. In short, enterprise IT should be positioned so it can participate in business development.

In order to do so, enterprise IT has to understand the domain and its language, and be able to discuss it. This means the fundamental relationships in the respective industry as well as the industry-specific terminology must be understood. Enterprise IT should also understand the company, the way it functions and its market position, challenges, and strategy. It should be familiar with the regulatory context and understand likely exogenous influencing factors. While this is not required for developing and operating software in the narrow sense, it makes the development of new business models easier and simplifies communication between operating departments and enterprise IT. Efficient and cooperative business development is only possible if this communication flows smoothly.

23.6   Knowledge of Business Processes, Business Models, and Partnerships

The New School of IT means focusing on lean software. Building as little software as possible is the goal. Rather than automating everything, the goal is to automate only what needs to be automated in order to become more productive and cost-effective in the interest of adding value to a company.

This can also mean that some activities, which only occur rarely, still have to be performed manually or that some reports that are rarely needed are no longer created. Perhaps it is not even possible to capture all data versions with dialogs, and one accepts that rare cases become actual exceptions with corresponding individual treatment. This follows the principle of data frugality (Akella et al. 2009). In order to consider where automation is sensible and where it is not, many things need to be known about the business processes being supported. What volume of business is being conducted where, what drives client and user satisfaction, what data inconsistencies can incur costs, how many administrators work with what functionality how often?

But even knowledge of all these relationships is not enough to assess whether delivering certain functionality is worthwhile. The costs of preparation and operation also have to be known to assess economic efficiency. It is essential for this reason alone that those stakeholders familiar with the application domain, and in particular with the operational handling of the business processes being supported, work together with software architects, developers, and operating experts. Great opportunities arise if they actually engage with each other. Such a cross-disciplinary team may, for example, identify that the desired functionality is too expensive and that minimal changes that could still be acceptable from a business perspective lead to more low-priced, economical solutions.

Truly lean software is the result: Developers and operating experts understand the essential requirements of the users and conceive lean implementations in cooperation with them—a lot of added value with little software. This requires the various competencies described above and the willingness to engage in an interdisciplinary debate to find the best solution. In fact, one not merely needs cooperation between development (Dev) and operation (Ops) according to the DevOps model (Bass et al. 2015), but also an understanding of the business. In other words, the New School of IT is not satisfied with DevOps but demands BizDevOps (Gruhn and Schäfer 2015).

Yet sometimes cooperation between enterprise IT and operating departments is not sufficient to improve support for business processes. Specialized knowledge is required in some cases to develop new business models. Perhaps customer behavior has to be observed and evaluated, and perhaps new products need to be delivered or maybe the pricing schema has to be adapted. Maybe unusual requirements apply in terms of security, mobility, or the user experience. Perhaps there is a trend in favor of service-based transaction models. Enterprise IT may not have all the required competencies in such situations. Here, it may be wise to get partners involved rather than developing the missing competencies from the ground up. If they provide support for central aspects and understand the business domain, the question arises whether they should not merely act as suppliers but as true partners—partners who participate in the potential business success but then also bear part of the risk. Of course this is no panacea. Maintaining sole control of a new business model is often more important than sharing the risks and opportunities. Sometimes, new business models are also used for practice. Many suppliers are not eligible as partners. But in the time of the New School of IT with its focus on new business models and the convergence of systems of records with systems of engagement, involving partners (formerly called suppliers) more closely should at least be considered. Possibly some business models are easier to establish when all competencies are exploited so they focus solely on the success of the business model. In general, this consideration is more applicable the more it falls into the context of the digital transformation [the use of technologies to fully digitalize aspects of the business (Westerman et al. 2014)].

23.7 Insights and Experiences

An enterprise IT department with all the knowledge discussed above appears to be perfectly equipped to practice tamed agility and the New School of IT. But it is also useful for the enterprise IT department—or a sufficient number of its members—to have gained experience and learned some lessons, including the following:

- **No one-size-fits-all projects**: Every project is different. This does not mean that no generally applicable methods and instruments exist. However, it means that changes are required every now and then, that flexibility is essential, and that there is no reason for method and process dogmatism.
- **Central importance of expectation management**: People want to know what awaits them, even if we are only talking about new software. This means one has to explain what is happening to them. Expectations are only adjusted if the explanations are also understood. Expectation management therefore means to explain circumstances as long and as thoroughly as it takes to make them understood, and not only as long as it should take to make them understood.
- **Lean and good-enough software**: Ideal solutions cannot be built, especially not at first try. Most of all they are too expensive. Software that fulfills its purpose is entirely sufficient, pays off more quickly, and is readily used. Additional financial resources may then be made available in order to get closer to ideal software, even though this is usually unattainable in the end.
- **People want to be valued and included**: In the end, *people* do the work in a project. People want to be appreciated for their contribution to project work, and they want to know how their contributions are integrated into the overall system.

- **Communication is the key**: Whether we are talking about delays or quality problems, project success, or sensitive measures—at least half of a project's success depends on appropriate communication. Being able to talk to the right people in the right order and suitable tonality is eminently important.

All experience shows that software projects succeed or fail with the ability of all stakeholders to correctly grasp, understand, assess, and implement the system context and system requirements. Especially in socio-technical systems in the context of the New School of IT, which are closely interwoven with existing business process and technology landscapes, the ability of the team members to communicate is central: Based on the most well-founded possible technology and domain knowledge, they have to make the right decisions about prioritizing requirements, designing system structures, adapting business processes and the integration of many different components and interfaces.

With the Interaction Room, we have introduced a method that supports the understanding, evaluation, and discussion of many different aspects of a system. True to the agile philosophy, it encourages healthy pragmatism with a focus on the aspects that are essential for understanding the project and ensures that value and risk drivers remain in view during the entire project term. The adVANTAGE contract model ensures that such a pragmatic, agile approach does not remain a theoretical ideal that is forced back into an advance planning corset by classic delivery contracts. Since adVANTAGE gives both the client and the supplier leeway for adjustments but fairly distributes risks at the same time, the contract model ensures that agility can actually be practiced in a flexible innovation process guided by value and risk considerations.

References

Akella J, Buckow H, Rey S (2009) IT architecture: Cutting costs and complexity. http://www.mckinsey.com/business-functions/business-technology/our-insights/it-architecture-cutting-costs-and-complexity. Accessed 1 Mar 2016

Bass L, Weber I, Zhu L (2015) DevOps: A software architect's perspective. Addison-Wesley

Davenport TH, Patil DJ (2012) Data scientist: The sexiest job of the 21st century. Harvard Business Review 90(10):70–76

Duvall PM, Matyas S, Glover A (2007) Continuous integration: Improving software quality and reducing risk. Addison-Wesley

Griebe T, Gruhn V (2014) A model-based approach to test automation for context-aware mobile applications. In: Kim S, Hung CC, Hong J (eds) SAC 2014: Proc 29th Annual ACM Symposium on Applied Computing, pp 420–427. doi:10.1145/2554850.2554942

Gruhn V, Schäfer C (2015) BizDevOps: Because DevOps is not the end of the story. In: Fujita H, Guizzi G (eds) SoMet 2015: Proc 14th Intl Conf on Intelligent Software Methodologies, Tools and Techniques. Communications in Computer and Information Science, vol 532. Springer, pp 388–398. doi:10.1007/978-3-319-22689-7_30

IREB e.V. (2016) Certified professional for requirements engineering (CPRE). https://www.ireb.org/en/cpre/basics/. Accessed 1 Mar 2016

Westerman G, Bonnet D, McAfee A (2014) Leading digital: Turning technology into business transformation. Harvard Business Review Press

Outlook: Twelve Hypotheses

24

Enterprise IT must and will undergo tremendous change. This change is not triggered by one single megatrend, buzzword, or idea. Rather, numerous developments are intertwining, jointly causing radical change. This change can be formulated in twelve hypotheses:

- **IT is no longer driven, but becomes the driver**: The importance of IT in the company will grow beyond merely supporting business. It is going to determine new business models. More and more often, new products and services will be the result of new possibilities in IT. All of a sudden, business development takes place in enterprise IT.
- **The world goes mobile**: The centralist world view of IT starts to totter. Infrastructure and applications are needed where business happens, not the other way around. Mobility will not merely constitute a specialization of IT, but become the basic pattern for the (further) development of IT.
- **Application development for the mobile world is a new discipline**: IT for mobility is far more than bridging the physical distance between mobile devices and companies. Software engineering for mobile applications is more difficult than software engineering for stationary software. Complexity increases and has to be managed.
- **Neat interfaces are not just for games**: A pleasant user experience will not be reserved for consumer applications and gaming. Users have become accustomed to elegant, well-functioning interfaces, and expect these in business life and daily work as well.
- **What is "in" today is "out" tomorrow**: The boundaries between enterprise IT and external contractors are going to shift significantly. More and more often, the risks of application development and operations are being passed on to contractors. They become specialists in the industry of the client. Internal IT becomes specialized in technically driven business development, requirements engineering, and test management.

© Springer International Publishing Switzerland 2016
M. Book et al., *Tamed Agility*, DOI 10.1007/978-3-319-41478-2_24

- **The client and contractor share joy and pain**: New cooperation models will define relationships with contractors. The client and contractor become partners and commit to lean processes, lean software, and lean operating models. Risks and opportunities are shared. The price is not determined by the size and complexity of the application, but by efficiency as the ratio between effort and benefits.
- **Everything in software development becomes agile, including the price**: The change in cooperation between the client and contractor in custom development leads to new commercial models. The time and materials basis is too risky for the client. Fixed prices are not affordable due to high risk surcharges. As a result, commercial models are designed based on agile development processes.
- **Software development becomes value-oriented**: There is only one true measure of productivity in application development: few function points per desired functionality. This becomes the control quantity in portfolio planning and the determination of success. Efficiency is the ratio of the benefits achieved to the effort expended. This leads to a focus on value-added features.
- **Software development increasingly becomes a process of gaining insights**: All progress in software engineering notwithstanding, specifying information systems fully is not possible and therefore will not be attempted. Instead one has to accept that some insights and requirements will not be known until late in the process.
- **Knowledge becomes a central element of application development**: The knowledge in the minds of the people in the business and IT departments is complementary. Value-added applications are created when both sides are willing and able to exchange and combine this knowledge. This requires mutual respect and communication skills.
- **Development and operations become one**: The increasing agility of application development radiates to deployment and operation. Short iteration cycles and the rapid availability of new software versions are only useful if they can be put into production quickly as well. The divides between application development and operations are bridged by necessity. Development operation organizations will be created for particularly dynamic domains.
- **IT remains human—but differently**: Automation, increased efficiency, mobility, agility, and flexibility—all the changes and evolution in IT also mean that the role of people in IT is going to be transformed. Social, communication, and creative skills are needed in addition to technical expertise in order to handle the new opportunities and reap the full benefits.

The New School of IT is a novel challenge and new responsibility rolled into one for enterprise IT. Rising to the challenge requires not only pragmatic methods and instruments, but also most of all capable people such as domain and technology experts who contribute their ideas, talk to each other, respond to each other, and look for new business and technical solutions.

Appendix A
Interaction Room Workshop Agendas

A.1 Interaction Room Workshop Agendas

The agendas suggested below can serve as guidelines for conducting Interaction Room workshops. The specified timeframe should only be interpreted as a rough orientation. Depending on the complexity of the project and which questions have to be resolved most urgently, it is conceivable to only apply certain elements of the methodology, or to spread the workshops over several days or even weeks. For example, it can be helpful to plan dedicated workshop days for the population of individual canvases, conducted at intervals of several days to give the stakeholders time for reflection, more in-depth understanding and preparation between the workshops.

A.1.1 IR:digital Workshop Agenda

Day 1

9:00 a.m.	Introduction of the stakeholders, overview of the IR:digital methodology
9:30 a.m.	Establishing the workshop objective
10:30 a.m.	Population of the partner canvas
12:00 p.m.	Lunch break
1:00 p.m.	Annotation of the partner canvas, discussion, and establishment of no more than the five most important partners
2:00 p.m.	Technology overview (presentation)
3:00 p.m.	Population of the physical object canvas (focus on identification of the OoIs)
4:30 p.m.	Annotation of the physical object canvas, discussion, and establishment of no more than the ten most important OoIs
5:00 p.m.	Summary of the day, establishing the focal points for day two
5:15 p.m.	Conclusion of the day.

© Springer International Publishing Switzerland 2016
M. Book et al., *Tamed Agility*, DOI 10.1007/978-3-319-41478-2

Day 2

9:00 a.m.   Population of the physical object canvas (focus on life cycles of the most important OoIs)
11:00 a.m.   Technology overview (presentation)
12:00 p.m.   Lunch break
1:00 p.m.   Population of the touchpoint canvas for the five most important partners (including establishment of the touchpoint lanes)
2:30 p.m.   Annotation of the touchpoint canvas, discussion
3:30 p.m.   Establishing the top five digitalization proposals
4:00 p.m.   Parallel preparation of "press releases" for the top five realization proposals
5:00 p.m.   Presentation of the "press releases"
5:30 p.m.   Summary of the results, feedback session
6:00 p.m.   Conclusion of the day.

A.1.2   IR:scope Workshop Agenda

Day 1

9:00 a.m.   Introduction of the stakeholders, overview of the IR:scope methodology
9:30 a.m.   Establishing the workshop objective, formulating the "press release"
10:30 a.m.   Population of the feature canvas, annotation and prioritization of the features
12:00 p.m.   Lunch break
1:00 p.m.   Population of the process canvas[1]
3:00 p.m.   Coffee break
3:30 p.m.   Annotation and discussion of the process canvas
4:45 p.m.   Brief summary of the insights, establishing the focal points for day 2
5:00 p.m.   Conclusion of the day.

Day 2

9:00 a.m.   Recap of key insights from day 1 and plan for day 2
9:15 a.m.   Completion of the object canvas
10:30 a.m.   Annotation and discussion of the object canvas
12:00 p.m.   Lunch break
1:00 p.m.   Completion of the integration canvas
2:00 p.m.   Annotation and discussion of the integration canvas
3:00 p.m.   Coffee break

---

[1]Depending on the project requirements, another canvas may also be chosen as the leading canvas.

3:30 p.m.	Analysis of the overall picture, elimination of gaps/inconsistencies, first more in-depth examinations
4:30 p.m.	Summary of the insights, establishing the next steps
5:00 p.m.	Conclusion of the day.

A.1.3   IR:mobile Workshop Agenda

Day 1

9:00 a.m.	Introduction of the stakeholders, overview of the IR:mobile methodology
9:30 a.m.	Establishing the workshop objective, formulating the "press release"
10:30 a.m.	Formulating, presenting, and weighting the personas
12:00 p.m.	Lunch break
1:00 p.m.	Population of the portfolio canvas
3:00 p.m.	Coffee break
3:30 p.m.	Annotation and discussion of the portfolio canvas
4:45 p.m.	Brief summary of the insights, establishing the focal points for day 2
5:00 p.m.	Conclusion of the day.

Day 2

9:00 a.m.	Recap of the key insights from day 1 and the plan for day 2
9:15 a.m.	Population of the touchpoint canvas
11:00 a.m.	Annotation and discussion of the touchpoint canvas
12:00 p.m.	Lunch break
1:00 p.m.	Population of the interaction canvas
3:00 p.m.	Coffee break
3:30 p.m.	Annotation and discussion of the interaction canvas
4:30 p.m.	Summary of the insights, establishing the next steps
5:00 p.m.	Conclusion of the day.

A.1.4   IR:tech Workshop Agenda

Day 1

9:00 a.m.	Introduction of the stakeholders, overview of the IR:tech methodology
9:30 a.m.	Establishing the workshop objective
10:30 a.m.	Population, annotation, and discussion of the feature canvas
12:00 p.m.	Lunch break

1:00 p.m.   Population of the object,[2] integration, and process canvas (current state)
3:00 p.m.   Coffee break
3:30 p.m.   Annotation and discussion of the canvases (current state)
4:45 p.m.   Brief summary of the insights, establishing the focal points for day 2
5:00 p.m.   Conclusion of the day.

Day 2

9:00 a.m.   Recap of the key insights from day 1 and the plan for day 2
9:15 a.m.   Population of the object canvas (target state)
10:30 a.m.   Population of the integration canvas (target state)
12:00 p.m.   Lunch break
1:00 p.m.   Population of the process canvas (target state)
2:30 p.m.   Annotation of the target canvases
3:00 p.m.   Coffee break
3:30 p.m.   Discussion of the canvases, deriving technology implementation potential and hurdles
4:30 p.m.   Summary of the insights, establishing the next steps
5:00 p.m.   Conclusion of the day.

---

[2]Depending on the project requirements, another canvas may also be chosen as the leading canvas.

Appendix B
Interaction Room Annotations

B.1 Interaction Room Annotations

The annotations that were briefly introduced in the chapters on the individual canvases are presented and explained in more detail in the following sections. This list is intended to help the IR coaches choose the most suitable annotations for a specific context. In addition to describing the meanings of the annotations, detailed questions are also listed to help coaches with precisely pinpointing and specifying the annotated issues in their project context.

B.1.1   Value Drivers

Value drivers are indicated by the symbols shown in Fig. B.1.

Business value

User value

Innovation

Fig. B.1 Value driver annotations

B.1.1.1   Business Value

From a service provider's perspective, value creation by a system or process element can express itself in many ways. While financial contributions to the sales objective are the most obvious and easiest to measure (e.g., sales via a shop platform), contributions to other business objectives can be more difficult to comprehend, which means they can be easily lost in prioritization approaches. Contributions to objectives such as customer loyalty, the external image, or quality are difficult to measure may not be directly attributable to concrete features. The business value annotation encourages the explicit exploration of these points.

© Springer International Publishing Switzerland 2016
M. Book et al., *Tamed Agility*, DOI 10.1007/978-3-319-41478-2

The following questions can be used to state the annotated business value more precisely:

- What system/process element has a particular influence on the business value?
- What company objectives are positively influenced by the annotated element, which ones negatively? (customer loyalty/sales/competition/market share/ external image/marketing/sustainability/company development/costs/quality/ productivity/other);
- What is required to achieve a positive influence or prevent a negative influence?

B.1.1.2   User Value

A question of added value also arises from the perspective of the system's user. While the expectations of the user and service provider may complement each other in some cases (e.g., the user benefits from a certain function, the provider from the usage fee), they may also contradict each other in other cases (if the user expects a function that is unattractive for the provider, e.g., the link to a comparison portal). To uncover such areas of conflict, the perception of the user is highlighted by the distinct user value annotation.

Since value dimensions as clear and generally applicable as the various company objectives used for the business value annotation typically cannot be defined for users, the Kano (1984) classification is used here. The intensity of value creation is defined according to whether the annotated system or process element is a must-be, one-dimensional, or attractive quality, i.e., a characteristic that is expected as a matter of course, one that is perceived to improve performance, or one that positively surprises the user and may enhance acceptance of the system.

To state this assessment more precisely, the following questions should be answered for each user value annotation:

- What system/process element has a special influence on user value?
- What are the expectations for this element? (basic/performance/enthusiasm characteristic);
- What is required to achieve a positive influence or prevent a negative influence?

B.1.1.3   Innovation

The innovation annotation identifies process sections, system elements, features, or general ideas that are especially innovative, for instance novel from a business or technical perspective. It therefore constitutes an interface between value and effort drivers:

Innovation implies a special business value on the one hand—if there was no prospect of this, one would hardly be inclined to expend the effort and accept the risk of the innovation (see below). The innovation annotation usually also identifies a user value, often even in the sense of an enthusiasm characteristic. The feature offers a novel function or realizes a known function in a new way that positively surprises the user, thereby differentiating itself from the competition and improving user acceptance.

But on the other hand, the innovation annotation also implies effort: Implementing an innovative solution is usually more resource-consuming than using established solution templates, since new approaches to solutions first have to be developed and evaluated. Risks are also inherent in every innovation—regarding the feasibility of the technical implementation, the time and budget required for implementation, and the ultimate acceptance by the user.

This combination of characteristics makes the innovation annotation an important anchor point for discussions. It requires especially diligent estimates of effort and prioritization as well as particularly competent development and quality assurance.

For a more precise definition, the following questions should be answered for every innovation annotation:

- What system/process element constitutes a special innovation?
- What is the innovation in this element?
- Is it a technology or business innovation? Is it disruptive in nature?

B.1.2 Effort Drivers

Effort drivers are indicated by the symbols shown in Fig. B.2.

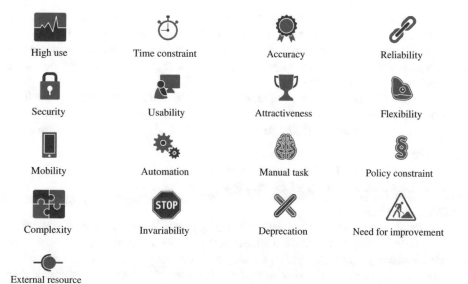

Fig. B.2 Effort driver annotations

B.1.2.1   High Use

Parts of a system may be permanently or temporarily subject to high use—perhaps due to a high number of users, voluminous batch processing, spikes due to deadlines or unforeseen events. Architectural and infrastructure precautions have to be taken in order to be prepared for such cases and ensure reliable functioning of the system even under heavy load. For example, usage peaks require a flexible infrastructure that can adapt to different load levels, rather than permanently providing resources for a peak load that is only required rarely. Providing such a scalable architecture is not only a question of hardware, but can have far-reaching consequences, for example, on the conceptual design of replication mechanisms, ensuring data and code portability. The conceptual design of this infrastructure, its implementation and testing requires significant effort which can be identified by the high use annotation.

The type of requirement—and therefore also the subsequent solution—is essentially based on how the load is distributed over time and what system components it is concentrated on. Therefore, the stakeholders are asked to answer the following questions in the annotation discussion:

- What system/process component is expected to be subject to high use?
- What is the type of load? When, how often, and for how long is it expected?
- What would the effects of overloading be?

B.1.2.2   Time Constraint

Time constraints in information systems typically apply to prescribed processing or response times (e.g., the maximum time required to make a decision, or the deadline for filing an application). The time-constraint annotation can therefore indicate that developers have to meet real-time requirements or that certain business deadlines have to be observed by the system.

In view of later finding a solution, one has to differentiate whether the time limit is expressed as a *deadline* (point in time) or a *window*. Both are recorded as subtypes of the annotation. The following questions also have to be answered:

- What is the required time frame?
- What is supposed to happen within the time frame?
- What would the effects of exceeding the time frame be?

B.1.2.3   Accuracy

Accuracy appears a trivial requirement at first glance, which should be met by all components of a system. But although correctness in the implementation is an obvious goal, especially high requirements for the precision, timeliness, or consistency of the processed data apply to certain components. For example, components that calculate interest or life insurance premiums decades in advance have to round monetary amounts according to precise specifications, and different implementations (such as a premium calculator in the insurance's back-end system and one in the mobile app at the point-of-sale) have to deliver exactly the same results. High requirements for the timeliness of data also apply, e.g., to the processing of securities prices. In designing user interfaces in particular, there is often a need to ensure the correctness of data input through suitable validations as well. These requirements (and the risks associated with the failure to meet them) are indicated by the accuracy annotation which is differentiated into the subtypes *precision*, *timeliness*, and *consistency*.

The following questions should also be answered when discussing the annotation:

- What processes/data are supposed to be as precise/timely/consistent as possible?
- What degree of precision/timeliness/consistency is required?
- What is the expected benefit of precision/timeliness/consistency?

B.1.2.4 Reliability

Reliability also sounds like a basic requirement that should be satisfied by any software system. In fact, however, the same reliability standards do not usually apply to all parts of a system: While it is always annoying when an expected system function is not available, the actual consequences can be more or less dramatic. In the most harmless case, there is merely a delay in executing a function. In more critical cases, data is lost. How critical such a loss of time or even data is depends on its severity and the application domain: Delays or the loss of messages can be tolerated in a chat application, but may cause damages in the millions in a financial application. This annotation is therefore intended to identify system elements where reliability is especially critical to support the business domain.

The following questions should also be answered when discussing the annotation:

- What processes/data need to be as reliable as possible?
- What degree of availability is required?
- What benefits are expected from the high reliability?

B.1.2.5 Security

The nature of security requirements can vary widely. For example, they include the digital signing of datasets in order to guarantee authenticity and non-repudiation, the anonymization of datasets prior to evaluation or ensuring the confidentiality of certain datasets. Implementing these requirements often affects both business processes and data structures. The security annotation symbolizes process and system components where specific security precautions have to be taken that go beyond the company's normal security standards. They are differentiated into the subcategories *protection against unauthorized access* and *protection against data loss*.

The following questions also have to be answered for a more precise definition:

- What is to be protected against unauthorized access/loss?
- What is the type of threat? How strong is the protection supposed to be?
- What would the effects of a lack of protection be?

B.1.2.6 Usability

Clearly, any software system with a user interface should meet fundamental usability requirements. It should be as intuitive as possible to understand, easy to use, suitable for the tasks of the user and so on. Yet there are often process steps or components that pose special usability challenges for business or technical reasons —perhaps because especially complex material has to be displayed (*visualization* subtype) or because special operating steps or user interface elements are required (*interaction* subtype), for example, gesture control on a touch screen. The challenges that require special attention in the interaction design (but possibly also in the process design) are identified by the usability annotation.

To define the usability requirement more precisely, the following questions have to be answered:

- What is supposed to be as understandable/easy to use as possible?
- What makes usability a special challenge in this element?
- What benefits are expected from usability in this element?

B.1.2.7 Attractiveness

The desire to make certain system or process elements as attractive as possible is related to the usability requirement at first glance. However, the attractiveness annotation can be used to identify a requirement that goes beyond an appealing user interface design. In some cases, a special incentive should be created to execute certain activities—whether this is through technical or business means. Examples are bonus systems or gamification techniques that reward certain activities beyond the fundamentally positive user experience.

The definition of attractiveness can be stated in more concrete terms by answering the following questions:

- What is supposed to be especially attractive?
- How is this incentive supposed to be created?
- What benefits are expected from the incentive?

B.1.2.8 Flexibility

For some process or system elements, it is already known at the time of conception that a single implementation cannot cover all requirements of the users, usage contexts, and basic conditions. An adequate measure of flexibility has to be planned in these cases, which can be achieved in various ways:

Minor adaptations of the system functionality to user-specific requirements or changed basic conditions can be realized through a suitable configuration of the system at runtime without requiring additional development effort (*configurability* subtype).

In other systems, certain (mainly technical) basic conditions may require realizing more than one version of a system from the outset to cover different applications. The versions are mutually independent instances of the system but typically developed in close dependency on each other—for example, the realization of an Android and an iOS version of a mobile app (*variability* subtype).

Finally, it may already be known in the design phase of a system that the current implementation will have to be adapted or replaced in the foreseeable future (e.g., when changes in legal regulations are pending). The future change should be taken into account in the system from the outset in this situation—both in regard to the architecture and in allocating effort to future obsolete functions (*design for change* subtype).

The following specifying questions serve to improve understanding of the background that makes flexibility necessary:

- What system/process element needs to be designed for flexibility?
- What configurations/variants/evolution paths are required?
- What would the effects of inflexibility be at this point?

B.1.2.9 Mobility

Accessing an information system or executing a business process using a mobile device such as a smart phone poses a number of challenges for the mobile components, which are not as prominent in classic information systems. In addition to the diversity of platforms already discussed under the flexibility annotation, the primary mobile effort drivers are mainly the unreliability of the network connection and the inclusion of location data (including fallback mechanisms if these are not available).

The mobility annotation is therefore stated more precisely by the following subtypes: *mobile availability* (to identify functions or process segments where mobile availability is desired), *off-line availability* (to identify functions that are supposed to work even if a network connection is lacking) and *location dependence* (to identify functions that depend on location information).

The mobility requirements are defined in more concrete terms with the following specifying questions:

- What system/process element is to be available in mobile use, off-line, or location-dependently?
- Under what circumstances can functionality restrictions be expected?
- What are the expected benefits of mobility/off-line availability/location dependence?

B.1.2.10 Automation

The objective of developing information systems is often the automation of process segments that were previously performed (semi-)manually. Such an automation project brings up a number of business and technical questions. Automation is usually no trivial mapping of activities to a technical solution, but requires the adaptation of processes and data, the definition of interfaces and—often the most difficult—establishing the extent of automation: To what degree will the process be automated? What special cases or errors are to be handled automatically, which ones are supposed to prompt for human intervention? What interfaces are used for such intervention? How can the process be simplified to avoid special cases as far as possible? Clarifying these questions and the resulting implementation requires significant effort and upheaval, which is highlighted by the automation annotation in the diagram.

For motivation and to state these requirements more precisely, the following questions should be discussed:

- What is to be automated?
- What degree of automation is desired?
- What does the user expect from the automation?

B.1.2.11 Manual task

The counterpart to the automation annotation is the manual task annotation. It indicates that a certain process segment will continue to be performed manually since it is not suitable for automated processing. This may be because specific expert knowledge is required, because it is based on an expert assessment that cannot be implemented algorithmically, or because human processing is preferable to automation for social reasons. Even a manually executed process step is a challenge for the realization of the information system, since one has to consider how manually and automatically processed data and process steps will be linked.

To define the requirements for manual processing steps more precisely, the following questions have to be asked:

- What requires human action/decision-making capability?
- How can the interface between the human and the system support/integrate manual tasks as well as possible?
- What effects would errors in manual processing have?
- Why is manual processing preferable to automation of this task?

B.1.2.12 Policy Constraint

Both the development and the operation of software systems take place in a project context that usually defines a number of different constraints. In general, most of these constraints are not formulated as dedicated requirements. This may be because they are assumed to be known to all stakeholders, or conversely because they are not known to any of the stakeholders, or they may be formulated somewhere but not be actually practiced or enforced.

The approach of not formulating all constraints as explicit requirements is initially due to a certain pragmatism. Since it is obvious that a patient file management system for a health insurance company has to comply with the applicable legal regulations, one is not going to include the entire text of the law in the requirements documentation. Yet it is important for the project stakeholders to be aware at what points in a process or system special attention must be paid to certain constraints—especially those that express more of a quality than a functional requirement.

Beyond that, projects are often subject to a number of constraints that cannot be formulated as product requirements, but rather define specifications for the system's design process—these may be technology decisions specified by existing system landscapes or quality assurance measures that apply throughout the organization.

The policy constraint annotation serves to highlight system or process elements where taking such constraints into account for the conceptual design or operation is especially critical or resource-consuming. According to the preceding discussion, one can differentiate *legal*, *technical*, and *organizational* constraints.

The following questions serve to state the constraint and its implications more precisely:

- What system/process element is subject to a constraint?
- What constraint has to be observed?
- Can this become a show stopper?

Since respecting any existing constraints is typically unavoidable, the question examining benefits is replaced by a risk-focused question for this annotation: A constraint may impose requirements that cannot be adequately implemented within the scope of the project and therefore endanger the success of the project. The question of the show-stopping character of a constraint helps identify such fundamental risks early on, which provides an opportunity to manage them.

B.1.2.13 Complexity

Some system or process segments that make a comparatively simple impression in the model can actually harbor a high degree of complexity which is not apparent to all stakeholders at first glance. This may be business complexity such as extensive calculation or decision rules, but also technical complexity such as major conversion or integration challenges. Such complexity may only be foreseen by a few domain experts or experienced developers, while stakeholders who are less familiar with the business or technology specifics typically underestimate the inherent effort and risks. The complexity annotation can be used to let all stakeholders know that the implementation of a certain system or process element requires expert knowledge and possibly extensive research or prototyping effort.

In stating the complexity annotation more precisely, one differentiates between the *business* and *technical* complexity subtypes since the solution typically requires the involvement of different stakeholder groups. The following specifying questions should be posed as well:

- What system/process element is especially complex?
- What does the complexity consist of?
- Can this become a show stopper?

B.1.2.14   Invariability

In extensive, organic system landscapes, there are typically numerous dependencies between components in different life cycle stages and with different development histories, technologies, and interfaces. While some legacy systems can be maintained and further developed, others may be facing imminent replacement.

A development stop may be imposed on especially critical legacy systems. Even though they continue to be used in productive operations, changes to the system are no longer permitted. This decision may, for example, be made because the system continues to work reliably, but certain decades-old knowledge about implementation specifics has eroded over time so that the effort and risk of re-engineering and adaptation of the code (which may, e.g., be written in COBOL) is considered unreasonably high. The invariability annotation can be used to notify all stakeholders that an existing system cannot be adapted to new conditions (e.g., in the course of process changes or the integration of additional components), but has to be encapsulated with suitable adapters.

To define the background and effects of the invariability decision more precisely, the following questions should be answered by stakeholders when this annotation is used:

- What system/process element is supposed to remain unchanged?
- How is this element supposed to be integrated into the changed system/process landscape?
- Why and on whose initiative is this element supposed to remain unchanged?

B.1.2.15   Deprecation

While some legacy components have to be considered invariable, other components may be easier to replace. Components slated for replacement or elimination can be identified with the deprecation annotation in the models. It indicates that the respective component will no longer be available in the future, so that the system under development cannot rely on it. Procedural or technical alternatives have to be developed for the deprecated component instead.

To state the background and effects of a component's deprecation more precisely, the following questions have to be answered:

- What system/process component is deprecated?
- How will its tasks be implemented in the future (if at all)?
- Why and on whose initiative is the component designated as deprecated?

B..1.2.16   Need for Improvement

In the course of the maintenance, adaptation or new development of system components, changing existing functions or processes is sometimes expedient in order to optimize them or adapt them to new conditions. This may involve *adaptation, expansion,* or *simplification* of a *business* or *technical* nature. In all of these cases, the "need for improvement" annotation indicates that work is required on a certain component or process step, thereby giving the stakeholders an overview in especially complex system landscapes of where "construction sites" are located and what areas remain stable.

The background of the planned improvement can be captured more precisely by answering the following questions:

- What system/process element is supposed to be adapted/expanded/simplified?
- What change is planned?
- Why and on whose initiative is this change being made?

B.1.2.17   External Resource

Interfaces to external resources often constitute effort drivers for two reasons: When the system being developed provides services for external components, the interface has to be designed with special care to optimize it for the current purpose but also be prepared for future expansions. When an existing interface is being expanded, one has to ensure that components already using this interface are not affected by the adaptations.

If the system being developed depends on external components, one should consider what happens if these components are temporarily or permanently unavailable, if their interfaces are altered or the technical or business conditions for their use change (e.g., regarding terms and conditions of use, prices etc.). In addition to the need to clarify these questions, the external resource annotation indicates that a fundamental make or buy decision regarding the externally linked functionality may have to be made.

External resources also prompt the question of the possibilities for influence on the resource provider. This is an important aspect since possible integration problems are much easier to solve through collaboration with the provider instead of assuming that the external interface cannot be changed.

- To what external resource does an interface exist?
- What information is exchanged with the external resource?
- What is the benefit/purpose of the connection for us and for the resource provider?
- What are the possibilities for influence on the resource provider?

B.1.3   Uncertainty

Uncertainty is indicated by the symbol shown in Fig. B.3.

Fig. B.3 Uncertainty
annotation

Uncertainty

The annotations introduced in the previous sections serve to highlight challenges of which at least some team members are already aware. However, it is just as important to be aware of points where there is still uncertainty in the team. These may be *business* aspects that are not fully understood yet, or open questions about the *technical* implementation. Such uncertainty is normal in any team, especially in early project phases. In classic system models, however, there is no possibility of expressing it. Quite to the contrary, the formality and precision of the modeling language suggest certainty about the modeled aspects which may not actually exist in the team. Once circumstances are modeled, they may no longer be sufficiently questioned even when they merely constitute initial ideas born out of uncertainty.

The uncertainty annotation addresses this problem by allowing all team members to clearly define the points of a system or process design where they still see a need for clarification. The respective uncertainties usually cannot be clarified immediately in the Interaction Room. Rather, they serve as an indication of where more extensive research is required or where hidden effort and risks may lurk.

Unlike the specifying questions for the preceding annotations, the focus with uncertainty is on strategies to record and clarify the points in question:

- What is the topic of uncertainty?
- What has to be done to eliminate the uncertainty?

B.4   Documenting Annotations

In practice, pads with self-adhesive annotation symbols have proven useful for conducting the annotation rounds in practice. The annotation characteristics (what does the annotation mean, where is it localized, why is it important) can be documented with forms like the one shown in Fig. B.4.[3]

For each annotation that is affixed to an element on a canvas, the IR domain coach records associated background information in one of these forms:

- In the "annotation ID" field in the top right corner, the annotation is numbered. This number is also noted on the annotation symbol affixed to the canvas.
- Next to the "stakeholders" heading, the name(s) of the stakeholder(s) who proposed this annotation are recorded in the "pro" field. If there are stakeholders opposing the annotation, their names are noted as well in the "con" field. This information is helpful for returning to these stakeholders later in the project for more information on dealing with the annotation.
- Under the "value drivers," "effort drivers," or "uncertainty driver" heading, the IR domain coach marks the type of annotation that is being documented. For most annotations, a subtype that provides more information on the nature of the challenge can be marked. (The preceding sections provide more information on categorizing these subtypes.)

---

[3]Annotation stickers and documentation forms are available at www.interaction-room.de.

STAKEHOLDERS	pro:	con:	Annot. ID:

VALUE DRIVERS

Business value
- [+] [−] Customer loyalty
- [+] [−] Sales
- [+] [−] Competitiveness
- [+] [−] Market share
- [+] [−] External image
- [+] [−] Marketing

- [+] [−] Sustainability
- [+] [−] Company development
- [+] [−] Costs
- [+] [−] Quality
- [+] [−] Productivity
- [+] [−] other: _____

User value
- [ ] Must-be quality
- [ ] One-dimensional quality
- [ ] Attractive quality

Innovation
- [ ] Business
- [ ] Technology
- [ ] disruptive

EFFORT DRIVERS

- [ ] **High use**

- [ ] **Time constraint**
  - [ ] Deadline
  - [ ] Window

- [ ] **Accuracy**
  - [ ] Precision
  - [ ] Timeliness
  - [ ] Consistency

- [ ] **Reliability**

- [ ] **Security**
  - [ ] Access protection
  - [ ] Loss protection

- [ ] **Usability**
  - [ ] Visualization
  - [ ] Interaction

- [ ] **Attractiveness**

- [ ] **Flexibility**
  - [ ] Configurability
  - [ ] Variability
  - [ ] Design for change

- [ ] **Mobility**
  - [ ] Mobile availability
  - [ ] Offline availability
  - [ ] Location dependence

- [ ] **Automation**

- [ ] **Manual task**

- [ ] **Policy constraint**
  - [ ] Legal
  - [ ] Technical
  - [ ] Organizational

- [ ] **Complexity**
  - [ ] Business
  - [ ] Technology

- [ ] **Invariability**

- [ ] **Deprecation**

- [ ] **Need for improvement**
  - [ ] Adaptation
  - [ ] Expansion
  - [ ] Simplification

- [ ] **External resource**

UNCERTAINTY DRIVER

- [ ] **Uncertainty**

Which system or process ELEMENT is affected by the annotation?

Which REQUIREMENT or CHALLENGE is expressed by the annotation?

Which BENEFIT is sought or which RISK is impending?

Potential benefit/risk: [S] [M] [L]   Frequency: [S] [M] [L]   Difficulty: [S] [M] [L]

Fig. B.4 Template for the documentation of annotation characteristics

- In case we are dealing with a business value annotation, the IR domain coach can indicate whether the aspect that the stakeholder wanted to highlight has a positive (+) or negative (−) influence on a number of business goals.
- For each annotations, the three boxes in the lower half of the form should be filled with notes regarding

- in the "element" box, the precise model element (i.e., system component, process step or similar) that the annotation is referring to, e.g., "submission of previous period's transaction data to regulatory authority";
- in the "requirement/challenge" box, the precise challenge or requirement that the annotation conveys, e.g., "data must be submitted by 20th of the month, or the preceding weekday if the 20th falls on a weekend or holiday";
- in the "benefit/risk" box, the positive or negative consequences of heeding or ignoring the annotation (whatever the dominant aspect is), e.g., "late filing of data will lead to significant fines."

The IR domain coach should obtain this information from the stakeholders as they are discussing the annotation.

- In the three groups of fields on the bottom of the form, the IR domain coach should record

  - the team's impression of the magnitude of the benefit or risk associated with this annotation,
  - the prevalence of the annotated challenge (e.g., its frequency of occurrence in a process—this might be every time the process is executed, or only in rare instances), and
  - the expected difficulty of addressing the annotated challenge.

Since these impressions can only be "gut feelings," they are just indicated in the three qualitative categories "small," "medium," and "large" rather than attempting to quantify them. If there is significant disagreement over the qualification of some criteria, the IR domain coach can choose to mark all options that different stakeholder groups are arguing for (e.g., "S" and "L", thereby indicating that the annotation is subject to particular contention and needs to be analyzed in more detail.

Together, these three criteria can be valuable indicators of an annotation's impact and the priority with which it should be addressed, and thus help in project planning.

The documentations of all annotations should be made available to the team together with photographic records of the annotated canvas. This will help the stakeholders later in the project to refer back to the knowledge recorded with the annotations and consider it in their search for appropriate solutions.

References

Kano et al (1984) Attractive quality and must-be quality. J Japanese Society for Quality Control 14 (2):39–48, ISSN 0386-8230 (in Japanese)

Appendix C
adVANTAGE Contract Template

C.1 adVANTAGE Contract Template

This chapter presents a contract template for projects conducted according to the adVANTAGE model. We point out that the contract model described in detail in Chaps. 14 and 15 is a template that can be used as a foundation for concrete projects but that considerable adaptations may also make sense, depending on the project requirements or partner constellation. Therefore, the following contract template should not only be reviewed and negotiated by a legal practitioner, but also by the persons in charge of commercial and technical matters for the client and contractor. The contract was developed for the German legal system, which naturally means it needs to be adapted if it is to be applied in a different legal system.

Section 1:   Object of the Contract

1. The object of this contract is the development of custom software and the granting of usage rights to this software by the contractor.
2. The individual software development steps—from determining the requirements to specification, design, and implementation to delivery to the client—are being performed in an agile development process.

Section 2:   Agile Process Model

The parties have agreed on the application of an agile, iterative project model for software development. The adVANTAGE model applied for the performance of this contract is based on the following principles:

1. Proceeding in sprints
   The design and implementation of the software takes place in several cycles called sprints. Specific requirements jointly defined by the parties are implemented in a

© Springer International Publishing Switzerland 2016
M. Book et al., *Tamed Agility*, DOI 10.1007/978-3-319-41478-2

sprint. The requirements are derived from features and refined in the conceptual design. Working software is delivered at the end of each sprint.

2. Service descriptions
   Before design and implementation commences in the project, the parties roughly establish the features desired by the client. This description must be established in sufficient detail so the effort needed for the development of the features can be estimated. A detailed description and specification of the requirements to be developed in a sprint is prepared at the beginning of each sprint.

3. Prioritizing the functions for the sprint
   The features to be developed in the respective sprint are prioritized by the client before the start of the sprint. This means the client decides which requirements corresponding to the features will be designed and implemented in which sprint. The client can change the prioritization of the features again before each sprint and therefore define the features to be developed in the next sprint after the end of a sprint.
   If more features are added in the course of the project, the total effort budget is increased accordingly. The parties jointly establish whether these features are implemented in an additional sprint (the team size established in advance remains unchanged). Replacing features with others of the same or lower value is possible after each sprint without affecting the budget. The principles for the addition of new features apply when features are replaced with others of higher value.

4. Flexibility
   After the end of a sprint, the client can terminate the project, define new features, or decide whether specific features will be developed or not. The client therefore has flexibility in responding to new insights and possibly changed requirements in the course of the project.

5. Duties to cooperate
   Even more so than other project models, the adVANTAGE project model requires the active participation of the client. The approach and influence the client can exert on design and implementation in the course of the project require a high level of client availability and participation.

6. Settlement after every sprint
   Settlement of the services provided takes place after every sprint. The compensation is made up of a base rate for analysis and project management, and effort-based compensation for feature development.

Section 3: High-Level Specification at the Start of the Project

1. At the start of the project, the parties jointly prepare a high-level specification for the software being developed. The high-level specification defines the purpose, field of application, function, future users, and similar parameters of the software being developed in general terms.

2. The business and (if applicable) also the technical requirements of the client are roughly described in the high-level specification in the form of features. A feature encompasses one or more functions of the software and can in principle be used on its own or together with one or more other features.

3. Features have to be described in sufficient detail so the contractor can estimate the design and implementation effort. Whether the initial high-level specification already meets these requirements or a more detailed specification is required has to be decided by the contractor for each feature. The contractor shall notify the client what information is required for the purpose of estimating. Should establishing a sufficient level of detail not be possible, the parties shall establish the compensation model for the respective feature by mutual agreement.

4. The contractor shall provide the client with an estimate of the design and implementation effort for each feature based on the high-level specification. This estimate shall be in person-days.

5. The contractor shall coordinate the high-level specification and estimated effort with the client. The high-level specification and estimated effort are part of this contract and form the basis for subsequent contractual performance. The high-level specification is included with this contract as Attachment 1, the estimated effort as Attachment 2.

6. If the high-level specification and/or estimated effort has already been prepared, coordinated, and approved by the parties before this contract is concluded (e.g., in the course of the quotation process, in the context of a workshop conducted in advance of the project or as the result of a proof of concept), the provisions of the two preceding subsections nevertheless apply correspondingly. The high-level specification and corresponding estimated effort agreed in this way, that is to say the documents containing them, are included with this contract as Attachment 1 and 2, respectively.

Section 4:   Sprints: Prioritization, Target Budgets, and Detailed Specification

1. The features described in the high-level specification are prioritized by the client following the approval of the high-level specification, estimated effort, and base rate. In coordination with the contractor, the client decides which features are most important to the client and which ones are assigned a lower priority. While the client is largely free to assign the priorities, possible business and technical dependencies between different features must be taken into account. The contractor supports the client in establishing a reasonable prioritization. The result of this prioritization is recorded by the parties in a list. This list is included with the contract as Attachment 3 and is therefore part of the contract.

2. The features (currently) having the highest priority are developed in the course of each sprint.

3. After this (initial) establishment, each sprint is assigned a fixed duration as well as the budget derived from the base rate and estimated effort for developing the features of the respective sprint.
4. At the start of each sprint, the features assigned to the sprint are established in concrete terms and detail in a detailed specification. For the second and all subsequent sprints this is done by the product owner during the currently ongoing sprint as far as this is possible.
5. The contractor designs and implements the requirements derived from the features in the detailed specification during the respective sprint and tests whether the software meets the requirements. Then, the contractor provides the software to the client for testing. The client tests the software and confirms acceptance. Acceptance is also deemed to be declared if the client puts the software into operation without reservations.
6. At the end of the project, after the final sprint is concluded and following the handover to the client, the client is given the opportunity to perform a final review and final comprehensive test. Once this is concluded, the client declares

   - that the project is complete,
   - that the software conforms to the contract, or
   - if deviations are noted, the desired rectification of defects.

7. The duration of the respective sprint and therefore the time budget for delivery for testing are fixed (known as time boxing). This means an individual sprint is not extended under any circumstances. Instead features for which requirements were not implemented in the software are shifted to another sprint, usually the following one (referred to as "carryover" in the following sections).

Section 5:   Subcontractors

The contractor is authorized to employ one or more subcontractors in the performance of this contract.

Section 6:   Principles of Cooperation, Project Organization, and Escalation

1. The success of the project depends on close cooperation between the parties and a constructive communication culture. Therefore, the parties within the scope of the applicable legal regulations declare their unrestricted readiness for mutual consideration, comprehensive information, precautionary warning of risks, joint and constructive resolution of differences in opinion and protection against disruptive third-party influences. This does not make the parties affiliated under company law.
2. The responsible product owner on the contractor side is named in Attachment 5 to this contract. The contractor may change the product owner and will inform the client accordingly if this is the case.

3. The responsible project manager on the client side and its deputy are also named in Attachment 5 to this contract. Both the project manager and deputy must have the required business and technical expertise for the tasks to be performed by them in the course of project implementation.
4. The contractor shall perform the design and implementation work pursuant to the contract at its own premises. However, performance may also be on site with the client or at the location of the hardware to prepare for delivery for the purpose of review and testing.
5. The project language is German.
6. Differences in opinion and disputes that arise or develop in the course of the project and that may endanger the successful realization of the project are initially discussed and clarified at the level of the contractor's project owner and the client's project manager. The resulting arrangements and agreements are jointly recorded immediately and exchanged in text form as a minimum. If timely resolution cannot be achieved at this level, the matter is immediately escalated to the steering committee for the project. The members of the steering committee are listed in Attachment 5 to this contract and are asked to resolve difficulties that arise promptly and in good faith.

Section 7: Duties to Cooperate

1. Active participation of the client is of particular importance under the chosen project model. The client therefore not only considers this a project of the contractor, but also its own project and is aware that adequate own resources of the client have to be scheduled on an ongoing basis for the successful real-ization of the project. The parties agree that the duties of the client to cooperate are actual obligations to perform.
2. The client obligates itself to promptly and at all times provide the business and technical information, deliver the documentation, and perform the acts required for the realization of the project, especially for the preparation of the detailed specifications for the individual sprints, for development and programming of the features and for testing.
3. The project manager and deputy are always available to the contractor for all questions related to the realization of the project. They can be reached by the contractor at any time by e-mail and telephone on working days between 8:00 a.m. and 8:00 p.m. and are authorized—to the extent obligated—to make all required decisions for the realization of the project.
   The client is authorized to replace the project manager or deputy with another person having equal qualifications and availability. However, the contractor must be notified of such measures in advance. Replacing the project manager and deputy at the same time is excluded.
4. In view of the fixed schedule for each sprint (time boxing), the parties agree to respond to inquiries and requests of the contractor within no more than 24

hours and to provide the respective information, take the required actions or make decisions. In cases where neither the client's project manager nor deputy meets this obligation in a timely manner, or if neither the project manager nor deputy is deployed at the respective time contrary to the obligations, the contractor shall make all decisions and take actions that are due itself subject to the principle of good faith. Decisions made in this way are binding for the parties.

5. In addition, the client's project manager or deputy is available to the contractor's staff responsible for the project, in particular for preparation of the detailed specification for the next respective sprint, and shall develop this detailed specification jointly with the contractor and approve it following coordination.

6. Furthermore, the client shall prepare and deliver to the contractor all data required for development, programming, and conducting functional verifications and tests of the software. This applies in particular to test datasets and test content to verify the functions of the respective software. The client shall also generate corresponding test cases in coordination with the contractor.

7. By request of the contractor, the client shall also enable the contractor to test the implemented software in a production equivalent test environment of the client prior to delivery for testing. The client shall provide corresponding access for this purpose.

8. The client shall promptly report failures, disruptions, and impairments in the operation of the software, including an error description, whether before or after testing.

9. Failed, late, defective, or incomplete performance of the duties to cooperate shall be borne by the client. The contractor shall notify the client in case of default on duties to cooperate contrary to duty, if applicable with a grace period to make up or repeat performance by the client. Due to the strict schedule for the sprints, verbal notification is sufficient.

If the client fails to meet the respective duty to cooperate within the grace period, the contractor is authorized to provide the service based on the information already available or to proceed according to subsection 7.4, sentences two and three of this contract. If neither one nor the other is possible, the contractor can stop the corresponding work until the duty to cooperate is met. Damages incurred by the contractor due to failure to meet the contractual duties to cooperate, in particular by keeping resources available (especially in the form of wait times by employees scheduled for the project), are billed to the client at the regular daily rates pursuant to Attachment 7 to this contract. In this context, the parties agree that the contractor based on the chosen project model is not able to otherwise deploy the employees assigned to the project in the course of an ongoing sprint.

Features that could not be completed in the respective sprint due to the failed, late, defective, or incomplete performance of duties to cooperate are transferred to the following sprint. The effort-based budget for the features is also transferred on a pro-rata basis, but without impairing the rights of the contractor pursuant to subsection 7.9, second paragraph, sentences three and four of this contract. The corresponding delays in the project are fully borne by the client.

10. The client is solely responsible for the adequate, if applicable continuous backup of its data according to the importance of the respective data. In particular, the client in this context has to ensure that all possible affected data is backed up again on an external system or data carrier prior to all previously announced work of the contractor performed on the systems of the client as intended.

Section 8:   Usage Rights

1. Custom development

    (a) The client acquires all exclusive usage rights to the software being developed as well as the documentation that is prepared, in particular the rights to duplication, dissemination, making available to the public and editing including the unrestricted exploitation of editing using all and even unknown exploitation methods. The contractor shall provide the client with the source code on one or more conventional data carriers.

    (b) The client can transfer these usage rights to third parties in whole or in part, and/or grant simple usage rights to them to third parties, without additional consent of the contractor.

2. Third-party software
    The type, contents, and scope of usage rights granted to the client by the provider of third-party software are determined by the provisions agreed between the provider and the client.

Section 9:   Compensation and Payment Terms

1. Compensation for performance and its settlement is based on the following principles according to the chosen project model:

    (a) A total effort budget for the project is established before the start of the project. It is based among other things on the number and duration of the sprints, size of the project team and estimated effort for the realization of the features.

    (b) Before the start of each sprint, the amount of compensation is established together with the joint estimate of effort in reference to the specific feature.

    (c) Settlement takes place after the conclusion of each sprint.

    (d) Compensation for the services provided in a sprint always consists of:

        (i) The fixed base rate, which covers all services of project management (product owner), the scrum master, developing and preparing the detailed specification, the development and integration tests performed by the contractor and preparation of the release, and the warranty and

(ii) Effort-based compensation for the conceptual design and development work in the sprint, which was previously estimated by the contractor and approved by the client

The base rate and approved estimated effort constitute the sprint budget.

Definition of roles:

The *product owner* is the business and organizational contact person for the client. S/he then provides the team with the requirements to be realized in the form of features and is available for business questions.

The *scrum master* ensures the optimization of the process, transparency, and improving the productivity of the team.

A *team member* develops the requirements of the corresponding features and actively implements value-oriented solutions in the course of the sprints. This results in usable software.

(e) In principle, compensation is paid for all design and implementation effort expended during the sprint for software that has been tested or made available for testing.

This includes effort that goes beyond the estimated effort and therefore exceeds the target budget, and/or for possible error corrections and comparable activities. However, the parties agree on three different daily rates based on this background, namely:

(i) A regular daily rate for effort of the product owner expended within the target budget,

(ii) A regular daily rate for effort of the Team Members expended within the target budget,
and

(iii) A lower daily rate for all effort that goes beyond the estimated effort **[OPTIONAL:** and for all design and implementation effort expended in the course of error correction and similar measures during an iteration]. The reference value for determining deviations is the respective feature.

All effort within the approved estimated effort is deemed to be within the target budget. Features completed within the target budget are settled at the regular daily rate according to the effort actually expended.

Effort that goes beyond the jointly estimated effort is settled according to the effort actually expended. The contractor informs the client if the target budget for a feature is exceeded.

This differentiation between the regular and lower daily rate also applies when a feature is not pursued further in the project (e.g., if it was not completed at the end of a sprint and not added to the next sprint).

The lower daily rate applies for additional effort expended after the conclusion of the last sprint (see section 4.6).

(f) After the conclusion of a sprint, settlement in addition to the base rate is only for the features that were tested or made available for testing. Carry-overs are also transferred to the next sprint in regard to the time already expended.

2. The agreed daily rates are established in Attachment 7 to this contract.
A person-day is defined as 8 working hours. Fewer or more hours worked on the respective day are settled on a pro-rata basis. Settlement is based on performance records. With the invoice, the client receives a printout of the activities of the corresponding employees recorded in the contractor's IT system for review. Once two weeks have elapsed since submission with no objections, the activity report is deemed to be approved.

3. **[OPTIONAL:** Bonus provision
The contractor receives a bonus payment for on-time delivery.
The total amount of the bonus is **[AMOUNT]** percent of the billed services.
The contractor is entitled to payment of the bonus when the following requirements are met:

- Meeting the deadline **[DATE]**.
- Readiness for acceptance of the services to be provided by the specified dates.

Upon meeting the deadline **[DATE]**, the contractor is entitled to an installment payment of **[AMOUNT]** € plus VAT as required by law. The installment payment is deducted from the bonus payment.
The entitlement to the bonus payment is not eliminated in case of failure to meet the deadlines because the client fails to meet its contractual duties to cooperate. In this case, the deadlines are postponed accordingly.**]**

4. Travel to the registered office of the client is already included in the quotation. Travel costs and expenses incurred for travel to other deployment locations by request of the client are reimbursed upon the presentation of vouchers or at the respective maximum amount according to tax laws.
[ALTERNATIVE: Travel and incidental costs required for the performance of the contact are reimbursed to the contractor by the client upon the presentation of vouchers. Travel time expended is billed to the client at 50 percent of the daily rate pursuant to this contract.**]**

5. The requirement for payment is the submission of a verifiable invoice in proper form. Invoices are due for payment 30 days after the invoice is received by the client. A three percent discount may be deducted in case of payment within eight days. The due date of incorrect invoices is delayed accordingly.
[ALTERNATIVE: Invoices are generally due for payment within 30 days after receipt of a verifiable invoice, with no deductions.**]**

Section 10   Termination

1. Ordinary termination of this project contract by the client is permitted pursuant
   to Section 649, sentence one of the German Civil Code (BGB). The following
   applies in this case:

   (a) Compensation paid for sprints that have already been completed remains
       with the contractor in any case.
   (b) If compensation has not been paid yet for a sprint that was already com-
       pleted, this compensation is due for payment immediately upon receipt of a
       corresponding invoice from the contractor.
   (c) If requirements for features have already been implemented in software that
       has been made available for testing at the time termination takes effect, but
       testing by the client is still pending, the client has to perform these tests
       notwithstanding termination and declare acceptability if the conditions are
       met. If the client fails to do so even after the contractor grants a period of
       grace, it is assumed that the corresponding requirements were properly
       implemented. This also applies if the client puts the software to use without
       reservations. In this case, the contractor is authorized to bill for the com-
       pleted features of the ongoing sprint; the client is obligated to pay the
       corresponding compensation.
   (d) For ongoing sprints, the client compensates the contractor for effort already
       expended at the time termination takes effect, according to the agreed daily
       rates in Attachment 7 to this contract and the base rate for the current sprint.
       The contractor provides proof of employee deployment by submitting
       corresponding activity records and delivers the software at the current state
       of development to the client.
   (e) For services not yet provided, the client pays additional compensation equal
       to the planned effort to be expended until the end of the current sprint
       according to the daily rates agreed for the sprint in Attachment 7. The
       actually expended effort for any carryovers from previous sprints has to be
       compensated in addition. However, the contractor has to permit the
       deduction of any savings realized by the contractor by the waiver of per-
       formance, and any proceeds gained or maliciously failed to be gained by
       otherwise deploying its employees.

2. Either party has the right to extraordinary cancellation if the respective legal
   conditions are met. In regard to compensation for services already provided in
   whole or in part, the preceding sections of this contract apply correspondingly.
   Subsection 10.1.d, however, applies subject to the limitation that compensation
   is waived in regard to services for which the client states within four weeks after
   the notice of cancellation that they are of no interest to the client.
3. A notice of cancellation must be in written form in order to be effective. Sub-
   mitting the notice by fax does not meet this written form requirement.

Section 11:   Warranty for Material Defects

1. The contractor warrants that the software meets the contractually agreed characteristics.
2. The warranty term is one year. This short warranty term does not apply to claims for compensation based on a material defect pursuant to Section 634, No. 4 BGB in case of intent or the malicious concealment of a defect by the contractor, in case of the loss of life, physical injury, or the impairment of health, or in case of claims pursuant to the Product Liability Act (ProdHaftG).
3. Defects not already listed in the declaration of acceptance have to be reported by the client to the contractor promptly and no later than within two weeks after they are discovered. If a notice is not submitted in a timely manner, the object of performance is deemed to be approved in regard to this defect. Insofar asserting warranty claims is excluded.
4. As far as possible and to the extent reasonable for the client in view of the effects of the defect, the contractor is authorized to provide an interim solution to work around the defect until it is rectified. Such an interim solution blocks possible rights of the client pursuant to Section 634, No. 2–4 BGB.
5. The warranty obligation is waived if the client alters the object of performance itself or has it altered by third parties, unless the defect is not due to the alterations that were made.
6. If the contractor is not able to rectify a material defect after two attempts, the client is authorized to assert the additional statutory warranty claims.

Section 12:   Warranty for Defects of Title

1. The contractor warrants that the software is free of third-party proprietary rights and that, to the best knowledge of the contractor, no other rights exist that limit or exclude use by the client pursuant to the contract.
2. In warranty cases, the contractor to an extent reasonable for the client has the right to either modify the software so that it no longer falls within the protection of the asserted right but still meets the requirements pursuant to the contract, or to obtain authorization so it can be used without restrictions pursuant to the contract and without additional costs for the client.
3. The warranty period is one year and begins with acceptance. However, in Subsection 11.2, sentence two of this contract applies correspondingly.
4. The parties shall inform each other promptly in writing if claims for the violation of proprietary rights are asserted against them.

Section 13:   Liability

1. For damages of the client caused by intent or gross negligence, the lack of a guaranteed characteristic, a culpable violation of essential contractual obligations (known as cardinal duties), a culpable impairment of health, physical injury or the loss of life, or in case of liability pursuant to the Product Liability

Act (ProdHaftG), the contractor is liable pursuant to the applicable legal regulations.

2. Cardinal duties are contractual duties, the performance of which makes the proper performance of the contract possible in the first place, for which the contractual partner is entitled to trust in regular performance, and the violation of which endangers achieving the purpose of the contract by the other side.

3. If a cardinal duty is violated, liability insofar as damages are based merely on simple negligence and not on death, physical injury, or the impairment of health is limited to damages that can be typically expected to occur within the scope of a contractual relationship such as this one.

4. In case of simple negligence, liability insofar as damages are not based on death, physical injury, or the impairment of health nor a promised guarantee is also fundamentally limited to an amount of 2 million €.

5. Any other liability is excluded regardless of the cause in law, both on the part of the contractor and its assistants and vicarious agents.

6. In case of damages incurred by the client due to the loss of data, the contractor is only liable insofar as the damages would not have been prevented by a backup of all relevant data by the client as described in subsection 7.10 of this contract.

Section 14: Confidentiality

1. In regard to all information about the respective other party that has become or becomes known to them in the context of this contract, identified as confidential or identifiable as business or trade secrets of the respective other party based on other circumstances, the parties are obligated to permanently maintain secrecy even after the end of this contract and to refrain from dissemination to third parties, recording or any other form of exploitation, unless the affected party has consented to disclosure or exploitation expressly in writing.

2. Insofar as legally possible, the parties through suitable contractual agreements with their employees and all other persons working for them shall ensure that these persons also refrain from any disclosure, exploitation, dissemination, or recording of the confidential information.

Section 15: Data Privacy

1. The parties shall observe the applicable legal regulations for the collection, processing, and use of personal data within the scope of this contract.

2. [OPTIONAL: Test data used by the client may not include actual personal data.]

3. Should a situation corresponding to Section 11, Paragraph 5 of the Federal Data Protection Act (BDSG) arise in the course of performance pursuant to this contract, the parties shall conclude a job-order data processing agreement according to the requirements of Section 11 BDSG.

Section 16:   Advertising and Investor Relations

1. With the consent of the client and no sooner than after the commencement of operation, the contractor is authorized to issue a press release regarding conclusion of the contract. The client shall not refuse consent without justifiable cause.
2. With the consent of the client and no sooner than after the commencement of operation, the contractor is authorized to name the client on the Web site and at the exhibition stands of the contractor as a client and to use the client's company logo for these purposes. The client shall not refuse consent without justifiable cause.
3. Furthermore, the client with consent and no sooner than after the commencement of operation permits the publication of a project report. The client shall not refuse consent without justifiable cause. The client shall also be available to future prospects of the contractor as a reference contact.

Section 17:   Choice of Law, Jurisdiction, and Place of Performance

1. For this contract and in regard to all legal relationships arising from the contract, the parties agree on the application of the laws of the Federal Republic of Germany. The application of the United Nations Convention on the Interna tional Sale of Goods as well as German and European international civil law is excluded.
2. The jurisdiction for all disputes arising from or in the context of this contract, and the place of performance, is **[PLACE]**.

Section 18:   Ranking

1. The ranking of the contractual agreements is as follows:

   (a) Individual amendments and/or endorsements to this contract after it is concluded
   (b) This contract without attachments
   (c) Attachment 4 to this contract with the appendices to Attachment 4 and all documents equivalent to these appendices
   (d) All other attachments to this contract

2. In case of contradictions, the provisions named first always take precedence over those named last. Gaps are filled by the respective subordinate provision. The same applies to amendments contained in the subordinate provisions. In case of documents with the same ranking, the more recent document takes precedence over the older document.

Section 19:   Final Provisions

1. This contract including its attachments contains the entire agreement between the parties regarding the object of the contract. In particular, the general business terms and conditions of the parties do not apply.
2. Amendments or endorsements as well as the cancellation of this contract must be in written form. This also applies to the waiver of the written form requirement itself.
3. Should provisions of this contract become ineffective in whole or in part, the remaining provisions of this contact shall remain unaffected. The ineffective, incomplete, or infeasible provision shall be replaced by the applicable laws. If a suitable regulation or suitable legal principle to amend the contract is lacking, and eliminating the clause does not offer a solution that protects the interests of the parties, the gap shall be filled by the supplementary interpretation of the contract. In this case, a provision is deemed to be agreed that comes as close as possible to the original object and purpose of the ineffective, incomplete, or infeasible provision.

Signatures

Contractor	Client

Place, date	Place, date

(Name in block letters)	(Name in block letters)

Attachment 1: High-Level Specification

[…]

Attachment 2: Initial Estimate of Effort and Base Rate

[…]

Attachment 3: Prioritization of the Features

If the prioritization of the requirements formulated in the features changes by request of the client or if new features are added, the changes are recorded in an appendix to this Attachment 3. The parties agree that the prioritization details required for the sprints can also be recorded in other documents on a case-by-case basis and that these documents do not necessarily have to be physically connected to this Attachment 3 to the project contract insofar as they expressly or implicitly refer to this Attachment 3 to the project contract.

[…]

Attachment 4: Duration, Planned Budget, and Detailed Specification for the Individual Sprints

For each sprint, the appendices attached to this Attachment 4 to the project contract contain:

1. The duration of the sprint
2. The planned budget for the sprint
3. If applicable, a description of the features for the sprint

The parties agree that the information required for the sprint can also be recorded in other documents on a case-by-case basis and that these documents do not necessarily have to be physically connected to this Attachment 4 to the project contract, insofar as they expressly or implicitly refer to this Attachment 4 of the project contract or Section 4 of the project contract.

[...]

Attachment 5: Project Organization

1. The project manager on the contractor side is Mr./Ms. **[NAME]**.
2. The project manager on the client side is Mr./Ms. **[NAME]**.
   His/her deputy is Mr./Ms. **[NAME]**.
3. The members of the steering committee are:
   Mr./Ms. **[NAME]**
   Mr./Ms. **[NAME]**
   [...]

Attachment 6: Software and Corresponding Licenses Provided by the Client
[...]

Attachment 7: Daily Rates

1. As the regular daily rate for all development and programming effort within the target budget, the parties agree on the net amount of **[AMOUNT]** €.
2. As the reduced daily rate for all development and programming effort expended outside the target budget and all error correction and similar measures during an iteration, the parties agree on the net amount of **[AMOUNT]** €.

[ALTERNATIVE: The daily rates according to the quotation apply.]

Index

A

Abstraction, 17, **18**, 41
Accuracy (annotation), 302
  on interaction canvas, 136
  on object canvas, 108
  on partner canvas, 72
  on physical object canvas, 80
Actual effort, **160**, 218, 268
adVANTAGE, **205**
  applicability, 236, 278
  example, 229, 269
  principles, 206
  procedures, 213
AE. *See* actual effort
Agile development, **8**, 49, 150, 178, 205
Agility, **5**, 206, 287, 294
Annotation, **43**, 56, 154, 299
  analysis, 45, 260
  documentation, 310
  in IR:digital, 84
  in IR:mobile, 137
  in IR:scope, 114
  in IR:tech, 145
  method, 46, 275
  on feature canvas in IR:scope, 94, 245
  on feature canvas in IR:tech, 143
  on integration canvas in IR:scope, 112, 259
  on interaction canvas, 135
  on object canvas in IR:scope, 106, 255
  on partner canvas, 72
  on persona canvas, 123
  on physical object canvas, 79
  on portfolio canvas, 125
  on process canvas in IR:scope, 99, 252
  on touchpoint canvas in IR:mobile, 83, 129
Application developer, **92**
Architecture, 283
Attractiveness (annotation), 304
  on interaction canvas, 136
  on touchpoint canvas in IR:mobile, 130

AugIR. *See* Interaction Room, augmented
Automation, 60, 284
Automation (annotation), 305
  on object canvas, 108
  on process canvas, 102

B

Backlog, 56
Base rate, **214**, 218, 234, 269
Big data, 288
Billing, **221**, 269
BizDevOps, 290
BR. *See* base rate
Business data, 103
Business department, 25
Business developer, **121**
Business object, 103
Business process, 69, 78, 95, 134, 154
Business value (annotation), 299
  on feature canvas in IR:scope, 94
  on feature canvas in IR:tech, 143
  on interaction canvas, 136
  on object canvas, 108
  on persona canvas, 124
  on physical object canvas, 80
  on portfolio canvas, 126
  on process canvas, 101
  on touchpoint canvas in IR:mobile, 130

C

Canvas, **41**, 56, 155, 168, 275
  in IR:digital, 84
  in IR:mobile, 137
  in IR:scope, 114
  in IR:Tech, 145
Change request, 185, 210, 222, 232
Channel, 81
Clarity, 25
Client, 154, 179, 181, 294
Client object, 75

Cloud computing, 3, 6, 288
Coach, **51**
    Domain expert. *See* domain coach
    Method expert. *See* method coach
Communication, **19**, 25, 167, 171, 292
Company boundary, 177, 181
Completeness, 23
Complexity (annotation), **307**
    on feature canvas in IR:scope, 94
    on feature canvas in IR:tech, 144
    on integration canvas, 113
    on object canvas, 108
    on physical object canvas, 80
    on process canvas, 102
Computer scientist's forecast, **161**, 270, 276
Context boundary (of system), 22
Context (of touchpoint), 81
Continuous integration, 6, 287
Contract for work and labor, 183
Contract model
    agile, **195**, 202
    multi-stage, 200
    traditional, **181**, 191
Contractor, **179**, 181, 190, 294
Cooperative performance structure, 179
Cost forward progressing, 33, 155, **159**, 270, 276
Customer journey map, 81
Customer safari, 81
Cyber-physical system, **61**

D
Daily rate, **211**, 232, 269
    reduced, 221, 223, 234
    regular, 215, 234
Daily scrum, 214
DE. *See* detailed estimate
ΔDE. *See* deviation (average), between *AE* and *DE*
Definition of Done, **207**, 222, 236, 268
Deprecation (annotation), **308**
    on integration canvas, 113
    on object canvas, 109
Detailed estimate, **160**, 218, 267, 269
Development risk, 192, 210, 222
Deviation (average), 276
    between *AE* and *DE*, **162**, 270
    between *DE* and *IE*, **161**, 271
Device, 286
DevOps, 290, 294
Dialog, 132
Dialog flow, 134
Digital business expert, **65**
Digital company, **60**, 74

Digitalization, 3, 48, **59**, 284
Digital technology expert, **67**
Disaster, 33, 153
Disaster point, **157**, 265, 277
Display, 168
DoD. *See* definition of done
Domain coach, **53**
Domain knowledge, 20, 273, 289, 294
DR_1. *See* daily rate, regular
DR_2. *See* daily rate, reduced

E
Earned value analysis, 219
Efficiency incentive, 211, **223**, 234
Effort, 154
    actual. *See* actual effort
    detailed estimate. *See* detailed estimate
    initial estimate. *See* initial estimate
    overall estimate. *See* overall estimate
    remaining. *See* remaining effort
Effort driver, 26, **45**, 301
Effort tracking, 218
EI. *See* efficiency incentive
Elasticity, 3, **5**, 49
Enterprise architect, **142**
Enterprise IT, **vii**, 3, 25, 283, 289, 291, 293
Estimate, 218, 276
    detailed (effort). *See* detailed estimate
    initial (budget). *See* initial budget
    initial (effort). *See* initial estimate
    overall (effort). *See* overall estimate
External resource (annotation), **309**
    on integration canvas, 114
    on object canvas, 109
    on process canvas, 102
External service provider, 179

F
Feature, 159
Feature canvas, 274
    example, 245
    in IR:agile, **150**
    in IR:scope, **93**
    in IR:tech, **142**
Feature point, 197
Fixed price, 183, 190
    per iteration, 195, 201
    per point, 196, 201
    per project, 184, 192
Flexibility, 288
Flexibility (annotation), **304**
    on feature canvas in IR:tech, 144
    on interaction canvas, 136
    on object canvas, 108

on physical object canvas, 80
on process canvas, 101
Follow-up activities
example, 261
IR:digital, 86
IR:mobile, 138
IR:scope, 116
IR:Tech, 146
Function point, 197, 199

H
Health insurance benefit system, 241
HIB system. *See* health insurance benefit
system
High use (annotation), 302
on feature canvas in IR:tech, 143
on integration canvas, 113
on partner canvas, 72
on physical object canvas, 80
on process canvas, 101

I
IB. *See* initial budget
IE. *See* initial estimate
ΔIE. *See* deviation (average), between *DE* and
IE
Improvement, need for (annotation). *See* need
for improvement (annotation)
Industry 4.0, 62
Information technology, vii
In-house development, 179
Initial budget, **215**, 269
Initial estimate, **159**, 213, 218, 263
Innovation (annotation), **300**
on feature canvas in IR:tech, 143
on interaction canvas, 136
on portfolio canvas, 126
on touchpoint canvas in IR:mobile, 130
Insurance benefit, 241
Integration, 287
Integration canvas, **132**, 274
example, 258
in IR:scope, **109**
in IR:tech, **145**
Interaction channel, 128
Interaction engineer, **68**
Interaction process, 134
Interaction Room, 17, **40**
applicability, 172
augmented, 168
coach, 51
distributed, 167, 169

follow-up activities, 56
for agile project monitoring, 49, **149**, 263
for digitalization strategy development, 48,
59
for mobile application development, 48,
119
for software project scoping, 49, **91**, 243
for technology evaluation, 49, **141**
layout, 18, 165
method, 40
principles, 18
results, 56, 276
temporary, 165
variant, 48, 171
workshop, 55, 295
Interaction trigger, 128
Interface, 69
Invariability (annotation), **308**
on integration canvas, 113
on object canvas, 109
IR. *See* Interaction Room
IR:agile. *See* Interaction Room, for agile
project monitoring
IR:digital. *See* Interaction Room, for
digitalization strategy development
IR:mobile. *See* Interaction Room, for mobile
application development
IR:scope. *See* Interaction Room, for software
project scoping
IR:tech. *See* Interaction Room, for technology
evaluation
IT. *See* information technology
Iteration, 196

K
Kano model, 94

L
Lean software, v, 8, 13, 18, 27, 29, 153, 277,
290, 291

M
Manual task (annotation), **306**
on object canvas, 108
on process canvas, 102
Maturity level, 190
Method coach, 46, **52**
Mobility, 3, **4**, 48, 60, 119, 284, 293
Mobility (annotation), **305**
on integration canvas, 113
on object canvas, 108
on portfolio canvas, 126

on process canvas, 102
Mobility expert, **121**
Modeling, 23
Money for nothing, change for free, **197**, 201
Monitoring, 35, 49, 149
Multi-stage contract model, 200

N
Need for improvement (annotation), **308**
    on integration canvas, 113
    on object canvas, 109
    on portfolio canvas, 126
    on process canvas, 102
    on touchpoint canvas in IR:mobile, 130
New School of IT, **3**, 6, 283, 291, 293
Note area, **41**

O
Object canvas, 274
    example, 255
    in IR:scope, **103**
    in IR:tech, **145**
Object of interest, **73**, 275
OE. See overall estimate
OoI. *See* object of interest
Operations expert, **92**
OS. *See* overspend
Overall estimate, 161
Overhead, 213
Overspend, 218, 268

P
Partner, 69, 81
    contractual, 181
Partner canvas, **69**, 274
Pay per use, **188**, 192
PD. *See* person-day
Persona, **122**, 127
Persona canvas, **121**
Personal injury manager, 241
Person-day, 233, 267
Physical object, 74
Physical object canvas, **73**, 275
Plan-driven development, **7**, 34, 178
Planning poker, 263
Platform, 286
Policy constraint (annotation), 306
    on feature canvas in IR:tech, 144
    on integration canvas, 113
    on object canvas, 108
    on process canvas, 102
Portfolio canvas, **124**
Pragmatism, 12, 23, 25
Precision, 25

Press release, **55**, 243
Price, 294
    in adVANTAGE contracts, 210, 211
    in agile contract models, 201
    in fixed price contracts, 186
    in fixed price per iteration contracts, 196
    in fixed price per point contracts, 197
    in Money for Nothing, Change for Free
        contracts, 198
    in pay-per-use contracts, 189
    in shared pain/shared gain contracts, 199
    in time and materials contracts, 187
    in traditional contract models, 183, 191
Prioritization, 95, **216**, 226
Process canvas
    example, 248
    in IR:scope, **95**
    in IR:tech, **145**
Process owner, **54**
Product backlog, 159, 215, 263
    in IR:agile, **150**
Product brief, 178, 186
Product object, 75
Product owner, 269
Progressive contracts, 196
Progress tracking, 158
Project controlling, 219
Project vision, 243

Q
Quality (Kano model), 94

R
RE. *See* remaining effort
Relevance, 23
Reliability (annotation), **303**
    on feature canvas in IR:tech, 144
    on integration canvas, 113
    on partner canvas, 72
    on physical object canvas, 80
    on process canvas, 101
    on touchpoint canvas in IR:mobile, 130
Remaining effort, **219**
Requirement, 93, 95, 154, 186, 213, 283
    early, **29**, 152, 277
    late, vii, **27**, 152, 185, 225, 277
Requirements exchange, 30, **152**, 155, 198,
    226, 270, 277
Risk, 23, 33, 179
    in adVANTAGE contracts, 209, 210, 222,
        228
    in agile contract models, 202
    in contracts for work and labor, 183
    in fixed price contracts, 185

in fixed price per iteration contracts, 195
in fixed price per point contracts, 196
in Money for Nothing, Change for Free
    contracts, 197
in multi-stage contracts, 200
in pay-per-use contracts, 189
in service contracts, 184
in shared pain/shared gain contracts, 198
in time and materials contracts, 187
in traditional contract models, 191
Risk driver, 216
Risk management, 157
Risk map, 34, **153**, 263, 265, 277
Role, 52, 54

S
SaaS. *See* software-as-a-service
Scope, 21
Scrum master, 214, 269
Security, 286
Security (annotation), **303**
    on feature canvas in IR:tech, 144
    on integration canvas, 113
    on object canvas, 108
    on partner canvas, 72
    on process canvas, 101
Semantics, 25
Service blueprint, 81
Service contract, 183
Settlement, **221**, 269
    fully completed sprint, 222
    partially completed sprint, 224
Shared pain/shared gain, **198**, 201
Skill, 283
Socio-technical system, **vi**, 177, 186, 292
Software, v
Software-as-a-service, 188
Software development. *See* software
    engineering
Software engineering, v, 283
Software metrics, 27
Software process, vi
Sprint, 160, 196
Sprint backlog, 160, 216, 267
Sprint completion
    full, 221
    partial, 224
Sprint planning, 151, 155, 160, 166, 226, 267
Sprint scope, 216, 233, 267
Stakeholder, **51**, 54, 167, 283, 291, 294
    example, 244
    in IR:digital, 64
    in IR:mobile, 120

in IR:scope, 92
in IR:tech, 142
Statistician's extrapolation, **161**, 270, 276
Storyboard, 132
Story point, 197
Supplier, **179**, 181
System
    boundary, 22, 154
    context, 21
    of engagement, 22
    of records, 21

T
T&M. *See* time and materials
Tailoring, 56
Tamed agility, 9, **11**, 13, 291
Team, 51
    distributed, 167
Team room, 166
Technology expert, **142**
Telecommunication, 285
Termination, 198, 226
Testing, 287
Time and materials, 183, **187**, 190, 192
Time constraint (annotation), **302**
    on feature canvas in IR:tech, 143
    on physical object canvas, 80
    on process canvas, 101
Timeline, 81
Touchpoint, **81**, 127
Touchpoint canvas, 275
    in IR:digital, **81**
    in IR:mobile, **127**
Touchpoint event, **81**
Touchpoint lane, **82**
Transparency, 19
Trust, **34**, 200, 207, 222, 228, 230
Trust point, **81**, 127

U
Uncertainty, vi, **30**, 177, 273
Uncertainty (annotation), 46, 47, **309**
    on feature canvas in IR:scope, 94
    on feature canvas in IR:tech, 144
    on integration canvas, 114
    on interaction canvas, 136
    on object canvas, 109
    on process canvas, 102
    on touchpoint canvas in IR:mobile, 130
Underspend, 218
US. *See* underspend
Usability (annotation), **304**
    on interaction canvas, 136

User, **93**
User experience, 132, 284, 285, 293
User journey, 127
User value (annotation), **300**
    on feature canvas in IR:scope, 94
    on feature canvas in IR:tech, 143
    on interaction canvas, 136
    on object canvas, 108
    on physical object canvas, 80
    on portfolio canvas, 126
    on process canvas, 101
    on touchpoint canvas in IR:mobile, 130
UX. *See* user experience

V
Value, **19**, 26
Value driver, 26, **45**, 154, 197, 216, 294, 299
Value risk, 192, 210, 222

W
Whiteboard, 39, 168
Workshop, 165, 168, 295
    IR:digital, 86, 295
    IR:mobile, 138, 297
    IR:scope, 116, 296
    IR:tech, 146, 297
    preparation, 55

Printed in the United States
By Bookmasters